Wings of the Gods

Wings of the Gods

Birds in the World's Religions

PETER (PETRA) GARDELLA
AND
LAURENCE KRUTE

OXFORD
UNIVERSITY PRESS

Oxford University Press is a department of the University of Oxford. It furthers
the University's objective of excellence in research, scholarship, and education
by publishing worldwide. Oxford is a registered trade mark of Oxford University
Press in the UK and certain other countries.

Published in the United States of America by Oxford University Press
198 Madison Avenue, New York, NY 10016, United States of America.

© Oxford University Press 2024

All rights reserved. No part of this publication may be reproduced, stored in
a retrieval system, or transmitted, in any form or by any means, without the
prior permission in writing of Oxford University Press, or as expressly permitted
by law, by license, or under terms agreed with the appropriate reproduction
rights organization. Inquiries concerning reproduction outside the scope of the
above should be sent to the Rights Department, Oxford University Press, at the
address above.

You must not circulate this work in any other form
and you must impose this same condition on any acquirer.

Library of Congress Cataloging-in-Publication Data
Names: Gardella, Peter, 1951– author. | Krute, Laurence, author.
Title: Wings of the gods : birds in the world's religions / Peter (Petra) Gardella, Laurence Krute.
Description: New York, NY, United States of America : Oxford University Press, [2024] |
Includes bibliographical references and index.
Identifiers: LCCN 2023040832 (print) | LCCN 2023040833 (ebook) |
ISBN 9780197691878 (hardback) | ISBN 9780197691885 (epub)
Subjects: LCSH: Birds—Religious aspects. | Animal worship.
Classification: LCC BL442 .G37 2024 (print) | LCC BL442 (ebook) |
DDC 202/.12—dc23/eng/20231114
LC record available at https://lccn.loc.gov/2023040832
LC ebook record available at https://lccn.loc.gov/2023040833

DOI: 10.1093/oso/9780197691878.001.0001

Printed by Sheridan Books, Inc., United States of America

*For all birds flying, swimming, running, and brooding everywhere,
that we humans might see and hear them and continue to be led by them.*

Contents

Acknowledgments ix

1. Birds and Religions 1
2. Birds in Creation, Evolution, and Creation Stories 12
3. Birds and Humans in Each Other's Rituals (and Costumes) 42
4. Bird Heroes and Villains 77
5. Bird Spirit Guides 110
6. Extinctions and Apocalyptic Birds 137
7. Birds in Romantic Arts, Sciences, and Religions 169
8. Birds Leading Humans to Another New World 203
Epilogue: How the Cover of This Book, the Artist Who Painted It, and the Albatross He Painted Embody a Religion of Nature 257

Bibliography 265
Index 279

Acknowledgments

Peter (Petra) Gardella

My thanks for this book go first to my coauthor, Laurence Krute, who introduced me to birding and whose perspective on evolution and anthropology informs the whole. Larry and his family have also supported my shifting between Peter and Petra as I came out as trans and gender fluid in the midst of this work, and so gained new intellectual perspectives on birds and religious history.

Two colleagues and friends, Professor Colleen McDannell of the University of Utah and Professor Emerita Theresa Sanders of Georgetown University, encouraged this project and reviewed early material. Without a final reading by Professor Sanders, the work might never have ended! Professor McDannell brought Zeyn Joukhadar's *The Thirty Names of Night*, a 2020 transgender version of the Sufi Muslim classic *The Conference of the Birds*, to my attention, with good effects I hope.

Cynthia Read, who edited my first book in 1985 and its revised edition in 2016, brought the project to Oxford University Press seven years ago, and Theodore Calderara, who edited my fourth book in 2014, brought it home despite Larry's and my reluctance to let go. Jessica Tubis of the Beinecke Rare Book and Manuscript Library at Yale University helped to obtain the rare version of Audubon's Golden Eagle that appears in Chapter 7. Avi Gitler, an art gallery owner and bird art entrepreneur, showed me the Audubon Murals Project in New York City and connected me with Kathryn Heintz, whom I interviewed when she was president of New York City Audubon, and with bird sculptor Nicholas Holiber and with Andrew Maas, whose photograph appears in Chapter 8. Bird guides Meredith Sampson and Cynthia Ehlinger, the founder and frequent leader of first Sunday bird walks at Greenwich Point Park in Connecticut, nurtured my connection with birds over fifteen years.

My wife, Professor Lorrie Greenhouse Gardella of Southern Connecticut State University, has read every word of the text more than once and advised regarding every detail of the project. In 2017, Lorrie and her cousin Sharon Cohen Ferraguto and Phil Ferraguto went with me to a four-day celebration of birds, art, and music by the Boston Symphony Orchestra called "Tanglewood Takes Flight." That weekend culminated at the Mass Audubon Museum of Bird Art, where we found the painting by Arthur Singer that appears on the cover and in the epilogue. I have had a good flock.

Laurence Krute

Without my coauthor and indeed lead author, Petra Gardella, there would be no book. This version of the book is far from the work that I, at least, originally envisioned, but it's a much better and more needed work, thanks to Petra.

Our two very fine editors at Oxford University Press, Cynthia Read and Theodore Calderara, materially shaped the book and helped us come to the point where the book was actually completed. We'd still be writing if not for them.

Petra and I began discussing religion about thirty years ago, when I suggested that we coteach a course on Native American religions. The roots of my view of religion rest in the historical materialism of the late Marvin Harris, whom I had the great fortune to interact with as a graduate student at Columbia University. It is his insistence on connecting social structure and cultural superstructure to physical reality that underlies my thinking.

As I listen to two red-shouldered hawks shouting at each other while I write this, I realize that the birding autobiography of Kenn Kaufman inspired me to take my previously lackadaisical birding to a higher level.

Finally, there is no way I can adequately acknowledge the contributions of my spouse, Julie Dolphin, and my children, Jayce and Maia Dolphin-Krute. They are pretty much the reason I have accomplished anything.

1
Birds and Religions

When the idea of a book on birds in the world's religions first arose, we hoped to connect the birds in sacred stories, rituals, and laws with accounts of how humans and birds have adapted to their environments. We did not know how much of the joy of discovery awaited us. The volume of material has been both exhilarating and daunting. It seems that every religion in the world reveres birds, usually in several ways.

Most importantly, we found that religions reveal how birds and humans evolved together, with potential lessons for overcoming the current worldwide crises of heat, pollution by plastics and oil, and contagious disease. By the end of our research, we became convinced that a new religious attitude—one that sees birds as active agents with rights, listens to birds as bearers of messages that reveal the condition of the world, and treats birds as elder forms of life with whom humans have relationships—can save the world that humans and birds made together. Birds connect the realms of earth, water, and air and so signify the whole system's health. Birds also transcend, and so can lead the world beyond, the human divisions over gender and sex, race, and political boundaries that prevent humans from solving the crises we have created.

We have concluded that, as humans track bird migrations on weather radar and watch birds in an explosion of citizen science, the foundations for a religion of nature focused on birds are being laid. Like the ancient religions of Africa, India, China, Israel, and the Americas, the religion of birds has no single founder, no authoritative hierarchy or creeds. To show how this new religion works, we need to start with birds themselves.

Birds have many rituals, and may even have religions that humans will never know, but bird behavior definitely belongs in any account of how human religions began and how they developed. Many books present symbolic uses of birds by humans. From Edward Armstrong's *The Folklore of Birds: An Enquiry into the Origin and Distribution of Some Magico-Religious Traditions* (1958) to *Birds and People* (2013), an encyclopedia by Mark Cocker with photography by David Tipling, such compilations provide many facts, images, and stories. In 2020, David Sibley added a new classic in the genre of explaining birds to humans, *What It's Like to Be a Bird*. Sibley's work is a worthy modern successor to John James Audubon's *Birds of America* (1827–1838) and *Ornithological Biography* (1831), which served as founding scriptures in the religion of birds.

Birds have always inspired people. Birds have magic—or in other words, startling emotional power—for people because birds fly, make dramatic sounds, appear suddenly, and look beautiful in many ways. As one scholar has recently written, crying out "Lord God" at the sight of a pileated woodpecker "is a shout-out to all of creation" that "a visage of God" has appeared.[1] And bird magic includes communication. They sing and speak to each other, to all other animals, and to us; they probably inspired the first humans who made music. Since long before written history began, people have regarded birds as messengers of gods, and often as gods themselves. Among the Stone Age goddess figurines categorized by archaeologist Marija Gimbutas,[2] bird goddesses abound, outnumbering goddesses that are also snakes or bears.

Although birds are magical, they are also familiar. Birds resemble people: they have two legs, two wings in the positions of arms, and they build homes where they raise families. Many birds live closely enough to us to be regarded as neighbors. People keep birds as pets, feed wild birds, watch birds for entertainment, and take their feathers to decorate themselves. For human hunters and gatherers, groups of crows and ravens have acted as traveling companions and collaborators in seeking food.[3] Humans can train birds to carry our messages or to hunt with us. We also hunt birds, raise birds for food, eat the eggs of birds, and sacrifice birds to gods or to the cosmos.

Though literate people focus on words and tend to think of religions as systems of beliefs or ideas, religions are also systems of behavior. "Religion" was defined in one of our books, *Domestic Religion* (1998), as "a system of nonrational commitments that holds life together."[4] Within religions, we eat and dress and have sex in certain ways; we recall that our ancestors lighted this fire and made that gesture when they set up camp. Different beliefs about why we do these things are often tolerated more easily than different behaviors. Derived from the Latin *ligare*, to bind,[5] religion deals with what is obligatory.[6] Behaviors become obligatory because they connect people to or protect people from some aspects of the world that have undeniable power, such as food and water, fire and air, intoxicating substances, and sources of fear and sexual attraction. In the development of human languages and societies, some behaviors have helped groups of people to survive and to flourish. It seems likely that the behaviors that have best promoted human life, joined together into systems, have become religions.[7]

All religions have rules and wisdom regarding the most important features of life, and birds are among these features. Questions such as which birds are good to eat, which birds are friends, and which are competitors or pests, operate on a basic level. On a higher cultural plane, there are birds who inspire us with their songs, birds who predict the weather or the future with their flight, birds whose feathers give higher status to the person who wears them, and birds who remind us of heroes or ancestors or gods. In postindustrial civilizations, the immediate impact of birds on human life has been mediated by layers of culture and technology, and the usefulness of birds has changed, but their symbolic heritage remains.[8] The stories, rituals, and languages of religions often preserve and reflect experience over thousands of years.

Besides organizing social and individual life, religions can inspire a sense of transcendence, of participation in higher or broader life and harmony with a power that informs all things. Religions set boundaries but also break them, telling stories of heroes and saints who went beyond. Religions foster and record moments of expanding the boundaries of consciousness through sex and death, meditation and drugs. And birds are boundary-breaking animals, the only animals that move between the sky, the sea, and the land. To follow a hawk in rapid flight or a soaring bird is to see and to feel transcendence.

Birds also connect people with transcendent moral standards. As historians, sociologists, and psychologists have lately argued, belief in gods who see everything has helped people in many societies to attain higher degrees of trustworthy behavior and peace, at least within their groups and sometimes beyond.[9] Birds often personify the all-seeing gods or inform those gods. In ancient Egypt, the eye of Horus the Hawk (who was also the reigning pharaoh) watched the people from the walls of many temples. The eagle stood for Zeus or Jupiter the sky god and his authority in Greece and Rome, and the eagle Garuda serves as the mount of Vishnu, the peaceful and universal sky god of India. In Scandinavia, the chief god Odin had two ravens, Hugin and Munin, who flew throughout the world and told Odin what humans did. As the Hebrew Bible warns, "Do not curse the king, even in your thoughts, or curse the rich, even in your bedroom, for a bird of the air may carry your voice, or some winged creature tell the matter" (Ecclesiastes 10:20, NRSV). In our own age of universal surveillance in the name of peace, the United States (which took the eagle as its symbol) calls its highest-flying and widest-ranging reconnaissance drone the Global Hawk (Figure 1.1).

Figure 1.1 Birds probably inspired ideas of all-seeing gods. That power of observation is approached by the Global Hawk, a reconnaissance drone that flies halfway around the equator, stays at sixty-five thousand feet for thirty hours, and refuels autonomously.
J Marshall – Tribaleye Images / Alamy Stock Photo.

Birds that watch humans may also stand as guards. Japanese torii, the gates at the entrance of Shinto shrines, derive their name from *Tori*, the word for a perch for birds.[10] Torii gates evoke roosters who greet the sun goddess Amaterasu. Before those roosters a great guardian was Simorgh, the Persian name of a female bird who renews her life forever, cousin of the Phoenix of China and likely antecedent of Zoroaster's male Creator with enormous wings, Ahura Mazda (Figure 1.2).[11]

The history of birds and religions will be told here in topical chapters, with each chapter organized chronologically. While acknowledging the competitions between religions, the controversies among scientists, and the sometimes difficult relations between religion and science, this text will seek to express an attitude of comprehension and acceptance. Scientists constantly revise and refine their accounts of creation and evolution, historians change their narratives of history, and religious adherents vary in their interpretations of traditions. We make allowances for disagreements and for growth.

Figure 1.2 The ruins of Persepolis, built around 600 BCE and destroyed by Alexander the Great, feature a figure identified either as Creator God Ahura Mazda or a Fravashi, one of the human spirits who save creation in a final battle with evil.
Suzuki Kaku / Alamy Stock Photo.

On the other hand, the sacred stories and rituals and moral teachings of religions remain fairly constant, and science has reached some points of consensus in describing how humans have interacted with birds. Chapter 2, on creation stories and how they may relate to historical evolution, allows equal weight to the truths of the Iroquois creation story and those of the book of Genesis, as well as to those of ancient Egypt and Finland, Japan and India, Mongolia and Mexico. All of these stories are considered in relation to the physical and social lives of the humans and birds who lived in the eras and places where the stories arose. On the scientific side, the chapter discusses how birds helped to create our world, not only by replanting forests after ice ages but also by spreading food grains and guiding the humans who crossed continents to fill the earth.

Chapter 3, on birds in religious rituals and costumes, abstains from judgments about the ultimate effectiveness or harmfulness of any ritual, but it does describe some controversies over bird sacrifices and using birds in captivity for rituals. Rituals including birds extend over the whole range of ancient human history, from vulture funerals of the Stone Age to the bird observations (called auguries) of ancient Etruscans and Romans. Birds modeled some rituals that humans have copied and developed, such as the flamenco (or flamingo) dance in Spain, honeyguide dances in East Africa, and eagle and sage grouse dances in the American West. Chickens are still being sacrificed by West Africans who share them with gods and by Orthodox Jews who pass chickens over their heads for purification at Yom Kippur. Just before Thanksgiving in the United States each year, two turkeys are brought to the White House and "pardoned" (not freed from punishment for crime, but exempted from being eaten) by the president of the United States. Doves were released by Pope Francis on New Year's Day and attacked by hawks in the Rome of 2014 and by seagulls in 2015 before the pope wisely gave up this ritual. When performing rituals, humans often dress in costumes made from or inspired by the feathers, wings, and colors of birds.

Chapter 4 deals with stories of birds intervening as heroes or villains in human events, as recounted in history and legend. Bird interventions include the geese that saved Rome from the Gauls in 390 BCE; the sparrows that saved Mecca from an army with elephants in 570 CE, the year when Prophet Muhammad was born; and the seagulls that ate grasshoppers to save the crops of Mormons in their first year at Salt Lake City, 1848. Contemporary Christian media sources report that in the Yom Kippur War of 1973, a dove came to one Israeli commander and stood on his shoulder, protecting him for ten days of fighting in the Golan Heights.[12] Many interventions by birds take place in the Bible and in sacred stories of Hindus, the Chinese Ming dynasty, and several Native American nations, among others.

In Chapter 5, birds appear as spiritual teachers, as examples of spiritual life, and as spiritual companions. That chapter begins with biblical images of the Spirit of God becoming incarnate in doves, as at the baptism of Jesus, then moves through the ancient roots of spiritual friendships between predatory birds and human hunters and between roosters and humans who engage in cockfighting. Birds of all kinds become spiritual teachers in *The Conference of the Birds* (Figure 1.3), written in the 1100s of our era by the Muslim author known as Attar, and in tales of the relations of St. Francis of Assisi with birds from the 1200s. Several legends of St. Francis preaching and listening to birds were made into the center of an opera by Olivier Messiaen in the twentieth century.

The role of birds as spiritual companions and teachers arose from evolution. Millions of years before humans appeared on Earth, our mammalian

Figure 1.3 Patterns of flight and tail feathers and the crest of the Eurasian hoopoe (*Upupa epops*), chief of birds in the Sufi epic *The Conference of the Birds* and national bird of Israel, make it a likely model for the spirit of Zoroastrianism.
Daniele Occhiato / AGAMI Photo / Alamy Stock Photo.

ancestors evolved brains that associate birdsong with safety. And as of 2021, a children's hospital in Liverpool began playing recordings of the dawn chorus of birds from a park near the hospital in order to calm the anxiety of its patients. It has been suggested that birdsong relaxes people physically while stimulating them cognitively, so that "the body relaxes while the mind becomes alert."[13] A primary school, also in Liverpool, is playing birdsong in its classrooms after lunch break, and Amsterdam's Schipol Airport is using birdsong recordings for the same ends. As we learn more about listening to birds, humans will find more therapeutic uses for birdsong and more ways for humans to converse with birds.

The sixth chapter deals with extinctions and with birds of apocalyptic prophecy. It considers the fate of the passenger pigeon, which went from flocking in billions that blackened the skies over North America to collecting dust in museums in a few decades. Today, less dramatic declines threaten the survival of many other species. The stories of real extinctions and the roles of birds as executors of judgment in the biblical books of Ezekiel and Revelation teach that life is fragile but resilient, subject to forces that seem both forgiving and vengeful. At the height of the Cold War, film director Alfred Hitchcock hinted that nature might turn against humanity in *The Birds* (1963). But birds have also been helpers during apocalyptic times, as in the flood stories from the Bible and ancient Mesopotamia, or in Hopi and other Native American stories of how people found their way from the destruction of previous worlds to this one.

The seventh chapter begins the story of birds in a new religion of nature. It explores the roles of birds in the 1800s, when scientific breakthroughs in geology and then in biology, breakthroughs largely based on discoveries of bird fossils in the Connecticut River and observations of birds on the Galapagos Islands by Charles Darwin, rewrote the story of life on Earth. Just as Romantic poets and composers turned away from rationalism and civilization to celebrate medieval themes and nature, so Romantic scientists turned to the past and discovered the vast antiquity of Earth and the evolution of life.

As reverence for nature became the primary commitment that holds life together for many people, a literature and a network of social organizations developed to express that reverence in social and environmental policies. According to historian Carolyn Merchant, these organizations have exhibited a pattern of males and females succeeding each other in leadership, a "gendered dialectic" in which male founders began conservation efforts that failed, but have been succeeded by female organizers who achieved more success and then handed over leadership to men. Our account carries Merchant's analysis through male reactionaries of the mid-twentieth century to Rachel Carson, the independent scientist who evoked a world without birds and saved eagles from extinction with her *Silent Spring* (1962). During Chapter 8, the narrative enters our era, a time when many are trying to transcend the limits of gender, often finding that birds can offer models and inspiration.

In the 1970s, millions of seekers were inspired by an illustrated children's book, *Jonathan Livingston Seagull*, a very masculine story that grew from the female-centered 1875 insights of Mary Baker Eddy and Christian Science and made birds into vehicles for an individualist human quest. Jonathan the Christlike (and magical Daoist) gull seemed silly thirty years later, but by then leaders of religion and culture had moved on to *The March of the Penguins*, an Academy Award–winning documentary of 2005 that became part of a national debate over gender and family in the United States. By November 2020, in the aftermath of the presidential election, Joe Biden used the popular hymn "On Eagles' Wings," which evokes birds in both male and female roles, in his victory speech. The fall of 2020 saw Carolyn Merchant's "gendered dialectic" resolved through gender transition in *The Thirty Names of Night*, a novel by a transman named Zeyn Joukhadar that relocates the Sufi Muslim epic poem *The Conference of the Birds*, within the community of Muslims who have fled from Syria to New York City.[14]

Toward the end of Chapter 8, we describe how artists and birdwatchers have worked together both to mourn and to resist extinctions of birds in recent decades. We recommend practical steps, such as abolishing factory farms, transforming the aviaries of zoos into nurseries to rebuild bird populations, and landscaping oases for birds in our cities and along migration flyways. Even in recent controversies over John James Audubon's ownership of slaves and possibly mixed-race ancestry, it appears that birds are leading people to see beyond categories of race, nation, and gender to glimpse new possibilities for a balanced and healthy world.

The hopeful ending of Chapter 8 is punctuated, and its hope partly punctured, by two simultaneous waves of disease in the summer of 2021. A global wave of human infections by a new variant of the Covid-19 virus prolonged the pandemic of 2020. During the first waves of that pandemic, millions of humans had become birdwatchers because watching birds was a rare activity that could still be pursued, in the safety of outdoor air and sometimes even in groups. People who stayed in their homes could still see birds outside their windows, and bird feeders became more popular. But 2021 brought a global infection of birds by a disease that attacked their eyes and nervous systems and killed many, causing Audubon societies and government conservation agencies to warn that bird feeders should be taken down because they caused birds to congregate closely and spread the germ.

The double assault of disease underlined the solidarity of birds and humans. In a *New York Times* opinion column, Ben Crair wrote that "rather than looking at wild animals as symbols of hope or freedom," the twin plagues showed that we should "recognize them simply as fellow creatures with only the cruel hand of natural selection to balance the benefits of community and cooperation against the risks of disease."[15] *Atlantic* magazine writer Elizabeth Breunig recalled the apology she offered her backyard birds as she took down her feeders and the tears she shed after burying a blue jay. "*Oh Lord, please don't make me do this again*," she prayed.[16] Religions deal with issues of life and death, and the global pandemics showed humans and birds caught in similar nets of deadly illness. Sometimes, as in previous epidemics of bird flu,

West Nile virus, and SARS, human and bird illnesses are caused by the same pathogen.

In her 2016 book, *Culture and Activism: Animal Rights in France and the United States*, sociologist Elizabeth Cherry described two attitudes toward religion among groups working for animal rights. In France, these groups have avoided religious language and associations, while in the United States, religion has provided positive cultural tools.[17] Cherry concluded that American animal rights groups have had more success than those in France in part because the American activists have made more use of the whole repertoire of arguments and appeals that their culture has provided.[18]

And now, as forests burn and glaciers melt and plagues afflicting both humans and birds spread across the world, we need a less anthropocentric religion, a religion focused on healing the whole Earth. Birds led our ancestors to honey in East Africa and across Siberia to the Americas, and our ancestors had the wisdom to follow. We offer this book in hope that it may foster a religious consciousness that will help people to reach a new world together with birds.

Notes

1. Mark I. Wallace, "The Pileated Woodpecker: Avian Divinity in a Time of Chaos," *Kosmos: Journal for Global Transformation*, Summer 2021, https://www.kosmosjournal.org/news/the-pileated-woodpecker-avian-divinity-in-a-time-of-chaos/ (accessed August 13, 2021).
2. Marija Gimbutas, *The Civilization of the Goddess* (San Francisco: HarperSanFrancisco, 1991).
3. Bernd Heinrich, *Ravens in Winter* (New York: Summit Books, 1989), 21–27.
4. Peter Gardella, *Domestic Religion: Work, Food, Sex, and Other Commitments* (Cleveland, OH: Pilgrim Press, 1998), 1.
5. Charlton T. Lewis and Charles Short, *A Latin Dictionary* (1879; Oxford: Clarendon Press, 1969), 1556.
6. This approach to religion is especially prominent in the work of sociologist Émile Durkheim and in that of anthropologists such as Clifford Geertz. A definition of religion as "a system of nonrational commitments that holds life together" is set forth in Gardella, *Domestic Religion*, 1–2.
7. Robert N. Bellah, *Religion in Human Evolution: From the Paleolithic to the Axial Age* (Cambridge, MA: Harvard University Press, 2011), xiii *et passim*.
8. Edward A. Armstrong, *The Life and Lore of the Bird: In Nature, Art, Myth, and Literature* (New York: Crown Publishers, 1975), 76–99 and 200–221.

9. Most recently, this has been argued by Ara Norenzayan, a Lebanese/Canadian social psychologist, in *Big Gods: How Religion Transformed Cooperation and Conflict* (Princeton, NJ: Princeton University Press, 2013). Similar arguments have been made by historian Karen Armstrong and sociologist Robert Bellah.
10. Kay Bradway and Barbara McCoard, *Sandplay: Silent Workshop of the Psyche* (London: Routledge, 1997), 101.
11. Aileen Kawagoe, "On the Trail of the Torii's Origins," *Heritage of Japan*, 2013, https://heritageofjapan.wordpress.com/2013/02/01/on-the-trail-of-the-toriis-origins/ (accessed June 12, 2021).
12. David McCaine, "Israel's History Is Inundated with Examples of Supernatural Protection from God," *San Jose Christian Perspectives Examiner*, September 13, 2013, http://www.examiner.com/article/israel-s-history-is-inundated-with-examples-of-supernatural-protection-from-god (accessed August 8, 2014). Also reported by the Christian Broadcasting Network, at http://www.cbn.com/cbnnews/insideisrael/2013/September/Fmr-Israeli-Commander-God-Protected-us-in-Battle--/ (August 8, 2014).
13. Bob Sundstrom, "Birdsong Therapy," *BirdNote*, broadcast in the United States August 13, 2021, https://www.birdnote.org/listen/shows/birdsong-therapy (accessed August 20, 2021).
14. Zeyn Joukhadar, *The Thirty Names of Night* (New York: Simon & Schuster, 2020).
15. Ben Crair, "What Birds Taught Me about Covid," *New York Times*, August 15, 2021, SR7.
16. Elizabeth Breunig, "Then the Birds Began to Die," *The Atlantic*, July 22, 2021, https://www.theatlantic.com/ideas/archive/2021/07/the-bird-pandemic/619521/ (accessed August 26, 2021).
17. Elizabeth Cherry, *Culture and Activism: Animal Rights in France and the United States* (New York: Routledge, 2016), 33–42.
18. Cherry, *Culture and Activism*, 145–146, also 101–102.

2
Birds in Creation, Evolution, and Creation Stories

Birds as Gods in Creation Stories

The Bible story of creation begins with the act of a bird. Although picturing God as a bird may seem primitive, or contrary to the biblical law against images of God or of any animal, such verbal pictures occur in the Bible from Genesis to Jesus. Sometimes the images of God as a bird are explicit, and sometimes they stand just under English translations of the text.

When the world was without form, "the spirit of God hovered over the face of the waters," says the American Jewish Version of Genesis 1:2. The New International Version, popular among evangelical Christians, agrees with a slight difference: at the beginning the world had no form, there was darkness over the deep, "and the Spirit of God was hovering over the waters." The Hebrew verb *rachaf*, the word translated as "was hovering," occurs here in past imperfect tense, *merachefet*. The same verb occurs in the present tense in Deuteronomy 32:11, which describes the creation of God's people Israel, when God took the nation from Egypt and led it through the desert. The God of Israel was "Like an eagle that stirs up its nest, and hovers (*yeracheif*) over its young, that spreads abroad its wings to catch them, and carries them aloft" (NIV). The Bible does not flinch from describing God as a nesting bird.

Birds come in two sexes, female and male, and so do the birds that personify God in these verses. In Genesis, the "spirit" who was hovering translates the Hebrew *ruach*, a feminine noun. In Deuteronomy, the "eagle" who teaches the chicks to fly translates the Hebrew *nesher*, a masculine noun for any large predatory bird.[1] By using bird images for God, the Bible includes both sexes in the divine. Birds enable the biblical creation to transcend the limits of sex and gender.

God creates in Genesis 1 by speech, in a series of orders beginning with the third verse: "Let there be light." And just before the first of those spoken orders comes the second verse, *veruach elohim merachefet*, "and the spirit of

God was hovering." This hovering of God's breath or spirit over the waters has been compared by both Jewish and Christian thinkers to a preparation for creation, the "brooding" that precedes hatching, or the gentle breath that precedes speech.[2] As a brooding bird beats gently with its wings over the nest, circulating air over the eggs, so the Genesis account pictures God breathing gently in the darkness, over the formless deep, before the spoken command. One scholar notes the parallel between the only two times this verb is used, at the creation of the world and the beginning of Israel, and concludes that the spirit is said to hover: "At the very beginning of things, when God is about to give shape to what is shapeless."[3]

The tenderness of this image corresponds with the way that Jesus is said to have used the metaphor of a hen to describe God in the Gospels of Matthew and Luke. In passages probably written after the Romans had destroyed the city of Jerusalem, those gospel writers picture Jesus lamenting the city's fate. They quote Jesus saying, "Jerusalem, Jerusalem. . . . How often have I desired to gather your children as a hen gathers her brood under her wings, and you were not willing!" (Matthew 23:37, NRSV; also Luke 13:34).

Hens and roosters, female and male chickens, began to appear in creation stories as people took up agriculture. Chickens were among the first animals domesticated for food by humans. Domestication of chickens apparently began in Southeast Asia, particularly in the area that is now Thailand, and quickly spread throughout Asia toward Europe.[4]

Creation stories reflected the role that chickens played as people began to settle into sedentary lives. For example, the persistently nomadic Mongols explained why there are so many more Han Chinese than Mongols by saying that their Mongol ancestors were hunters who began to mate with swans, or with sheep, while the Chinese were descended from hens, which breed more rapidly.[5] Among the Yoruba, who set up cities and began the use of iron in West Africa, guinea fowl were domesticated in a separate line of development from the Asian chicken, and the creation of land was said to have resulted from the scratching of a rooster who scattered earth over the primordial water.[6]

There are now about as many breeds of chickens, the results of selective breeding by people, as there are breeds of dogs. In these days of factory farming and supermarkets, it may be hard to realize that people for millennia have had intimate relations with chickens, sometimes treating as pets the birds they fed every day and whose eggs they might eat for years. But whether the particular bird was the domestic hen of the Gospels, the wild eagle of

Deuteronomy, or the nameless bird who "hovers" in Genesis, the actions of a bird nurturing its young seemed to biblical writers and to other ancient people to be an appropriate image of how their God related to the world.

One historical precedent for this image of God came from the moment of creation that was commemorated in Egyptian temples. The ancient Hebrews, whose name derived from the word for "wanderer," were seminomadic traders and herders who traveled between the realms of Mesopotamia (now Iraq) and Egypt. As the biblical stories of Abraham and the patriarchs suggest, the Hebrews began in Mesopotamia but often visited or even lived in Egypt, and their culture reveals elements borrowed from both of those empires. And every Egyptian temple, according to historian Michael Wood, included an altar representing the original mound of earth that emerged from the water at the birth of the world,[7] just as the Nile flooded and retreated every spring to reveal new earth in which to grow crops. On that first mound of earth grew reeds, and upon a column of papyrus reeds stood a divine bird, Horus the Hawk.

Horus embodied the principle of order, a ruler emerging from chaos. Every pharaoh reigned as Horus, and the temples had statues of Horus standing on the mound and wall paintings of the same scene. The hawk also stood for rebirth after death, because Horus was begotten by his father, the god Osiris, even after Osiris had been murdered by his evil brother Set. The body of Osiris was recovered after that murder by his wife Isis, a goddess who used her powers to revive her husband long enough to conceive by him. In the imagery of Egyptian gods, Isis often appeared as a woman with the wings of a bird (usually a kite, another large bird of prey, but sometimes a falcon, a hawk-like kestrel, or a swallow) lifted in protection. There was some violence in the Egyptian creation—the murder of Osiris, and a long battle between Horus and Set—but the overall message was a triumph of peace, under the sheltering authority of a noble bird. Even today, the flag of Egypt features a large eagle, called the Eagle of Saladin after the general who ruled Egypt and recovered Jerusalem from the Christian Crusaders in the 1180s.

The tendency of Egypt to identify its rulers with birds of prey may relate to the ancient status of Egypt as a rich agricultural nation, the breadbasket of the Mediterranean world. For farmers who worry about small birds and mice and rabbits eating their crops, hawks and eagles must appear in the sky as noble allies. Those altars of Horus on the reeds depicted the hawk protecting the rich land. That land, in turn, nurtured many birds to protect itself. Egypt and its neighbors to the south provided habitat for so many birds that the upper Nile was called "the land of whirring wings" by the Hebrew prophet Isaiah (Isaiah 18). About five hundred species of birds are associated with Egypt today. In recent years, an estimated 2.8 billion birds follow migration paths from Europe over Egypt toward Africa each fall.[8]

The ancient religion of Egypt teems with birds. The vulture is Nekhbet, goddess of Upper Egypt and protectress of women in childbirth; the ibis (a waterbird, falsely celebrated by the Greek writer Herodotus for protecting Egypt from snakes) is Thoth, the Egyptian god of wisdom and writing; even the solar disk has wings in the Egyptian cosmos.[9] Birds connect the sky over Egypt, the Nile that creates Egypt, the rich Egyptian farmland, and the people.

All over the world, creation stories describe the emergence of land from water, and in those stories birds frequently play a role. The power of flight makes it possible for birds to mediate between the orderly heavens and the chaos of the sea. Because waterbirds need land to nest, they also link the air and water to the land. A large waterbird, a swan or a goose, was said to have laid the golden egg from which the world developed in some Hindu stories (Rig Veda 10.121).

Eggs contain the world in several Hindu creation stories. According to one Hindu text, the Chandogya Upanishad, dating from about 700 BCE, the original egg had a shell of two parts, one of silver that became the earth, and one of gold that became the sky. The outer membrane of the egg became the mountains, the inner membrane became clouds and mist. Veins in the egg became rivers, and its fluid became the ocean. The story reflected extensive knowledge of eggs and understanding of the life cycle. Centuries before that text about the egg, the Rig Veda, a collection of poems from about 1200 BCE, had traced the beginning of the world to a golden embryo, and a sacrifice in which Prajapati, the first man, cut himself into pieces to make the gods and the castes or divisions of humanity. The Brahmanas, written about 1000 BCE to provide prose instructions on how to perform sacrifice, said that it was Prajapati who broke open the original egg. In a sense these Hindu stories make humans into birds, because they teach that the ancestor of all humans was born from an egg in the manner of a bird.

In many creation accounts, animals or spirits dive below the surface of the water to find land, and several types of birds have the power of water divers. The Yakuts of Siberia tell a story of a mother goddess who asked a white-billed diver (also called the "yellow-billed loon") to seek earth from beneath the waters that covered the earth, and all across the north from Mongolia to

Norway water divers are seen as messengers to the spirit world.[10] According to another Siberian people, the Samoyed, creation began with seven men in a boat who retrieved land that had stuck to the beak of a loon, then threw the land into the water, where it grew. Loons dove to recover land after a great flood, according to legends of the Ojibwa (or Chippewa) people who have lived around Lake Huron and Lake Superior in North America since long before Europeans arrived, and who live there today.[11]

For the Iroquois or Haudenosaunee, the coalition of five Native nations who live in what is now upstate New York along the border of Canada from Montreal to Lake Erie, creation began with a need for birds to rescue a pregnant woman who fell from the heavenly realm through a hole in the sky.[12] At that time this lower world was covered in water, and nothing lived here but the waterbirds and creatures of the water. Seeing the woman falling, the birds flew up to catch her. Some versions of the story say that the loons caught her and used their loud voices to call out for help; other versions say it was the white swans who used their great size to catch the woman. Ducks are also mentioned. Whichever birds were responsible, "Flying wingtip to wingtip, they made a great feathery raft in the sky to support her."[13]

In Japan, a small and notably active bird called the wagtail, because of a long tail that moves almost constantly, is said to have beaten the water away from the earth with its tail and feet and so created dry land, according to the creation stories of the Ainu people (the natives of Hokkaido, northernmost island of the Japanese archipelago).[14] Japanese myths also report that the original pair of gods learned how to do sexual intercourse by watching a pair of wagtails, who have a striking mating dance. Because of this story, the wagtail is called "the love-knowing bird," and a place called "Wagtail Rock" is visited by pregnant women for good luck.[15]

Another waterbird, the teal duck, takes a more direct role as the source of all things in the Finnish creation poem, called the *Kalevala*. When the world was all water, "the beauteous teal" flew this way and that, searching for a place to lay her eggs.[16] This would have been especially difficult with the world covered by water, because the Eurasian teal is a ground-nesting bird. The Mother of Waters saw the teal and lifted her knee above the surface. The bird made her nest (from what it is not clear) on the knee and laid six golden eggs and a seventh egg of iron. She brooded on the nest, warming the eggs, for three days, but the heat caused the Mother of Waters to move her knee, so that the eggs rolled into the water and broke. Part of the shell of an egg became the sky, the yolks became the sun, the whites the moon, and spots in the eggs became other creatures. From the black yolk of the iron egg came the thunderclouds.

This story continues to inspire Finns today. In May 2013, the nation opened a new Finnish Nature Centre, named "Haltia," or "spirit of the land," to celebrate the natural wonders of Finland. The center is housed in a wooden building, designed as a modern evocation of a duck, with a tower at one end representing the duck's neck and head and a world egg standing in its exhibit hall. According to the center's website, "Haltia settles into the steeply sloping lot and landscape as naturally as a bird in its nest."[17]

Social Birds Helping to Create Human Societies

Humans and birds are closely allied in many Siberian and Native American stories of how ravens, and sometimes their smaller cousins the crows and magpies, took part in creation. Ravens and crows as creators may seem strange to moderns with a scientific worldview. Such stories would also seem odd to settled agriculturalists, or to the traders who travel between such civilizations, but stories about how ravens took part in creating the world have made sense to hunter-gatherers. After all, ravens and crows themselves live as hunter-gatherers, in groups of nine or ten composed of a mating pair, some offspring of the pair up to about three years old, and isolated birds that have attached to the group. Such groups of birds often accompany, sometimes following and sometimes leading, groups of people or groups of wolves. The birds are attracted to the same sources of water and food that indicate where prey animals are, and in return for their help in locating prey they share in what is left from the kill, because they are both omnivores and scavengers. For farmers, crows and ravens are pests, voracious eaters of grains—hence the famous figure of the "scarecrow" in the fields—and for city dwellers, crows can seem like flying rats, attracted to garbage and dropping their feces on every surface, but for hunter-gatherers, crows are allies.

Humans observing ravens or crows might have noticed that the young of these birds resemble human babies because they emerge from their eggs nearly naked, with only a few pinfeathers. They do not become feathered for five or six weeks.[18] After emerging from the nest, crows resemble humans in other ways. Exhibiting great intelligence, ravens and crows will recognize particular people and animals and respond to their previous behavior. For example, years after an experiment for which students trapped crows that were later released, the crows were still mobbing and cawing at the students who had trapped them.[19] Crows imitate sounds made by other birds, animals, and people in their neighborhoods. They sometimes work together in groups of two or three to distract other animals, such as otters catching fish or dogs with meat, in order to steal their catch, or to "mob," attack, and harass predators such as hawks. Swedish ice-fishermen report that crows lift up unattended lines and take their fish. Experiments show that crows will not only use sticks or pieces of metal to get food, but will also bend a straight piece of metal into a hook to make it more efficient for picking up objects.[20]

Because ravens and crows have a deserved reputation as socially intelligent animals and opportunistic thieves, the role they play in creation stories is usually that of a trickster god, a god who uses guile to defeat evil and who teaches people useful skills. According to a widespread story among Native Americans of the Pacific Northwest, particularly the Kwakiutl, Raven stole the sun from a miserly shaman, a powerful magician who had hidden the sun in a cedar box, so that the whole world was dark. Observing that the shaman's weakness was his love for his daughter, Raven lurked near the stream where the girl went to get water. He transformed himself into a hemlock needle and fell into the water, where the girl scooped him up. She swallowed the needle while drinking, and Raven entered her body and turned into a human baby boy. He was born from the girl in the shaman's house, and the shaman loved him as a grandson and the son of his beloved daughter. When the boy (whose nose still looked a bit like a beak) asked for the glowing box, the shaman could not refuse him. Raven opened the box, changed back into a bird, and carried the sun up into the sky.[21]

Such a story must have had natural appeal in northern climes, where the sun did disappear every winter. According to an account from 1896, the Tlingit nation of Alaska told a similar tale of Raven releasing the sun.[22] Tlingit also give Raven a more basic role, because they have a tradition that Raven found human beings hidden inside a clamshell and brought them out into the world. According to the Haida, a nation of what is now the Northwest of Canada, Raven made their homeland, the Queen Charlotte Islands, by dropping pebbles into the sea.[23]

A creation story with more social implications, in which Crow saved all the animals from a harsh winter by obtaining fire, arose among the Lenape, the original inhabitants of what is now New York City and its environs. In the Lenape version, long before humans arose, the first snow that fell at creation nearly killed all the animals.[24] After the mice and the rabbits disappeared in the deep snow, the other animals held a council to decide whom to send to the Creator to ask that the snow be stopped.

A crow volunteered, but it was not the crow that we know. This was Rainbow Crow, a bird with feathers in the colors of the rainbow and a sweet singing voice. He flew for days to reach the Creator, then got his attention with that voice. But when the crow asked the Creator to stop the snow, the Creator said that he could not, because the snow has its own spirit and would only stop on its own. Nor could the Creator stop the wind or the cold. He did offer Rainbow Crow the gift of fire. He lit a stick and gave it to the bird. But as Rainbow Crow flew the three days' journey back to earth, on the first day his tail was blackened by the smoke, and on the second day the rest of his feathers were blackened, and on the third day the smoke blew into his throat and made his voice harsh. By the time he reached the earth, all the animals were buried by snow, and he flew around and around with the fire and set them free. Then all of the animals praised him with a song and dance, and the fire he had brought became the grandfather of all fire.

But Rainbow Crow was sad, because he had changed. Seeing his sadness, the Creator consoled him. Soon humans would come to the earth, the Creator said, and humans would hunt other birds for their feathers and their flesh, but they would not hunt the crow because his feathers were black and his flesh, burned from the fire, tasted bad. Some birds would be captured for their beautiful songs, but no one would keep the crow in a cage to hear it sing. Nor had his feathers completely lost the rainbow, because if he looked at them closely, he could still see tiny rainbows within the shiny black. So the crow was satisfied.

In this story, the social character of the crow is evident. He volunteers to help, he saves his fellow animals. And in fact, observers of crows and ravens note that they are very social. They do not steal from birds of their own groups; they bring food to injured colleagues; and they are even said to mourn when one of their group dies.

Because they can imprint on humans as fledglings, and sometimes adopt a human group as their own, crows have also been seen to guard human babies and to discriminate between strange humans and members of a family. When the Bible tells the story of the prophet Elijah fleeing into the wilderness east of the Jordan River to avoid the wrath of idolaters during a drought that Elijah had called down upon Israel, it notes that God commanded the ravens to feed the prophet (1 Kings 17:4), and reports that "The ravens brought him bread and meat in the morning, and bread and meat in the evening" (1 Kings

17:6, NRSV). Perhaps some ravens really knew Elijah and followed him. They probably would not have fed him, though they might have showed him food or traded with him, especially if the prophet had fed them first.

By fleeing over the Jordan, Elijah was entering territory that was beyond the normal boundaries of Israel, over the river that Israel crossed to enter into its Promised Land on the way up from Egypt. He was metaphorically retreating to a place before the creation of the chosen people, so that he could bring about their rebirth. In that recreation, the ravens were his helpers. All effective creation stories explain the origins of important cultural practices, and the ravens function in the Elijah story as helpers of the one who is recreating the correct religion of Israel, the worship of their one God alone.

In a biblical text much closer to the first creation story of Genesis, ravens helped to remake the world after the Flood. In Genesis 8:6–7, Noah sends a raven out from the ark after forty days of flood, and according to the text, the raven "went to and fro until the waters were dried up from the earth" (Genesis 8:7, NRSV). This action of the raven has been seen in recent scholarship as participation in drying up the waters.[25] The raven flies "to and fro" until the waters are dried up, just as the spirit of God "hovered" over the waters in Genesis 1 until it brought forth the land.

Because Noah sends a dove from the ark after the raven, to see if the land has appeared, the role of the raven has often been interpreted negatively by older scholars; the raven has been seen as evil and the dove as good. At first, the dove returns with no evidence of land; then it returns with an olive branch; and finally it does not return at all, so Noah concludes that the flood is over. But the text never says that Noah sent the raven to look for land, just that Noah released a raven before releasing any doves. By flying over the waters until they were dried up, the raven may have performed the land-creating role that many stories attribute to birds.

The different roles of raven and dove may also reflect phases in the history of ancient Israel and older civilizations of Mesopotamia. In the flood story of the Gilgamesh epic from ancient Babylon, written down more than a thousand years before the flood story of Genesis, the Babylonian Noah (Utnapishtim) first sends out a dove and a swallow from the ark, and both birds return with no evidence of land; he then sends a raven, who does not come back, showing that the flood was no longer complete. The Israelite author of Genesis 8:6–7, who is believed by scholars to be a Jerusalem priest of the sixth century BCE reworking stories that began much earlier, retains the role of the raven as a bird that did not return and magnifies the role of the dove. This probably reflects the status of the dove as a pure (kosher), vegetarian bird who could be sacrificed in the rituals of the Jerusalem Temple, while the raven was a scavenger who could neither be eaten nor sacrificed by Jews. For the priestly author, the raven's old role in signaling the end of the Flood (and possibly in recreating the world) could not be left out, but the role of the domesticated dove had to become more important.

Slight differences in culture probably explain the small but striking difference in the roles that the magpie—a black-and-white member of the same corvid family with the crow and the raven—plays in two variants of the same creation story told by neighboring Plains Indian nations. Among both Lakota and Cheyenne, the Black Hills are the original land, where all animals emerged from the earth. Both nations say that the buffalo at first ate humans and other animals, but humans protested. It was decided that there would be a great race around the Black Hills to decide whether humans or buffalo would rule, and other animals also raced to decide their rank. This race was about two hundred miles, extending from Buffalo Gap, at the southeast corner of the Black Hills, to the northeast corner at Mato Tipila, a famous butte that is also called Devil's Tower, and that attracted aliens in the movie *Close Encounters of the Third Kind*. Because buffalo had the advantage of four legs over only two for the humans, humans were allowed to pick four birds to race for them. The buffalo chose their fastest runner, Running Slim Buffalo Woman, and the humans picked a hummingbird, a meadowlark, a hawk, and a magpie.

Although the little hummingbird flew fast, the race was far too long for him to keep up a fast pace, and he dropped away early. At about the halfway point, the Lodge of the Bear, the lark was too tired. Then the hawk passed the buffalo, but again the long distance caused him to tire and he could not stay ahead.

Here the Cheyenne and Lakota stories diverge. According to the Cheyenne, the magpie was the slowest flier among the birds but also the most determined. It kept going steadily, and as the Buffalo Woman tired toward the end of the race, magpie slowly and painfully caught up with her, gaining the lead when the two animals were only a hand-breadth away from the finish line. By winning the race, magpie not only secured humans the right to hunt buffalo, but also won a home for magpies in the Black Hills, where magpies live all year, although crows migrate away in winter.

The Lakota story reaches the same ending by a different route. Lakota say that the magpie made up for her slower flying by hitching a ride on Buffalo

Woman until near the end of the race, when "that clever bird flew ahead" and won. Some Lakota versions of the story say that magpie was punished for cheating by being made to eat the leavings of other animals.[26]

These different endings of the story may reflect how Cheyenne and Lakota people found the strengths of their own cultures embodied in magpies. Both nations lived on the Great Plains, but the Cheyenne tended to be more settled and to have central authorities, while the Lakota lived more nomadic lives in smaller bands. For the Cheyenne, magpie's persistence and loyalty to home were admirable, while the Lakota saw magpie's tricky intelligence as the bird's most important characteristic. But both ascribed to this cousin of the crow a basic role in the beginning of their world.

Far to the south of the Great Plains, in Central America, a more distant relative of the crow featured prominently in the creation account of the Mayans, who built a great urbanized civilization more than a thousand years ago. The Mayan sacred epic, the Popul Vuh, describes an original creation that failed and was destroyed by a flood, after which the first humans became monkeys and things began anew. The world after the flood was dark—like the world of the Siberian and northwestern Indians after the shaman hid away the sun—until a giant macaw, a great parrot called Itzam Yeh, gave the world light with its plumage, perching at the top of a great tree. *Itz* was the Mayan word for the force of life, found especially in fluids like blood and spit, and the word *Itzam* connotes one who can work with *itz*, a shaman, while *Yeh* means "giver." The macaw who is called Itzam Yeh became proud and arrogant after its accomplishment, identifying itself with the sun and the moon and demanding worship, but the human hero twins whom the Mayans called their founders shot the bird out of its tree. Later, the twins fooled the bird by offering to heal it. When it agreed to let them operate, they took its teeth (the Itzam Yeh bird had teeth) and left white corn meal in their place, and left metal in place of its eyes. The story of this cruel trick is seen by some scholars as a symbol for the sacrifice of the blood of the ruler, the ritual by which Mayans tried to release *itz* to renew the life of the world. Mayan rulers wore the feathers of the macaw as they stood atop pyramids and wounded themselves in order to offer blood.

Just as the macaw resembles the raven and crow and magpie in being a social, long-lived, intelligent bird that can imitate the human voice, so the role the macaw plays in the Mayan view of creation and cosmic renewal bears some resemblance to the role of raven, crow, and magpie for northern Native Americans. But Mayan society was far more concentrated, settled, and elaborated than the societies of northern Indians who told their stories of raven, crow, and magpie. Mayans needed a more elaborate and formal religion to hold their world together. The Mayan world had full-time kings and priests, regular sacrifices, massive temples, astronomical observatories, and complex calendrical scheduling. Their cosmic macaw, Itzam Yeh, had more developed connections with more numerous dimensions of life than did the corvids of North America.

Sometimes, the Mayan macaw was pictured with the body of a serpent to go with its wings and beak. This symbolism connected Itzam Yeh with the feathered serpent Quetzalcóatl, of the Aztecs, and with the phoenixes and dragons, the birds who rise from the dead and the flying serpents, of China and elsewhere. Such dramatic creatures will be discussed further in the chapter on birds of apocalypse.

Here, in relation to birds of creation, the differences between the Mayan macaw and birds of the later Aztec empire again demonstrate how creation stories express the social character and worldviews of the cultures that tell them. The aggressive Aztecs preferred two more aggressive species of birds, the hummingbird and the eagle, to the social macaw and the feathered serpent as heroes of creation. Aztec kings wore hummingbird feathers to personify Huitzilopochtli, the hummingbird god of the sun who defeated the stars of night and completed the process that Quetzalcóatl had begun. According to Aztec myth, Huitzilopochtli had thrown the heart of his last enemy into Lake Texcoco, on the site where the Aztec capital of Tenochtitlán and later Mexico City would stand. The hummingbird god told the Aztecs that they would know the site because they would see an eagle standing in a cactus and eating a serpent at that place. This striking image, representing the birth of the Mexican nation, has appeared since 1821 on the flag of Mexico.

The tiny, energetic hummingbird, which migrates across the American continents and fiercely defends its territory in its seasonal neighborhoods, has been widely regarded as a creator and founder of cultures by Native American nations. For the Mohave of Southern California, the hummingbird served as the guide who led the members of the nation from deep underground to live on the sunlit surface. It brought the staple crop of corn to the Navajo, a seminomadic people who themselves had come down from the Arctic to settle in the North American Southwest. The same bird was credited with bringing tobacco to the Arawak and Carib nations of the Caribbean and to the Cherokee of what would become the southeastern United States.[27] Because corn and tobacco were so basic to these cultures, the bird that brought them contributed a vital aspect of creation.

But there was also a much more personal aspect to the way the hummingbird took part in creation, at least in the semitropical climates of Mexico and southeast South America, where the most numerous varieties of hummingbirds live. In many stories from Mayan and Aztec cultures, and from regions including modern Belize and Guatemala as well as various parts of Mexico, a hummingbird mates with a human woman to produce legendary kings and aspects of the world such as cotton and many kinds of animals.

Sometimes the hummingbird is the sun and the woman is the moon. Sometimes hummingbird is a human who disguises himself as a hummingbird to attract the woman, who is almost always being guarded by jealous parents who do not want her to marry at all. The woman is engaged in weaving, creating sustenance that the parents want. To gain access to her, the male must distract her from weaving, and approaching her as a hummingbird helps to deceive the parents and to attract the woman's attention. When the woman takes the hummingbird under her clothing or brings him to bed with her, sometimes after he has been trapped or shot with a blowgun or injured by the girl's father, the marriage is consummated. There are variants of the story in which the hero animal is a quetzal bird or macaw, a grackle, or even a mosquito, but a hummingbird is most often the suitor. The basic subject is "the hierogamy [sacred marriage] that variously resulted in the birth of the sun, the moon, and human sustenance."[28] This hummingbird and human hierogamy is reenacted in sacred dances that continue to this day. Behind the stories and the dances probably lies much observation of real hummingbird mating, which involves the bird couple flying in intricate patterns and approaching each other with force sufficient to knock the partners to the ground.

At every point in this survey of birds in creation and evolution, cooperation between birds and humans has been a common theme uniting all types of human cultures, from Paleolithic hunter-gatherers to modern horticulturalists, and from ancient nomads or merchants to farmers and city dwellers. No nation's creation stories and subsequent worldview have stressed cooperation more than those of the Hopi, a nation still living in its ancestral villages of more than a thousand years ago, in the "four corners" section where the borders of Utah, Colorado, New Mexico, and Arizona meet. For the Hopi, creation has always involved cooperation with birds. It was a swallow that found the entrance to this world, the passage from the previous realm where the Hopi had lived under the earth. When they emerged, they found that they had left their vital corn seed behind, but a swallow went back and retrieved it. Once Hopi began to live in this world, they learned their traditional songs, the songs for rituals that maintain the cycles of the sun and the seasons, by listening to the mockingbird. Mockingbirds also taught the Hopi how to speak.[29]

Birds and Humans Evolving and Creating Together

Birds came into the world more than one hundred million years before people and helped to make the environment that gave birth to humanity. Wherever humans have lived, there were birds already in the skies, on the shores, in the grasses and forests. Whether *Homo sapiens* looked at birds and thought that birds had godlike powers or that gods had birdlike powers, birds remained ubiquitous and prominent as humans spread through the world and dominated many ecosystems.

The roles that humans have given to birds in creation stories reflect the ways that humans have perceived birds acting as their helpers and companions in shaping the world. It is no accident that in the world's religions, birds appear alongside the gods and sometimes before the gods, or as gods themselves. The stories told by religions did not spring from abstract thinking, mathematical logic, or pure imagination, but reflect the physical world that humans experienced, a world of sky and water and trees, all filled with birds. The stories of creation make much more sense once we comprehend how birds and humans have really worked together to make the world.

Today, scientists estimate that there are approximately two hundred to four hundred billion individual birds (between thirty and sixty birds for every individual human, depending on the time of year), comprising nine to ten thousand species.[30] There are more than twice the number of bird species than mammal species and 50 percent more bird species than reptile species. Birds live on all continents, including Antarctica, which humans only visit. But bird population is in long-term decline because of ecological changes and human-caused extinctions.[31]

Many are familiar with the notion that birds evolved from dinosaurs, or from species that resembled the dinosaurs. More precisely, most scientists interpret the evidence from fossils and physiology as demonstrating that the ancestors of birds evolved from the theropods, one type of bipedal, agile, upright-postured, toothed, carnivorous dinosaur with short forelimbs, during the Jurassic geological period between 130 and 160 million years ago. The famous archaeopteryx and its cousins (two genera of *Archaeoterygidae* are known) walked with its feathers fluttering, around 150 million years ago, but these creatures still had somewhat mobile hands, teeth in their jaws, long bony tails, and small crania.[32] By the late Cretaceous period, down to 65 million years ago, the ancestors of more familiar modern birds shared spaces with swimming toothed birds and flying toothed "anti-birds" (the Enantiorthinines). Birds were helped by and helped the rise of flowering plants, called angiosperms, which radiated widely across the globe and finally replaced conifers (trees that have their seeds in cones) in many ecosystems, with angiosperms forming forest canopies in the Upper or late Cretaceous (about 75 million years ago).[33] Birds and flowers flourished and evolved together.

Some birds survived the event that killed the dinosaurs: the catastrophic meteor strike at Chicxulub in the Yucatan of Mexico, approximately sixty-five million years ago.[34] This meteor strike was accompanied by flood basalt eruptions on the other side of the world that sent rock oozing from fissures and rents in the surface and flowing like honey over tens of thousands of acres for tens or even hundreds of thousands of years. Ancestors of the mostly flightless "ratites" (ostriches, emus, and their flying kin, the tinamous), ducks and other shorebirds, terrestrial fowl, and less well-known ancestors of the modern flying birds survived the long blockage of sunlight caused by debris from the meteor strike and subsequent fires. Probably, birds survived as the early mammals did, successfully competing with reptiles because they were more capable than dinosaurs of living on a diminished supply of large plants. Birds later helped to recreate the world, planting forests by spreading the seeds of trees. Today, jays and nutcrackers will carry seeds up to thirteen miles and leave some caches of seeds that they never consume. Many scientists think that this behavior helped to establish new forests after ice ages in the areas that became Siberia, Alaska, and Canada.[35] Birds created the forests in which they live.

By seven million years ago, members of all modern families of birds were walking, flying, and swimming through the world. These included the very large and diverse group of perching birds or "Passeriformes," which have the special feature of a tendon connecting legs and toes that causes their toes to lock onto a branch whenever their legs bear weight, so that they can perch even as they sleep. At roughly the same point about seven million years ago, the first direct ancestors of *Homo sapiens*, primates distinct from the ancestors of modern chimps and gorillas, had also emerged.

By the time *Homo sapiens* entered the world, between 1.5 and 1.2 million years ago in sub-Saharan Africa, some fifteen hundred species of birds inhabited the "Ethiopian" zoogeographical realm (also known as "Afrotropical") that includes Africa south of the Sahara and the southern Arabian Peninsula. As humans migrated out of Africa into Asia, they found many (about one-third) of the same general types of birds that they knew in Africa. First in Asia and later globally, humans also encountered "cosmopolitan" types of birds that had already attained worldwide distribution. These included hawks, swifts, and woodpeckers.[36]

Based on anthropological study of contemporary hunters-gatherers, shifting horticulturalists, and similar societies that have been described historically, early humans had an extremely detailed knowledge of their local environments, from flora and fauna to wind, cloud patterns and weather, water and rock, and of course birds. The Piaroa, for example, a contemporary society of horticulturalists and hunters in the Venezuelan Amazon who have been studied by anthropologists including Laurence Krute, one of the authors of this book, can name in their language around one thousand types of plants and 130 types of birds.

We say "type" here, rather than "species," because Piaroa and other pre-agricultural societies do not have a concept of "species" in a scientific sense. Rather than biological criteria such as skeletal formation and genetics, Piaroa distinguish types of creatures by the external observable criteria of appearance, behavior, and location, which for them include much more detail than for most modern humans. Piaroa understand and can discuss feeding preferences, locations, and timing of activity, mating rituals, nest building and brooding behavior, family and flock patterns, preferred habitats, and the songs, sounds, and calls of many different types of birds. They have learned these details not simply because they are interesting, but also because they reveal other aspects of the environment.

When scientists discuss birds with people from traditional societies, differences in what counts as knowledge can lead to difficulties in communication. For example, anthropologist Steven Feld reported that his attempt to identify the species of birds that a member of the Kaluli people of New Guinea was imitating once led to the Kaluli man exclaiming, "Listen—to you they are birds, to me they are voices in the forest."[37] Understanding the messages of the voices was more important to the Kaluli man than creating a system of classification.

This detailed local knowledge is gained through intensive observation, continuous, almost obsessive attention to nature, and follow-up discussion and teaching. It is very likely that early humans who carefully observed birds in their environs survived and thrived better than those humans who were less observant of birds. Bird alarm calls could alert a group of humans to the presence of a predator (or a hostile group of humans). Bird flocking and chattering could attract human attention to a short-term, rich patch of food, a fruiting tree or berry-bearing shrub, a school of fish that could be harvested immediately, or to a carcass that could be scavenged. Lions have been observed to keep track of vultures as the vultures forage aerially (and vultures watch lions and follow them).[38]

Unlike lions, birds have rarely provoked fear in humans. As Edward A. Armstrong wrote, birds are "unique, in that no member of this huge group of animals has ever been a direct menace to man." Armstrong noted that snakes, insects, and bacteria have often proven deadly, and that sharks, crocodiles, lions, and tigers (not to mention bears and wolves) have reputations as man-eaters, "But even the largest and most powerful birds have never been a serious threat"[39] to humans. In fact, there are Mongolians who train eagles to serve them in hunting, and hunters of many cultures have trained hawks and falcons. Powerful birds can make powerful allies, and small birds can be friends and neighbors who have never joined together to attack us.

It seems indisputable that humans glean survival benefits from close and ongoing observation of their avian "eco-companions." In many oral traditions worldwide, bird behavior is interpreted as foretelling changes in weather. Folk traditions in various areas of the United States, for example, claim that seagulls flying inland, geese walking east but flying west, crows flying alone (not usual for a highly social species such as crows), or petrels gathering under the stern of a ship all indicate storms. By way of a possible explanation, gulls, for example, are known to be sensitive to small changes in barometric pressure, changes often associated with the arrival (and departure) of storms. This may explain why birds notice storms before they start and why humans who noticed birds would have some warning.

Bird behavior probably also predicts natural disasters such as hurricanes, tsunamis, and earthquakes, though the evidence is much more speculative. There are numerous anecdotal reports of predictions by birds, from

Indonesian pheasants known as *kuwau* (*Argusianus argus*) giving warning of the 2004 Christmas earthquake and tsunami in the Indian Ocean to flamingoes in the National Zoo in Washington, DC, flocking in agitation just before the earthquake of August 2011 in Virginia.[40] Mechanisms to explain these behaviors have been suggested, including sensitivity to the faint vibrations of P-waves (the first, weak, very fast-moving vibrations from an earthquake) or to infrasonic (below the frequencies that humans can hear) sounds produced by hurricanes as well as earthquakes, or to detection of chemical changes in groundwater or regional tilting of the surface, but these all remain unproven. One possible explanation particularly applicable to birds is detection of changes in the regional electrical or magnetic field of the planet, caused by changing subterranean stresses. Many migratory birds are thought to navigate at least partly by detecting magnetic fields, and experiments with homing pigeons do bear this out.[41] The physiology of magnetoreception by birds is poorly understood, so this line of thinking is still a hypothesis. At any rate, it is likely that birds can detect natural events before humans and that humans can be warned of dramatic, dangerous events by observing birds.

Apart from storms and disasters, in normal times the presence of birds in numbers and variety could help humans find a suitable environment, rich in a variety of resources. Ecological research makes it clear that birds occur in greater variety in environments with greater primary productivity. Primary productivity is a measure of the growth (and hence richness) of plants and other photosynthetic organisms, such as algae. Primary productivity correlates with such factors as temperature, precipitation, solar radiation, and potential evapotranspiration (how much water is lost from leaves as plants "breathe," which is a measure of the availability of water). In Africa, the highest densities of bird species and hence the highest levels of primary productivity, the richest environments, are found along the forested uplands and lake districts of eastern Africa through Malawi, across central Africa north of the Congo rainforest into the West African forests, and along the southeastern coasts of modern South Africa and Mozambique. Groups of humans who followed birds would have found their way into the most suitable environments and thrived.

It is interesting in this regard to note that heavily forested environments present themselves to our human senses first of all as a soundscape. Before we humans begin to pick out visual details in the forest itself, standing in a clearing or approaching a forested riverbank, we may hear the sounds of water and wind, insect and possibly animal calls, and we almost always hear the songs and calls of birds. From a boat or canoe on a river, rainforest presents a solid wall. It is difficult to see more than a few feet, if that, into the forest, but the forest is always noisy. Many Indigenous Amazonian languages, for example, capture this in a very rich set of onomatopoetic words for sounds, including bird calls. Amazonians, such as Piaroa, and of course other Indigenous peoples of forested landscapes also imitate birdcalls to communicate in these environments. Piaroa coordinate the movement of dispersed hunters during a hunt and link up with traveling companions from whom they have become separated, by calling out bird calls. There is a "double whoop" that signals "We here are Piaroa," for example.

As early humans learned to live in various environments, birds were among their teachers. Humans found water and plants, fish and other animals by watching birds. Birds warned people of predators and storms, and perhaps of volcanoes and earthquakes. Arrivals, departures, and mating cycles of birds marked the seasons.[42] Bird calls and birdsongs inspired humans to imitate their forms of communication.

Only in recent decades have scientists documented that birds communicate with each other when they sing, rather than singing as a reflex bodily function. Ornithologist Peter Marler, who died in 2014, was among the first to establish that some songbirds learned their songs as they grew and had different songs to warn or to alert others to specific aspects of the world. He also demonstrated that birds of the same species developed different dialects in different areas. These dialects are "so well marked that if you really know your white-crowned sparrows, you'll know where you are in California," Marler said in 1997.[43] Some humans in traditional societies must have had similar knowledge fifty thousand years ago.

Beyond the immediately utilitarian benefits of observing birds, birds gave humans a constant source of companionship and a mirror in which to observe their own lives. Birds helped humans not only to survive in the environments that birds and humans shaped together, but also to think about what the world and the lives of all who lived in the world meant. Birds became symbols for humans, because birds resemble humans in many ways. Early humans saw in detail that birds walked on two legs and stood upright, with two "arms" (in the form of wings) at their sides. They saw that birds mated monogamously and took care of their young in shelters they constructed. People saw that some birds used tools (rocks to crack open shellfish, for example) and had traditions (such as returning to the same nest spots, year after year). Birds generally lived socially, and often hierarchically, as in the proverbial "pecking order" among members of a flock. They were obviously very much like us.

Humans also, of course, saw that birds adorned themselves with gorgeously colored and patterned feathers. The use of feathers in religious ritual is discussed in more detail later. With regard to creation and evolution, it should be noted that humans began adorning themselves at least seventy thousand and possibly up to one hundred thousand years ago. It is likely that some of the earliest two-dimensional art was intended to be attached to clothing as a social badge, a function shared by human decoration and a bird's feathers.

Perhaps most importantly, birds spoke to one another. They sang and called to warn of predators or to defend a territory or a mate, to attract a mate in the first place, to guide their young, and seemingly for the sheer pleasure of singing and calling. Consider a nightingale at dusk or a mockingbird sitting high up in a tree on an exposed branch pouring out song. Some have thought that the efforts of humans to make music resulted from our experience of birds. In the 1980s, Steven Feld found that the Kaluli people he studied in New Guinea said that anyone who sang and danced became a bird.[44]

Listening to birds and observing the powers of birds must have often inspired humans with wonder and led humans to think about the other powers that make the world. Birds have powers that humans do not, most notably the ability to fly. For people living in many areas, the power of birds to fly great distances results in the seasonal appearance and disappearance of birds through migration that must have seemed magical, and bird migration still provokes emotional responses in humans facing winter, spring, and summer.

Other powers of birds must also have impressed our ancestors. Some birds, such as whippoorwills, can enter extended periods of torpor that approximate hibernation. Birds are seemingly little affected by most storms (although major storms may disrupt migrations), or by naturally occurring wildfire. To maximize the usefulness of flight in finding food, birds have a sharpness of vision, especially in the case of raptors and scavengers, far beyond the capacity of humans.

Beings with suprahuman powers may be gods. Possessing these powers, birds were and are, at the very least, highly appropriate analogies for comprehending and explaining the gods that rule the world and for carrying the weight of human wishes. Gods as birds (or birds as gods), however, were not only analogies, metaphors, or other symbols; before birds were gods, they were birds.

Birds in Prehistoric Art and Religions

Beginning with the experience of birds as guides to food sources and as signs of rich habitats, and developing our ideas as we listened to birds singing and communicating, watched them fly, appear and disappear seasonally, "marry" and rear their young, humans have been thinking about birds for a very long time. Birds have clearly figured in religious thought since at least the "Paleolithic creative explosion" some thirty-five thousand years ago, when the arts of two-dimensional painting and engraving and three-dimensional sculpted figurines first flourished. The particularities of the representation of birds in Paleolithic art lends credence to the idea that birds featured in the creation of human cultures.

One of the most discussed images of a bird in Paleolithic cave art is the figure labeled the "Dead Man" or the "Bird-Headed Man with Bison," or sometimes the "Raven Priest," in the well-known and spectacular cave of Lascaux, France, which dates from about seventeen thousand years ago (Figure 2.1). The scene includes a large bison with its entrails bulging out of its body facing a human figure that is stretched out rigidly, with its arms held or lying straight by its sides. Next to the human figure lies a broken spear, stick, or branch. In a cave containing some six hundred paintings of horses, stags, aurochs (a member of the bovine or cattle family), ibexes, other bison and a few carnivores, this is the only painting of the full body of a person. One of the things that makes it seem clearly meaningful is its location, in a small chamber that can be reached only by dropping down about sixteen feet. The effort of reaching the parts of caves where paintings are often found—crawling through narrow, sometimes muddy, sometimes stream-filled passages, shimmying up or down chimneys, squeezing through very narrow openings, crossing chasms, all the while carrying ropes or other climbing devices, pigments and containers, sources of light, and possibly food and water—can only indicate the great importance of these paintings and accompanying activities to the people who painted them.

What makes this scene relevant here is that the human figure has a bird's head. This is clearly not a mask or covering; there are images in other caves of humans inside an animal figure or wearing a headdress of some kind, but this

Figure 2.1 These paintings in a cave near Lascaux in France were found in 1940 and dated to over seventeen thousand years ago. The bird-headed figure may depict a ritual using the bird scepter. Ravens lead and follow wolves and human hunters.
Chris Howes / Wild Places Photography / Alamy Stock Photo.

is not a headdress or mask. This figure has the head of a bird. Additionally, a bit to the left and below the figure, there is a stick with a bird on one end, where the stick could even be taken to be the bird's long legs, like the legs of a wading bird. These are the only depictions of birds in Lascaux.

All interpretations are speculative, but this scene clearly has some deep significance. Is it a representation of an actual event or a dream? If the picture is a narrative, does it represent a recurring event, such as a ritual, or a seasonal hunt, or a particular, actual one-time hunt? Is the figure a shaman in trance, or is it a hunter, either supernatural or "mere" human, killed in the hunt? Is the stick an atlatl (a spear-thrower) carved with a bird head (atlatls are weighted on one end) or a ritual object? Does it represent a bird as a "spirit helper"? One source notes that wooden posts topped by birds are still used in funerals by Alaskan Eskimos and by Yakuts (an Indigenous people of Siberia) in animal sacrifice ceremonies.[45] This may indicate a deep and direct continuity in religious beliefs and human thinking about birds, as mediators between living and dead humans, from Paleolithic France to Siberia. Whatever the meaning, the "Bird-Headed Man with Bison" is not just doodling. Far too much effort was involved in its creation.

There are very infrequent but important images of birds in other Paleolithic painted caves in France. The infrequency and isolation of these images could mean that the sites where birds were depicted were especially sacred. There are penguins in the cave at Cosquer, unidentifiable birds incised or traced in Cussac Cave, and an owl with its head rotated 180 degrees in Chauvet.

These birds are not part of larger scenes, but they have distinctive positions. The owl in Chauvet Cave, from about thirty thousand years ago, is looking into the cave, so the picture testifies to human admiration of the power of the owl to see in the dark. It is also suggestive that bird figures are also painted in Les Trois Frères Cave, which contains two fully modeled three-dimensional sculpted bison and the painted figure known as the Shaman, a human figure inside a deer, complete with horns, walking upright. This cave was chosen by ancient humans as the site for very important art, and it included birds.

In other rock art traditions, birds appear in equally significant contexts, even in those traditions where images of birds are rare. On the Cumberland Plateau in eastern Tennessee, birds are common in cave art but not in exposed art on rock walls. They are sometimes depicted in flight with the individual flight feathers visible on extended wings. Images include a bird of unidentified species holding a ritual cane or club and a ritual ax, possibly at the moment of transforming into a human. The Indigenous peoples in Tennessee were known in historic times to see flying birds as intermediaries between the upper world of the heavens and the middle world of humans, serving as messengers and members of both worlds.[46]

Another example of birds as messengers among the ancient peoples of the Americas appeared among the Mayans of what is now Mexico. In the classical tradition represented in Mayan writing and painting, the King Vulture (*Sarcoramphus papa*)—a white bird, larger than the more familiar turkey vulture, with a bald and wrinkled, purple, red, and yellow head—was described and depicted both as a bird and as a god with a human body and bird head, functioning as a messenger between humans and gods. Mayan stories describe the King Vulture helping to recreate the world after a great flood by eating the dead, reviving some humans, and even eloping with one of the first women.[47]

In South Africa, at sites in Western Cape Province, east of Cape Town, there are part-human, part-ostrich figures heavily decorated with stripes and dots on their torsos and faces, painted by the San peoples (known as

"Bushmen"). Otherwise, birds are fairly rare in San rock art, except for one other image. There is an Ethiopian snipe (*Gallinago negripennis*) painted in outline, plunging downward with wings rounded and tail flared. As part of snipe mating ritual, male snipes dive through the air in a stylized posture, which is clearly depicted, while vibrating their tail feathers to make a "drumming" sound. The San name for the snipe (*woer-woer*) is also their term for the bull-roarer, the musical instrument used in some San rituals. These mating rituals occur at dusk, and snipe are generally crepuscular (active at dusk and dawn). Snipe can see in the dark, so that they become, for San, creatures with actually and symbolically powerful vision. The figure is also largely surrounded by painted red spots, with some on the body as well. Red color and spots themselves as part of the "aura" or penumbra of a painted figure are symbols of power and reproductive potency for the San (as for other traditions, such as aboriginal Australia). Perhaps the snipe paintings marked a site of San marriage or fertility rituals, or a place where previous San generations were remembered.

In Australia, among many richly painted aboriginal sites, probably dedicated to religious rituals, there are two striking examples of painted birds. At Djulirri Rock Shelter, in Arnhem Land in the north, there are hundreds of small birds stenciled by blowing pigment (red ocher, an iron oxide-based pigment) from the painter's mouth around the outline of the image.[48] These birds appear to be a species of honeyeater. Honeyeaters are a large group of acrobatic birds found across Australia and New Guinea and outward to New Zealand and nearby Polynesia. Some can hover for short periods of time like hummingbirds, to sip nectar. These stenciled, possibly hovering birds may be ancestral spirits, but the people who made these paintings rarely stenciled their ancestors. In 1982, anthropologist Steven Feld reported that the Kaluli of New Guinea still listened to the birds of the forest as the voices of their ancestors.[49] Were the hundreds of birds immortalized at Djulirri Rock Shelter pets? Dinner? A rare species? An artist's signature (like a graffiti tag)? A record of a rare, flocking event? It seems more likely that the site was used for a ritual that connected people with ancestral forces, perhaps from the time of creation.

Also in Arnhem Land in Australia, to the southwest of Djulirri, there is a depiction of a bird that has been identified by paleontologists as *Genyornis*, a heavy, large-beaked, thick-necked, thick-legged, flightless emu-like bird. The oldest pigment on rock in Australia is dated to around twenty-two thousand years ago, and most rock art is less than five thousand years old.

One remarkable fact of this picture is that *Genyornis* has been extinct since fifty thousand years ago (at the latest, possibly forty thousand years ago).[50] The paleontological evidence for that date of extinction seems to be quite solid. Whether the resemblance of the painting from at most twenty thousand years ago to the bird from fifty thousand years ago is a coincidence or demonstrates real continuity in aboriginal religious "Dreamtime" beliefs, the painting is clearly important to the aboriginal practitioners.

The Kaluli of New Guinea now tell the story that flightless birds helped to create the world by stamping on mushy ground to harden it.[51] Mating and nesting rituals of some birds involve a great deal of foot stamping, and bowerbirds will prepare small tracts of ground for the bowers where they nest. Perhaps some distinctive behavior of the flightless *Genyornis* led to a legend of creation that preserved the image of the *Genyornis* among native Australians long after the bird had become extinct. A large flightless bird also figures in the creation stories of another Australian native nation, the Yuwaalaraay of New South Wales, who describe the sun as an emu's egg that was thrown into the sky.[52]

Before people began to live in cities, humans maintained similar relations with birds in their natural surroundings over long periods of time. The forest and the mountain, the river and the plain changed slowly or not at all, and the humans and birds who lived in and around those natural settings interacted in similar ways for thousands of years. As hunting and gathering and light gardening gave way to systematic agriculture, human societies became wealthier and larger and more complex, and people built city walls to safeguard the large harvests. The city was a human creation, a countercreation or alternative world in contrast to the natural world of the gods. People left nature to live behind the walls of cities after the invention of agriculture, which took place at the end of the last Ice Age, about twelve thousand years ago.

Within the cities new inventions, especially writing and arithmetic, would open a distance between human culture and nature. But in the religions of those who lived in cities, birds did not lose their importance. Birds of the forest were joined by domestic birds, and predators gained a role as guardians of crops. In fact, the creation stories preserved by the new writing and the rituals practiced by the literate priests often made birds into important mediators.

Gobekli Tepe, to consider only one instance, emerged by the tenth millennium BCE on a ridge in southeastern Anatolia (modern Turkey), amid the hilly flanks of the Fertile Crescent, where hunters and gatherers were becoming sedentary and learning to rely on farming. There is no direct estimate of the population of Gobekli Tepe, but geographically close and culturally related sites such as Catal Huyuk probably held six thousand to eight thousand inhabitants. These were some of the first cities. Gobekli Tepe is marked by over two hundred standing stone monolithic pillars arranged in groups of double concentric circles in a number of structures. These often T-shaped pillars weigh from ten to fifty tons, stand up to sixteen feet in height, and were moved as far as a quarter of a mile from their source. They are carved in high relief with animal figures, generally of lions, bulls, boars, foxes, spiders, and snakes, but also birds such as cranes, ducks, and many vultures. On one pillar, there are ostrich-like birds accompanying two boars. The site also yields a three-dimensional freestanding sculpted head of a vulture.

Vultures played an essential role in the practice of open-air burial, whereby the flesh was removed from unprotected cadavers by scavengers (especially vultures), weather, and decay, liberating the bones and hopefully the spirit. It has been hypothesized that such ways of dealing with the dead were practiced also at Catal Huyuk and early Jericho, where vultures are frequent in the iconography. Today, the Parsees, or Zoroastrians, the few surviving practitioners of the pre-Islamic religion of Persia or Iran, still rely on vultures to dispose of dead bodies that they place in stone "Towers of Silence."

These Parsees are now an urban people, merchants who live in western India, who are trying (despite the near extinction of vultures in their area) to maintain a funeral practice that began when they were nomadic herders on the high deserts of Iran. Their sense that birds connect humans with life beyond death resembles that of the Paleolithic artists who made the Lascaux cave and the Kaluli rain forest dwellers of New Guinea. When Parsees depict the God of their creation story, who is named Ahura Mazda, or the *favrashi* or soul of a human, they usually give the figure of God or the soul the wings of a large bird. Their sacred writings were among the first writings in their language, originating in the millennia around 3000 to 1000 BCE, when written languages were being born. Their religion influenced that of the Jews, because it was the Persians who conquered Babylon and released the Jews from their captivity, at the same moment when the Jews were first writing down their own stories and codes and editing them into what has become the Hebrew Bible and the Christian Old Testament.

Birds, Cooperation, and Consciousness

Nature writer Colin Tudge, in a book titled after the admonition of Jesus, "Consider the birds," makes the point that competition has been overemphasized in accounts of evolution, despite the fact that cooperation within and across species is at least as important a factor.[53] For example, only recently have human biologists begun to investigate the vital role of the one hundred trillion bacteria that inhabit every human being, vastly outnumbering the ten trillion cells of the human body, in maintaining human life, including the functioning of the brain. These bacteria and the human body must have evolved together, affecting each other at every step.

More than half a century ago, the Jesuit theologian and paleontologist Teilhard de Chardin argued in many books that consciousness should not be understood as a phenomenon confined to individual humans, but as a dimension of existence that constitutes the "inner lining" of the whole material world.[54] To really appreciate the roles that birds have played, and continue to play, in creating the world that birds and humans share, perhaps we need to admit that birds participate along with us in the common consciousness, the spirit of this world. Sometimes the birds are really singing and calling to us, as well as to each other. The roles played by birds in creation stories can seem ridiculous in a human-centered worldview, in which only people reflect the image of a creator God. How can the waterbirds save the life of the falling Sky Woman if the world has not yet been made? How can a raven have set the sun in its place? And yet, because the world is a system in which humans form only a small part, these stories do show how the parts of that system work together.

Animals other than birds certainly appear in creation stories. The snake has its place in the Garden of Eden, the python is important in West Africa, and in Babylon the sea was a great female monster, a Leviathan. But no animal or class of animals, including the mammals among which we humans are found, has as many prominent and positive roles in creation stories as the birds.

Notes

1. Scott A. Ellington, "The Sustainer of Life: The Role of the Spirit of God in Creation," *Australasian Pentecostal Studies*, 2009, https://aps-journal.com/index.php/APS/article/download/5/2?inline=1 (accessed July 7, 2021). Also Melissa Tzp, "Ha-azinu: A

Hovering Bird," in *Midrash Torah*, September 18, 2017, https://mtorah.com/?s=nes her (accessed July 7, 2021).
2. Michael Hornum, "Asis Rimoni," *asisrimoni.blogspot.com*, February 3, 2012; Wayne Simpson, "And the Spirit of God Moved upon the Face of the Waters," *jasher.com*, September 19, 2010.
3. Johanna W. H. van Wijk-Bos, *Reimagining God: The Case for Spiritual Diversity* (Louisville, KY: Westminster John Knox Press, 1995), 73.
4. Joseph Barber, *Chickens: A Natural History* (Lewes, UK: Ivy Press, 2012), 14–15.
5. Nassen-Bayer and Kevin Stuart, "Mongol Creation Stories: Man, Mongol Tribes, the Natural World, and Mongol Deities," *Asian Folklore Studies* 51 (1992): 325.
6. David Adams Leeming and Margaret Adams Leeming, *A Dictionary of Creation Myths* (New York: Oxford University Press, 2009), 298.
7. Michael Wood, *Legacy: A Search for the Origins of Civilization* (London: Network Books, 1992), 136.
8. Adam Welz, "Jonathan Franzen: Egypt Is the Worst Place to Be a Migratory Bird," *The Guardian*, July 19, 2013, http://www.theguardian.com/environment/nature-up/2013/jul/19/jonathan-franzen-egypt-migratory-bird (accessed August 6, 2014).
9. Foy Scalf, "The Role of Birds within the Religious Landscape of Ancient Egypt," in *Between Heaven and Earth: Birds in Ancient Egypt*, ed. Rozenn Bailleul-LeSuer (Chicago: University of Chicago Press, 2012), 34.
10. Peter Tate, *Flights of Fancy: Birds in Legend, Myth, and Superstition* (New York: Delacorte Press, 2007), 30–35.
11. Mark Cocker with David Tipling, *Birds and People* (London: Jonathan Cape, 2013), 97.
12. This story appears in many forms and in many sources. Those consulted here include James Axtell, ed., *Indian Peoples of Eastern America: A Documentary History of the Sexes* (New York: Oxford University Press, 1981), 174.
13. Axtell, *Indian Peoples*, 174.
14. John Batchelor, *The Ainu and Their Folklore* (London: The Religious Tract Society, 1901)
15. Geoffrey Parrinder, *Sex in the World's Religions* (New York: Oxford University Press, 1980), 104.
16. W. F. Kirby, trans., *Kalevala: The Land of the Heroes*, vol. 1 (London: J.M. Dent, 1907), 5–7. Selection in Barbara C. Sproul, *Primal Myths: Creation Myths around the World* (New York: HarperOne, 1979), 176–178.
17. See http://www.haltia.com/haltia-the-finnish-nature-centre/architecture/ (July 23, 2013).
18. Catherine Feher-Elston, *Ravensong: A Natural and Fabulous History of Ravens and Crows* (Flagstaff, AZ: Northland Publishing, 1991), 116–117
19. J. Marzluff, Jeff Walls, Heather N. Cornell, John C. Withey, David P. Craig, "Lasting Recognition of Threatening People by Wild American Crows," *Animal Behavior* 79 (2010): 699–707, https:doi.org/10.1016/j.anbehav.2009.12.022
20. See http://news.nationalgeographic.com/news/2002/08/0808_020808_crow.html (accessed July 23, 2014).

21. Feher-Elston, *Ravensong*, 19–24.
22. Eliza Ruhamah Scidmore, "Tlingit Customs," http://www.arcticwebsite.com/Tlingit Customs.html (July 23, 2014).
23. Cocker and Tipling, *Birds and People*, 394.
24. Hitakonanu'laxk (Tree Beard), *The Grandfathers Speak: Native American Folk Tales of the Lenape People* (New York: Interlink Books, 1994), 72–75.
25. R. W. L. Moberly, "Why Did Noah Send Out a Raven?," *Vetus Testamentum* 50, no. 3 (2000): 353–354.
26. Leonard Little Thunder, "The Legend of Red Clay," as told to him by his grandfather, Frank Comes from War, who heard the story from his own grandfather in 1900 http://www.siouxpottery.com/display_story.php?id=13 (August 10, 2013).
27. Cocker and Tipling, *Birds and People*, 301.
28. Oswaldo Chinchilla Mazariegos, "Of Birds and Insects: The Hummingbird Myth in Ancient Mesoamerica," *Ancient Mesoamerica* 21 (2010): 58.
29. Cocker and Tipling, *Birds and People*, 421 and 454.
30. Kevin W. Gaston and Tim M. Blackburn, "How Many Birds Are There?," *Biodiversity and Conservation* 6 (1997): 615–625. Kevin Drum, "How Many Birds?," *Mother Jones*, March 23, 2011, http://www.motherjones.com/kevin-drum/2011/03/how-many-birds (accessed July 9, 2014).
31. There is a common estimate that the bird population has decreased by 25 percent in the last five hundred years, and that it will decrease further in the future. See, for example, http://news.stanford.edu/news/2005/january12/birds-011205.html (accessed August 5, 2014).
32. See a general account of archaeopteryx as an ancestor of birds at http://www.bbc.co.uk/nature/life/Archaeopteryx (accessed July 29, 2014). A spirited alternative from the consensus that birds evolved directly from dinosaurs like archaeopteryx has been mounted by Alan Feduccia, in works such as *The Origin and Evolution of Birds* (New Haven: Yale University Press, 1996). Feduccia exalts the direct ancestors of birds to equal status with dinosaurs.
33. For a geologic timeline, see http://www.ucmp.berkeley.edu/help/timeform.php (August 9, 2014).
34. Douglas Palmer, *A History of Earth in 100 Groundbreaking Discoveries* (Buffalo, NY: Firefly Books, 2011), 261.
35. Cocker and Tipling, *Birds and People*, 392.
36. Alan Feduccia, "Big Bang for Tertiary Birds?," *Trends in Ecology and Evolution* 18, no. 4 (April 2003): 172–176. Also see Feduccia, *Origin and Evolution*.
37. Steven Feld, *Sound and Sentiment: Birds, Weeping, Poetics, and Song in Kaluli Expression*, Thirtieth Anniversary Edition (Durham: Duke University Press, 2012), 45.
38. See http://www.scienceworldreport.com/articles/14375/20140501/human-interactions-scavengers-vultures-drove-evolution.htm (July 29, 2014); the site refers to Marcos Moleon, Jose A. Sanchez-Zapata, Anthoni Margalida, Martina Carrete, Norman Owen-Smith, and Jose Donazar, "Humans and Scavengers: The Evolution of Interactions and Ecosystem Services," *BioScience*, May 2014, 394–403.

39. Edward A. Armstrong, *The Life and Lore of the Bird: In Nature, Art, Myth, and Literature* (New York: Crown Publishers, 1975), 6.
40. On the National Zoo flamingoes in 2011, see http://nationalzoo.si.edu/scbi/animalcare/news/earthquake.cfm (accessed July 29, 2014). On the 2004 tsunami, see http://unesdoc.unesco.org/images/0018/001831/183133e.pdf (accessed July 29, 2014).
41. Robert C. Breason, "Mechanisms of Magnetic Orientation in Birds," *Integrative and Comparative Biology* 5, no. 3 (2005): 565–573. Also see http://www.birds.cornell.edu/allaboutbirds/studying/migration/navigation (accessed July 29, 2014).
42. Feld, *Sound and Sentiment*, 61.
43. Paul Vitello, "Peter Marler, Graphic Decoder of Birdsong, Dies at 86," *New York Times*, July 28, 2014, A18.
44. Feld, *Sound and Sentiment*, 220.
45. Tate, *Flights of Fancy*.
46. Jan Simek, Alan Cressler, Nicholas P. Herrmann, and S. C. Sherwood, "Sacred Landscapes of the South-eastern USA: Prehistoric Rock and Cave Art in Tennessee," *Antiquity* 86, no. 336 (2013): 430–476.
47. Elizabeth P. Benson, "The Vulture: The Sky and the Earth," *Palenque Round Table* 10, no. 310 (1996), http://mesoweb.com/pari/publications/RT10/Vulture.pdf (accessed August 12, 2014).
48. Paul S. C. Tacon, M. Langley, S. May, R. Lamilami, W. Brennan, and D. Guse, "Ancient Bird Stencils Discovered in Arnhem Land, Northern Territory, Australia," *Antiquity* 84, no. 324 (2010): 416–427.
49. Feld, *Sound and Sentiment*, 218.
50. Emma Masters, "Megafauna Cave Painting Could Be 40,000 Years Old," *ABC News*, May 30, 2010, http://www.abc.net.au/news/2010-05-31/megafauna-cave-painting-could-be-40000-years-old/847564 (accessed August 11, 2014).
51. Feld, *Sound and Sentiment*, 52.
52. Cocker and Tipling, *Birds and People*, 25.
53. Colin Tudge, *Consider the Birds: Who They Are and What They Do* (London: Penguin Books, 2008), 251–259.
54. Pierre Teilhard de Chardin, S.J., *The Phenomenon of Man*, trans. Bernard Wall (New York: HarperCollins, 1959), 79.

3
Birds and Humans in Each Other's Rituals (and Costumes)

Birds and the Roots of Ritual

Birds have a role in the ritual of inaugurating a president. The word "inauguration" comes from the Latin *augurium*, the ritual for reading good or bad fortune by observing the flight, singing, or behavior of birds. Whenever new leaders started their terms in Rome, a special rite of augury called *inauguratio* was done.[1] The leader only took office if the augur, the priest who performed the augury, could announce, *Aves admittunt!* (The birds allow it).[2] This chapter explores rituals of hunting, funerals, dancing, and other forms of augury that the birds allow, and some rituals of sacrifice and purification birds probably would prefer to stop.

Like religion, ritual can be defined in several ways. We understand rituals here as patterns of action deliberately repeated for purposes that are not simply functional.[3] To raise food repeatedly to the mouth in order to eat or to swing a scythe repeatedly to harvest grain is not to perform a ritual, if the actor only intends to eat or to harvest. Ritual patterns also involve an attempt to express meanings, to induce states of mind in participants and observers, and/or to influence the world by connecting with cosmic forces or spirits. Any action, including eating or harvesting grain, can be ritualized, but not every repeated action is a ritual. When the commitment to perform a ritual seems to hold life together for a person or a community, that ritual becomes obligatory, or religious (from Latin *ligare*, to bind). By this measure, a presidential inauguration is a religious ritual, part of the civil religion that holds the nation together. And the roots of this ritual, as of others too numerous to describe, involve birds.

Birds repeat many actions, some in elaborate patterns, and birds appeared in the world hundreds of millions of years before humans. It seems that many patterns of bird behavior became models for human ritual. People adopted avian patterns of action in their religious rituals, just as they adopted feathered costumes to wear in some of those rituals.

As early humans made their livings in a world filled with birds, they observed birds carefully. Humans probably watched birds more than they watched other animals because birds are more visible, flying overhead and perching in trees, confidently allowing themselves to be approached by people because they can escape easily. Also, as we have noted and our ancestors surely did, humans and birds resemble each other as two-legged creatures who build shelters, raise small families, and communicate with elaborate sounds and songs and dances.

People have not only watched birds forage for food, they have sometimes partnered with birds in foraging. For example the Hadza, a nation of hunter-gatherers in East Africa, the original home of humanity, both call and respond to calls by birds called "honeyguides" in English, who bring the Hadza to the hives of bees. These humans and birds communicate, whistling and chirping specific calls back and forth, and the humans follow the birds who fly from tree to tree to the tree where the bees live. Then Hadza men climb the trees, subdue the bees with smoke, and open the hive.[4] The humans collect and consume the honey and larvae, while the birds eat the adult bees and leftover wax. Without the birds, the humans would rarely see these well-hidden hives high in trees, and the birds would find it much harder to open and eat the hives without the humans. The bird species that works with humans is the greater honeyguide (*Indicator indicator*), ten inches long with gray-brown upper sides and white undersides, in a family related to woodpeckers. On the island of Mozambique, this same species of bird works in the same way with a different human society called the Yao.[5]

Like most hunter-gatherers, the Hadza have a simple life with almost no religious rituals, but one ritual that has been described by anthropologists is a dance by men called the *epeme* (meaning manhood or hunting) dance, which is performed on the nights when no moon appears in the sky, and with no campfire, in complete darkness. In this ritual, the influence of birds is apparent. Men take turns wearing a headdress of ostrich feathers and anklets of bells as they dance, and they whistle to call the women with the same notes they use to call the honeyguide birds.[6] Groups of women get up and dance around each man, answering him and commenting on his dance and his appearance. Their comments in the Hadza language include words with "click consonants," unusual consonants present in only a few African languages, which resemble the sounds that honeyguide birds make while hunting honey.

Figure 3.1 The greater honeyguide (*Indicator indicator*) has spoken and listened to humans for thousands of years, leading members of the Hadza nation of Tanzania and others to beehives they share. Courtship dances of the Hadza mimic the honeyguide.
Alf Jacob Nilsen / Alamy Stock Photo.

The Hadza have continued their ancient hunter-gatherer lives into the modern world, and in recent years they have even allowed tourists to accompany them as they seek honey with the birds and use poisoned arrows to hunt baboons and giraffes. The presence of outsiders and government pressure has resulted in their beginning to bury their dead, modifying another custom incidentally involving birds. Decades ago, the dead bodies of Hadza who died in the open were left there for vultures and hyenas to eat. If a person died inside one of the temporary shelters the Hadza make from branches, the shelter and the body were burned together. Now the bodies are buried in shallow graves, with ostrich feathers from the *epeme* dance placed on the grave of a man and a broken gourd on the grave of a woman.[7]

Exposing bodies to be eaten by birds was apparently one of the first rituals used by people to deal with death. One of the earliest known cities, dating from about 6000 BCE, a city called Catal Huyuk in what is now Turkey, features a shrine room with wall paintings of vultures attacking headless figures, apparently human corpses. It seems that the people of Catal Huyuk exposed their dead to vultures on the roofs of their houses. When the vultures finished removing the flesh from the bones, a task they can accomplish without disturbing ligaments holding the bones together, the skeletons were brought into the shrine, folded into a fetal position, tightly wrapped in cloth, and then stored under platforms on which the families of the deceased slept.[8] The scavenging birds were probably Egyptian and cinereous vultures, but may have been lappet-faced vultures. Lappet-faced vultures, the vultures with the longest wings and largest bodies in the world, are clearly identifiable in Egyptian iconography.

A similar ritual with vultures prevails among Zoroastrians, followers of the ancient religion of Persia (now Iran), which dates from about three thousand years ago and now survives in western India. The Parsis, as followers of Prophet Zoroaster are often called, believe that burying or cremating dead bodies pollutes nature.[9] They expose their dead to vultures atop structures called Towers of Silence, concrete or stone buildings several stories tall. The participating birds include three species of the genus *Gyps*, smallish vultures, and the red-headed or Indian vulture, with a wingspan of almost nine feet and a huge black beak. Old World vultures hunt by sight and not smell, so exposing bodies on tower-tops serves to make them prominent to the scavengers, who also certainly learn where the towers are located. Since the 1990s, a sudden, near extinction of these vultures, especially *Gyps*—a plunge from a population of forty million in the 1980s to about one hundred thousand now—in India has made this practice much more difficult, because only vultures have the capacity to clean the bodies of flesh quickly enough that they do not rot. It has been discovered that diclofenac, a pain-killing drug given to cattle, was killing the birds, and bans on this drug in parts of India are helping the vultures to recover.[10] Special breeding programs are also underway to enable this partnership of humans and birds in ritual to continue, but the success of these efforts is still uncertain.[11]

Another variety of funeral involving birds is practiced by the Vajrayana Buddhists of Tibet, Nepal, China, and Mongolia, where the large (up to twenty-eight pounds) and aggressive Himalayan vulture (*Gyps himalayensis*) dominates a number of other vulture species. These Buddhists burn jasmine incense to attract vultures, then chop the bodies of their dead into pieces with cleavers and throw the pieces to the birds on the ground. Dozens of vultures make short work of the flesh, stripping a human corpse in about thirty minutes. Any bones remaining are pulverized with mallets and mixed with *tsampa* (a compound of barley flour, tea, and yak butter or milk), then fed to the crows and hawks that have also gathered. Here the goal is not to avoid polluting the world with death, as with the Parsis, but to be generous to the birds and to any small animals the birds might otherwise eat.[12] The monks who chop up the bodies, fling the body parts to the vultures, and pulverize the bones work with laughter and gestures of happiness, to express their joy in giving to the birds and to help the spirit of the deceased person to let go of the body and to move on. Although the monks do not encourage filming or casual attendance at these ceremonies, still photographs accompany the reference above, and a vivid re-enactment of a Buddhist "sky burial," as this ritual is sometimes called, appears at the beginning of Martin Scorsese's film about the life of the Dalai Lama, *Kundun* (1997).

In recent years, humans have begun to recognize that some birds, particularly crows, appear to hold funerals of their own. Crows have been reported to gather in groups of up to a hundred around a single dead bird on the ground. They perch in trees and call out, then "march" in silence, grasping and ungrasping the branches. They fly and walk in circles around the corpse. Some have been reported to touch the dead bird, to groom the corpse, and even to simulate copulation with the dead crow. Perhaps the long history of humans enlisting birds as participants in human funerals began with our ancestors observing and imitating such phenomena.[13] Many other human rituals reveal the inspiration and agency of birds.

People Imitating Birds in Rituals

Early humans also often saw avian intelligence and planning, extending to patterns of action that involved pretense and imitation. For one example, humans in what is now Namibia could have watched, as people do today, the birds now called common drongos (*Dicrusus adsimilis* (glossy black birds with heavy bills, resembling small ravens) cry out alarm calls warning of eagles. Other birds and some small mammals, especially meerkats, also respond to the warnings. The drongos next watch the meerkats capturing insects and issue false alarm calls even though no eagle is near, frightening the meerkats away from their catch, so that drongos can swoop in to consume the abandoned prey. When the meerkats learn to stop responding to drongo alarm calls, the drongos begin to imitate meerkat alarms, and go on pilfering insects from the mammals. Humans observing such repeated behavior would have rightly seen birds as intelligent, intentional, purposeful actors, with humanlike capacities for forethought and social manipulation of others.

Beyond seeing birds deceiving and imitating other animals, seeking and building shelter, and caring for their young, along with other functional behavior, humans saw birds engage in apparently unproductive, purposeless actions. They saw birds, individually and in groups, repeat actions for no immediate material benefit. Such rituals occur particularly in relation to mating.

Consider flamingoes, to pick one striking example. On the seasonal salt lakes of southern and eastern Africa and of the Andean high plateau, groups of flamingoes (two African species and four South American species of *Phoenicopterus*) numbering from fifteen or so to as many as fifty individuals, will suddenly, at apparently random times in the breeding season, begin to dance. Members of these small breeding groups (within a flock that could be several thousand strong) will simultaneously begin stretching their necks straight up, then waving their heads and flapping their out-stretched wings. With wings held cocked out over their backs, the group begins to run in a very tight huddle straight ahead through the shallows or on the mudflats of the lakes for up to fifty yards and then repeat the process.[14] Other groups may be dancing at the same time or shortly after. Individuals in the moving troupe do not seem to be showing off to specific other individual birds.

Humans in a scientific age have interpreted this ritual as behavior that emerged, evolved, and survived because it helps unattached flamingoes find mates, or allocates scarce nesting sites, or triggers nesting. For prehistoric people, the movements of the flamingo groups would have been interpreted as intentional dances (as they almost certainly are). Given the obvious intelligence of birds, early humans might also have inferred that the dancing flamingoes intended to influence the world through ritual, perhaps protecting the flock or bringing on good weather or a change of seasons. Seeking similar results, humans might have decided to adopt similar behaviors. As anthropologist Pascal Boyer has written, "Human rituals are generally recognized as such by virtue of features that apply to many types of animal displays as well." Boyer cites "stereotype, repetition, and the rigid sequencing of elementary actions" as "aspects that make animal and human ritual structurally similar."[15]

In Spanish, the word *flamenco* designates both the *Phoenicopterus* bird and the most famous form of Spanish dance. The origins of flamenco dancing are murky, but most accounts associate the dance with Africa, where the flamingo birds do their own most vivid dances. In southern Spain, flamingoes do not dance in groups, but individual birds stomp and circle as they try to dislodge shrimp and other crustaceans from the beds of shallow salt lagoons. Some say that the flamenco dance was brought to Spain by Roma (also called Gypsies) or by Moors; it has also been associated with Jews and with Muslims, and with the dark, passionate states of spiritual possession described by the word *duende*. Dance historians note that flamenco was not originally performed with songs or melodies played on instruments, but only with simple cries and chants by the dancers and with rhythms made by the dancers' feet or by simple instruments like walking sticks. These dances, called *palos secos*, or "dry styles,"[16] closely resemble the movements of individual flamingo birds. "Dancing" flamingoes in groups also turn their heads and call out, and tame flamingoes will dance as individuals and call in response to instrumental music.[17]

A Chilean flamingo born in captivity at Busch Gardens in Tampa, Florida, in 1996 entertained visitors with her dances, featuring varied foot rhythms and turning, head dipping and raising, for many years before she was killed by a human criminal assault in August 2016.[18] "Pinky," as this flamingo was called, was not taught to dance by humans, but invented her own moves. Of course, flamingoes have not communicated any meaning they may ascribe to their dances to humans. It seems very likely, however, that this dignified human art form, sometimes regarded as a ritual associated with religions and with spiritual possession, arose from the inspiration of a bird.

Almost certainly, the shift of human perspective from natural intimacy with other animals to the distanced view of urban civilizations has obscured the roles of birds in the development of human rituals. For example, it was only after a 2008 study of Snowball, a white cockatoo whose obvious dancing to music had become an internet sensation, that scientists have agreed that animals are capable of hearing human music and synchronizing their movements to the beats, or in other words intentionally dancing.[19] Civilized humans have displayed strong tendencies to deny any agency to animals, much less to admit influences of birds on people.

And yet, in Mexico and Central America, the abundance and beauty of birds has clearly inspired many rituals and costumes. Males of the aptly named resplendent quetzal species (*Pharomachrus mocinno*) have two or three tail feathers that extend up to three feet below the bodies of the birds, extending behind in flight and twitching in slow whipping motions when the bird sits and seeks to attract a mate.[20] Normally green, these feathers may also look blue depending on the angle of light, so that a crown or robe made of them enabled the Aztec kings who wore such crowns and robes appear to transform as they walked or danced in rituals. A headdress given by the last king of the Aztecs, Moctezuma (or Montezuma), to the conquistador Hernando Cortés, has four hundred tail feathers from quetzals as well as bright pink and magenta feathers from the roseate spoonbill (*Platalea ajaja*), brilliant turquoise and blue feathers from the lovely cotinga (*Cotinga amabilis*), and long brown tail feathers from the squirrel cuckoo (*Piaya cayana*). Cortés gave the headdress to his uncle, Holy Roman Emperor Charles V, and it now rests in an Austrian museum while Mexico seeks its return. It was so little appreciated that the earliest surviving European record of its existence, dating from 1596, calls the headdress a "Moorish hat."[21] But the surviving art of the Aztec and Mayan civilizations shows that such gorgeous feathered crowns and robes belonged to the essence of kingship, because they were worn in rituals that identified and connected the king and the nobility with the gods.

In her study of Late Preclassic (about two-thousand-year-old) Mayan monuments, Julia Guernsey found that "an image of the ruler, transformed into a bird," seated on a throne and being blessed by a "Principal Bird Deity, that hovers above the head of the ruler" was prominent at the Mayan site of Izapa, on the Pacific coastal plain between Chiapas and Guatemala.[22] Fifteen hundred years after the Mayans built Izapa, when Moctezuma gave the headdress to Cortés, both rulers and sacrificial victims were apparently dressed as birds for enthronement, in battle, and as participants in rituals ending in death on high altars. For the Aztecs, the most important god was Quetzalcoatl, the Feathered Serpent,[23] who sacrificed himself and was transformed by death and fire into the "Lord of the Dawn."[24]

Today, the heritage of ritual transformation of humans into birds and gods is continued in Mexico by the *Voladores*, or Flyers of Papantla, a small town in Veracruz, on the eastern coast. Every day, tourists can witness a ritual that was traditionally performed once a year, as described in Aztec codices and by the Spanish priest Torquemada around 1612. It was performed from central Mexico to northern Nicaragua, in a variety of forms shaped by local peoples, but always associated with rain, solar gods, the spring equinox, and, of course, with birds.

In the modern Veracruzan version, five men dressed as birds—parrots, macaws, quetzals, or eagles—with feathery capes and crests on their heads, climb a pole 130 feet tall to a square framework at the top. Four of the men secure ropes around their waists, while the fifth sits on the middle of the frame, playing a traditional tune resembling the call of a quetzal on a flute and keeping up a rhythm with a small drum. Then the four men fall backward into the air, their heads facing the earth and their arms extended as wings. Streamers as long as quetzal tail feathers, attached to each of their hats, wave in the wind as they descend, turning thirteen rotations around the pole. Just before their heads hit the ground, they flip upright on their ropes and land running, after which the flute player wraps his legs around one of the ropes and slides down to join them.

The meaning of this ritual has been explained in several ways and clearly varied across different Mesoamerican societies and centuries. Looking at pictures in the Aztec codices named (for historic Mexican politicians) *Porfirio Diaz* and *Fernandez Leal*, anthropologist Rosemary Gipson speculated that the pole with ropes was originally a way to prepare humans to be sacrificed. She concluded, following a scholar named Walter Krickeberg, who first published the codices, that once the divine birdmen fell from the sky, they were tied to a scaffold and shot with arrows and flayed, after which their bodies were flung to the earth.[25]

In a less violent interpretation of the ritual, sources from the Totonac ethnic group who perform it today say that they first performed the flight in an attempt to end a drought, and that it was given to one of their shamans in a vision. The drought ended, so they continue to perform the ritual for the sake of their crops ever since. As early as 1612, less than a century after the conquest of Mexico by Cortés, the priest Torquemada wrote accounts of the ritual that lament its persistence and support the idea that the ritual went on with reference to fertility and the cycle of the year without any association with human sacrifice.[26] Perhaps there were both Aztec and Totonac versions of the ritual from the beginning. As of 2013, the BBC reported that 250,000 Totonac speakers remained in Mexico, and that the ritual of the *Volodares* remained important as the center of their cultural identity.[27]

In 2009, UNESCO placed the *Voladores* ritual on its Representative List of the Intangible Cultural Heritage of Humanity. The description of the ritual on the UNESCO website calls it a "fertility dance," and represents it with a ten-minute video featuring men in plain white clothing without feathers or plumes, bearing no resemblance to any other description from native codices, historical accounts, or contemporary videos.[28] In contrast, the tourist website of Puerto Vallarta advertises the daily flight of the *Voladores* with exultation in every avian detail, including the sacrifice of a black chicken and seven eggs under the 130-foot pole. Toward the end of a description that runs to fourteen paragraphs, the website says that "the bird-men have become mortals again" when they land, and rejoices that "once again the sacred covenant between men and their gods, between man and the universe, has been renewed."[29]

Direct, explicitly admitted imitation of birds prevails in the eagle dance ritual of the Hopi, a nation of Native Americans that has lived for a thousand years in pueblos, villages of multistory, mud and adobe dwellings that resemble townhouses, atop mesas in the Four Corners area where the modern states of Utah, Colorado, New Mexico, and Arizona meet. Growing corn in the flat ground at the base of these mesas, without irrigation from any nearby river in this dry climate, the Hopi developed a religion attuned to nature in all of its aspects, especially the turning of seasons and the spirit of life in plants and animals. Their ritual year begins near the winter solstice, when rituals involving the kachina (alternatively katsina) spirits embodied by men and boys wearing elaborate and highly stylized masked costumes begin. At high summer, a few weeks after the summer solstice, the cycle of rituals ends when the kachinas are said to leave the villages and return to their home in the San Francisco Peaks to the southwest. There is an eagle kachina, a masked costume said to be inhabited by an eagle spirit and worn during rituals for clans and ceremonial associations within the kivas, or underground ritual rooms, in the pueblos. There are also eagle dancers, who are not masked but costumed as eagles with their faces showing under headdresses with beaks, who perform an all-day ritual called the eagle dance for the whole people in the public plazas of the pueblos.[30] In the arid country where the Hopi build their pueblos and plant their corn, the golden eagle (*Aquila chrysaetos*) is more common than the similarly colored, slightly smaller bald eagle (*Haliaeetus leucocephalus*), which prefers water edges and a diet of fish.

The Hopi eagle dance in its traditional form (as opposed to small samples done at festivals or for tourists) is quite demanding. It involves long passages of quick, sliding movements of the feet to create a gliding, flying motion, while the arms, covered in eagle feathers to simulate wings, are held out at the sides. When the American ballet dancer and choreographer Ted Shawn was a young man touring as a dancer hired to entertain at stations of the Santa Fe Railroad, in 1914, he was allowed to witness the eagle dance in a Hopi pueblo, and he later wrote, "There is no living white man today (and that includes all the greatest of the Russian Ballet, as well as American dancers, including myself) who, after spending a year studying this dance, would be able to reproduce it. There was the most extraordinary rapidity of movement that I have ever witnessed."[31] Shawn created his own interpretation of the eagle dance as one part of a 1923 ballet, *Feather of the Dawn*.

Controversy has surrounded the ritual use of eagles by the Hopi for more than a century. In 1912, anthropologist H. R. Voth published a short article, "Notes on the Eagle Cult of the Hopi," that detailed the annual capture of eaglets by members of ten clans of Hopi from the pueblo of Oraibi (Arizona). Voth counted thirty-five eaglets in that village in one year. They were tied by one leg on the roofs of the flat house tops of the pueblo and fed rabbits and mice until July, when they reached full size. On the holiday of *Niman* (Farewell), the day when the kachinas return to the San Francisco Peaks, these eagles were taken down from the roofs and quickly smothered in a blanket and choked during the descent. Their feathers were then removed, to be used in many rituals and costumes, and the bodies were buried in a ceremonial manner, with rolls of thin blue piki cornbread and a kachina doll, in an eagle cemetery more than half a mile from the pueblo.[32] Voth's article went on to list many uses of the eagle in Hopi ritual, from feathers on the corners of a bride's costume to prayer offerings on human graves to whistles made from eagle bones.

Attacks on these customs have come from Christian missionaries seeking to convert the Hopi, from the US government seeking to protect eagles, from animal rights activists denouncing Hopi cruelty, and from other Native American nations, particularly the Navajo and Apache, objecting to Hopi taking eagles from nests on their land.[33] But defenders of the Hopi have also spoken out. In 2013 Peter Whiteley, the curator of North American ethnology at the American Museum of Natural History in New York, wrote that "self-righteous blame of Hopi eagle-gathering is myopic scapegoating." This was part of the conclusion of an article that cited Percy Lomaquahu, a Hopi whose name translates as "beautiful eagle," for the insight that Hopi see eagles as humans in another form, and as the "lifeline" of their nation. According to Whiteley, each clan takes eaglets only from nests in its own area, along the route used by the clan in its legendary migrations more than a thousand years ago, where the ruins of ancestral pueblos mark the way. The eaglets are seen as reincarnations of ancestral spirits, born to answer the prayers of their descendants. When they arrive in the pueblo, the eaglets have their heads washed, just as the Hopi wash the heads of their newborns, and they are given personal names and baby gifts. On the roofs, they are fed with honor by boys of the pueblo. After their deaths and burials in the eagle cemetery (no other nonhuman animal has a cemetery), they are expected to return with the kachinas in the following year.

The bald eagle and golden eagle were both protected from all hunting by federal law in 1962, but Hopi have been granted permits by the government to continue their capture. In Peter Whiteley's view, the Hopi pose no threat to eagle populations, because Hopi strictly limit the number of eaglets they take and have even commissioned biologists to monitor the numbers of birds. Whiteley points to "residential and municipal development on the Navajo Reservation . . . and industrial development throughout the West" as the true threats to eagles. He urges non-Hopi to take the Hopi perspective, seeing the Hopi and the eagles together as two native nations endangered by the arrival of European Americans and Navajo on their land.

Reading the Messages of Birds: Augury in Kenya, Borneo, Rome, India, and Tibet

In Africa, a very different but in some ways analogous ritual role for eagles has developed among the Waso Boorana people of Kenya. A subgroup of the large Oromo ethnic and language group of Ethiopia, Somalia, and Kenya, the Waso Boorana live in the Isiolo District of Kenya, a flat semidesert northeast of Nairobi, with green hills on its northern horizon. Although the Waso Boorana are Muslims, they have integrated eagles into their own special religious practices, particularly with regard to healing and divination.

Both red-tailed eagles (*Bateleur terathopius*) and augur or jackal buzzards (*Buteo rufofuscus*) frequently appear overhead or landing in the occasional trees around the settlements of the Waso Boorana. Both species are called *Hajj Riisa*, or "pilgrim eagles" sent by God to speak to the people and named for the Muslim pilgrimage to Mecca, the hajj.[34] If one of these birds stays in a tree for a time, the Waso Boorana will bring meat as an offering, at the same time regarding the bird with some anxiety as a possible harbinger of illness or death. If the bird soars in the air and screams above people as though about to dive for prey, then does not dive, it may be regarded as choosing one of the people for a message through spirit possession.[35] People who are so chosen may give messages and healings during ceremonies held at night within a sacred enclosure called a *molla*, a circular hut built around a tree and open in the middle. The eagle becomes present by possessing a human who goes into trance, makes animal sounds, then asks questions about the relations of the people to God and to each other. The possessed person may spit on the sick, request an animal sacrifice and a communal meal, lead prayers, give directions to repair broken social relations, or proclaim that the eagle will carry away any particular evil afflicting the community. At the climax of the ceremony, the participants chant *Hajj Riisa Ijole Mijje Riisa*, or "Pilgrim Eagle, Pilgrim Eagle like a child." Like the American Hopi, these Africans call eagles their children. Both children and eagles are regarded as free from sin and as able to communicate with God, according to Mario Aguilar, the author of several studies of Waso Boorana religion.[36]

The Waso Boorana do not always require possession to receive messages through birds. Flying birds mediate between heavens and earth, carrying the messages of gods or responding to cosmic forces. When the Waso Boorana see an eagle crossing their path from right to left, it is an indication of bad fortune, but an eagle crossing from left to right is a good sign for the future. This is the practice of augury, and one of the birds the Waso Boorana call *Riisa* or eagle is commonly called the augur buzzard.

In another form of augury, the Kantu' people of Borneo traditionally decided where to do their slash-and-burn agriculture and what crops to plant each year by taking a day of abstinence from work and ritually observing seven species of birds.[37] These are not eagles or other raptors, but birds that eat seeds or insects on plants in the rainforest, especially the maroon woodpecker (*Blythipicus rubginosus*) and the crested jay (*Platylophus galericulatus*), both threatened species. Anthropologists hypothesize that making the decision on where to slash and burn and plant by observing the birds has good ecological effects, because it randomizes the destruction involved in this kind of farming, prevents consolidation of large farms, and gives cleared plots a chance to recover. This would make communities of Kantu' who practice augury consistently more successful farmers than those who do not.[38]

Among the ancient Romans, divination by augury was practiced and regulated by an order of priests, the augurs. Most versions of the founding story of the city of Rome include augury. When the twins Romulus and Remus disputed with each other over who should lead and where the city would be built, they left the decision to the birds. Romulus stood on the Palatine hill and Remus on the Aventine, and the brothers waited for vultures. Six vultures quickly landed on the Aventine, and Remus claimed victory, but then twelve vultures landed on the Palatine, so Romulus prevailed.[39]

As the government of Rome transformed itself from a dynasty of kings to a republic to an empire, all of its leaders continued to rely on augury. Before every military campaign, as every new consul or emperor took office, and at the foundation of every building project, an augur took his place at the Auguraculum, at the top of the Capitoline Hill, and looked at the sky, asking Jupiter to send the birds with a message and pouring a libation to the god. The priest raised his staff, the *lituus*, a straight piece of wood with no knots and a curving top end. Gesturing from west to east and north to south, he created a space in the sky called a *templum*.[40] He sat down on a chair facing south,[41] looked to the center of the *templum*, and waited for a stated amount of time: perhaps an hour, measured by a sundial, or perhaps from dawn to noon or noon to dusk, or even as much as an entire day. He looked for birds that flew through the *templum*, basing his judgments of their meaning on the species, numbers, and direction of the birds. Birds entering from the priest's left (the east) or from his front (the south) were regarded as good omens; birds from the priest's right (the west) or from behind (the north) were signs of ill fortune.[42] Not all birds had equal weight in determining the message. Eagles, the birds of Jupiter, were most important. Hawks were next, followed by ravens, crows, woodpeckers and any smaller birds. A rare or unexpected bird was more important, either for good or ill. Bird calls were also important, and similarly judged by their direction and number, with the calls of ravens and owls more important than those of woodpeckers or hens. Records were made of all observations and consulted in the interpretation of meaning. What had proven to be a good omen in the past was likely to portend good again.

Among the Romans, augury was not limited to public occasions. The eldest male of every family, the paterfamilias, would do an augury before important family events such as marriages and the building of new houses.[43] And as in the state, families kept records of auguries to consult from one generation to another.

The use of birds to determine whether good or bad fortune awaited an action was not limited to observing free birds in flight. Before a battle, Roman generals had the sacred chickens that accompanied the army fed, and took it as a good sign if they ate so eagerly that some food fell from their beaks to the floor or the ground, but as a bad omen if they refused to eat. During the first Punic War in 249 BCE, when Hannibal of Carthage was defeating one Roman army after another, the Carthaginians held a port on the western coast of Sicily. The consul P. Claudius Pulcher wanted to attack that port with a Roman fleet, but the chickens on Pulcher's ship would not eat. Notoriously, Pulcher declared, "Let them drink, since they won't eat" (*Bibant, quoniam esse nolunt*) and threw them into the sea to drown.[44] After suffering a disastrous defeat, Pulcher was tried by the Senate for failing to obey the augury and retired from politics, apparently going into exile from Rome.

Scholar Susanne Rasmussen explains that the theory of augury was not to attempt to control fate or the gods, but to try to act in harmony with the powers of the cosmos. The birds observed in Roman augury were not agents controlling the future, but signs of how well a proposed action would suit the disposition of things in the present.[45] And as Pulcher's unfortunate example indicated, augury could also be manipulated. Just before the Roman republic turned into an empire, as the orator and philosopher Cicero (an augur himself) and others attested, augury by observation of flight gradually declined in favor of the more easily manipulated augury by feeding.[46]

On the other hand, Augustus the first emperor, revived the traditional rituals of bird observation to claim divine favor for his rule. After defeating Marc Antony and Cleopatra at the Battle of Actium, returning to Rome, and paying off his troops, Augustus (then still known as Octavian, the adopted son of Julius Caesar), had the ritual called *augurium salutis*, the augury for closing the doors of the Temple of Janus and declaring an end of war, performed. In 28 BCE, Octavian asked the Senate to authorize the even more important ritual of *inauguratio*, also called the *augustum augurium*. This amounted to a symbolic refounding of the city, re-enacting the augury of Romulus. Within a year after that, in 27 BCE, the Senate conferred on Octavian the new name of Imperator Caesar Divi Filius Augustus (Emperor Caesar Son of God Augustus). It has been plausibly argued that the name of the first Roman emperor, and in a sense the concept of empire itself, derived from these rituals of augury.[47]

Although augury has almost disappeared in the West, its heritage remains. The staffs of Christian bishops, commonly called crosiers and often understood to be symbolic of shepherds' staffs, are also modern forms of the *lituus*. The word "auspicious," used to denote something with a favorable aspect, derives from *aves*, birds, and *specere*, to look, with the preposition *ad*, toward: *ad aves specere* turned into "auspicious."[48] The name of the augury by feeding chickens, which the Romans called the *tripudium* or three-step (derived from the happy stamping of the birds), has become a form of processional favored in some churches.[49] Just as flamenco dancers may be unconsciously imitating flamingoes, so Episcopalian and Orthodox Christians who do the *tripudium* have (unconsciously) inherited their formal steps from chickens.

Perhaps the Romans obtained augury from the East, where they could find the origins of many of their religious practices. Texts discovered in Hittite sites of the 1300s BCE, dating from six centuries before the foundation of Rome, describe officials watching birds for oracles in ways that resemble the Roman augurs. The Hittite lands in eastern Anatolia (modern Turkey) are traversed by many rivers, including some that flowed down to Mesopotamia and the Persian Gulf. Instead of standing on a hill as the Romans later did, the Hittites stood facing a river. They divided their field of vision into eight triangles, with the river as the main horizontal line and a perpendicular line from the observer to the river. Although some of the birds mentioned are not identifiable, the eagle and the raven appear to have been important. As in Rome and among the Waso Boorana of Kenya, Hittite augurs thought that it was good for the bird to fly from the left of the observer to the right.[50]

Farther to the east from Rome, in India and in Tibet, the calls of crows and ravens were regarded as prime sources for augury. The oldest Hindu collection of scriptures, the Rig Veda (usually dated to about 1000 BCE), extols the raven's voice as "auspicious, bearing joyful tidings" (Rig Veda 2.42.4).[51] It urges the raven, "Let not the falcon kill thee, nor the eagle, let not the arrow-bearing archer reach thee" (2.42.3). Some Romans later believed that of all the birds of augury, only the raven understood what its message to humans was.

As for the raven's smaller cousin the crow, a Tibetan text of the 800s CE so humanizes crows as to ascribe castes to them: the intelligent crow is a Brahmin or priest; the "red-eyed" crow is a Kshatriya or warrior; the crow that flaps its wings a great deal is a Vaisya, or merchant; and the crow shaped like a fish or "subsisting on filthy food" is a Shudra, or laborer.[52] Any of these crows might bring a message, the meaning of which depended on the direction from which it came and the time of day, with the day divided into five periods. Here the augury was not, like the Roman, simply a yes or no to a proposed action. Rather, the crows of Tibet were heard as predicting specific events: the arrival of a friend, the arrival of a stranger, obtaining property, a storm, a conflagration, a great wind, an outbreak of disease, et cetera. All these and more depended on the time of day and the direction of the call.[53] A separate section of the text deals with the meaning of crows observed while the human is making a journey.[54] In addition, where the crow built its nest and the specific sounds of its call (transcribed in the English version as *ka-ka*, *da-da*, *ta-ta*, or *gha-gha*) had predictive meanings.[55] In a different ninth-century Tibetan text, the calls of a raven are similarly translated. That text begins, "The Raven is the protector of men."[56]

Birds as Food and Rituals of Sacrifice: Jews, Africans, Egyptians, and Hindus

Neither ravens nor crows (or eagles or vultures, for that matter) are normally eaten by humans. The expression to "eat crow" is a negative, because the crow's flesh tastes bitter, so that to have to eat crow is regarded as a sign of defeat and a punishment for pride. The same lack of human interest in eating some birds has extended to eagles, vultures, hawks, and owls. In the Hebrew Scriptures (Leviticus 11:13–19 and Deuteronomy 14:11–17), a long list of birds is called unclean, so that it is forbidden for Israelites to eat them: eagles, vultures, ospreys, kites, falcons, ravens, ostriches, nighthawks, seagulls, hawks, owls, cormorants, ibises, water hens (a small long-legged waterbird, related to the rail), pelicans, storks, herons, and hoopoes (a magnificently crested bird, the national bird of modern Israel). No reason is given for forbidding the eating of these birds, but all the birds listed as unclean eat mammals, fish, and carrion, unlike the largely vegetarian and insectivorous chickens, ducks, geese, pigeons, doves, sparrows, and (since the Americas were discovered) turkeys that are the primary kosher (proper, clean) birds.

Eating and sacrificing are closely related, and so are the rituals surrounding them. But eating answers simple biological need, from which rituals of eating have evolved, while the origins of sacrifice remain unclear. Among theorists, some argue that sacrifice begins only after animals have been domesticated and human societies have developed beyond the hunter-gatherer stage.[57] In Frank W. Marlowe's book-length study of the Hadza of East Africa, who gather honey with birds (2010), as discussed above, no sacrifices are described, although the Hadza do practice a ritual sharing of the meat of large animals killed in the hunt. Following René Girard, others have argued that sacrifice developed from a need to displace aggression arising from envy or "mimetic desire";[58] that sacrificial rituals emerged alongside kingship, agriculture, and cities; and that such rituals began as human sacrifices, with animals later accepted as replacements for human victims. We know by written records, including the Vedas of India and the Hebrew Torah, that patriarchal nomads of the Bronze Age who had no cities of their own, no kings, and no agriculture practiced animal sacrifice and attributed great power to these rituals. But since those nomads lived in a world of cities and kings and agriculture, it could be argued that they imitated the practices of other cultures.

Perhaps offering food to the cosmos or to spiritual beings, in the way that one offers food to human guests or allies, is an attempt to create a bond of debt, through which the gods or ancestors or the natural world could be induced to return the favor. If this is the origin of sacrifice, then edible foods, including edible birds, would be the primary offerings. Remembering that, symbolically, birds and humans make excellent analogues of each other, we also recall that various birds, including the bower bird of Australia and New Zealand (*Ptilorynchus violaceus*), offer gifts of food or bright objects to potential mates.[59] Observing male bower birds constructing the elaborate enclosures (not nests) in which they place gifts for females may have inspired humans to make special settings for their sacrifices.

When humans sacrifice birds, identifying humans very personally with the bird victims seems to play a role. Consider two cases from an account of sacrifice among the Yoruba of West Africa in 1973. In the first instance, a man with a sick child came to an oracle, who told him to prepare some water with crushed herbs and to bring the water, along with the child and a chick a few days old, to a crossroads at midnight. The man then bathed the child with the water. Next he held the chick by the legs and swung it around the child's head three times, then dashed the chick to the ground so that it instantly died. Explaining this action, a Yoruba scholar wrote that the man believed his child was afflicted by witches, and that the death of the chick would appease them and lead them to accept a substitute, so that the "chick thus died, as it were, the child's death."[60]

The second modern Yoruba case identifies bird and human even more closely. The scholar recounted a man being instructed by the oracle to gather a small group of friends and family and to bring a bowl of cold water, some salt, a pigeon, and a kola nut. After washing the nut in the water, he held and touched it to his head, praying that his personal Ori, or spirit, would bring him good things. Then he touched his head with the pigeon, prayed again, wrung the head off the pigeon, and smeared his head with its blood. Everyone next took part of the kola nut and touched it to the salt and prayed that the man's life should be good and sweet. The pigeon was then prepared, fried, and eaten by the man and those he invited to what the scholar called a "sacrifice."[61] In his analysis, the scholar noted that pigeons are suitable for rituals for "good luck and longevity." This is because "The bird is noted for its serenity in flight, its neatness of appearance and its smartness in movement."

He quoted a Yoruba chant: "The pigeon will always be prosperous, / The dove will always find peace; / So let me be prosperous, / Let everything be well with me."[62] The bird referenced in this song is probably the rock dove, the now-global bird we think of as the pigeon (*Columba livia*), but may have been a laughing dove (*Spilopileia senegalensis*), a more reddish-brown bird that is the most widespread dove of sub-Saharan Africa.

Of course, all sacrifice must involve some identification of humans with the animals or plants killed, or else the deaths could not do the humans any good. But in the case of birds, identification seems particularly intense. The Bible is filled with passages that express this identity. "I am like an owl of the wilderness, like a little owl of the waste places," laments the psalmist, reflecting the afflictions of King David and of later Israel, in Psalm 102 (NRSV). That Psalm continues, "I am like a lonely bird on the housetop. All day long my enemies taunt me." Celebrating a national victory in Psalm 124:7, the writer identifies all Israel with the bird, exulting, "Blessed be the LORD who has not given us as prey to their teeth. We have escaped like a bird from the snare of the fowlers; the snare is broken, and we have escaped." In the New Testament, Jesus is quoted as urging his hearers to identify with birds. Don't worry about what you will eat or wear, says Jesus in the Gospel of Luke, but "Consider the ravens: they neither sow nor reap, they have neither storehouse nor barn, and yet God feeds them" (Luke 12:24 NRSV). Seeking to quiet the fears of his disciples that the authorities might kill them, Jesus uses the image of sparrows skewered and cooked and sold for meat. "Are not five sparrows sold for two pennies? Yet not one of them is forgotten in God's sigh. t. . . Do not be afraid; you are of more value than many sparrows" (Luke 12:6–7 NRSV).

While neither the owl nor the raven could be eaten or sacrificed by biblical standards, the sparrow was kosher and could also be used in ritual. The Hebrew word translated as "bird" in the Psalms, the bird sitting lonely on the housetop and escaping the fowler, is *tsippor*, or "sparrow." In the rituals for cleansing a leper and cleansing a leper's house given in Leviticus 14, the same word appears. When the leper's skin appears to have healed from the disease, the priest is instructed to go to the leper with two living sparrows, a clay pot with fresh water, a piece of cedar wood, a branch of hyssop (an herb still used as an antiseptic), and a crimson thread. He then kills one bird over the earthen vessel so that its blood flows into the water. He dips the hyssop, the crimson thread, the cedar, and the living sparrow into the same water, next sprinkles the water seven times over the healed leper, who is to be declared clean. The living bird is then released into an open field, after which the former leper washes his or her clothes, shaves off all hair including the eyebrows, and bathes (Leviticus 14:1–9). A similar ritual cleanses the home of the leper (after all of its plaster has been replaced), with the difference that it is the home that is sprinkled with water mixed with the blood of one sparrow, while the other sparrow is again dipped in the bloody water and set free (Leviticus 14:48–53). Incidentally, it might be noted that the term translated as "leprosy" in Leviticus (Hebrew *tsaraath*) was probably used for many diseases of the skin, not simply for the modern disease called leprosy, or Hansen's disease.[63]

The Torah prescribes animal sacrifice for many infractions of the law and instances of pollution, ranging from failure in one's duty as a witness to inadvertent swearing, contact with impure substances such as dead human bodies or the bodies of impure animals, and childbirth (impure because of its unusual fluids and blood). In most cases "animals of the flock," sheep or goats, are the preferred sacrifice, but birds may be offered as a substitute by those who cannot afford the larger and costlier animals. No bird substitutes were allowed for some of the graver sins, in which the cost of sacrifice could be borne by the whole nation. A bull was the costliest sacrifice, and two bulls were offered when the whole people of Israel was guilty of some unintentional breach of the law (Leviticus 4:13–21). One bull was the prescribed offering for an unintentional sin by the high priest (Leviticus 4:3–12). On the Day of Atonement (Yom Kippur), a bull and a ram were sacrificed on behalf of the whole people, and two goats were also involved: one to be sacrificed, the other sent into the wilderness after the priest laid his hands on its head and confessed "all the iniquities of the people of Israel, and all their transgressions, all their sins, putting them on the head of the goat." This was the famous "scapegoat," who escaped being sacrificed, just as one of the sparrows escaped in the cleansing of lepers and their homes.

Besides leprosy, the only infractions for which birds were the prescribed sacrificial animals were bodily emissions. When a male had an emission of seed outside of sexual intercourse, or a woman had emission of blood outside the normal course of her period, they had to wait seven days, then on the eighth day offer the priest two turtledoves or two pigeons. In these cases neither bird lived. Both were killed by having the priest snap their necks with his thumbnail, and their blood was sprinkled on the corner of the altar at the Temple, but one was then burned completely and the other cooked and eaten by the priests and their male children (Leviticus 7:1–6 and 15).[64] This was the normal difference between a "burnt offering" or *olah* (from which the word Holocaust comes) and a "sin offering" or "guilt offering," both of which could be eaten.

Another indication of the direct identification of people with birds appears in the fact that the only sacrifices of the Bible in which birds are the prescribed animal are the most personal cases: skin disease and bodily emissions. The birds involved are also very human-oriented, tameable birds, turtledoves and pigeons and sparrows. Turtledoves (*Streptopelia turtur*) are smaller and more distinctively marked than the common pigeon and have been expanding their range from southern Europe. According to a modern manual for Jewish sacrifice, published in 1993 in the hope that the Jerusalem Temple might be rebuilt and Jewish sacrifices resumed, the turtledove must be mature: "Long and shining goldish feathers are the sign of having reached adulthood." If a pigeon is used, on the other hand, it must be young. "If blood gathers at the spot from which a feather was plucked, it is a sign that the pigeon is still young."[65]

Although no birds have been killed at the Jerusalem Temple since the Romans destroyed it in 70 CE, many Jews still partner with birds in a ritual every fall at Yom Kippur. Orthodox and Hasidic Jews have a custom on the day called *kaporos* (or *kaparot*) that involves saying a prayer while swinging a live chicken over one's head. According to the handbook of the Lubavitcher school of Hasidim, men should use a rooster, women a hen, and pregnant women should use three birds: a hen for themselves and a hen and a rooster to cover a child of either sex. The prayer says: "This is my exchange, this is my substitute, this is my expiation. This hen [or rooster] shall go to its death and I shall proceed to a good, long life and peace." The person performing the ritual then hands the bird to a kosher butcher, who chops off its head and deposits the body in a box. Controversy rages over what then happens to these chickens, with some saying they are given to the poor to eat and others that they are simply wasted, taken to a landfill. As consciousness of animal rights and sensitivity to cruelty rise, the places in Hasidic neighborhoods where this ritual takes place have become targets of protest. In 2016, it was estimated that fifty thousand chickens were killed in Brooklyn, New York, alone in the ritual of *kaporos*. Alternatives abound: for example, the Lubavitcher website allows for the *kaporos* prayer to be said while waving money over one's head and then donating the money to the poor, or for performing *kaporos* with a live fish.[66] Neither money nor fish would seem to offer the human-bird connection of the chicken. Rebbetzin Leah Zelwig, creator of a series of advice videos on Jewish customs, performs the ritual with a live hen that she holds very gently and strokes, and she does not kill the bird.[67]

An analogous and more dramatic use of chickens appears in the voodoo rituals honoring Damballah, the serpent god, and Gede, the god of death. Recorded by Maya Deren in a classic documentary film from 1951, *Divine Horsemen: The Living Gods of Haiti*, these sacrifices involve first allowing a pair of birds (a black rooster, in these cases, and a white or black and white hen) to eat grain that has been scattered on the *vever*, the intricate chalk design on the ground where the ceremony is performed, to show the birds' consent, then waving them over the heads of each member of the congregation to absorb their sins. Next, voodoo priests break the wings and legs of the chickens so that the sins cannot fly free. They kill the birds by twisting their necks, twirling them by the head and dropping the bodies onto the *vever*. In the sacrifice to Damballah, a god represented by the serpent, all this goes on to the complex, rapid beat of drums and increasingly vigorous dance, until the god takes possession of one of the dancers and "rides" that person, distributing healing energy to the others in the circle. Here the point of sacrifice is to feed the gods so that they come to their people. The birds are eventually cooked and eaten.

These practices came to Haiti with the Yoruba of West Africa, whose ritual sacrifices of chicks and pigeons were described above. In the Yoruba diaspora to the Americas, similar uses of chickens came to Cuba and Puerto Rico, where the religion is called Santeria, and to Brazil, where it is called candomblé. Just as *kaporos* has caused controversies in Brooklyn, the killing of chickens in Santeria and voodoo rituals has met resistance in Miami, New Orleans, and New York. In a 1993 decision, *Church of the Lukumi Babalu Aye, Inc. v. City of Hialeah*, the US Supreme Court unanimously ruled that a Florida statute banning animal sacrifice was unconstitutional.[68] Later in 1993, during the World Parliament of Religions in Chicago, radio host Aaron Freeman interviewed a voodoo priest who defended such rites by emphasizing how rarely they are performed and how reverently he prays for the soul of the sacrificed bird.[69]

Even less pleasant examples of bird cults have been noticed in the borough of Queens in New York City, where living roosters and hens are abandoned, some with their feet cut off, under the North Channel Bridge near Howard Beach.[70] This practice of "loosing" birds is attributed to followers of the Hindu goddess Kali, some of whom have come to New York. In India and in Nepal, followers of Kali sacrifice chickens, as well as goats and water buffalo, on her altars.

With regard to the scale of bird deaths, the cult of Kali, *kaporos*, and voodoo all pale in comparison to the ancient Egyptian practice of killing and mummifying birds. Archaeologists have found that every city of Egypt in the 500s BCE had animal necropolises, and those of the sacred ibis are particularly large. Feeding areas in lakes were maintained to attract the birds and to keep them nearby. At Tuna el-Gebel, a necropolis near ancient Hermopolis Magna, a city at the border of Upper and Lower Egypt, about halfway between Thebes and the Nile delta, approximately fifteen thousand ibises per year were mummified. The total number of bird mummies remaining in the necropolis today is estimated at a million, with ninety species represented, although the vast majority of mummies are sacred ibises.[71] Apparently, the site was used as a place of pilgrimage for members of an ibis cult and as a source for devotees who purchased mummified birds for their homes, as pledges for their own resurrection and immortality (another example of human-bird identification).[72] For those who worked at Tuna el-Gebel, the killing and mummifying of a bird, or the taking of eggs from a nest to mummify them, would not have seemed an act of harm or disrespect, but the deliverance of the soul of the bird to everlasting life.[73] At that time, Egyptian law made mistreatment of ibises or falcons punishable by death. Because the sacred ibis is easy to semidomesticate on feeding grounds, mummification made that bird a year-round resident rather than a migrant at Tuna el-Gebel, and its population survived, but the numbers of hawks and falcons in ancient Egypt dwindled.[74]

Modern Rituals: Thanksgiving, Bird Releases, and Yawar, Peruvian Independence Day

The most prominent ritual involving birds in the United States today is Thanksgiving. The turkey is the star of the holiday, as evidenced in Norman Rockwell's painting to illustrate Freedom from Want, one of the Four Freedoms announced by President Franklin Roosevelt as the aims of the United Nations in World War II.[75] And on the day before Thanksgiving, there is another ritual: a traditional turkey pardon by the president at the White House. This was foreshadowed by Abraham Lincoln's writing a reprieve for a turkey at the urging of his son Tad, who had made the bird a pet, just before Christmas of 1864.[76] Turkeys became strongly associated with the presidency and Thanksgiving from the 1870s, when a poultry dealer named Harold Vose gained publicity by sending a bird every year to the White House until his death in 1913, but those turkeys were not pardoned.[77] Since the Truman administration, the National Turkey Federation, a lobbying group for the turkey industry, has selected the White House turkey from among those raised by the farmers it represents.[78] In 1963, President Kennedy looked at the forty-pound bird, which had a sign saying, "Good eating, Mr. President" hung around its neck, and said, "Let's let this one grow." Richard Nixon sent a turkey to a petting zoo in 1969, and Ronald Reagan did the same in 1987, but these were all one-off actions, as much polite acknowledgments of the gift from the Turkey Federation as pardons.[79] The tradition of calling the action a pardon began with George H. W. Bush in 1989, and it has continued since. At this point, the ritual has become so elaborate that the bird—now normally a pair of birds—is brought to the White House in a limousine manned by people pretending to be Secret Service agents, decorated with presidential seals that feature a turkey wearing a Pilgrim hat and the words, "National Turkey of the United States."[80]

Figure 3.2 A farm-bred, white turkey is presented by National Turkey Federation chairman John Reicks to President Barack Obama, and "pardoned" from service at Thanksgiving dinner, in an annual White House ritual in 2016.
White House Photo / Planetpix / Alamy Live News.

Unfortunately, the humor of the turkey pardon covers a less pleasant reality. The pardoned turkeys are products of intensive breeding and factory farming, and their lives are short. Only about four months old when they are pardoned, they are already too massive for their bone structure and on the brink of organ failure. Even though sent to Virginia Tech's Animal and Poultry Sciences Department, they rarely live as much as a year after the pardon. Only three pardoned turkeys were alive at Thanksgiving of 2016; one that had just died, named Courage and pardoned in 2009, had been put on a weight reduction diet at Disneyland and lived to be six years old.[81]

In the wild, turkeys are intelligent, lean, and social birds who hunt snakes together and who can bond with humans. This was well illustrated in the PBS Nature documentary *My Life as a Turkey* (2011), in which biologist Joe Hutto chronicled his raising of a family of turkeys. Turkeys are good food for humans, and in the New England of the Pilgrims they were so numerous that they were easy to hunt. They did form part of the menu at the three-day harvest festival the Wampanoag Indians and Plymouth settlers held in 1621, but they were not as central to that feast as the five deer donated by the Indians.[82] Immediately popular in England and Europe, they became strongly associated with Christmas after Charles Dickens pictured his character Ebenezer Scrooge giving a turkey to the Cratchit family to replace their skinny goose in 1843.[83] Turkeys remained expensive luxuries in England and Europe (where France and Italy are now major growers of turkeys) until modern times. Dickens's readers would have understood the generosity of the gift.

Because geese are more aggressive and better fliers than turkeys, they do not take as easily to factory farming, and their popularity at holidays decreased while the turkey gained. European Jews traditionally served goose on Hanukkah, using its abundant fat to cook potato pancakes and its feathers for pillows and beds, but Jewish immigrants to America soon switched to chicken and turkey,[84] both bred into forms that could never survive in nature, and that almost certainly do not enjoy their lives very much. A Perdue "oven-stuffer" roasting chicken has more room while being cooked in an oven than it ever had in its life.

In this context, the presidential turkey pardon is a cruel joke. It seems as futile as the papal release of doves for peace on the last Sunday of January, a tradition begun by Pope John Paul II in 1985. Raised in captivity, the doves have often (in 2005, 2011, and 2012) flown back into the papal apartment. In 2013 and 2014 they were immediately attacked by seagulls and crows, so that in 2015 Pope Francis released balloons instead.[85] Animal rights activists pointed out that the balloons would be likely to be eaten by wild birds, and this January tradition has apparently ceased.

Another questionable ritual interaction between humans and birds has emerged in Peru, around Peruvian Independence Day, July 28. During a three-day festival called Yawar, a ritualized fight between a condor and a bull symbolizes the survival of native culture despite the Spanish conquest. The Spanish brought cattle to Peru after their arrival in 1528, and the Andean condor (*Vultur gryphus*), a New World vulture with a wingspan of almost eleven feet, is native to the area. Luring condors to the ground with dead horses, the people of many villages capture a male and a female bird, bathe them and feed them for weeks before the event, then parade them through the street with their enormous wingspans on display, a man holding each wing out while another holds the harness of the bird. The harness on the feet of one condor is then sewn into the hide of a bull's back, and the bull is released to run around a ring. Men, sometimes professional bullfighters, spur the bull on with red targets and capes. Although the bull is not killed, it is tormented by the condor, and the condor flaps and struggles on its back. After some time (about seven minutes in this reported instance), the first condor is released from the bull and the second attached for another set of bucking and fighting. After the bull is exhausted, the birds are released, given some of the sour fermented corn drink that is enjoyed at the festival, and encouraged to fly away. This can be difficult, because these birds are so heavy that they need an updraft from a peak or a running start down an incline to take off.[86] If the condors are injured or killed in the bull ring, it is regarded as a bad sign for the year and it can bring a fine to the village, because the Peruvian central government has forbidden this ritual, although there are provinces and towns that still support it.

At the end of a successful festival, the birds soar away and demonstrate the victory of the Natives over the Spanish. Some find a deeper symbolism in the ritual, saying that it represents the union of sky and earth and has roots in native culture before the Spanish ever came. Others say that it has much more recent origins, taking its current name from a novel published in 1941, and that it has spread from village to village as Peruvians have grown wealthier and sought to gain prestige and income for their villages by promoting the ritual for tourists.[87]

Estimates of how endangered Andean condors are, and of how much the spread of these festivals contributes to endangering their survival, vary wildly. Without doubt, however, these ritual fights are not natural or pleasant

68 WINGS OF THE GODS

Figure 3.3 In the 2012 Yawar festival, the people of Cotabambas, Peru, cast a condor in the role of natives fighting the imported European bull. The condor is meant to survive the ritual.
Jan Sochor / Alamy Stock Photo.

for the bulls or for the birds. Cockfights at least express something of the nature of the birds and probably contributed to the spread of domesticated chickens across the world, but condor festivals address nothing more than human needs for entertainment, affirmation of national identity, and contact with magnificent animals.

Birdwatching as Ritual and Potential Cooperation between People and Birds

Since the 1950s, people in the United States have taken up bird feeding and birdwatching at increasing rates. Scholars at Stanford University and at the Cornell University Laboratory of Ornithology estimate that about forty million American households, or sixty-five million people, are now feeding birds in their backyards, and birdwatching has become the second most popular "passive sport" (after gardening).[88] Birdwatching has its rituals, beginning with the keeping of a record (or "life list") in notebooks often small enough to carry in a pocket. The Christmas bird count, sponsored by the National Audubon Society, began in 1899 and has grown steadily to include, by 2018, almost seventy-seven thousand counters in more than twenty-five hundred groups covering North and South America, the Caribbean, and the Pacific Islands.[89] The tradition of the Big Year, in which individual bird watchers try to see how many different species they can record on the North American continent—or, now, in the world—from January 1 to December 31, has grown since its birth in the 1930s into a subject for books, movies, and media coverage. An official "Big Year" must conform to rules set by an organization, the American Birding Association.[90]

Meanwhile, research on bird cognition has made mutuality more possible. Only a few years ago, people used the phrase "bird brain" as an insult. Now, scientists know that crows and pigeons (and many other birds) recognize particular humans,[91] that crows not only use but make tools, and that all of the birds in the backyard communicate with each other with alarm calls that distinguish between cats, people, dogs, and hawks.[92] People who feed birds are encouraged to make "phish" sounds as they fill the feeders to call the birds,[93] and bird watchers carry phones that can play bird calls. All this interaction can lead to abuses: overfeeding with suet from winter into spring, when the suet melts, may result in damaged feathers, and birders may confuse and frighten away birds by overusing recorded calls. But the overall trend is toward new forms of cooperation and new rituals, in which both humans and birds participate as partners, learning to recognize each other as agents with spiritual gifts and needs. Facebook and Instagram have encouraged people to post photos of birds feeding from their hands, and birding books include many stories of how birdwatching, bird feeding, and bird rehabilitation have led to personal rituals of bonding between humans and birds.

A poignant example of ritual interaction between birds and people takes place every fall on Martha's Vineyard, a famous resort island off Cape Cod, Massachusetts. At Aquinnah, a town on the island, the Wampanoag nation of Native Americans—the nation that greeted the English Pilgrims who came ashore at Plymouth Rock in 1620—has a reservation and tribal office. They hold an annual powwow where people from many nations do many dances. One dance imitates a local bird, the heath hen, which went extinct in 1932. Todd McGrain, the resident artist at the Cornell Lab of Ornithology, described this dance as he saw it recently, in the midst of a crowd of dancers and singers:

> One tall male dancer, adorned in layers of intricate beadwork and feathers, is moving like no one else. He struts, jerking this head forward beyond his rounded shoulders. His arms are arched to his side. His moccasins touch softly. Toe to heel he pats the ground and then shifts to a quick, gentle flat-footed tamping. The bells at his ankles join the music, softening the edges of the beat. A small hop and then a circle, he pauses. Lifting one knee high, he holds still as if offering himself for admiration. Again, he joins the rhythm.[94]

That man was paying tribute to a spring mating dance that heath hen males long performed on that same open field, called a lek. "Balanced over their stout legs, the males inflated preposterous, ballooning orange throat sacs and raised dark horn-like feathers high above their heads," McGrain wrote, reflecting eyewitness descriptions. He concluded that the extinct heath hen males, like the contemporary human male, "alternated between very rapid intervals of fluttering steps and moments of complete stillness, as if to give the females a chance to take in the marvel of their display."[95]

McGrain had come to Martha's Vineyard to install and to dedicate a shiny black, bronze statue of a male heath hen about six feet tall, with its beak open in the midst of its dance, on a lek where the last bird of its kind was last seen on March 11, 1932. Once so abundant from New England to the Carolinas that domestic servants bargained not to be fed heath hen more than three times per week, the bird was hunted to elimination everywhere but on Martha's Vineyard, where a few hundred survived in the 1870s. The government of Massachusetts established a reserve for the bird in 1908, banning hunting and planting crops for the birds. Unfortunately, a fire and the arrival of goshawks, "a serious Heath Hen predator," ravaged the population until a single surviving male, nicknamed "Booming Ben" by human neighbors because of the sound he made with his air sacs, was flying to the tops of trees and calling out, but receiving no response, in 1929. Ben apparently lived the last three years of his life alone.

Eighty years later, the ritual of installing the heath hen statue brought Ben's call back to the lek on Martha's Vineyard. With the statue there to be seen and touched, the powwow including the heath hen dance took on new meaning. Next came the music: McGrain's collaborator and brother-in-law, neurologist Andrew Stern, gathered glass bottles to replicate the call of the male heath hen, following an old description that their call resembled the sound made by blowing across the mouth of a "two drachm [about eight ounce] apothecary bottle."[96] With the attention and cooperation of a second-grade class of children and their music teacher, Stern told the story of Booming Ben; then he and the children filled the old heath hen lek with the sound of "a full flock of Heath Hens."

Although rituals cannot replace environmental activism, this ritual inspires hope that the emotional impact of rituals might lead to action in the future.

Notes

1. Rosalinde Kearsley, "Octavian and Augury: The Years 30–27 B.C.," *Classical Quarterly*, new series, 59, no. 1 (May, 2009): 159. Mary Beard, John North, and Simon Price, *Religions of Rome*, vol. 1, *A History* (Cambridge: Cambridge University Press, 1998), 23.
2. Susanne William Rasmussen, *Public Portents in Republican Rome* (Rome: L'Erma di Bretschneider, 2003), 162–163.
3. Ronald L. Grimes, *The Craft of Ritual Studies* (New York: Oxford University Press, 2014), 188–189.
4. Mike Carter, "In Tanzania with Africa's Last Hunter-Gatherers," *Financial Times*, August 21, 2015, https://www.ft.com/content/0054e202-44c3-11e5-af2f-4d6e0e5ed a22 (accessed January 4, 2016). Also, see video at https://www.youtube.com/watch?v= 6ETvF9z8pc0 (accessed January 3, 2017). Also, BBSRC video, "How Honeyguide Birds Talk to People," published July 21, 2016, https://www.youtube.com/watch?v= hGC4nG0RqYI&t=114s (accessed January 3, 2017).
5. Ian Johnston, "Humans and Wild Birds 'Talk' to Each Other as They Hunt for Bees' Honey," *The Independent*, July 21, 2016, http://www.independent.co.uk/news/scie nce/birds-bees-honey-honeyguides-mozambique-niassa-national-reserve-animal-communication-a7148896.html (accessed January 5, 2017).
6. Frank W. Marlowe, *The Hadza: Hunter-Gatherers of Tanzania* (Berkeley: University of California Press, 2010), 59.
7. Marlowe, *The Hadza*, 65.
8. Kristina Killgrove, "These Ancient Headless Corpses Were Defleshed by Griffon Vultures," *Forbes*, June 9, 2017, http://www.forbes.com/sites/kristinakillgrove/2016/ 06/09/griffon-vultures-defleshed-corpses-to-create-headless-burials-in-ancient-anatolia/#57b468132705 (accessed January 5, 2017). Also Ian Hodder, "Mysteries of Catalhoyuk," Science Museum of Minnesota, 2003, https://www.smm.org/catal/ mysteries/burial_practices/ (accessed January 6, 2017).
9. Elliott Hannon, "Vanishing Vultures a Grave Matter for India's Parsis," *All Things Considered*, September 5, 2012, http://www.npr.org/2012/09/05/160401322/vanish ing-vultures-a-grave-matter-for-indias-parsis (accessed January 5, 2016).
10. Madhura Karnik, "India Has a Grand Plan to Bring Back Its Vultures," *Quartz India*, June 8, 2016, https://qz.com/700998/india-has-a-grand-plan-to-bring-back-its-vultu res/ (accessed January 12, 2017).

11. Ian Burfied and Chris Bowden, "South Asian vultures and diclofenac," Cambridge Core blog, September 27, 2022, https://www.cambridge.org/core/blog/2022/09/28/south-asian-vultures-and-diclofenac/ (accessed November 14, 2023).
12. "Chopped Up and Fed to the Vultures," *Daily Mail*, July 24, 2013, http://www.dailymail.co.uk/news/article-2376190/Chopped-fed-vultures-glimpse-closely-guarded-tradition-Tibetan-sky-funeral.html (accessed January 5, 2017).
13. BirdNote, "A Funeral for Crows," February 6, 2015, https://www.audubon.org/news/a-funeral-crows (accessed July 3, 2019). Also Jason Bittel,"Think Crow Funerals Are Strange? Wait Until You See the Wake," *Audubon*, July 23, 2018, https://www.audubon.org/news/think-crow-funerals-are-strange-wait-until-you-see-wake (accessed July 3, 2019).
14. PBS Nature, "Andes: The Dragon's Back," June 24, 2010, http://www.pbs.org/wnet/nature/andes-the-dragons-back-video-dance-of-the-flamingos/3104/ (accessed January 6, 2017).
15. Pascal Boyer, *The Naturalness of Religious Ideas: A Cognitive Theory of Religion* (Berkeley: University of California Press, 1994), 189.
16. Michelle Chaplow, "Flamenco History," http://www.andalucia.com/flamenco/history.htm#4 (accessed January 6, 2017).
17. Unknown source, saved to Internet Archive under "Flamingo Flamenco." Visual and auditory evidence is compelling: https://www.youtube.com/watch?v=w_-1V0jcKTM (accessed January 7, 2017).
18. Kelli Bender, "Dancing Flamingo 'Pinky' Killed by Busch Gardens Visitor," *People*, August 5, 2016, http://people.com/pets/dancing-flamingo-pinky-killed-by-busch-gardens-visitor/ (accessed January 6, 2017). The dances of Pinky are also available: ABC Action News, August 3, 2016, https://www.youtube.com/watch?v=IOG_xh60b60 (accessed January 7, 2017).
19. Ed Yong, "Not a Human, but a Dancer," *The Atlantic*, July 8, 2019, https://www.theatlantic.com/science/archive/2019/07/what-snowball-dancing-parrot-tells-us-about-dance/593428/ (accessed July 15, 2019), reporting on study by neuroscientist Anirrudh Patel from 2008. July 2019 stories also appeared on BBC and in the *New York Times*, because a student of Patel released videos documenting many of Snowball's moves.
20. Jeffrey Dietrich, "Nesting Male Resplendent Quetzal at Mount Totumas Cloud Forest," May 22, 2011, https://www.youtube.com/watch?v=BrXjCoJXieE#t=31.475896 (accessed January 7, 2017).
21. "Feathered Headdress," Khan Academy, https://www.khanacademy.org/humanities/art-americas/early-cultures/aztec-mexica/v/feathered-headdress-aztec (accessed January 7, 2017).
22. Julia Guernsey, *Ritual and Power in Stone: The Performance of Rulership in Mesoamerican Izapan Style Art* (Austin: University of Texas Press, 2006), 93.
23. Quetzalcoatl may be a translation of Mayan names for this deity, meaning Feathered Serpent, as German translates English skyscraper into "sky scratcher." The Nahua (Aztec) root *quetz* refers to "erect feathers" or plumes in general, and then specifically to the resplendent quetzal.

24. Molly H. Bassett, *The Fate of Earthly Things: Aztec Gods and God-Bodies* (Austin: University of Texas Press, 2015), 37–38.
25. Rosemary Gipson, "Los Voladores, the Flyers of Mexico," *Western Folklore* 30, no. 4 (October, 1971), 270–271.
26. Gipson, "Los Voladores," 272–274.
27. Frederick Bernas and Amado Trevino, "Voladores Ritual Is Flight for Survival for Mexico's Totonacas," *BBC News Magazine*, October 11, 2013, http://www.bbc.com/news/magazine-24439200 (accessed January 8, 2017).
28. "Ritual Ceremony of the Voladores," http://www.unesco.org/culture/ich/en/RL/ritual-ceremony-of-the-voladores-00175 (accessed January 8, 2017). Direct link to video at https://ich.unesco.org/en/RL/ritual-ceremony-of-the-voladores-00175.
29. "The Papantla Pole Flyers in Puerto Vallarta," http://www.puertovallarta.net/fast_facts/the-papantla-birdmen.php (accessed January 8, 2017).
30. John M. Goggin, "Notes on Some 1938–1939 Pueblo Dances," *New Mexico Anthropologist* 3, no. 2 (November–December 1938): 30–32. An eagle dance is noted for January 6, 1939. Also see Tom Bahti and Mark Bahti, *Southwestern Indian Ceremonials*, 10th ed. (Las Vegas: KC Publications, 1997), 24, 40.
31. Ted Shawn, *The American Ballet* (New York: Henry Holt, 1926), 16. Quoted in Jane Sherman, "The American Indian Imagery of Ted Shawn," *Dance Chronicle* 12, no. 3 (1989): 376.
32. H. R. Voth, "Notes on the Eagle Cult of the Hopi," *Publications of the Field Museum of Natural History. Anthropological Series*, Vol.11 No. 2 (February, 1912), 105–109.
33. For example Dylan Forest, "Cannibalism, Sacrifice, and Hunting in National Parks," *Animal People*, April 2001, http://newspaper.animalpeopleforum.org/2001/04/01/cannibalism-sacrifice-and-hunting-in-national-parks/ (accessed January 13, 2017).
34. Mario I. Aguilar, "The Eagle as Messenger, Pilgrim and Voice: Divinatory Processes among the Waso Boorana of Kenya," *Journal of Religion in Africa* 26, no. 1 (1996): 59.
35. Aguilar, "Eagle as Messenger," 62–63.
36. Aguilar, "Eagle as Messenger," 63–66.
37. Michael R. Dove, "Uncertainty, Humility, and Adaptation in the Tropical Forest: The Agricultural Augury of the Kantu'," *Ethnology* 32, no. 2 (Spring 1993): 148.
38. Dove, "Uncertainty, Humility, and Adaptation," 149–154.
39. Account from Livy, *The History of Rome*, 1.6.3–1.7.3. Text of Livy appears in Steven J. Green, "Malevolent Gods and Promethean Birds: Contesting Augury in Augustus's Rome," *Transactions of the American Philological Association* 139, no. 1 (Spring 2009): 150–151.
40. Varro, *On the Latin Language*, VII.8–10. Text of Varro appears in Mary Beard, John North, and Simon Price, *Roman Religion*, vol. 2, *A Sourcebook* (Cambridge: Cambridge University Press, 1998), 86–87.
41. Rasmussen, *Public Portents*, 151.
42. Jerzy Linderski, *Roman Questions: Selected Papers* (Stuttgart: Franz Steiner Verlag, 2007), 17.
43. Linderski, *Roman Questions*, 11.

74 WINGS OF THE GODS

44. R. G. Grant, *Battle at Sea: 3,000 Years of Naval Warfare* (New York: Penguin, 2011), 45; Cicero, *On the Nature of the Gods*, 2.7–8.
45. Rasmussen, *Public Portents*, 160–161.
46. Federico Santangelo, *Divination, Prediction and the End of the Roman Republic* (Cambridge: Cambridge University Press, 2003), 26–28.
47. Kearsley, "Octavian and Augury," 159–160 and 165–166.
48. Linderski, *Roman Questions*, 10.
49. Definition at http://latinlexicon.org/definition.php?p1=1016781 (accessed September 25, 2023). Example of procession at St. Greory's Episcopal Church, San Francisco at https://www.youtube.com/watch?v=ByI_6kzoIk8 (accessed January 20, 2017).
50. Richard Beal, "Hittite Oracles," in *Magic and Divination in the Ancient World*, ed. Leda Ciraolo and Jonathan Seidel (Leiden: Brill, 2002), 70–71, 73. Also see Hethitologie Portal Mainz, "Oracles and Omens: Hittite Divination," https://www.hethport.uni-wuerzburg.de/HPM/hpm-en.php?p=divin-en#_RefHead_1 (accessed January 19, 2017).
51. Translation at http://www.ancientvedas.com/chapter/2/book/42/ (accessed January 19, 2017).
52. Berthold Laufer, *Bird Divination among the Tibetans* (Leiden: Brill, 1914), 8–9. Laufer's pioneering work is hailed and contextualized in Eric Mortensen, "Raven Augury from Tibet to Alaska: Dialects, Divine Agency, and the Bird's-Eye View," in *A Communion of Subjects: Animals in Religion, Science, and Ethics*, ed. Paul Waldau and Kimberly Patton (New York: Columbia University Press, 2006).
53. Laufer, *Bird Divination*, 9–15.
54. Laufer, *Bird Divination*, 15–17.
55. Laufer, *Bird Divination*, 18.
56. Laufer, *Bird Divination*, 33–34.
57. Jonathan Z. Smith, "The Domestication of Sacrifice," in *Violent Origins: Walter Burkert, René Girard, and Jonathan Z. Smith on Ritual Killing and Cultural Formation*, ed. Robert G. Hampton-Kelly (Stanford, CA: Stanford University Press, 1987), 199–201.
58. Smith, "The Domestication," René Girard, 121–129.
59. BBC Earth, "The Crazy Courtship of Bower Birds," November 20, 2014, http://www.bbc.com/earth/story/20141119-the-barmy-courtship-of-bowerbirds (accessed July 16, 2019).
60. J. Omosade Awolalu, "Yoruba Sacrificial Practice," *Journal of Religion in Africa* 5, no. 2 (1973): 82–83
61. Awolalu, "Yoruba Sacrificial Practice," 83–84.
62. Awolalu, "Yoruba Sacrificial Practice," 87.
63. Giuseppe Minunno, *Ritual Employs of Birds in Ancient Syria-Palestine* (Münster: Ugarit-Verlag, 2013), 99 n. 581.
64. Rabbi Yaakov Fruchter and Rabbi Sholom Dov Steinberg, *An Illustrated Guide to Kobonos and Menochos* (Brooklyn, NY: Torah Umesorah Publications, 1993), 61–63.
65. Fruchter and Steinberg, *Illustrated Guide to Kobonos*, 21; "Text of Kapparot," http://www.chabad.org/holidays/JewishNewYear/template_cdo/aid/320228/jewish/Text-of-Kapparot.htm (accessed January 21, 2017).

66. Op. cit., note 57.
67. Leah Zelwig, "The Rebbetzin on Kaparos," https://www.youtube.com/watch?v=kz4I HEE3hqA (accessed January 22, 2017).
68. Linda Greenhouse, "Court, Citing Religious Freedom, Voids a Ban on Animal Sacrifices," *New York Times*, June 12, 1993, http://www.nytimes.com/1993/06/12/us/supreme-court-animal-sacrifice-court-citing-religious-freedom-voids-ban-animal.html (accessed January 22, 2017).
69. Peter Gardella, "Two Parliaments, One Century," *Cross Currents* 44, no. 1 (Spring 1994): 104.
70. Pearl Gabel, "The Chickens under the Bridge," *New York Daily News*, August 21, 2015, http://interactive.nydailynews.com/2015/08/chickens-under-the-bridge/ (accessed January 22, 2017).
71. Angela von den Driesch, Dieter Kessler, Frank Steinmann, Véronique Berteaux, and Joris Peters, "Mummified, Deified and Buried at Hermopolis Magna—the Sacred Birds from Tuna el-Gebel, Middle Egypt," *Ägypten und Levante / Egypt and the Levant* 15 (2005): 203, table of species 216–217.
72. Driesch, "Mummified, Deified and Buried," 239–241.
73. John Owen, "Egyptian Animals Were Mummified Same Way as Humans," *National Geographic News*, September 15, 2004, http://news.nationalgeographic.com/news/2004/09/0915_040915_petmummies.html (accessed January 22, 2017).
74. Jane O'Brien, "Unwrapping the Ancient Egyptian Animal Mummy Industry," *BBC News Magazine*, November 17, 2011, http://www.bbc.com/news/magazine-15780427 (accessed January 22, 2017).
75. Peter Gardella, *American Civil Religion: What Americans Hold Sacred* (New York: Oxford University Press, 2014), 262–265.
76. Gilbert King, "The History of Pardoning Turkeys Began with Tad Lincoln," *Smithsonian.com*, November 21, 2012, http://www.smithsonianmag.com/history/the-history-of-pardoning-turkeys-began-with-tad-lincoln-141137570/ (accessed January 22, 2017).
77. Betty C. Monkman, "Pardoning the Thanksgiving Turkey," White House Historical Association, https://www.whitehousehistory.org/pardoning-the-thanksgiving-turkey (accessed January 22, 2017).
78. Domenico Montanaro, "The Strange Truth behind Presidential Turkey Pardons," *NPR: WSHU*, November 25, 2015, http://www.npr.org/2015/11/25/457253194/the-strange-truth-behind-presidential-turkey-pardons (accessed January 22, 2017).
79. Domenico Montanaro, "Why Presidents Pardon Turkeys—a History," *PBS: CPTV*, November 26, 2014, http://www.pbs.org/newshour/updates/presidents-pardon-turkeys-history/ (January 22, 2017).
80. Montanaro, "Why Presidents Pardon Turkeys."
81. Montanaro, "Why Presidents Pardon Turkeys.".
82. Megan Gambino, "What Was on the Menu at the First Thanksgiving?," *Smithsonian.com* (November 21, 2011), http://www.smithsonianmag.com/history/what-was-on-the-menu-at-the-first-thanksgiving-511554/ (accessed January 22, 2017).
83. Michelle Tsai, "Wherefore Turkey?" *Slate*, November 25, 2009, http://www.slate.com/articles/news_and_politics/recycled/2009/11/wherefore_turkey.html (accessed January 22, 2017).

84. Jeffrey Yoskowitz, "Goose: A Hanukkah Tradition," *New York Times*, December 24, 2016, https://www.nytimes.com/2016/12/24/opinion/goose-a-hanukkah-tradition.html?_r=0 (accessed January 22, 2017).
85. Lindsey Bever, "How Killer Birds Forced Pope Francis to Change a Vatican Tradition: Releasing Doves of Peace," *Washington Post*, January 26, 2015, https://www.washingtonpost.com/news/morning-mix/wp/2015/01/26/how-killer-birds-forced-pope-francis-to-change-a-vatican-tradition-releasing-doves-for-peace/ (accessed January 22, 2017).
86. Thomas Munita, "Pitting Heaven and Earth in a Fierce Andean Rite," *New York Times*, August 10, 2013, http://www.nytimes.com/2013/08/11/world/americas/pitting-heaven-and-earth-in-a-fierce-andean-rite.html (accessed January 22, 2017).
87. Jonathan Watts, "Fight of the Condor: Peru Bull Fiestas Threaten Future of Rare Andean bird," *The Guardian*, January 29, 2013, https://www.theguardian.com/world/2013/jan/29/condor-peru-bull-fight-andes (accessed January 22, 2017).
88. Paul R. Ehrlich, David S. Dobkin, and Darryl Wheye, "Feeding Birds," 1988, https://web.stanford.edu/group/stanfordbirds/text/essays/Feeding_Birds.html (January 23, 2017). Also Cornell Laboratory of Ornithology, "Winter Bird Feeding," 2001, http://www.birds.cornell.edu/AllAboutBirds/notes/BirdNote01_WinterFeeding.pdf (accessed January 23, 2017).
89. Geoffrey S. LeBaron, "The 118th Christmas Bird Count Summary," *Audubon Magazine*, November 29, 2018, https://www.audubon.org/news/the-118th-christmas-bird-count-summary (accessed July 3, 2019).
90. American Birding Association, "ABA Big Year Rules," http://listing.aba.org/big-year-rules/ (accessed January 23, 2017).
91. Claudia Stephan, Anna Wilkinson, and Ludwig Huber, "Have We Met Before? Pigeons Recognise Familiar Human Faces," *Avian Biology Research* 5, no. 2 (2012), https://doi.org/10.3184/175815512X13350970204867 (accessed January 23, 2017).
92. Jon Young, *What the Robin Knows* (Boston: Houghton Mifflin, 2012).
93. Melissa Mayntz, "Sounds That Attract Birds," *About Home*, November 7, 2016, http://birding.about.com/od/attractingbirds/a/Sounds-That-Attract-Birds.htm (accessed January 23, 2017).
94. Todd McGrain, *The Lost Bird Project* (Hanover, NH: University Press of New England, 2014), 71.
95. McGrain, *The Lost Bird Project*, 72.
96. McGrain, *The Lost Bird Project*, 74.

4

Bird Heroes and Villains

Many birds—as various as swallows, geese, seagulls, ravens, hoopoes, eagles, vultures, robins, and wrens—have intervened in the histories, legends, literary dreams, and fantasies of human religious life. When humans first planted crops and made nations, birds took part as protectors and pests. When civilization has broken down in war, pigeons and doves have taken part. When prophets like Noah, Elijah, and Muhammad appeared, other birds helped them. A magpie landing on the head of the founder of the Manchu dynasty of China caused enemies to mistake him for a dead tree at a distance and so saved his life.[1] Since the magpie almost certainly did not think the emperor was a tree, and we know that birds recognize individual people, it may be that the bird chose him and landed on him deliberately. Such capacities have been especially important for birds in wars and other crises. But birds have also become heroes in human religions just by acting in their own environments, without direct concern for people.

Bird Saviors and Creators of Crops, Bird Guardians of England

In May 1848, more than four thousand members of the Church of Jesus Christ of Latter-Day Saints, colloquially known as the Mormons, were about to harvest the second set of crops they had planted near Salt Lake City, Utah.[2] These crops were far more varied than the winter wheat they had already harvested. A mild winter had encouraged them to plant early. The new settlers hoped for corn, beans, pumpkins, squash, cucumbers, and melons, as well as more wheat. Their hopes were damaged by frosts in April and May, but seemed in danger of perishing on May 22, when hordes of insects swarmed over their fields. Called "Mormon crickets," these invaders were small-winged, flightless members of the katydid family. For more than a week, the insects ate the crops. Desperate Mormons tried beating and burning the bugs, to no avail.

Early in June, flocks of California gulls (*Larus californicus*) arrived and began to eat the insects. As a letter to Brigham Young described it, the gulls "sweep the crickets as they go; it seems the hand of the Lord is in our favor." Miraculously, as it seemed to the settlers, the gulls were insatiable. When they were full of crickets, they flew to the Salt Lake, drank some water, regurgitated something, and then returned to eating the insects on the crops. The seagulls saved the Mormon settlement by defending the first full harvest in Utah. By the fall of 1848, Mormon writers were crediting the gulls for the food that remained and praising God for sending them in what they saw as a special act. In 1913, the Seagull Monument was dedicated on Temple Square in Salt Lake City. It features a bronze sculpture group of three active gulls on top of a tall stone cylinder, and a base with four bronze relief panels showing the story of the Mormon farmers, the crickets, and the gulls.

In recent decades, many have discounted any supernatural claim for the "Miracle of the Seagulls." Some have pointed out that on their arrival at Salt Lake in 1847, before they had planted any crops, the Mormon settlers saw the native Ute Indians driving millions of crickets into fires, roasting them, and storing them in baskets for winter food.[3] If the Mormons had consulted their Bibles, they might have noted that locusts are kosher to eat. Two Mormon scholars, David B. Madsen and Brigham R. Madsen, suggested in 1995 that their ancestors would have been better off eating the crickets and killing the gulls.[4] As for the presence of gulls, even the article "Seagulls, Miracle of" in the 1992 *Encyclopedia of Mormonism* points out that the California gulls regularly pass the Great Salt Lake in spring, on their way to their summer breeding grounds in western Canada, so that the 1848 appearance of gulls was "not unusual."[5] Meanwhile, the Mormon crickets or katydids (*Anabrus simplex*) swarm through the Rocky Mountain region regularly, three times every ten years, and their swarms still pose problems for crops and for automobile traffic and for the general pleasantness of life.[6] Even the most miraculous aspect of the gulls' behavior to the Mormon settlers, the fact that they went to the lake and disgorged about a pint of crickets then went back for more, has the natural explanation that the birds cannot digest the exoskeletons of the insects, so they absorb the soft inner bodies and rid themselves of the shells before eating more. The whole story can be reduced to a natural phenomenon: flocks of birds wanting lots of food on their way to mate hundreds of miles inland, meeting swarms of insects doing their own periodic foraging before they lay their eggs and die, so that their kind can rise and swarm again.

On the other hand, natural explanations meant little to the settlers who saw their first big harvest threatened and then partly saved, or to the descendants who passed the story on. For Mormons driven out of the United States and seeking a new land, the intervention of the gulls to defend their crops confirmed that God favored them. In a survey of more than 1,112 Mormon respondents in 1997, including 889 history students at Brigham Young University, researchers found that the seagull miracle story was far more widely known and believed (for example, by 87.6 percent of the BYU students) than any other out of twelve well-known stories from Mormon history (no other story reached 80 percent).[7]

A more scientific—yet also in its way religious, because it grew more from nonrational love of birds than from measurement—appreciation of bird interventions to save crops appeared among biologists and anthropologists in the nineteenth and early twentieth centuries, when the science of ornithology was also first emerging. As C. D. Howe, the state ornithologist of Vermont, wrote in 1915:

> The birds are the farmers' and horticulturists' hired men. They work day and night, seven days in a week.... These hired men do not ask wages, do not ask lodgings, and they board themselves except occasionally they may take a little cultivated fruit.... And do you horticulturists and farmers realize it and do you make a definite concerted effort to protect and attract the birds?[8]

Other experts praised the agricultural contributions of particular birds. In 1893, Albert K. Fisher recognized that farmers erect scarecrows in an attempt to protect their corn from crows at planting time, but argued that as the corn grew, the crow became a useful partner, who changes into "an exemplary member of bird society, and the war he wages on the cutworm earns him no scanty need of praise from the grass farmer."[9] An Ontario naturalist, William Saunders, noted in 1938 that a dead owl had lately been found with thirteen field mice in its stomach. Saunders estimated on that basis that every owl was worth "nearly a hundred dollars a year" (more than two thousand dollars today) to farmers in the neighborhood.[10] The US Department of Agriculture had a Division of Economic Ornithology that published (for example) studies of the diet of woodpeckers and the relative harmfulness or helpfulness of imported English sparrows.

After the 1940s, the convenience and human control offered by new chemical pesticides diminished interest in developing human cooperation with birds in agriculture. By 1962, when Rachel Carson published *Silent Spring* and touched off a reaction against pesticides, birds were valued only for their songs and visual beauty, not as potential saviors of human crops. But as our own age develops its ecological consciousness, some scholars are reconsidering the value of "economic ornithology."[11] It has been suggested that the defense of crops by birds helped to make the beginnings of agriculture possible, and that the domestication of pigeons and chickens may have preceded or even helped to cause the development of plant agriculture.

Across many islands in eastern and southeastern Asia, folk tales attribute the beginning of rice cultivation to the intervention of birds, sometimes as messengers of gods. The Ryuku Islands between China and Japan, among which Okinawa is the largest, have a story that a government official went to China and stole some heads of rice and tied them to the leg of a crane, who flew to Okinawa, where they were planted. In another version of that story the bird is a hawk, a more frequent seasonal visitor than the crane to Okinawa.[12] Among the Rampi people of Indonesia, a sky god is said to have entrusted rice to the wagtail bird to bring to their island.[13] In Malaysia, a more earthly explanation attributes the first rice to a turtledove who deposited its excrement, including a grain of unhusked rice, on the floor of a palace.[14] The king noticed the grain, had it planted, and so began the cultivation of rice. On Madagascar, various stories describe the bringing of rice from a heavenly kingdom to earth by the cardinal, the sparrow, and the skylark. Because they brought the rice, all these birds are also allowed to eat some of it, with the cardinal and the sparrow being allowed to eat in the rice fields and the skylark on the roads or other parts of the earth.[15] The idea that birds brought rice to these islands has some plausibility in scientific terms. As we saw in Chapter 2, distribution of seeds by birds is credited for the recovery of forests after the last ice age.

In England, birds have been regarded as protectors of the kingdom itself. The word "Bran," the name of a legendary king who conquered England for the British, means "raven" in Gaelic, and names with the elements of "Bran" or "raven" abound in the United Kingdom. Legend has it that the head of Bran, who was decapitated as he died by his own wish, was brought back from war on the continent of Europe and buried under Tower Hill in London, facing France.[16] When a later quasi-legendary king, King Arthur, died, he was said to have been turned into a raven (*Corvus corax*), or into a relative of ravens, the related red-billed chough (*Pyrrhocorax pyrrhocorax*). Chough in particular are emblems of fidelity, mating monogamously for life and returning to the same nesting site annually. One day, Arthur will return to lead his nation, but in the meantime the raven and the chough are to be respected.[17]

Among the ruins and walls of Tower Hill in London, where so many notables were imprisoned and executed over the centuries, eight ravens are now kept as somewhat troublesome guardians. The ravenmaster and his assistants, wearing uniforms that bear a coat of arms with a raven's head and a tower, release the birds from their night cages every morning at dawn, and the birds disperse to different territories within the small park of Tower Hill.[18] Their wings have been clipped so that they cannot fly far away, though since 2017 Ravenmaster Chris Scaife has been clipping less and allowing the ravens more freedom, relying more on the birds' bonding to him to keep them returning to their roosts.[19] According to the current folk belief, the kingdom will fall unless at least six ravens guard the Tower, so it is imperative that they remain. Visitors are warned not to try to feed them, because they are quite territorial and likely to bite a hand extended toward them with food. Signs warn that ravens can unzip bags. But even without contributions from tourists, the ravens' diet is rich enough in bloody meat and the occasional whole rat or chick.[20] All of them have names, and their ages are noted.

Occasionally a raven escapes, sometimes coming to harm outside. One named Thor, very popular with tourists because he often said, "Good morning" and answered a handler's "That's for you" with "That's for me" when he was fed, killed himself in 2010 trying to fly from a tower. In 1981, a raven who chronically escaped took down five television antennas in the Tower neighborhood and had to be sent to a zoo, and in 1995 two others were banished to a zoo for unspecified crimes.

This captivity of the Tower ravens is attributed to (or blamed on) King Charles II (reigned 1662–1685), who lived through the execution of his father, Charles I, in 1649 and thirteen years of exile in France before the republic set up by the English Revolution collapsed. Although Charles II agreed to return and to reign, he naturally never felt entirely secure. According to the story told at the Tower today, the royal astronomers who used the Tower for observing the heavens objected to the presence of ravens, but Charles insisted that they must remain lest his kingdom fall.[21] Instead of moving the birds, he moved the Royal Observatory to Greenwich, where it still keeps Greenwich Mean Time. Charles II may have been motivated in part by the usefulness of ravens in raising alarms against rebels and saboteurs. Some say that Guy Fawkes, the Catholic spy who tried to blow up James I, the grandfather of

Charles II, and his entire Parliament on November 5, 1605 (he succeeded in filling the basement of Westminster with barrels of gunpowder), was caught because of the cries of ravens.[22]

Whatever truth may support the connections of the ravens with Charles II, ravens have not continuously been kept at the Tower since his time. Evidence of guidebooks and journalism indicates no cultivated presence of pet ravens in the Tower until 1883.[23] By then, wild ravens had largely disappeared from London, and indeed from England.[24] But the emphasis on the ravens as protectors became much more pronounced during World War II, and it has remained strong to the present.

In the perilous times of the Blitz by German bombers, the yearning for protection by ravens intensified and extended beyond the Tower. Watney's Brewery in London prided itself on its mascot and guard, "Jackie the Lucky Raven," and requested a raven from the Tower when Jackie died near the end of the war. Unable to spare any ravens, having lost a pair in the bombings, the government refused Watney's request. From the 1600s on, many breweries in England had kept ravens to guard against rodents and insects eating their grain. But since the war, with beer production growing much more mechanized and sterile, ravens have not returned to the breweries.[25]

As sympathy for captive animals grows in contemporary culture, there have been proposals to set the Tower ravens free. If a nesting site were established atop a turret, some of the current ravens might be allowed to grow their wings, or raven infants imported. Between 1988 and 1994, a breeding program in the Tower resulted in eighteen surviving chicks, who were distributed to Scotland, Wales, and Lincolnshire.[26] One advocate for breeding and supporting free ravens based in the Tower has published the hope that "perhaps, some day, visitors to the White Tower will look up, see ravens soaring overhead, and feel confident that Britain is safe."[27]

Swallows Save Mecca, Geese Save Rome

In the Koran, Surah 105 reads:

> Don't you see how your Lord dealt with the Companions of the Elephant?
> Did he not make their treacherous plan go astray?
> And he sent against them flights of Birds,
> Striking them with stones of baked clay.

Then He made them like an empty field of stalks and straw (of which the corn) has been eaten up.[28]

Islamic tradition has generally taken this surah to refer to the attack on Mecca by Christian forces from Yemen, led by an African Christian named Abraha (or Abraham) who brought over elephants to strengthen his army. Since Prophet Muhammad had to defend his city of Medina against attacks from superior forces from Mecca during the years from 621 to 630, when the Prophet led Medina and before he took control of Mecca, these verses of revelation from God could have been meant as a consolation to the Prophet. Just as Mecca had been delivered from attack through "flights of Birds" sent by God, so God would find a way to defend Medina.

Muslims have other memories of the Yemeni attack. According to the accepted stories, the entire motivation of the attack was religious. Abraha of Yemen wanted a new church he had built in his capital, Sanaa, to displace Mecca as the focus of pilgrimage in the Arabian peninsula.[29] His main aim was to destroy the Kaaba, the cubical building in Mecca that Adam had built to worship God, and which had been reduced to rubble in the Flood and then restored by Abraham, where the tribes of Arabia had been coming to worship Allah (and 360 other gods and spirits) long before Prophet Muhammad. As the army approached, seizing camels and other property on its way, the inhabitants of Mecca fled to the surrounding mountains. The leader of the Quraysh clan that ruled Mecca, Abdul Muttalib, met with the Yemenite Abraha and asked for the return of his camels. Abraha scornfully asked Abdul Muttalib why he was seeking the return of a few camels but not defending the house of his God. Abdul answered Abraha that he asked for his camels because he owned them, and that the owner of the Kaaba would also defend it. Then Abraha joined the other Meccans on the mountains.[30]

Just as the Yemenites approached the walls of the Kaaba to destroy it, clouds of birds appeared. Most Arab traditions say that the birds were swallows, or *Ababil*. The swallows carried three stones, one in each claw and one in their beak. These would most likely have been barn swallows (*Hirundo rustica*), who are widespread across the globe, and resident in the Mideast, although more likely to be winter migrants to the eastern Arabian peninsula. Swallows are known for their ferocious mobbing behavior, flying quite close as they swoop on those birds or other animals who disturb them or approach their nests. The swallows of the Koran pelted the Yemenite soldiers and elephants with such force that they died on the march. Meanwhile, as one of the

Qurayshi women, Amina the wife of Abdullah, was hiding in the mountains, she gave birth to Muhammad bin Abdullah, who would become the Prophet of Islam and cleanse the idols from the Kaaba.

Modern historians have suggested that, given the lack of care with which birth dates were recorded through most of history, the birth of Prophet Muhammad was set at the same time as the Year of the Elephant by later Muslims, because the coincidence seemed fitting. History has raised little doubt of Yemenite hostility to Mecca or of the attack and its failure. On the other hand, an Indian Muslim scholar named Hamid al-Din al-Farahi (1862–1930) produced an entirely different meaning of Surah 105 in relation to the birds.

According to Farahi, the surah was addressed not by God to Muhammad, but by God *through* Muhammad to the Quraysh, to remind them that God defends his own chosen cities and people, perhaps in the days when the Quraysh were attacking the Muslims at Medina.[31] Farahi used contemporary Arab accounts of the battle to argue that the Quraysh did not abandon Mecca but hid in the mountains and attacked Yemen's superior army and elephants with stones, and that God completed the defense by raising a powerful wind that rained more stones and sand on the Yemenites to kill them, followed by flights of birds who ate the corpses and left the army lying empty on the ground, like fields of grain that had been stripped of its corn. Although there was still a miracle, in Farahi's view the miracle had more to do with wind than birds. As a contemporary scholar, Mustansir Mir of Youngstown State University, explained the mistake in 2005, "People find the idea of birds throwing stones fascinating and miraculous," and so "the idea struck root."[32] But whether the birds threw the stones or came and ate the dead Yemenis, an avian intervention remains associated with the salvation of Mecca from destruction by Christians and with the birth of Muhammad.

Almost a thousand years before the Year of the Elephant, in 390 BCE, the city of Rome repelled an attack by the Gauls. Legends say that the attack was thwarted because of an alarm raised by geese on the Capitoline Hill.[33] Geese were present because they were sacred to Juno, wife of Jupiter and patron of motherhood, whose temple (later known as Juno Moneta, or "Juno the Warner") stood on the Capitoline Hill.

According to the traditional stories, the Gauls were raiding all over Italy at the time, and the Romans had been defeated in the field. Many scattered, including an exiled former Roman commander named Camillus, and others barricaded themselves on the highest of the seven hills of the city, the Capitoline. Camillus gathered enough of the defeated Romans into an army to face the Gauls again, but he wanted authority from the Senate to act. He sent a messenger up the Capitoline by a secret path, and the Senate agreed to appoint Camillus as temporary military dictator. Unfortunately, the Gallic leader Brennus had his men watching, and the footprints of the Roman messenger revealed a hidden way to climb the Capitoline. Soon after, Brennus sent men up the hill in the middle of the night, to take the defenders of the Capitoline by surprise. They were so skillful and silent that no sentry noticed their climb and no dogs barked, but the geese of Juno were more alert and raised the alarm. The Roman consul Manlius was first to respond, throwing a Gaul from the Tarpeian Rock to his death. Then others awoke and successfully defended all that was left of Rome, the citadel on the Capitoline Hill.

The thwarting of their surprise attack dispirited the Gauls, and the Senate made an agreement with Brennus that the Gauls would withdraw if Rome paid a ransom. At the ceremony weighing out the gold, Brennus threw his heavy steel sword into the balance to make Rome's payment of gold heavier, calling out *Vae victis!*—"Woe to the vanquished!" But Rome was not to pay, because the dictator Camillus interrupted the ceremony with his army, telling the senators that Rome would win its freedom not with gold but with steel. Battle ensued, and the Romans won.

Scholars have doubted the story from many angles. In 1993, Adam Ziolkowski of the University of Warsaw called the warning by the geese "the last quasi-mythical event in Rome's history," and argued that the temple of Juno Moneta on the Capitoline was not dedicated until 345 BCE.[34] Nicholas Horsfall noted that the event of the warning was commemorated in a ritual every summer in which geese were carried on litters decorated with purple and gold, then fed by the censors of Rome, the guardians of public morals. In the same ritual, dogs were "impaled or crucified on alder-stakes,"[35] as punishment for their failure to warn. Horsfall was not convinced that the ritual began with the defeat of the Gauls, however. He called the sacrifice of dogs "common in Roman religion" and argued that the ritual developed because of "the patriotic appeal, the charm, the poignancy of the story, even though there always remained those who knew that the geese had never cackled."[36] Horsfall concluded that the Capitoline Hill had actually fallen in 390 BCE, and that the story of the geese was a cover for Roman shame at Rome's defeat. On the other hand, William McLoughlin, author of many articles on classical history for the *War History Online* website, noted that all of the ancient sources mention the geese, concluding that "geese are a common theme and their saving of the Capitoline is just crazy enough to be plausible."[37]

Anyone who has experienced how noisy, territorial, and aggressive geese can be has reason to think they might have been effective guardian animals for Rome. Equipped not with teeth but with hard serrations on the edges of their bills and on their tongues, geese can bite with formidable effect. Geese can also be domesticated, and are very protective of their nests, so their association with Juno, goddess of marriage and childbirth, seems appropriate. Although the Roman records from 390 BCE are imperfect, the story of geese intervening to save Rome fits the general pattern of relations between humans and geese.

Individual Bird Heroes of War

On Yom Kippur of 1973, Syria and Egypt attacked Israel. They sought to recover territory lost in the Six Day War of 1967, when Israel took the Golan Heights from Syria, Gaza, and the Sinai Peninsula from Egypt, and the West Bank territory of Palestine from Jordan. The attack by Syria and Egypt took Israel by surprise and nearly overran the Jewish state.

Efraim Eitan was twenty-one years old, patrolling the Golan Heights for Israel, when Syrian tanks began to roll. Eitan fought with a bazooka from a water ditch outside Nafa Camp of the Israel Defense Force. After a few days of fierce battle, he was ordered to take part in a raid on a Syrian bunker. He threw hand grenades ahead of his path in concrete corridors, trying to reach the Syrian command center. Then something came out of the smoke and dust. Eitan aimed his rifle at the movement, but it turned out to be a bird who landed on his right shoulder. When he tried to dislodge the bird, a dove, she (he called the dove she) moved to his left shoulder. He gave up trying to get rid of the dove and continued firing his gun and throwing grenades.[38]

After Eitan emerged from the bunker, the dove was still with him, and he tried to brush her away, but she returned. He put out his hand, and the bird stood on it. The dove remained with him through ten days of intense fighting. Even at night, when as Eitan noted, doves are not normally active, this dove patrolled with him, standing on this shoulder. During all the time when the dove remained, no member of Eitan's company was killed or injured. Only after two weeks, when Eitan got into the truck that took him off the Golan Heights and down from the front lines, did the dove fly away.

Eitan had a conversion from cultural to religious Judaism, partly as a result of this.[39] After serving for thirty years in the IDF, he rose to the rank of brigadier general, then joined the National Religious Party and became a Knesset member and a cabinet secretary in Ariel Sharon's coalition government until 2004, when he resigned to oppose Israel's withdrawal from the Gaza Strip. He became notorious for calling for the expulsion of almost all Arabs from Israeli-held territory, or what he called "Judea and Samaria," in a speech at a soldier's memorial service in 2006. He argued for pre-emptive Israeli attacks on nuclear programs in Iraq and Iran. In the summer of 2016, he was noted as the head of a company called Genie Energy that numbered former vice president Richard Cheney, media mogul Rupert Murdoch, former CIA director James Woolsey, and British Lord Jacob Rothschild among its investors. Genie Energy was searching for reserves in 153 square miles on the Golan Heights, an area still regarded as part of Syria under all international treaties but on which Genie Oil holds a lease from the Israeli government.[40]

According to Pat Robertson, the Christian talk show host of *The 700 Club* and 1988 presidential candidate who founded Regent University in Virginia, Eitan's dove was really an angel. The angel "chose not to present himself as a mighty warrior but as a symbol of peace, signifying that one day the hotly contested border of Israel will be part of a highway of peace,"[41] Robertson wrote. But more personal interpretations are available.

Days before Efraim Eitan saw the dove for the first time in the bunker, he was fighting outside Nafa Camp, stopping Syrian tanks with his bazooka and hiding in a water ditch. He reported years later that he had during those battles "a feeling of transcendence" and "a certain absolute satisfaction and joy." Clearly, the desperate but successful battle brought Eitan into a state of mind that predisposed him to see the bird as miraculous.

And what about this experience from the standpoint of the dove? The dove may have recognized Eitan. Recent research has shown that pigeons both in the wild and in the lab, along with members of the Corvidae family (a variety of similar birds, distinguished mainly by size and habitat, from smaller jackdaws to larger ravens), mockingbirds in urban environments, smaller black-and-white magpies (*Pica pica*), and even Antarctic (or South Polar) skuas (*Stercorarius maccormicki*, a whitish seabird about twenty-one inches long) can all identify and remember individual humans.[42] The value for an urban bird of the ability to remember which humans are resources and which are dangerous is clear. This intelligence may help account for the success of not only pigeons and doves, but also of mockingbirds and crows, in urban areas, where all these birds have been increasing in number in recent decades.

How might Eitan have looked in the battle, if he was being watched by a dove living near the camp? Did some action of his save a nest from destruction? Or did the bird first see Eitan at a moment when she was trapped in the smoke and noise of the bunker, or traumatized by the shock of an explosion, so that sitting on his shoulder seemed the best place to be? No doubt, the presence of the bird reassured Eitan, and probably others in his company. He said that the phenomenon might be doubted if he had been alone, but that it happened "in front of the eyes of thousands of soldiers."[43]

The cognitive abilities, emotional needs, and cultural contexts of this dove and this human somehow added together. Of course, the inhabitation of the dove by an angel, or the appearance of an angel in the form of a dove, cannot be disproven, but no angel is needed to give the story religious significance. Those whose religion, or system of nonrational commitments, embraces the whole world shared by humans and animals might see deeper meaning in a dove's intervention than in that of an angel.

Another dove intervened, perhaps at the cost of its life, when Israel made an incursion against Hamas in Gaza in 2014. According to an account by Yael Eckstein, the wife of a prominent rabbi, a soldier who had just returned from Gaza, speaking at a synagogue, said that his unit was told to take the house of a terrorist in a raid just before dawn. As they looked at the front of the house through binoculars, they were puzzled to see a dove sitting above the front door, not apparently supported by anything but also not flapping its wings. Closer inspection disclosed that the bird was perched on a thin, transparent fishing line. They hesitated, and a moment later the entire house blew up, turned to dust by explosives set to go off when the line was disturbed.[44] Whether that dove survived the blast is unknown.

World War I saw heroism by many homing pigeons, a variety of domestic pigeon and a first cousin of doves. One of these pigeons lived to be recognized by both the French and American governments. During the Battle of Verdun, as American troops were advancing through the Argonne Forest, roughly 550 men of three regiments of the Seventy-Seventh Division, under Major Charles Whittlesey, pushed too far and became surrounded by Germans. They were trapped from October 2, 1918, until October 4, despite attempts to fight their way back to American lines. They were running out of ammunition, and an attempt to drop them supplies by air failed. What was worse, their exact position was not known, and an artillery bombardment intended to help them break out on October 4 actually fell on what became known as the "Lost Battalion." Several of their carrier pigeons had been shot and killed trying to reach American lines. Only one carrier pigeon, a Black Check cock named Cher Ami, remained to them as the artillery fell. Major Whittlesey put a note into the silver canister on that pigeon's leg: "We are along the road parallel to 276.4 [a map designation]. Our own artillery is dropping a barrage directly on us. For heaven's sake, stop it."

Cher Ami took off, apparently perched in a tree for a moment amid the din of battle, but responded to his branch being shaken, along with urgent calls from the soldiers for him to "Fly home, Cher Ami, fly home!" Heading for his roost, Cher Ami was hit by a bullet and knocked to the ground in view of some troops, but the pigeon got up and flew again. After a flight of twenty-five miles in about sixty-five minutes, Cher Ami reached the American headquarters. His right eye had been lost, there was a hole in his breast, and the cylinder containing Major Whittlesey's note dangled from a ligament of his broken right leg. But the message came through, and the Americans began to bombard the Germans rather than their own men. On October 8, 194 men from the Lost Battalion finally fought their way back to the American lines.[45]

Cher Ami was patched up by medics—one even made him a wooden leg— and lived about nine months longer. When the war ended in November, he returned home to Fort Monmouth, New Jersey. France gave Cher Ami the Croix de Guerre with Palm, one of her highest military honors. After his death on June 13, 1919, his body was preserved, and Cher Ami now stands on one leg in the Smithsonian Museum of American History, on the National Mall in the District of Columbia (Figure 4.1). A French monument to the Lost Battalion in the Argonne Forest includes a one-legged statue of Cher Ami.

Although Cher Ami attained more fame than any other pigeon, many others became heroes and routine participants in the wars of the twentieth century. Cher Ami was one of 442 pigeons who flew messages for the Americans during the two-month Battle of Verdun. One American pigeon called "The Mocker" flew fifty-two missions before he was wounded. In World War II, the British gave thirty-two medals to pigeons. A British bird named William of Orange flew 250 miles to bring news of the ill-fated attempt to land in Europe called Operation Market Garden. King George V of England had his own flock of homing pigeons returning to their loft at Sandringham to bring him news of the war. British bombers, warships,

90 WINGS OF THE GODS

Figure 4.1 The pigeon called Cher Ami flew through enemy fire to get help for a trapped battalion of American soldiers in World War I. The bird now stands in the Smithsonian Museum of American History.
Photograph by National Museum of American History, Archives Center.

and even submarines carried pigeons to have a way to send a distress call or an alert when technology failed. Meanwhile, the Germans of World War II equipped pigeons with spy cameras strapped to their chests and appropriated a million birds from occupied Europe. Only in 1948 did the British give up their armed forces carrier pigeons. The United States continued to train pigeons until 1957, and the Swiss Army did not give up its birds until 1996.[46]

Biblical Bird Heroics

As we saw in the chapter on birds in creation stories, avian interventions in the Bible started with the Flood story of Genesis, when Noah sent out a raven and then a dove to see whether the floodwaters had receded. True to the homing instincts of doves (who are close relatives of pigeons, bred for whiteness), the dove returned to Noah with evidence of plant life, while the independent, nomadic raven never came back to the ark.

When Israel wandered in the desert, the people were fed by manna, a substance tasting like "cake baked with oil" (Numbers 11:8, NRSV) that appeared on the ground each morning. Strangely, the manna was preceded on the first day by a flight of quails:

> In the evening quails came up and covered the camp; and in the morning there was a layer of dew around the camp. When the layer of dew lifted, there on the surface of the wilderness was a fine flaky substance, as fine as frost on the ground. When the Israelites saw it, they said to one another, "What is it?" For they did not know what it was. Moses said to them, "It is the bread that the Lord has given you to eat." (Exodus 16:13–15, NRSV)

How the quails were connected with this bread is not clear, and later appearances of manna included no birds. The manna simply appeared with the dew each night (Numbers 11:9).

In the second year of their wandering after the departure from Egypt, the people grew tired of eating nothing but manna. According to the book of Numbers, they recalled the food of Egypt and asked Moses to provide them with meat. Moses complained to God, wondering how he could provide meat for such a multitude (about six hundred thousand people had left Egypt, according to Exodus). God's reply again began with a flight of quails:

> Then a wind went out from the Lord, and it brought quails from the sea and let them fall beside the camp, about a day's journey on this side and a day's journey on the other side, all around the camp, about two cubits deep upon the ground. (Numbers 11:31, NRSV)

Since a cubit is determined by the length from a man's elbow to the tip of his fingers, the quail on the ground were more than a yard or a meter deep. Numbers 11:32 reports that the people worked all day and all night and all the next day gathering quails. But when they began to eat, "while the meat was still in their mouths, before it was consumed," God struck Israel with a great plague, and they buried many there, calling the place "Graves of craving." The traumatic memory was recalled centuries after the wilderness journey, in a psalm dated to the era after King Solomon, when the kingdom had split into Israel and Judah. Psalm 78 retells the whole history of the people and gives six verses to this incident, repeating that God killed the quail-eaters "while the food was still in their mouths." The psalm laments that God "killed the strongest of them, and laid low the flower of Israel" (Psalm 78:30–31).

These birds would have been *Coturnix coturnix*, very widespread across Europe and Asia, with most European quail migrating into Africa through the Mideast and along the Red Sea and Nile River valley. A naturalistic explanation for the quail incident was offered by scholars G. R. Driver and E. W. Gurney Masterman.[47] According to them, quails migrate "annually in vast numbers from SE Europe by way of Sinai to the N. African coastal countries and back again." In both Exodus and Numbers, they believed, the children of Israel encountered quails during their migration to the north. Over the wilderness of Sinai, "carried with the wind" that the Bible ascribes to God, the quails would have been "flying very low and indeed often just skimming the surface of the ground." They commonly rest on the shore of the Red Sea, after following its shoreline from the south and crossing the water at its narrowest point. Therefore, the right translation for the passage from Numbers should be that the quails did not lie dead two cubits deep, but "fluttered over the camp ... all round the camp and about two cubits above the ground." In their long migration, these low-flying quails grow "so exhausted that they can be taken by hand in any number." Driver and Masterman concluded that "what was a miracle to the Israelites was in fact exactly in harmony with the quail's migratory habits." Unfortunately, so was the sickness resulting from their eating of the birds. It is reported that "if [quail] have eaten certain plants, although which plants is still in debate, the meat from quail can be poisonous, with one in four who consume poisonous flesh becoming ill with coturnism, which is characterized by muscle soreness, and which may lead to kidney failure." It is also reported that quail migration still helps to feed the poor in Gaza, providing meat, which is otherwise beyond their reach, at least seasonally.

More direct feeding of a human by birds occurs when the prophet Elijah is called to oppose the wickedness of King Ahab and Queen Jezebel of the northern kingdom of Israel. Ahab and Jezebel were encouraging idol worship in the kingdom of ten tribes of Israel that had rebelled against the house of David, which still ruled the tribe of Judah from Jerusalem. Oddly, when Elijah was called by God to oppose Ahab and Jezebel, he was at first told to flee into the wilderness east of the Jordan River, and he was assured by God that "I have commanded the ravens to feed you there." Two verses later, the story brings Elijah to the appointed place, where "The ravens brought him bread and meat in the morning, and bread and meat in the evening" (1 Kings 17:4, 6).

After a contest in which Elijah kills 450 prophets of the Canaanite storm god Baal (the prime god of Jezebel), the prophet again flees into the wilderness and is fed "a cake baked on hot stones" by an angel. Angels and ravens have analogous functions in the Elijah stories, but the ravens with their bread and meat come before the angel with his cake. Birds and angels are associated by their wings and abilities to fly, their sudden, seemingly miraculous appearances, and also by their roles as messengers between God and humans. Unlike angels, who only appear on special occasions and to special people in the Bible, ravens have been known to lead many nomadic humans (and packs of wolves) to food.

Because ravens also can pick up words in human languages, they may be one of the sources for a biblical warning against avian intervention. "Do not curse the king, even in your thoughts," warns the book of Ecclesiastes, "or curse the rich, even in your bedroom; for a bird of the air may carry your voice, or some winged creature tell the matter" (Ecclesiastes 10:20). The old saying that "a little bird told me" may derive from this verse, as well as many jokes about people having their secrets betrayed by talking pet birds who have heard them.

King Solomon, the son of David the Psalmist and the legendary author of Ecclesiastes, knew the language of birds, according to Jewish traditions and the Koran (Surah 27:16). A hoopoe (*Upupa epops*, now the national bird of Israel) described the Queen of Sheba (Surah 27:20–27) to Solomon, who then invited the queen to visit him. The hoopoe is a widespread Old World bird, strikingly colored (black and white stripes below light brown head and shoulder, topped with a black-tipped crest). It is familiar across Europe and the Mideast, including Egypt, and plays a role in much folklore, the call of the hoopoe being an omen of war in Scandinavia, for example.

Birds take part in the battles predicted for Israel's last days. After the northern kingdom of Israel disappeared and became the Ten Lost Tribes, and the kingdom of Judah saw Solomon's temple at Jerusalem burned and went into exile, becoming the people known as Jews, the prophet Ezekiel promised deliverance. Ezekiel 37–38 predicted the return of the Jews to their land under a king of their own, a descendant of David. Then the prophet described an attack on the regathered Jews by mysterious nations or princes, called Gog and Magog, who lead a coalition of identified nations such as Persia and Ethiopia and five others whose names are given but harder to decipher. This coalition is expected to attack Israel, but then God strikes the invading armies. Finally, Ezekiel is instructed to "speak to the birds of every kind" and to tell them to "assemble and come, gather from all around to the sacrificial feast that I am preparing for you, a great sacrificial feast on the mountains of Israel, and you shall eat flesh and drink blood . . . eat the flesh of the mighty, and drink the blood of the princes of the earth" (Ezekiel 39:17–18).

On a more peaceful note, the descent of a dove marks the baptism of Jesus in all four of the canonical Gospels. For example, Luke wrote that "the Holy Spirit descended upon him in bodily form like a dove" (Luke 3:22). In the Gospel of John, John the Baptist describes the most birdlike behavior when he relays the word of God that came to him as Jesus was baptized: "I saw the Spirit descending from heaven like a dove, and it remained on him. I myself did not know him, but the one who sent me to baptize with water said to me, 'He on whom you see the Spirit descend and remain is the one who baptizes with the Holy Spirit'" (John 1:31–33). The initiative of the dove in descending and remaining on Jesus revealed to John that Jesus was the Messiah he expected.

There could hardly be a more direct identification of God with a bird than these passages from the New Testament. In Genesis, the *ruach*, Hebrew for "wind," or in Latin *spiritus* of God is the creative force that parts the waters and enters the mouth of Adam to bring him to life. Here in the Gospels, the Spirit of God is personified as a creature of the wind, the dove.

This biblical picture is unique because the dove is far less formidable than other avian gods. Many religions have certainly pictured their gods as birds: for example Horus the Hawk and Isis (often a kite) in Egypt, as we saw in the chapter on creation. Ahura Mazda, creator god of the Zoroastrians, or Parsis, is pictured as a man with great wings. But after all of the eagles and ravens, vultures and ibises and owls of the world's religions, to settle on the dove as the highest avian persona for God makes a statement of peace, domesticity, even sacrifice and nutritional availability. Doves were sacrificed on the altar outside the Jerusalem Temple and consumed by the priests during the lifetime of Jesus. That sacrificial practice had just ceased when the Gospels were written, shortly after the destruction of the last temple by Rome in 70 CE. To say that God intervenes in history in the form of a dove was a radically pacifist statement.

As Christian art built on the biblical heritage, the dove took a role in images of the virgin conception of Jesus. Pictures of the Annunciation, probably the most frequently painted scene of Renaissance art, usually show the Holy Spirit in the form of a dove approaching the Virgin Mary as the angel Gabriel presents her the request that she become the Mother of Jesus, and so the Mother of God. Before Mary has answered, "Let it be with me according to your word" (Luke 1:38), the divine dove, God's Holy Spirit, is already flying toward her ear, where he will enter to impregnate her.

Birds as Gods, Men as Birds, and Birds as Villains and Heroes in Greece

At the opening of *The Birds*, a comedy from ancient Athens (first performed 414 BCE) by Aristophanes, two men are leaving Athens because they are sick of its chronic lawsuits and corrupt politics. Each man has a bird perched on his shoulder—one has a crow, the other a smaller corvid called a jackdaw. They bought the birds as guides to help them find Tereus, a former king of Thrace who raped his wife's sister and was punished by being turned into a hoopoe (perhaps the foul smell that nestlings and brooding female hoopoes have from a liquid that they excrete and rub on their feathers is relevant to the punishment here).

The men leaving Athens hope that, having lived as a bird, Tereus will have knowledge of many cities, and so will be able to guide them to find one where they will enjoy life more than in Athens. The two Athenians succeed in meeting Tereus, who appears with feathers and a beak, but none of his suggestions for cities in Greece or around the Aegean Sea appeal to them. During the discussion, Pisthetairos, the leader of the pair of Athenians, gets the idea of convincing the birds to create a new city in the air. Then the birds can intercept human offerings as they rise to the gods of Olympus, starve the gods, and take over their power. Tereus eagerly accepts the idea and wakes his wife, a nightingale, to sing so that birds will gather. He tells Pisthetairos that the birds will understand when the Athenian explains his idea, because Tereus has taught them human speech. The birds arrive: first a flamingo, then a peacock, and ultimately twenty-five species who are listed, including an imaginary Glutton bird. The birds who gather do not include an eagle, a hawk, or an owl, birds sacred to Zeus, Apollo, and Athena, respectively. Except for a kestrel and a vulture, the birds to make the new city are all primarily grain or insect-eating birds.

In his argument, Pisthetairos tells the gathered flock that birds originally stood in the place now usurped by the gods. He notes that the rooster still commands all humans to get up and go to work.[48] He points out that human kings still have bird emblems on their shields and standards, and that Zeus rules by the eagle, Athena by the owl, and Apollo by the hawk.[49]

Questioned by the birds about what birds as gods could do to help humans, Pisthetairos has several answers. First, the birds can protect vines and figs from locusts and gall wasps; then, they can show humans how to grow rich by seeking out sites for mines; and they can protect shipping by watching out for storms and warning seamen.[50] They can even add years to human life by borrowing from the crow: he quotes a saying, "Five human lifetimes lives the cawing crow," referencing a Greek folk belief about the longevity of crows. Convinced by the speech of the companion with whom he left Athens, the human character Euelpides exclaims, "My word, these birds are far more qualified to govern us than Zeus."[51] Pisthetairos concludes that having birds as gods will also be more convenient for humans, who will no longer need to travel to shrines like Delphi, but just stand beneath some trees offering their prayers and grain.

More than convinced, the leader of the bird chorus directly addresses the human audience of the play:

> Come now, you men out there, who live such dark, sad lives . . . now turn your minds to us, the eternal, deathless, air-borne, ageless birds, whose wisdom never dies, so you may hear from us the truth about celestial things, about the birds—how they sprang into being. . . . In broad Tartarus, Love had sex with murky Chaos. From them our race was born—our first glimpse of the light. Before that there was no immortal race at all.[52]

After the leader adds a few more details of the beginning and arguments about how humans already depend on birds (as gifts for their boy lovers, as signs to tell the seasons, and as metaphors to talk about each other and their lives), the bird chorus makes a more telling point. The birds remind the human audience that birds are more accessible than Olympians: "And we won't run away to a cloud and sit there like Zeus, who's so proud—we're ready to give, hang out where you live, and be there for you in the crowd."

From here the plot proceeds apace. Pisthetairos suggests the name of the city, Cloudcuckootown, and the birds build it quickly, herons carrying bricks and mortar and woodpeckers doing the carpentry. The two Athenians are given a root that helps them to grow wings so they can inhabit the city in the air. Because the birds invite humans to come and join them, potential immigrants arrive from Athens. The applicants personify the vices of the human city, and Pisthetairos rejects most after interviews, often administering comic beatings or throwing them off the stage. Some humans do get wings; one young man-bird is sent to establish a colony of Cloudcuckootown in Thrace.[53]

Prometheus then arrives to tell Pisthetairos that "Zeus is done for" because humans have stopped offering sacrifices to the gods.[54] When a delegation from Olympus, led by Poseidon and Hercules, tries to reason with Pisthetairos, he makes serious demands, following the suggestions of Prometheus. The former Athenian asks that Zeus present his scepter to the birds and give the Princess Basileia, who keeps his thunderbolts, to Pisthetairos in marriage. At first Poseidon is outraged, but Hercules is hungry to eat some birds (convicted as rebels against "the fowl democracy" according to Pisthetairos) that Pisthetairos is roasting.[55] Pisthetairos promises that in exchange for sovereignty, he will give an alliance to the Olympians. If any humans swear false oaths to Zeus, which they now can do under cover of clouds, the ravens will hear them and pluck out their eyes. If a human starts to offer a sacrifice to the Olympians and changes his mind, a kite will "grab his cash, the value of two sheep," and bring that to the gods.[56] On those terms, the scepter and the Princess of the thunderbolts are handed over, and the marriage of Pisthetairos and Basileia is celebrated. The birds and human-birds have triumphed over the gods as the comedy ends.

Far from mere fantasy, *The Birds* actually offered an acute diagnosis of the political situation in Athens. The play won second place at the dramatic contest of 414 BCE, while an enormous invasion force from Athens (about forty thousand men) was hoping for victory and spoil from the rebellious Greek colony on Sicily, centered at the city of Syracuse. Decades before, Athens had adopted an imperial policy, devised by the great leader Pericles, under which its navy extracted wealth from a few colonies and traded with the world while Athens pulled back from defending the peasantry on the farms of Attica, around the city.[57] Country people who wanted protection in the chronic wars

98 WINGS OF THE GODS

with Sparta and with Persia had to abandon their lands and move inside the city walls.

In a sense, Athens had become Cloudcuckootown, detaching itself from agriculture and living by intercepting goods. Like the city of the birds, it was transcending traditional peasant ways of life, and by extension the traditional gods to whom the peasants sacrificed. At the moment when the play was performed, the strategy had a chance of victory. If the rich Sicilian colonies, established by non-Athenian Greeks, could be brought under Athenian control, their strength might help to secure Athenian domination of the eastern Mediterranean. But part of the concept of Pericles had been for Athens to seize no more colonies, and so to take no big military risks that might provoke enemies. In 413, the force from Athens was utterly defeated on Sicily, with almost no survivors. By 404, Sparta defeated Athens, and Athens never regained its freedom or its glory. In 399, five hundred Athenian jurors voted to put the philosopher Socrates to death because they blamed him for corrupting the generation of Athenians that had dared to overreach, to challenge the gods.

The tragedy of Socrates's execution exposed deep sexual themes that also informed *The Birds*. Like all of the comedies of Aristophanes, *The Birds* is very explicit in its sexuality. When Procne, the wife of Tereus who was turned into a nightingale, appears, Eulpedies exclaims, "How I'd love to help that birdie spread her legs, if you catch my drift."[58] Later the Chorus of Birds tells the human audience,

> We fly around the place, assisting those in love—the handsome lads who swear they'll never bend for sex, but who, as their young charms come to an end, agree to let male lovers have sex with them, thanks to the birds, our power as gifts—one man gives a porphyrion [purple swamphen], another man a quail, a third one gives a goose, and yet another offers up a Persian Fowl [ancestor of our chicken].

Behind these lines lies the story of Alcibiades, a beautiful and talented young soldier and politician who had been a student (and rumored boy lover) of Socrates. Alcibiades dissented from the Periclean strategy for Athens,[59] appealing to the displaced peasantry in elections. He planned the campaign to conquer Sicily and sailed as a joint commander of the Athenian force, but then was recalled to the city for trial because someone had broken hundreds of good-luck phallic statues (called herms) that adorned front doors and public squares in Athens, on the night before the fleet sailed. It has been speculated that this may have been a protest by Athenian women, who had unusual freedom to roam the streets because of an Adonis festival, but Alcibiades had the reputation of a prankster and was blamed.[60] Refusing to face trial, Alcibiades betrayed Athens by going over to the Spartan, and finally to the Persian, side in the wars. It was this particular youth, the adopted son of Pericles, whom Socrates was killed for corrupting. On his shield Alcibiades displayed the winged god Eros, armed with the thunderbolt of Zeus.[61]

When *The Birds* was first produced, the fleet had already sailed to Sicily, but the disastrous defeat had not yet happened. Aristophanes was depicting, and satirizing, the phallic spirit that led the Athenians to their ambition to build a city detached from the earth, like the Parthenon on its cliffs. But the dramatist was also part of the circle that included Socrates and Alcibiades, and he had little piety for the old Olympian gods. Aristophanes clearly meant to skewer potential tyrants, along with the party at Athens that favored military rule, by showing Pisthetairos callously skewering some of his subject birds, but his play did not reject Athenian ambitions to soar beyond the earth, with the birds.

For his part, Socrates also seems to have shared these ambitions. Plato quotes him in the *Phaedo*, just before his death, saying that humans will never understand the world until they take the wings of birds and gain the capacity to see reality from beyond our atmosphere.

> We are dwelling in a hollow of the earth, and fancy that we are on the surface; and the air we call the heaven, and in this we imagine that the stars move. But this is also owing to our feebleness and sluggishness, which prevent our reaching the surface of the air: if any man could arrive at the exterior limit, *or take the wings of a bird and fly upward* [emphasis mine], like a fish who puts his head out and sees this world, he would see a world beyond; and, if the nature of man could sustain the sight, he would acknowledge that this was the place of the true heaven and the true light and the true stars.[62]

As he died from the hemlock he was made to drink, Socrates again invoked a bird, and the bird most associated with Eros. He asked his students to give a cock, a rooster, to the temple of Asclepius, the god of healing, in payment for his deliverance from the ills of life. The great questioner of Athens may not have been inspired by the Olympian gods, but he was inspired by the birds.

Legends and Dreams of Interventions by Birds

No presence of birds is noted in the Bible's accounts of the death of Jesus on the cross. According to European Christians, however, the red breast of the robin resulted from that bird trying to help the suffering savior by pulling the thorns from his crown. According to Swedish legend, the swallow also was present, flying over the cross and calling "Svala, svala," or "Be consoled."[63] These legends of intervention at the cross probably arose from the observation of both robins and swallows in northern climes at the beginning of spring, which is also the time of Good Friday and Easter.

Another tormented figure, Prometheus, has the eagle of Zeus for his torturer. After stealing fire from the gods for humanity, the titan Prometheus was punished by being chained to a rock on a mountain. Every day, the eagle of Zeus flew to the titan and ripped at his abdomen with his beak and claws. Being immortal, Prometheus healed at night, only to again be torn by the eagle the next day. On the other hand, the bird of Zeus could also intervene to help a human. When Psyche, who had been married in secret by Eros, the son of Aphrodite, was working on a set of hopeless tasks set by her mother-in-law, she faced defeat in getting a cup of water from the spring that fed the River Styx. The spring came from the top of a mountain covered by poisonous snakes. As Psyche approached the mountain in despair, the eagle came and took the cup, got the water, and brought it back to her.

In cultures that did not know Prometheus as bringer of fire, birds were frequently given credit for fire by legend. The Amahuaca of eastern Peru attribute this to the parrot, who stole fire from a giant who would not have shared the gift. Other Native Americans have attributed fire to the swallow or, as was seen among the Lenape of New York in Chapter 2, to the crow, whose feathers were charred while bringing it down, as a gift from the Creator.

Two vulture brothers, Jatayu and Sampati, intervened to save the goddess Sita and god Rama in the Hindu epic the Ramayana. Nephews of Garuda, the eagle who carries the heavenly god Vishnu, Jatayu and Sampati tried to fly to the sun in their youth. When Jatayu's wings began to burn, Sampati, the elder of the brothers, used his own wings to shield him. Both fell to earth, but the wings of Jatayu were only singed, while Sampati lost his wings.

BIRD HEROES AND VILLAINS 101

Many years later, when Rama (the seventh incarnation of Vishnu the heavenly god) and Sita were living as exiles in the forest because Rama's father, the king of Ayodhya, had vowed to allow another prince to take his throne for some time, the demon Ravana seized Sita while Rama was hunting a deer. Jatayu saw Ravana begin to fly off with Sita in his magical chariot and pursued them, attacking and injuring Ravana with his beak and his talons. But Ravana had twenty arms wielding swords, and he cut off both of Jatayu's wings and fatally wounded the noble vulture. Searching for Sita, Rama and his brother Lakshmana found Jatayu dying on the ground. He told them what had happened and in what direction Ravana went with Sita. In gratitude, Rama struck the ground with his arrow and called on the seven rivers of India to come to the spot, so that they could perform funeral rites and help Jatayu to attain moksha, release from rebirth. The spot is remembered as Lepakshi, in Andra Pradesh.

As the search for Sita went on, Hanuman, the monkey god, led an army of monkeys to try to find the goddess. At the southernmost end of the Indian subcontinent, the monkeys became exhausted and collapsed on the ground. Then the elder brother vulture, Sampati, appeared, without wings but with a huge body and beak, saying that he would enjoy the huge feast lying before him. They replied that unlike this vulture who seeks to devour helpless monkeys who are trying to do good deeds, there was a vulture Jatayu who gave his life trying to save the goddess Sita from a demon (Figure 4.2). Hearing the name Jatayu, Sampati asked what they meant. They told Sampati of his brother's sacrifice, and he cried. He then told the monkeys that he had seen Ravana's chariot, carrying the beautiful goddess, flying from the land of India to the island of Lanka. As a karmic reward for his good act, Sampati grew new wings. The Ramayana continued with an attack on Lanka by the monkeys and Rama's other allies and the rescue of Sita from Ravana.

Although vultures are among the unclean birds of the Hebrew Scriptures, and generally not highly valued in the West, they are also recognized as cousins of the eagle in the Bible and well respected in South Asia. As seen in Chapter 3, vulture burials were among the earliest ways of dealing with the dead in early human cities, and vultures became integrated into the funeral practices of Zoroastrians and Himalayan Buddhists. The Ramayana goes another step, making vultures into active agents who choose the right side in the struggle of gods against demons that runs through Hindu legends.

Back in Europe, avian intervention plays a large role in the legends of Siegfried and in the whole Ring cycle, which have taken many forms from

Figure 4.2 The vulture Jatayu, a hero of the Ramayana, tried to rescue goddess Sita from a demon. He fell, but helped the god Rama find his wife. At Jatayu Earth's Centre, Jatayu now defends women and the environment. Sculptor Rajiv Anchal.

Photograph Raul Arago / courtesy Cercle Jatayu.

the days of Norse pagans through the operas of Richard Wagner down to J. R. R. Tolkien and *The Lord of the Rings* movies. One important moment from that complex of stories came when Siegfried has killed the dragon Fafnir at the behest of Mime the blacksmith, in order to earn a wonderful sword. He did not know that the dragon was really the human brother of the smith, transformed into a dragon by greed for the treasure of gold, including a wondrous ring, which he guarded. After Siegfried hid in a ditch and stabbed the dragon from below through the heart, and after the dragon's blood bathed him (or alternatively, when he had eaten some of the dragon's flesh, or simply tasted the blood of the dragon), the hero found that he could understand the language of birds.

The birds then intervene, telling Siegfried that the smith sent him against the dragon hoping he would be killed. Led by the birds, Siegfried returns to the smith and kills him. Again led by the birds, he finds the goddess Brunhilde, who lies sleeping under a spell behind a wall of fire. He of course then fights through the fire, kisses her, and wakes her to be his love.

Birds take a more central role in another story of a hero named Siegfried that informs the late nineteenth-century ballet *Swan Lake*. There Siegfried meets his true love when he is out hunting swans. Near nightfall, as he aims his crossbow, one of the swans turns into a beautiful woman named Odette, who tells him that she can only be human at night. During the day, she lives as a swan, the queen of many swan maidens, under the spell of a magician Rothbart. Unless she can find a man who has never loved and who will love her forever, she will have to remain in this condition. Rothbart appears, and Siegfried wants to kill him, but Odette warns that if the magician dies before the spell is broken, she must remain a swan, no longer taking human form.

The next day, Siegfried goes to a ball at which, his mother told him, he must choose a wife. He sees a woman who appears to be Odette, and dances with her, but she is really Odile, the magically disguised daughter of Rothbart the magician. Fooled by the spell, Siegfried declares his love for Odile.

Rothbart then shows Siegfried an image of the true Odette, who is back at the lake. Siegfried rushes to her, but she is inconsolable; by falling for Odile, he has made himself ineligible to break the spell. Determined to be together anyway, Siegfried and Odette leap to their deaths. The swan maidens are released to be human again, and in a vision they see Siegfried and Odette transported together to heaven.

The preceding synopsis follows the 1895 libretto for *Swan Lake*; however, there are numerous variants. Many productions add a prologue, to show

Rothbart capturing Odette in his spell and making her a swan. Alternative endings also abound. In Soviet and Chinese versions, the couple marries and lives as humans. In others, Odette kills herself and Siegfried remains alone in grief; or Siegfried tries to kill Rothbart, misses, and kills Odette with his crossbow; or Rothbart and Siegfried fight and die, leaving Odette to live as a swan; or Siegfried dies in a struggle with Rothbart, leaving the magician to carry off Odette. There are extremes of fatalism and optimism in recent years. In 2006, the New York City Ballet presented a version that had Siegfried's declaration of love for Odile simply seal the fate of Odette, who had to remain a swan forever. On the other hand, in a 2015 English National Ballet production for children, the swan maidens rose up together as heroes against Rothbart, whose death breaks the curse, so that Siegfried and Odette live happily ever after.

Without doubt, the most active bird hero in a version of Swan Lake to date came in 2010, with the movie *Black Swan*. There both Odile and Odette act primarily as swans, competing for the heart of Siegfried, and the twist comes because the director wants to cast the same woman as both white and black swans. The prologue, with Natalie Portman playing a human ballet dancer transformed by the spell into a swan, introduces the plot. Development hinges on the virginal character played by Portman needing to find her capacity to become the black swan. At one point, the director demands that she touch herself at home to feel her sexuality. As she experiments with sex and with drugs (ecstasy, or 3,4-methyl enedioxy methamphetamine), the dancer experiences more and more vivid hallucinatory states. At one point, black feathers seem to be sprouting from her shoulder blades. As the climax of the ballet brings the black swan closer to victory, Portman spins while full wings with black feathers appear on her arms. Finally, Portman as white swan plunges off the back of the stage to what should have been her fictional death, and it appears that the ballerina has actually stabbed herself in the abdomen with a shard of glass. She dies to the tumultuous applause of the audience, whispering, "That was perfect." The fantasy of becoming the black swan has killed her.

Perhaps the most dramatic tale of avian villainy in the realm of legends and dreams is that of Leda and the swan, told by the Greek poet Hesiod. Leda was a queen, the wife of King Tyndareus of Sparta, and so beautiful that Zeus fell in love with her. He came to her as a beautiful, human-sized swan and in that form he raped her. On that same night, she had sex with her husband, so that the children she produced as a result of that day were mixed. One of them, the daughter of Zeus, became Helen of Troy, the wife of Menelaus whose abduction by the Trojan prince Paris caused the Trojan War. Another child of Leda from that night, the daughter of Tyndareus, became Clytemnestra and married Agamemnon, the leader of the Greeks at Troy. Clytemnestra killed her husband in a conspiracy with her lover, and she was killed in turn by her daughter Electra.

Of course, it could be argued that the rape of Leda was by the god Zeus, not a bird, but the god took the body of a swan, and Leda and Zeus both experienced the rape by means of that swan body. Imagining the physicality of an enormous swan having sex with a human woman, as well as the consequences of that sex, the Irish poet William Butler Yeats (1865–1939) wrote a sonnet that included these lines:

> A sudden blow: the great wings beating still
> Above the staggering girl, her thighs caressed
> By the dark webs, her nape caught in his bill,
> He holds her helpless breast upon his breast.[64]

Such sensuality, unsurpassed in English poetry, testifies to the power that the image of a bird with intentions of its own can excite in the human imagination. Here the whole saga of Homer, both *Iliad* and *Odyssey*, have arisen from a god talking the body of a bird to cause, as Yeats described it, a human "shudder in the loins."[65]

The dream of sex with a bird has a close affinity to the dream of sex with an angel, which was long forbidden in Western theology but which became a feature of popular culture, sculpture, music, and drama during the twentieth century. Dreams of bird and angel merged in the Broadway play and HBO movie *Angels in America*, by Tony Kushner, which made a dramatic and influential statement for gay rights in the 1990s, at the height of the AIDS crisis. In that play, the archangelic Principality of America who visits the human hero causes him (a gay AIDS sufferer) and a Mormon woman to have orgasms. That angel, in the form of a winged woman, beats her wings in the air and struggles against the hero seizing her and demanding a blessing with the statement, "I will not be compelled; I am a bird of prey!"[66]

Bird heroes and villains continue to fly through the religious experience of humans. That experience can surpass the intense crises of this chapter to become a more lasting relationship, in which birds become spirit guides for humans. Sometimes, birds embody the Holy Spirit.

Notes

1. Evelyn S. Rawski, *The Last Emperors: A Social History of Qing Imperial Institutions* (Berkeley: University of California Press, 1998).
2. Richard W. Sadler, "Seagulls, Miracle of," in *The Encyclopedia of Mormonism*, ed. Daniel Ludlow (New York: Macmillan, 1992), 1287–1288.
3. Sadler, "Seagulls, Miracle of."
4. David B. Madsen and Brigham D. Madsen, "One Man's Meat Is Another Man's Poison: A Revisionist View of the Seagull 'Miracle,'" in *A World We Thought We Knew: Readings in Utah History*, ed. John S. McCormick and John R. Sillito (Salt Lake City: University of Utah Press, 1995).
5. Sadler, "Seagulls, Miracle of."
6. National Geographic Society, "Giant Swarm of Mormon Crickets," videorecording, April 3, 2013, https://www.youtube.com/watch?v=Yy3dQJYquoY (accessed March 18, 2017).
7. Jessie L. Embry and William A. Wilson, "Folk Ideas of Mormon Pioneers," *Dialogue: A Journal of Mormon Thought* 31, no. 3 (Fall 1998): 93–94 and 98–99.
8. C. D. Howe, "Service of the Birds," in *Seventh Annual Report of the Commissioner of Agriculture for the State of Vermont, 1915* (St. Albans, VT, n.p.), 71.
9. Albert K. Fisher, *The Hawks and Owls of the United States in Their Relation to Agriculture*, Division of Economic Ornithology and Mammalogy, Bulletin no. 3 (Washington, DC: USDA, 1893), 9.
10. William E. Saunders, "The Value of Predatory Birds," in *Sixty-Ninth Annual Report of the Ontario Entomological Society* (Toronto: T. E. Bowman Printer, 1938), 120.
11. Matthew D. Evenden, "The Laborers of Nature: Economic Ornithology and the Role of Birds as Agents of Biological Pest Control in North American Agriculture, ca. 1880–1930," *Forest & Conservation History* 39, no. 4 (October 1995): 172–183.
12. Toichi Mabuchi, "Tales Concerning the Origin of Grains in the Insular Areas of Southeastern Asia," *Asian Folklore Studies* 23, no. 1 (1964): 13 and 13 n. 20.
13. Mabuchi, "Tales Concerning the Origin," 41.
14. Mabuchi, "Tales Concerning the Origin," 52.
15. Mabuchi, "Tales Concerning the Origin," 55–56.
16. Boria Sax, *City of Ravens: The Extraordinary History of London, the Tower, and Its Famous Ravens* (London: Duckworth Overlook, 2011), 26–30.
17. The story of King Arthur being turned into a raven is reported in Cervantes's novel *Don Quixote*, book 2, chap. 5. It is reported by a later Cornish source at http://www.sacred-texts.com/neu/eng/prwe/prwe162.htm (accessed March 19, 2017). The color of the red-billed chough's beak and claws are said to derive from the violent end of King Arthur's last human life: http://www.sacred-texts.com/neu/eng/prwe/prwe163.htm (accessed March 19, 2017).
18. Sax, *City of Ravens*, 94 and 103.
19. Olivia Rudgard, "Exclusive: Could the Legend Come True? Tower of London Raven Allowed to Fly Free," *The Telegraph*, May 15, 2017, https://www.telegraph.co.uk/

news/2017/05/15/could-legend-come-true-tower-london-ravens-can-fly-warden-reduces/ (accessed July 19, 2019).
20. Rudgard, "Exclusive," 103–104.
21. Historic Royal Palaces, "The Tower of London," 2017, http://www.hrp.org.uk/tower-of-london/visit-us/top-things-to-see-and-do/the-ravens/ (accessed March 19, 2017).
22. Sax, *City of Ravens*, 71.
23. Sax, *City of Ravens*, 50.
24. Sax, *City of Ravens*, 46–48.
25. Sax, *City of Ravens*, 62–70.
26. Sax, *City of Ravens*, 94–96.
27. Sax, *City of Ravens*, 164.
28. Abdullah Yusuf Ali, *The Qur'an: Translation* (Elmhurst, NY: Tahrike Tarsile Qur'an, 2000).
29. Simply Seerah Studios, "The People of the Elephant," videorecording, https://www.youtube.com/watch?v=ZZdrKfKe7Dk (accessed March 16, 2017).
30. Ahlul Bayt Digital Islamic Library Project, "The Year of the Elephant," https://www.al-islam.org/life-muhammad-prophet-sayyid-saeed-akhtar-rizvi/year-elephant (accessed March 16, 2017).
31. Mustansir Mir, "Elephants, Birds of Prey, and Heaps of Pebbles: Farahi's Interpretation of Surat al-Fil," *Journal of Qur'anic Studies* 7, no. 1 (2005): 33.
32. Mir, "Elephants," 40.
33. William McLaughlin, "How Holy Geese Saved the Republic during the First Sack of Rome (390 BCE)," *War History Online*, March 24, 2016, https://www.warhistoryonline.com/featured/how-holy-geese-saved-the-republic-in-390-bce-during-the-first-sack-of-rome.html/2 (accessed March 16, 2017).
34. Adam Ziolkowski, "Between Geese and the Auguraculum: The Origin of the Cult of Juno on the Arx," *Classical Philology* 88, no. 3 (July 1993): 209 and 213–219.
35. Nicholas Horsfall, "From History to Legend: M. Manlius and the Geese," *Classical Journal* 76, no. 4 (April–May 1981): 308.
36. Horsfall, "From History to Legend," 311.
37. McLaughlin, "Holy Geese."
38. Chris Mitchell, "Former Israeli Commander: God Protected Us in Battle," *CBN News*, September 16, 2013, http://www.cbn.com/cbnnews/insideisrael/2013/september/fmr-israeli-commander-god-protected-us-in-battle--/?mobile=false (accessed March 15, 2017).
39. Ari Shavit, "Dear God, This Is Effi," *Haaretz*, March 20, 2002, http://www.haaretz.com/dear-god-this-is-effi-1.49866 (accessed March 15, 2017).
40. Claire Bernish, "Drilling for Oil in the Israeli-Occupied Region of Syria's Golan Heights, a Violation of International Law," *Global Research*, June 25, 2016, http://www.globalresearch.ca/drilling-for-oil-in-the-israeli-occupied-region-of-syrias-golan-heights-a-violation-of-international-law/5532455 (accessed March 15, 2017).

41. Pat Robertson, *Miracles Can Be Yours Today* (Nashville: Integrity Publishers, 2006), 89.
42. Natali Anderson, "Brown Skuas Can Recognize Individual Humans, New Study Shows," *Sci News*, March 28, 2016, http://www.sci-news.com/biology/brown-skuas-recognize-individual-humans-03734.html (accessed May 8, 2017).
43. Mitchell, "Former Israeli Commander."
44. Christine Darg, "Two Miracle Dove Stories: From Gaza 2014 and Yom Kippur War 1973," *Jerusalem Channel*, February 12, 2017, http://jerusalemchannel.tv/two-miracle-dove-stories-one-gaza-2014-one-yom-kippur-war-1973/ (accessed March 15, 2017). Also see Lonnie Mings, "Dove Saves Soldiers from Death," *Israel News Digest*, August 2014. Ami Maimon, an Israeli radio reporter for the Haredi radio station Kol Barama, told the same story.
45. Adam Bieniek, "Cher Ami: The Pigeon That Saved the Lost Battalion," United States World War One Centennial Commission, http://www.worldwar1centennial.org/index.php/communicate/press-media/wwi-centennial-news/1210-cher-ami-the-pigeon-that-saved-the-lost-battalion.html (accessed March 16, 2017).
46. Jasper Copping, "Honoured: The WW1 Pigeons Who Earned Their Wings," *The Telegraph*, January 12, 2014, http://www.telegraph.co.uk/history/world-war-one/10566025/Honoured-the-WW1-pigeons-who-earned-their-wings.html (accessed March 16, 2017).
47. E. W. Gurney Masterman and G. R. Driver, "Quail," in *The Hastings Dictionary of the Bible*, ed. Frederick Grant and H. H. Rowley, rev. ed. (New York: Charles Scribner's Sons, 1963), 826.
48. Aristophanes, *Birds*, trans. Ian Johnston (Arlington, VA: Richer Resources Publications, 2008), line 490.
49. Aristophanes, *Birds*, lines 510–520.
50. Aristophanes, *Birds*, lines 590–600.
51. Aristophanes, *Birds*, line 610.
52. Aristophanes, *Birds*, lines 685–700.
53. Aristophanes, *Birds*, line 1369.
54. Aristophanes, *Birds*, lines 1515–1520.
55. Aristophanes, *Birds*, lines 1580–1590.
56. Aristophanes, *Birds*, lines 1610–1622.
57. William Arrowsmith, "Aristophanes' Birds: The Fantasy Politics of Eros," *Arion: A Journal of Humanities and the Classics*, New Series, 1, no. 1 (Spring 1973): 119–121.
58. Aristophanes, *Birds*, line 668.
59. Arrowsmith, "Aristophanes' Birds," 130 and 142 n. 13.
60. Christopher Miles with John Julius Norwich, *Love in the Ancient World* (New York: St. Martin's Press, 1997), 104–105.
61. Arrowsmith, "Aristophanes' Birds," 135.
62. Plato, *Phaedo*, trans. Benjamin Jowett (New York: P.F. Collier and Son, 1909), 605–606.

63. Cassandra Eason, *Fabulous Creatures, Mythical Monsters, and Animal Power Symbols: A Handbook* (Westport, CT: Greenwood Press, 2008), 73–74.
64. W. B. Yeats, "Leda and the Swan," public domain, https://poets.org/poem/leda-and-swan (accessed August 3, 2023).
65. Yeats, "Leda and the Swan."
66. Tony Kushner, *Angels in America: A Gay Fantasia on National Themes, Part Two: Perestroika*, act 5 (New York: Theatre Communication Group, 2005), 251.

5
Bird Spirit Guides

The Holy Spirit Incarnates as a Dove

Christians rarely notice that the New Testament describes two incarnations of God, one in the body of Jesus and one in the body of a bird. In Luke 3:22, after Jesus was baptized by John the Baptist, the Gospel says that "the Holy Spirit descended upon him in bodily form like a dove." The dove here is real: the Greek word translated as "form" in the New Revised Standard Version and as "shape" in the King James Version is *eidos*, which is the word Plato used for the real objects in his allegory of the cave, where humans without true understanding are pictured as seeing objects (*eidos*) only by their shadows projected on a wall by light behind them.

All four Gospels mention this dove, giving different physical details. In Matthew 3:16, the bird is seen "alighting on" Jesus. John 1:32 quotes the Baptist saying that he saw "the Spirit descending from heaven like a dove, and it remained on him [Jesus]." Then God told John, "He on whom you see the Spirit descend and remain is the one who baptizes with the Holy Spirit" (John 1:33). In Matthew, Jesus is the one who sees the dove, and in Luke, the whole crowd of those being baptized see the dove. In Mark, which most scholars believe to be the first Gospel to be written, only Jesus sees the dove, but the dove does more than simply land on him: "And the Spirit immediately drove him out into the wilderness." Behind this lies the likelihood that a bird would prefer the wilderness to a scene with humans crowding around a river.

Long before Jesus, biological lore connected birds with virgin births. Many ancient writers, including Homer and Aristotle, noted that hens would lay eggs without having sex and concluded that in some species of animals, females could become pregnant from the wind, without a male. Eggs of hens with no rooster are not fertile, and they were called *zephyria* or "wind eggs," but vultures were said to be capable of having viable, long-lived offspring from wind. Christian theologians including Origen, Ambrose, and Augustine concurred. When Gabriel tells Mary that she will become pregnant by the "spirit," the Greek word is *pneuma*, or wind, and the form of conception is familiar from birds.

The dove as embodiment of the Spirit has inspired Christian artists and architects. Doves have become central to most depictions of the Annunciation and the Pentecost over the last thousand years, although no dove appears in connection with those two events in the Bible. When the Trinity is pictured, the most common image is that of a bearded, crowned Father on a throne behind Jesus the Son on the cross, with a dove hovering in the space between them.

In recent decades, theologians have finally begun to follow the artists and to focus on the bird when reflecting on the Holy Spirit. As Mark Wallace of Swarthmore College has written, "Put simply, if God can become a loaf of bread or cup of wine, then why can God not become a bird...?"[1] Describing the bird in the baptism of Jesus, James Perkinson of the Ecumenical Theological Seminary in Detroit wrote that the Spirit "visits in the form of a passenger pigeon, spiraling above, landing with precision, and mission in its talons."[2]

Pigeons and doves belong to the same family, the Columbidae, of which there are at least three hundred species, including eight hundred breeds of pigeons alone, more than any other animal with possible exceptions of dogs, chickens, and goldfish. For more than three thousand years, Columbidae have lived in domestic relations with humans, as pets and as sources of food, and also as messengers and racing animals and producers of fertilizer and gunpowder (their dung is a good source of saltpeter, potassium nitrate).[3] In a blend of wild and domestic life, people have provided dovecotes or shelters for pigeons near human homes so that the birds are attracted to remain while retaining their freedom. As Perkinson's reference to "talons" above reminds, the roles of pigeons and doves as spirit guides have not always been peaceful. The last chapter of this book recounted how often these birds have gone to war, guiding soldiers.

When the Swiss psychologist Carl Jung (1875–1961) had just broken with Sigmund Freud, around Christmas of 1912, he dreamed of a dove that alighted on a table where he and his children were sitting. That dove turned into a girl of about eight years old who went off and played with the children, then turned again into a bird, came back to the table to stand before Jung alone, and spoke to him in a human voice: "Only in the first hours of the night can I transform myself into a human being, while the male dove is busy with the twelve dead." She flew off, and Jung awoke.[4] This led to several years of dreams and overpowering visions, sometimes described as a creative psychosis, which produced Jung's concept of a "mid-life crisis" during which "archetypes," or channels of energy and knowledge (the "twelve dead") formed in the brain by evolution return to life in the unconscious to correct unbalanced attitudes of the ego. In a Jungian view, the birds of religion, including the dove of Jung's dream, can be spirit guides because they mediate between everyday consciousness and the deeper mind. At the center of the collective unconscious lives the Self, which is not the personal ego but God, the "transcendent function." Jung transposed the traditional Christian role of the dove as Holy Spirit, linking humanity to the God of heaven, into his map of human psychology.

Predatory Spirit Guides and Shamans

Encounters with such spirit guides may be pleasant or frightening, experienced as inspiration or possession, depending on the life situation of the human and the attitude of the ego. One of the bestselling books of 2014, Helen Macdonald's *H Is for Hawk*, began with the longing the author felt to hunt with a goshawk as she lived through a depression following her father's death. Macdonald had been a falconer as a young woman, and when her father died suddenly during her thirty-seventh year, she felt a need for connections to a larger bird, harder to tame, with a reputation for savagery. A few months before her father died, she had encountered a goshawk in a tree and for a moment had mistaken the huge bird for a man.[5] She had just published a book called *Falcon*, which recounted none of her own experiences as a falconer but surveyed the rest of humanity's relations with falcons, all over the world, from ancient times to the present as well as in legend and myth. But her relations with the goshawk she named Mabel, and the resultant book, were deeply and relentlessly personal. Her reflections on Mabel were also intensely religious: "Looking for goshawks is like looking for grace: it comes, but not often, and you don't get to say when or how."[6]

Jung stressed that the archetypes of the unconscious had their own agendas, independent of the ego, and that is also true of the externally living birds people turn to as spirit guides. Early in her ownership of Mabel, Macdonald became acutely aware of the hawk watching her and reacting with alarm or pleasure to her physical actions. Deciding how to walk or

Figure 5.1 The intensity and violence of bonding as a hunter with a goshawk (*Accipiter gentilis*) helped British author Helen Macdonald deal with the death of her father in a bestselling book, *H is for Hawk*.
Ondrej Prosicky / Alamy Stock Photo.

whether to scratch her nose in front of Mabel, Macdonald was shocked by how sensitive she became to the bird's responses. "I was turning into a hawk," she wrote.[7]

When Mabel felled a rabbit that Macdonald pitied enough to kill by wringing its neck before the hawk began to eat it, Macdonald's feelings merged the personal and religious: "Kneeling next to the hawk and her prey, I felt a responsibility so huge that it battered inside my own chest, ballooning out into a space the size of a cathedral."[8] And the religious experiences she had with this bird spirit guide differed from the experiences provided by falconry:

> There is something religious about the activity of looking up at a hawk in a tall tree. Sir Thomas Shirley wrote in the seventeenth century that flying falcons turns one's eyes to the heavens, which is why falconry is a moral activity. This [hunting with the goshawk] seems more akin to falling to my knees begging redemption from an indifferent deity. Mabel flies on, deeper into the trees. I follow her.[9]

The relationship between hawk and woman did not always go smoothly. Mabel could not always be relied on to return to Macdonald's glove, and she once raked her owner's head with her talons, bathing Macdonald's face in blood. But when an earthquake terrified the woman one night, and she checked on the bird in her barn, Mabel provided reassurance. Macdonald found the goshawk unruffled by the quake, and wrote in wonder:

> She is not a duke, a cardinal, a hieroglyph or a mythological beast, but right now Mabel is more than a hawk. She feels like a protecting spirit. My little household god. Some things happen only once, twice in a lifetime. The world is full of signs and wonders that come, and go, and if you are lucky you might be alive to see them. I had thought the world was ending, but my hawk had saved me again, and all the terror was gone.[10]

But this relationship, however healing it was for Macdonald, did not last as long as the hawk's life; it endured only for a year. When Macdonald's depression lifted and she could work again, she gave Mabel to a friend. In a new preface to the 2016 edition of *Falcon*, Macdonald spoke of the "unconscious trap" of identification with the bird that she had fallen into "during that dark year with my own hawk Mabel." Macdonald learned that she was basically a scholar and teacher of history and literature, not a person who worked with falcons and hawks.

According to a career natural science writer, a woman named Sy Montgomery, raptors often inspire humans to identify with them, and to expect the birds with whom they hunt to love them. After training and hunting with a falcon named Jazz, Montgomery suggested another path: "For a human to love without expecting love in return is hugely liberating. To leave the self out of love is like escaping the grip of gravity. It is to grow wings. It opens up the sky."[11] For Montgomery, Jazz became a spirit guide granting personal grace, like the dove at the baptism of Jesus:

> I give Jazz a brief toss from my glove, and she sails into a pine. She looks down at us. Now I am worthy of Jazz's interest. She knows something is about to happen. For the first time, I am bathed in her sight. It's a baptism, and feels momentous, transforming.[12]

But on the other hand, there was a more transpersonal dimension in the gaze of the falcon. Working with a falcon expert, who taught Montgomery and

Jazz to hunt together, opened a realm of the spirit different from Christian love, the realm of Buddhist awareness:

> Birds' eyes gather more of life than ours do. Perhaps this is why I could feel Jazz so purely, densely full of life, filling up the moment—here, now, and nothing else. The Buddhists say there really *is* nothing else, because now is timeless; now is everything. Perhaps because of this, Jazz seems more immediately alive than any human I have ever known. To be in the gripping gaze of that bird is like looking directly into the sun. The class is a transforming experience.[13]

Avian raptors—eagles and goshawks and falcons—have guided the shamans, the religious leaders and medicine men, of Siberian hunter-gatherers for tens of thousands of years. At the end of the last ice age, twelve thousand years ago, some of those hunter-gatherers came down into North America and began the Native American nations, including the Lakota of the American Midwest. In the summer of 1890, a Lakota named Black Elk (1863–1950) took part in a ritual dance, called the ghost dance, at Wounded Knee in what is now North Dakota. After days of dancing in a circle and chanting, he felt as if he was lifted into the air, as though falling off a swing. Then, as he testified later, he had a vision:

> All I saw at first was a single eagle feather right in front of me. Then the feather was a spotted eagle dancing on ahead of me with his wings fluttering, and he was making the shrill whistle that is his. My body did not move at all, but I looked ahead and floated fast toward where I looked.[14]

Black Elk then saw a beautiful world, with Lakota eating from plentiful racks of meat and horses grazing on plentiful grass. He helped to paint ghost shirts for others to wear as they joined in the dance. But he soon had another vision, of a man "who was not a *Wasichu* [white man] and not an Indian," who stood against a "holy tree" with "arms held wide in front of him."[15] That man wore an eagle feather on the left side of his head. He told Black Elk that "all earthly beings and growing things belong to me," but then he disappeared. Twelve men who were with him warned Black Elk that his nation's life would be like that of the man with his arms held wide.

Decades after the slaughter of hundreds of Ghost Dancers by the US Seventh Cavalry (General Custer's former unit, which Black Elk's father had

116   WINGS OF THE GODS

helped to wipe out in 1876) at Wounded Knee in the winter of 1890, Black Elk became a Roman Catholic. He never ceased to be a Lakota shaman, however. Black Elk took part in Lakota rituals blessing Gutzom Borglum, the artist of Mount Rushmore, and his crew as they carved the heads of four presidents into the holy mountain where Black Elk had received his first visions as a child, a mountain that Lakota call the Six Grandfathers. Despite all the horrors and changes he witnessed, Black Elk still believed in the future that the eagle had shown him.

Beginning in the middle of the twentieth century, about the time when Black Elk died, many humans who were not shamans began to experience and to write about spiritual guidance by birds. This cultural phenomenon grew from several sources. Scientists discovered many new things about the capabilities of birds: for example, that their songs were not merely instinctive but learned, varying in birds of the same species who lived in different places.[16] Crucially, humans also learned that birds recognize and remember individual people, and that they communicate complex messages (warning of particular kinds of predators, for example) with other birds and with humans and with other animals.[17] Meanwhile, suburban neighborhoods grew, providing new environments where all kinds of birds could live in close proximity to humans.[18] Ecological consciousness, raised especially by Rachel Carson's *Silent Spring* (1962), led people to stop using the insecticide DDT, which killed birds by weakening eggs, and brought people to think about birds as their neighbors and as signs of how healthy their own air and water and food were. By the first quarter of the twenty-first century, a great age of avian guidance of humans had begun.

Modern Women Guided by Birds

For example, Sy Montgomery's *Birdology* (2010) detailed intense relations with chickens, cassowaries (enormous flightless, dinosaur-like birds of the South Pacific), hummingbirds, pigeons, parrots, falcons, and crows. Each of these birds taught her different lessons. Her book's title was borrowed from the title of a sermon by the Reverend Elaine Bomford, which Montgomery heard at the Universalist Church of West Chesterfield, New Hampshire. In the sermon, Bomford said that a birdologist "experiences the divinity of creation revealed in the birds."[19] And Montgomery had already found birds to be active teachers. She recalled that as a child, a parakeet in her parents' home had been "the first male ever to court me" when he threw up on her finger, and she understood that Jerry the parakeet was trying to feed her.[20] When she had her own home, Montgomery kept chickens and left a baby monitor in their coop, not only so that she could tell if a predator came but also so that "as I wrote my books, my words and thoughts would be bathed in the soothing sounds of the calm chicken voices in our barnyard."[21]

During the New Hampshire church service that gave Montgomery her book's title (*Birdology*), the congregation joined in reciting this passage from a book by Terry Tempest Williams, *Refuge*:

> I pray to the birds.
> I pray to the birds because I believe they will carry the messages of my heart upward. I pray to them because I believe in their existence, the way their songs begin and end each day—the invocations and benedictions of Earth. I pray to the birds because they remind me of what I love rather than what I fear. And at the end of my prayers, they teach me how to listen.[22]

Each of the thirty-six chapters of *Refuge*, a meditation on the family of the author and the Utah landscape where they lived, is named for a species of bird and for the level of the Great Salt Lake on the day when Williams encountered that bird and had the interactions with people that the chapter describes. The book ends with six pages listing types of birds associated with the lake.

Many prominent women—more women than men, at least among modern writers and thinkers—testify that birds have been their spirit guides. In "Animal Compassion," French philosopher Luce Irigaray recalled:

> The most precious and also the most mysterious aid has most often come to me from birds. The most decisive was that brought by a very little bird, probably a sparrow, who had come to perch on the sill of the balcony of my Paris apartment one December day when a storm was raging. How did that baby bird come there in winter and in such weather? I have no explanation, but he was there, a sign of life and friendship which was providential for me.

Irigaray went on to reflect that "birds are our friends. But also our guides, our scouts. Our angels in some respect." Besides accompanying lonely people, they sing without words, and unlike verbal song or logical speech, their song animates without turning flesh into abstraction. Birds call people to action. "It is not for naught that the bird appears as the spiritual assistant, even the spiritual master, in many a tradition. Most of the birds love us but want us inhabited by a subtle, divine breath."[23]

Alice Walker, the author of *The Color Purple*, took up raising chickens around 2010 and found that the act of caring for them and sitting with them brought intense memories of forgotten aspects of her childhood, when her mother had kept chickens. She eventually wrote a book of letters to the chickens, *The Chicken Chronicles* (2011), which included musings on life, death, and religion. Writing home to the chickens while on a trip to India, she wondered why no chickens appeared among the many animal gods and divine companions of Hindu temples. "I don't understand it. With your flesh and eggs, surely holy, you feed the world. Yet no one bows to you. How can this be?"[24]

Cockfighting and Learning to Face Death

But if hens were not worshipped in modern India, there is evidence of cock fighting in the archaeological remains of the ancient Indus Valley city of Harappa, which flourished before 2500 BCE.[25] Roosters or cocks, the consorts of hens, have been held in high esteem in many cultures since ancient times. At Athens, the lawgiver known as Solon (ca. 640–558 BCE) is said to have decreed that at least once a year, "all men of military age were required to assemble and watch birds fight to the utmost limit of exhaustion."[26] Although chickens have many breeds, all fighting cocks from Japan to Latin America to Africa share a genetic sequence called haplotype D.[27] Probably the domestic chicken and the custom of cockfighting were spread from southern Asia to China and west to the Levant and to Europe by passing through the Persian Empire, which touched all these places. In Persia, roosters were regarded as defenders against demons, and the zigzag crowns of kings all over the West were derived from copying the ridges of their combs. The statue of Athena in the Parthenon wore a helmet crowned with three plumes modeled from rooster combs, as were many helmets of Greece and Rome. The cock was a spirit guide for soldiers, but his guidance did not always lead to peace. The earliest detailed description of a cockfight from China dates from 517 BCE, when Confucius was thirty-four years old, and that fight resulted in a war between noble houses in the sage's native state of Lu.[28]

One of the classics of modern anthropological writing, an article by Clifford Geertz called "Deep Play: Notes on the Balinese Cockfight" (1972), stresses that the human males of Bali identify with their cocks, and that they use cockfighting as a way of enacting and understanding the status differences and conflicts of their culture. Geertz focused on individuals acting out—but not changing—their own places in the social whole.[29] On the other hand, Geertz did not deal with the many female dancers, male priests, and spectators who witnessed and participated in larger rituals surrounding the cockfight. As historian Andrew Lawler described the prelude to a cockfight in Bali in 2014: "There are prayers and a series of processions to honor the upper, middle, and lower worlds." Lawler went on to detail a religious ritual to begin the cockfight that included girls and hens as well as roosters and men:

> A clutch of a dozen young girls dressed in long gowns—premenstrual virgins, Windhu Sancaya [a Balinese anthropologist] explains—slowly begin to circle around an enormous oval of fruit and flower offerings laid in intricately shaped palm-leaf containers. The girls' stylized, birdlike dance reminds me of the female dancing spirits called *asparas* carved on the stone friezes of Cambodia's Angkor Wat temples. Attendants twirl huge black-and-white parasols. As one seated priest chants, another holds a chicken in his right hand and a bell in his left that he rings rhythmically. He takes up a short knife, slits the animal's throat, and pours the gushing blood into white bowls that are then emptied over the offerings. The two men kneel beside the mass of fruit and flowers and blood and play a game of egg toss until two eggs smash against each other and break. Everyone cheers.[30]

One of the priests explained to him that the sacrificed chickens and eggs fed the bodyguards of gods—earth demons—who were invited to the ceremony. The sacrifice protected the humans because the humans loved the chickens and the chickens belonged to the human families. Because of the spiritual relationship between chickens and humans, the chickens could stand for the humans and their deaths could protect the humans.

Clearly, there is a collective as well as individual dimension to the actions and uses of birds as spirit guides. Premodern literature and life abounds in examples. In the *Panchatantra*, a collection of Hindu teaching stories featuring animals compiled by a scholar named Vishnu Sharma about 200 BCE, but containing much older elements,[31] birds offer guidance to everyone.

When the enmity between owls and crows is discussed, for example, the crows decide (and teach human readers) that they must choose among six forms of action: to seek peace; to attack and then wage war; to retreat; to entrench or fortify; to seek the help of allies; or to employ intrigue and espionage.[32] The crows (as real crows surely would in a conflict with owls, whom they rightly see as stronger) settle on using intrigue and espionage.[33]

In a later story, a pair of doves embody the highest Hindu ideals of selflessness. A cruel hunter with the face of Yama, the god of death, traps the female of a pair of doves and puts her in a cage. Then the hunter loses his way in a terrible storm and takes refuge under a tree, where the male dove is worrying aloud about why his wife has not returned. Hungry and cold, the hunter begs anyone in the tree to help him. Meanwhile, the female dove in the cage hears her husband worrying about her, and from her cage she advises him that he must help anyone who comes to their home, because to refuse would mean he had to pay for all of the sins of his would-be guest and lose all the merits of his own good deeds. She tells him that she is imprisoned because of her own past actions, and he should "think of religion and welcome him according to our traditions." So the male dove welcomes the hunter, who begs for relief from the cold, because the storm has ceased but left him wet and cold in the night.

Flying off, the male retrieves a live coal and sets it into a pile of dry leaves to start a fire. But he regrets having no food to give the hunter, and he has an idea: "With joy in his heart, the pious bird flew once round the fire and then entered it, as if it had been his own nest." His sacrifice moves the hunter to see the error of his ways and to fear karmic punishment for taking lives, so he resolves to "give up all my pleasures and lead a life of discipline." He throws away his net and breaks open the cage that held the female dove.

Then she sees what her husband has done and wails, "What is the good of living without you? Widowhood results in loss of pride, loss of respect in the household and loss of authority over servants." She immediately flies into the same fire that had killed the male. Shortly after, she sees him exalted into the form of a god, "riding a chariot and wearing costly ornaments." He praises her for following him into the fire, and she also gains a divine form. Meanwhile, the hunter lives the life of a hermit in the forest until his mind becomes free of all desires. One day he sees a forest fire, walks into it, and also becomes divine. These doves exemplified, and taught a human how to recognize and practice, the Hindu idea of karma and the Hindu goal of obtaining release from rebirth through the denial of self.

Bird Models of Buddhist and Taoist Enlightenment

Centuries before Vishnu Sharma compiled the *Panchatantra*, the teachings of the Buddha (563–483 BCE) collected in verses 91–93 of the *Dhammapada* had already used birds as models of enlightenment:

> 91 Those who have high thoughts are ever striving: they are not happy to remain in the same place. Like swans that leave their lake and rise into the air, they leave their home for a higher home.

> 92 Who can trace the path of those who know the right food of life and, rejecting over-abundance, soar in the sky of liberation, the infinite Void without beginning? Their course is as hard to follow as that of the birds in the air.

> 93 Who can trace the invisible path of the man who soars in the sky of liberation, the infinite Void without beginning, whose passions are peace, and over whom pleasures have no power? His path is as difficult to trace as that of the birds in the air.[34]

About 360 BCE in China, the Taoist sage Zhuangzi (Chuang Tzu) compared the human who follows the Tao, the great Way that runs through all things to a legendary creature, which is first a fish in the Northern Sea called the Kun, hundreds of miles long. The Kun ("Kun" means "water") leaves the ocean for the air as the Peng bird, with wings hundreds of miles wide. Looking down, the Peng (which means "beautiful") sees both ocean and sky as "the same azure expanse,"[35] and the Peng then flies to the Southern Sea, "the heavenly pond." As the contemporary Taoist Derek Lin concluded in 2000 CE, the fish represents the spirit living blindly, and the bird represents the spirit that has seen the true oneness of the world and become free from limitations.[36]

Buddhism came slowly to Tibet, where the isolation caused by mountainous topography and the ferocity of the native Bon religion resisted the Buddha's dharma.[37] Even after a first Buddhist monastery in Tibet was established in 787 CE, repression by kings disrupted any organized Buddhist life until after 1000. By the 1400s, however, Tibet became the most Buddhist nation on earth, with monks dominating politics and culture.

Sometime in the 1600s, an anonymous Tibetan author wrote *The Buddha's Law among the Birds*. Its premise was that Avalokitesvara, the incarnation of the Buddha (a bodhisattva, one who has attained enlightenment but reincarnates to help others) who now lives as the Dalai Lama, once became a cuckoo and sat under a tree in Tibet "for many years day and night, immobile and in perfect trance."[38] A parrot approached the cuckoo offering seeds, and the cuckoo was then roused from his trance and told the parrot to gather all the other birds to hear his teaching. When they had gathered—Indian birds led by the peacock and Tibetan birds by the vulture—the cuckoo began to speak, punctuating each line with the exclamation, "Koo!"

> Reflect in earnest on impermanence and death, — Koo!
> Commit in no way any evil deed, — Koo!
> ....
> The objects of activities are altogether vain, — Koo!
> Put your inmost minds into a state of non-action, — Koo!
> ....
> For seven days meditate on these precepts, — Koo!
> And then return to me, — Koo![39]

When they gathered again after seven days, many birds, including the vulture, the great crane, the golden goose, the wagtail, the ruddy sheldrake, the white grouse, the pigeon, the dove, the jackdaw, the owl, the cock, the lark, the lagopus (a smaller grouse, often called a ptarmigan), the Chinese thrush, the peacock, the kestrel, and the parrot, spoke of the lack of permanence and satisfaction to be found in worldly activities. Cuckoo summed up the findings of their meditation and sent them to spread the teachings of Buddhism, with a plan to gather again in a year. At that meeting, they each promised some improvement of behavior that corresponded with their nature:

> The King Vulture then promised not to kill another living being. The White Grouse, the heavenly bird, promised henceforth to live only in mountain ranges, never to descend into the valleys. The Goose promised to seek his food only from the waters and the swamps. The Indian Kestrel promised to spend but one hour a day on food. The Pigeon promised to make his home in the hollow of a rock-cavern, and to respect the Stupas and the shrines [many were white with pigeon dung]. The Lark, one of the smaller birds, promised to offer worship to the Three Treasures [the Buddha; the dharma, or teaching; and the sangha, or community] with melodious song. The Cock, the domestic bird, promised no more to violate the dawn. The

Hoopoe promised to make the caves his winter home [hoopoe nests are notoriously smelly]. And all the birds, both large and small, promised not to gather food above their daily needs.

Only the Raven and the Kite, from habitual avarice, would make no promises at all.[40]

Cuckoo sang happily and urged all the others to sing and to dance, which they did for a day. Then he returned to India, and all the other birds to their own homes.

Sufism and Attar's *Conference of the Birds*

As Islam expanded from Arab lands into Asia in the 700s CE, it developed a mystical side among groups called Sufis, from the word "white" that designated the plain white robes they wore, as well as their hope for pure and unmediated absorption into God. Inspired by Sufism, a poet born in Iran in 1145 and named Abu Hamid bin Abu Bakr Ibrahim, who wrote under the name of Attar (or "the pharmacist"), wrote *The Conference of the Birds*. In this long set of poems (4,724 Persian lines), many kinds of birds sought their legendary king, Simorgh, who had the attributes of God.

The leader of Attar's birds is the hoopoe (*Upupa epops*), a very distinctive bird with black-and-white striped wings, a long thin beak, and a magnificent crest of orange feathers edged in black that can be laid back or fanned out. Famed as the companion of Solomon who was said in the Koran to have told Solomon about the Queen of Sheba (Surah 27:20–28), the hoopoe is now the national bird of Israel. When the hoopoe finds the other birds seeking a leader, the hoopoe introduces himself as "the Messenger Bird for the Visible and the Invisible" who can bring them to Simorgh.[41]

Although the birds have gathered to seek their king, Hoopoe's warning about how long and difficult the journey will be leads them to make excuses, each of which reveals the spirit of the bird who offers the excuse. Nightingale says that "the mysteries of love begin and end with me," that "I repeat love's teachings each night," and that he himself loves a rose he could not bear to leave.[42] The parrot wants "to sit tight in a corner of my cage."[43] The duck says, "Water is my life. How can I step away from it and find my way through deserts and valleys?"[44] The falcon boasts that he prefers to sit "on the king's forearm" and win his favor; the heron doesn't want to leave the sea; the goldfinch is too weak for such a long journey.[45] One by one, the peacock and the partridge, the owl and osprey, explain why they cannot go. Each bird is answered with a rebuke and a story about the shortcomings of their favorite things by Hoopoe, who praises the great Simorgh as far more valuable than anything else. Hoopoe's description of Simorgh owes something to the great Peng bird of Taoist legend. He says that "when that Great Beauty soared in full glory over China / A feather from its plumage swung to the ground / and triggered a titanic tumult in every land." Set into a Chinese museum, that feather inspired "all of science and art," which come from China.[46]

So convincing is Hoopoe that a hundred thousand birds set off on the journey, but they are quickly frightened by "the opening to the abyss of the Path."[47] In order to reach Simorgh, the birds have to abandon themselves completely. To console his followers, Hoopoe tells many stories about people who have given up all for love, among them referring to the story of Majnun and Layla that became a song of the 1970s by Eric Clapton. They have to pass through seven valleys: the valleys of the quest, of love, of knowledge, of detachment, of unity, of wonderment, and of poverty and annihilation. The journey takes years, and almost every bird dies. Some drown, some die of thirst, some are eaten by tigers and lions, and some starve. "Some were charmed by marvels and became distracted. / Others yielded to the sirens' songs and stayed behind." Of the hundred thousand who began, "Only thirty arrived at the door of the Great Abode."[48]

A door opens, and a herald of Simorgh emerges and tries to drive them away, but they insist, comparing their devotion to that of Majnun for Layla and of a moth to a flame. Finally they are admitted, and each is given a parchment scroll and told to read it from beginning to end. When they begin to read, they find that everything in their lives is on the scrolls, and that they have betrayed and abused themselves and others many times. But then, just as they see themselves as worth nothing, "The Sun of Proximity poured its rays on them and endowed them with new life."[49] The face of Simorgh is revealed to them in a reflection, and when they look into that reflection they see themselves, and notice for the first time that the name Simorgh is made of two words, *si* and *morgh*, which mean "thirty birds" in Farsi. A message comes to them wordlessly: "The valleys you traversed were in Me, the bravery you displayed was Mine." Then "the birds surrendered themselves to the Great One / and became utterly nothing. / Silence fell as both the pilgrims and their leader / became one with the Way."[50] Attar's spiritual epic used the differences between birds to teach that whatever unique attachments, weaknesses, and even sins block the path, the greatness of God overcomes all and unites all spirits.

Saint Francis of Assisi: Guidance by Birds and Guidance of Birds

The poet Attar died in Iran in 1221, at the same moment when Saint Francis of Assisi was being inspired by birds in Italy, and five years before Francis died. The *Little Flowers*, or legends of Francis, and the early biographies by Thomas of Celano and Saint Bonaventure recount several kinds of interactions. According to many sources, Francis was greeted and encouraged by birds, and he also sang with them, befriended them, set them free from traps, preached to them, urged them to be silent and to sing, praised them, and received praise from them (Figure 5.2).

Figure 5.2 One of the best-known stories of St. Francis of Assisi (1181–1226) involves preaching to the birds, who obeyed him by remaining quiet and by singing. The Renaissance painter Giotto depicted the miracle, including at least twelve bird species.
Lanmas / Alamy Stock Picture.

To start with simple inspiration: toward the end of his life, just before receiving the stigmata (the marks of Christ's crucifixion) on his body, Francis and a few followers went to the peak of Mount La Verna for a retreat. Francis sat under an oak tree to rest, and birds took note:

> A great number of all kinds of birds came flying down to him with joyful songs, and twittering and fluttering their wings. And they surrounded St. Francis in such a way that some of them settled on his head and others on his shoulders and others on his knees, and still others on his arms and lap and on his hands and around his feet. They all showed great joy by their tuneful singing and happy movements, as if they were rejoicing at his coming and inviting and persuading him to stay there. . . . St. Francis rejoiced in spirit and said to [his companions] "My dear Brothers, I believe it is pleasing to Our Lord Jesus Christ that we accept a Place and live a while on this solitary mountain, since our little brothers and sisters the birds show such joy over our coming."[51]

According to Edward A. Armstrong, a widely published writer both on birds and on Saint Francis, the model for this story probably came to Italy from Ireland, where crowds of welcoming birds were associated with the ancient folk hero Cú Chúlainn. Irish monks worked as missionaries in Europe centuries before Saint Francis, and the stories about Saint Columban (543–615), who founded an abbey at Bobbio less than two hundred miles from Assisi, describe wild birds and small animals perching on that saint and being fondled by him. Another Irish saint, Kevin (Coemghen, 498–618), was said to have stood so long with his arms outstretched in prayer that blackbirds nested in his hands. Although this caused the saint great pain, he bore the pain for six weeks until the eggs laid in the nest were hatched.[52] This suggests another, less joyful connection between birds and the wounds in hands called stigmata, though Armstrong does not make that connection.

As Armstrong notes, Francis was a lover of music, a singer and a friend of singers. The modern scholar finds plausibility in a story that the saint once sang a duet, an antiphonal music competition, with a nightingale:

> Once when Saint Francis was about to eat with Brother Leo he was greatly delighted to hear a nightingale singing. So he suggested to his companion that they should also sing praise to God alternatively with the bird. While Leo was pleading that he was no singer, Francis lifted up his voice and,

phrase by phrase, sang his duet with the nightingale. Thus they continued from Vespers to Lauds [from evening till morning] until the Saint had to admit himself beaten by the bird. Thereupon the nightingale flew on to his hand, where he praised it to the skies and fed it. Then he gave it his blessing and it flew away.[53]

Pointing out that human hunter-gatherers imitate birds and engage with them in calls and responses—as we saw in Chapter 3, with regard to the Hadza of East Africa and the honeyguide birds—Armstrong claims to have had a similar experience, whistling back and forth with a nightingale in Assisi.[54]

On two occasions, individual birds were said to have chosen Francis, in the way that animal spirit guides are often said to choose humans. Saint Bonaventure wrote that when Francis was recovering from an illness at Siena, a nobleman sent him a pheasant that had been caught alive. After the bird saw Francis and heard his voice, he refused to leave, even when taken outside the friary to the vineyard and set free. Eventually, the other friars gave the pheasant to a doctor who often came to see Francis, but the bird then refused to eat until he was returned to the saint. As Thomas of Celano put it, "As soon as the pheasant was put upon the ground, it saw its father, and putting off all grief, it began to eat with joy, and gave every sign of being delighted."[55] Later, when Francis was living on the mountain where he received the stigmata, a falcon nesting there "became a great friend of his and woke him every night with its song just at the time he used to rise to say the office." Francis appreciated that the bird would not allow him to be lazy. But the bird did not act automatically: when it saw that "he needed a longer rest than usual, the falcon had pity on him and did not wake him up so early." Instead of calling at Lauds, which take place at three in the morning, it would let Francis sleep until dawn before calling.[56]

According to the stories in the *Little Flowers*, Saint Francis once met a boy in Siena who had trapped several doves and was carrying them to the market to sell them. He said, "Good boy, please give me those doves so that such innocent birds, which in Holy Scripture are symbols of pure, humble, and faithful souls, will not fall into the hands of cruel men who will kill them."[57]

Inspired by God, the boy gave the doves to Francis, who spoke to them: "Sister Doves, why did you let yourselves be caught? I want to rescue you from death and make nests for you where you can . . . fulfill the Creator's commandment to multiply." Francis made the nests, and the doves laid their eggs, responding as if they were chickens who had "always been raised by the friars." To the boy, Francis prophesied that he would become a friar. "So St. Francis not only obtained comfort for those little birds in this life but also the joys of eternal life for that youth."[58]

No tale of Francis and birds is as well known as the Sermon to the Birds. Both early biographers describe Francis "journeying through the valley of Spoleto," in central Umbria, northeast of Rome and southwest of Florence, when he "came to a spot near Bevagna where a great number of birds of different sorts were gathered together." Thomas names some of the birds as doves, crows, and jackdaws (a smaller cousin of the crow). According to Thomas, Francis "left his companions in the road and ran eagerly toward the birds." What ensued struck Francis and his brothers as surprising:

> But, not a little surprised that the birds did not rise in flight, as they usually do, he was filled with great joy and humbly begged them to listen to the word of God. Among the many things he said to them were these words: "My brothers, birds, you should praise your Creator very much and always love him; he gave you feathers to clothe you, wings so that you can fly, and whatever else was necessary for you. God has made you noble among his creatures, and he gave you a home in the purity of the air; though you neither sow nor reap, he nevertheless protects and governs you without any solicitude on your part." At these words... the birds, rejoicing in a wonderful way, according to their nature, began to stretch out their necks, extend their wings, open their mouths and gaze at him. And Francis, passing through their midst, went on his way and returned, touching their heads and bodies with his tunic. Finally he blessed them, and then, after he had made the sign of the cross over them, he gave them permission to fly away to some other place.[59]

Walking again with his fellow friars, Francis "began to blame himself for negligence in not having preached to the birds before, seeing that they had listened to the word of God with such great reverence." After that, according to Thomas, "He solicitously admonished all birds, all animals and reptiles, and even creatures that have no feeling, to praise and love the Creator, for... he saw their obedience by personal experience."[60]

The affinity of Saint Francis with birds extended to the ability to silence birds by command and then to permit them to sing. According to Saint

Bonaventure, Francis and another friar were walking through marshes near Venice when "they came upon a huge flock of birds, singing among the reeds." Francis decided to join the birds:

> The saint said to his companion, "Our sisters the birds are praising their Creator. We will go in among them and sing God's praise, chanting the divine office." When they had gone into their midst, the birds stirred not from the spot, and when, by reason of their twittering, they could not hear each other in reciting the Hours, the holy man turned unto the birds, saying, "My sisters, stop singing until we have given God the praise to which he has a right." The birds were silent immediately and remained that way until Francis gave them permission to sing again, after they had taken plenty of time to say the office and had finished their praises. Then the birds began again, as usual.[61]

Stories of Francis preaching to birds became widespread and important during the saint's lifetime. According to a contemporary English Benedictine monk, Roger of Wendover (d. 1236), the Franciscan order owed its foundation partly to this power. Roger wrote that in 1209, when Francis first approached Pope Innocent III in Rome and asked for permission to preach and to recruit brothers, the pope famously rejected him because of his dirty brown robe and told him he was fit only to work with pigs. Then Francis left Rome and gathered "crows, kites, magpies and many other fowls" that were eating carrion just outside the city and made them stop and hear his sermon. People "rushed to see this strange sight . . . and joyfully escorted Francis back. . . . From that time his fame spread throughout Italy."[62]

On the other hand, the traditions about Saint Francis retain some sense of humility about his power over nature. A story in the Franciscan archives says that on another walk with Brother Masseo, who had been with Francis when he preached to the birds near Spoleto, the saint was less successful.

> Rapt in devotion, Francis once found by the roadside a large flock of birds, to whom he turned aside to preach. . . . But when the birds saw him approaching they all flew away. . . . Then he came back and began to accuse himself most bitterly, saying: "What effrontery you have, you impudent son of Pietro Bernadone"—and this because he had expected irrational creatures to obey him as if he, and not God, were their Creator.

When Francis died in 1226 at the age of forty-five, two years after receiving the stigmata, his passing was recognized by the bird he called his favorite, the lark.[63] According to the *Speculum Perfectionis* (*Mirror of Perfection*), perhaps the earliest source of written stories about Francis, "Above all birds he loved the little lark, known in the language of the country as *lodola capellata* (the hooded lark)." Francis used this lark's behavior, its song, and its color as examples for his brother friars. The *Speculum* quotes the saint:

> Sister lark has a hood like a Religious and is a humble bird, for she walks contentedly along the road to find grain, and even if she finds it among rubbish, she pecks it out and eats it. As she flies she praises God very sweetly, like good Religious who despise earthly things, whose minds are set on the things of heaven, and whose constant purpose is to praise God. Her plumage resembles the earth, and she sets an example to Religious not to wear fine and gaudy clothing, but cloth of a humble price and colour, just as earth is inferior to the other elements.[64]

The *Speculum* goes on to say that on the night when Francis died, after the evening prayer was said, "A great flight of larks assembled above the roof of the house where he lay." Although larks do not usually fly so late, "They circled around it in the form of a wheel, singing sweetly as they flew and seeming to praise God."[65]

Olivier Messiaen, Bird Music, and the limits of Human Appropriation

Olivier Messiaen (1908–1992) wrote one opera, *Saint François d'Assise*, which stretches to five hours in which almost all of the instrumental music is based on birds. Messiaen was a musical prodigy who taught himself the piano at eight and entered the Paris Conservatory at ten.[66] He transcribed birdsongs into musical notation as a teenager, wrote his first piece based on a bird, a two-minute piano prelude called *La Colombe* (*The Dove*) at twenty, and produced a three-hour *Catalogue des Oiseaux* (*Catalogue of Birds*) that uses solo piano to evoke seventy-seven different birds in thirteen regions of France when he was fifty. At age seventy-five, he completed, helped to stage, and witnessed the first performance of *Saint François d'Assise*.

A crucial moment in Messiaen's development was the nine months he spent as a prisoner of war, captured by the Germans on June 20, 1940, and released on May 10, 1941.[67] He was held at the border between Germany and Poland through the winter, one of thirty thousand French soldiers in the camp. Birdsong consoled him, and he was turning away from classical music, and even from the moderns, such as Debussy and Stravinsky, who had moved him in his youth. Birds helped him to survive and even to write new music in the camp. His *Quartet for the End of Time*, a piece in eight movements for piano, clarinet, violin, and cello, began with a clarinet solo inspired by a blackbird and a violin solo inspired by a nightingale, followed by other birds in a dawn chorus. Commenting in a preface to the score on the third movement, "Abîme des Oiseaux" or "Abyss of Birds," for solo clarinet, Messiaen wrote: "The Abyss is Time, with Its sadnesses and tediums. The birds are the opposite of Time; they are our desire for light, for stars, for rainbows and for jubilant outpourings of song!" For Messiaen, the end of time was not disaster but resurrection, eternal love after apocalypse. The quartet was performed in the camp for the first time, and the performance helped convince the camp commander (a music lover and anti-Nazi) to release the composer and two other members of the quartet.

Messiaen became a teacher at the Paris Conservatory after his release, but he was increasingly convinced that birds were the only true musicians:

> In my hours of gloom, when I am suddenly aware of my own futility, when every musical idiom—classical, oriental, ancient, modern, and ultramodern—appears to me as no more than admirable painstaking experimentation without any ultimate justification, what is left for me but to seek out the true, lost face of music somewhere off in the forest, in the fields, in the mountains or on the seashore, among the birds.[68]

Always a serious Catholic believer, Messiaen had written many religious works. In his opera on Saint Francis, he combined his religious vision and his increasing concentration on composing with birdsong. Here he used songs from forty-four different species, thirty species in the Sermon to the Birds alone, and many of these birds are used more than once. Seeking more striking songs to suggest holiness, the composer traveled to New Caledonia, a French colony in the South Pacific, to hear and to transcribe songs of such species as the gerygone (which underlie the music of an angel in the opera), the superb lyrebird, and the New Caledonian friarbird.

Messiaen made scene 6 of act 2, the Sermon to the Birds, the emotional turning point of the three-act opera. It comes after Francis has kissed and healed a leper, overcoming his extreme fear and distaste, then nearly died from the beauty of a visiting angel's music, and just before he receives the stigmata, dies, and returns to life. Where the early biographies of Saint Francis made the sermon a homely little miracle, involving doves and crows and a few lines of speech, the opera presents the sermon as a forty-minute exploration of the glories of the birds and the lessons they have for Francis and for his order of friars. Individual birds sing and are praised in turn: first the dove, who is said to have accompanied one of the brothers, then the winter wren, the European robin, and the Eurasian blackcap. Others sing without being named in the libretto, although their identities have been cataloged in Messiaen scholarship.[69] In an emotional climax not found in any lives of Saint Francis, the Francis of the opera praises an island where the leaves are red and the ocean green. He praises birds like "Brother Eopsaltria whose whistle tumbles from high to low," "Brother Philemon who moves his rainbow casque like jewels in twilight," and "Sister Gerygone who interrupts time with her staccato." When Brother Masseo, who accompanies Francis during this scene as he did in medieval accounts of the Sermon to the Birds, says he has never heard such birds "in our Umbria," Francis answers that he has not physically heard those birds either, but "they sang in my dream."

Following the medieval accounts, Francis then tells the birds to praise God for all he has given them, such as the air and clouds, sun and wind, "moss for your nests." The list of gifts is more extensive in the opera than in the lives of Francis by Celano or Bonaventure. As in the lives, the sermon ends with Francis blessing the birds with a sign of the cross, and they fly away.

But Messiaen again finds more lessons in the birds than his medieval sources. Brother Masseo notes that the birds flew away in four directions, and Francis says that they are the directions of the cross. "Will our announcement of the Cross also spread everywhere?" Masseo asks, and Francis says yes. Then the saint uses the birds as example:

> But do not forget my sheep, the wonderful example that these birds give us: they own nothing, and God feeds them. If we put our faith for caring for our lives in divine providence, if we look for the kingdom and its justice, then everything else will be bestowed on us as a matter of course.

A wild explosion of birdsong follows, and the scene and the act end.

Messiaen did not try to duplicate or to imitate birds in his music. Instead, he used birdsongs as models to compose music for the piano, the clarinet, the violin, and other human instruments, including many forms of percussion. His music poses great difficulties for performers and its degree of abstraction and lack of melody challenge audiences, but he is generally acknowledged as a master, and his long works are still regularly performed. In a sense, Messiaen's work is the logical extension of Vivaldi's *Il Gardellino* (*The Goldfinch*) flute concerto of 1729, a piece of about twelve minutes modeled on the European goldfinch's song.[70] Mozart's Piano Concerto in G Major no. 17 (1784) is sometimes said to have been partially written by his pet starling, and Beethoven used birdsong in Symphony no. 6.

On the other hand, the increasing sophistication of recording equipment and of electronic tools for slowing, altering, and mixing recordings of birds has led many composers to go beyond Messiaen and to integrate birdsong directly into their music. In *The Pines of Rome* (1924), Ottarino Respighi called for a recording of a nightingale to be played in the third movement. A few more recent examples are Bernard Fort (b. 1954), David Lumsdaine (b. 1931), and Ron Nagorcka (b. 1948), but there are many more.[71] Perhaps because Australia and surrounding areas in the South Pacific are so replete with birds that have elaborate songs, most of the composers using recorded birds in their music are Australian. Whether arrangements of recordings of birds deserve to be called music is debated, however, and unlike Messiaen's works, they have not found large audiences. David Rothenberg, a professor of philosophy at the New Jersey Institute of Technology who is also a jazz clarinetist and composer, has sought a third way by playing his clarinet with birds, eliciting responses from them, and recording those sessions.[72]

Starting with hunter-gatherers and shamans working with predatory birds tens of thousands of years ago, birds and humans have guided each other. In ancient cockfights, Hindu and Taoist legends, and Buddhist teaching tales, humans found models for themselves among birds. The Bible presents the Holy Spirit of God as a bird. Medieval mystics, Attar among Muslims and Saint Francis among Christians, related to birds as spiritual equals. For Carl Jung, one of the founders of modern psychology, a bird led to the depths of the soul. Contemporary musicians and writers, from Olivier Messiaen and others to Luce Irigaray, Terry Tempest Williams, and Alice Walker, testify that birds have given them spiritual truths and power. But there is also a limit and a dark side to the spiritual relationship of birds and humans, a story of extinctions and apocalypse told in the next chapter.

Notes

1. Mark I. Wallace, "The Wild Bird Who Heals: Recovering the Spirit in Nature," *Theology Today* 50, no. 1 (April 1993): 16.
2. James W. Perkinson, "Protecting Water in the Anthropocene: River Spirits and Political Struggles in Detroit, Standing Rock, and the Bible," *Cross Currents* 66, no. 4 (December 2016): 471.
3. Courtney Humphries, *Superdove: How the Pigeon Took Manhattan . . . and the World* (New York: HarperCollins, 2008), 10.
4. Carl Jung, *Memories, Dreams, Reflections* (New York: Vintage Books, 1961), 171–172.
5. Helen Macdonald, *Falcon* (London: Reaktion Books, 2016), 10.
6. Helen Macdonald, *H Is for Hawk* (New York: Grove Press, 2014), 5.
7. Macdonald, *H Is for Hawk*, 85.
8. Macdonald, *H Is for Hawk*, 196.
9. Macdonald, *H Is for Hawk*, 235.
10. Macdonald, *H Is for Hawk*, 296.
11. Sy Montgomery, *Birdology: Adventures with a Pack of Hens, a Peck of Pigeons, Cantankerous Crows, Fierce Falcons, Hip Hop Parrots, Baby Hummingbirds, and One Murderously Big Living Dinosaur* (New York: Free Press, 2010), 134.
12. Montgomery, *Birdology*, 124.
13. Montgomery, *Birdology*, 125.
14. John G. Neihardt, *Black Elk Speaks: Being the Life Story of a Holy Man of the Oglala Sioux* (Lincoln: University of Nebraska Press, 1979), 242.
15. Neihardt, *Black Elk Speaks*, 245.
16. Peter Marler, the British-born scientist credited with doing this work in the 1950s, first in England and then in the United States, died at eighty-six years of age in 2014. See his obituary in *The Telegraph*, August 4, 2014, http://www.telegraph.co.uk/news/obituaries/11011006/Peter-Marler-obituary.html (January 12, 2018).
17. Jon Young, *What the Robin Knows: How Birds Reveal the Secrets of the Natural World* (Boston: Houghton Mifflin, 2012).
18. John M. Marzluff, *Welcome to Subirdia: Sharing Our Neighborhoods with Wrens, Robins, Woodpeckers, and Other Wildlife* (New Haven: Yale University Press, 2014).
19. Montgomery, *Birdology*, 6.
20. Montgomery, *Birdology*, 1.
21. Montgomery, *Birdology*, 33.
22. Terry Tempest Williams, *Refuge: An Unnatural History of Family and Place* (New York: Vintage Books, 1992), 149.
23. Luce Irigaray, "Animal Compassion," in *Animal Philosophy: Essential Readings in Continental Thought*, ed. Matthew Calarco and Peter Atterton (London: Continuum, 2004), 197.

24. Alice Walker, *The Chicken Chronicles: Sitting with the Angels Who Have Returned with My Memories. Glorious, Rufus, Gertrude Stein, Splendor, Hortensia, Agnes of God, The Gladyses, & Babe. A memoir* (New York: New Press, 2011).
25. Andrew Lawler, *Why Did the Chicken Cross the World? The Epic Saga of the Bird That Powers Civilization* (New York: Atria Books, 2014), 34.
26. Jo-Ann Shelton, "Beastly Spectacles in the Ancient Mediterranean World," in *A Cultural History of Animals in Antiquity*, ed. Linda Kopf (Oxford: Berg, 2007), 104.
27. Lawler, *Why Did the Chicken Cross*, 84.
28. Robert Joe Cutter, *The Brush and the Spur: Chinese Culture and the Cockfight* (Hong Kong: Chinese University Press, 1989), 10–15.
29. Clifford Geertz, "Deep Play: Notes on the Balinese Cockfight," *Daedalus* 134, no. 4 (Fall 2005): 79.
30. Lawler, *Why Did the Chicken Cross*, 173–174.
31. Pandit Vishnu Sharma, *Panchatantra*, trans. G. L. Chandiramani (New Delhi: Rupa Publications, 1991), v.
32. Sharma, *Panchatantra*, 125.
33. Sharma, *Panchatantra*, 128.
34. *The Dhammapada: The Path of Perfection*, trans. Juan Mascaro (London: Penguin Books, 1973), 48.
35. Tsai Chih Chung, *The Tao of Zhuangzi: The Harmony of Nature*, trans. Brian Bruya (New York: Doubleday, 1997), chap. 1, p. 26.
36. Derek Lin, "Tao Living: The Giant Peng Bird," http://www.truetao.org/living/2000/200011.him (accessed January 17, 2018).
37. John Snelling, *The Buddhist Handbook* (Rochester, VT: Inner Traditions, 1991), 168.
38. *The Buddha's Law among the Birds*, trans. Edward Conze (Oxford: Bruno Cassirer, 1955), 17.
39. *Buddha's Law*, 20.
40. *Buddha's Law*, 45.
41. Attar, *The Conference of the Birds*, trans. Sholeh Wolpé (New York: Norton, 2017), 41.
42. Attar, *Conference of the Birds*, 47–49.
43. Attar, *Conference of the Birds*, 52.
44. Attar, *Conference of the Birds*, 56.
45. Attar, *Conference of the Birds*, 64–67, 71.
46. Attar, *Conference of the Birds*, 46.
47. Attar, *Conference of the Birds*, 109.
48. Attar, *Conference of the Birds*, 324.
49. Attar, *Conference of the Birds*, 330.
50. Attar, *Conference of the Birds*, 333.
51. *Little Flowers of St. Francis, Part Two*, trans. Raphael Brown, in *St. Francis of Assisi: Writings and Early Biographies: English Omnibus of the Sources for the Life of St. Francis*, ed. Marion A. Habig (Chicago: Franciscan Herald Press, 1983), 1435–1436.
52. Edward A. Armstrong, *Saint Francis: Nature Mystic* (Berkeley: University of California Press, 1973), 44–47.
53. Armstrong, *Saint Francis*, 1881–1882. From John R. H. Moorman, ed. and trans., *A New Fioretti: A Collection of Early Stories about Saint Francis of Assisi* (London, 1809).

54. Armstrong, *Saint Francis*, 68–70.
55. Armstrong, *Saint Francis*, 696. From Saint Bonaventure, *Major Life of St. Francis*, trans. Brenan Fahy, chap. 8.10.
56. Armstrong, *Saint Francis*, 696.
57. *Little Flowers*, 1352.
58. *Little Flowers*, 1352.
59. *Little Flowers*, 277–278. From Thomas of Celano *First Life of St. Francis*, chap. 21.58.
60. *Little Flowers*, 278.
61. *Little Flowers*, 695. From Saint Bonaventure, *Major Life of St. Francis*, trans. Brenan Fahy, chap. 8.9.
62. Armstrong, *Saint Francis*, 62–63.
63. Armstrong, *Saint Francis*, 1882–1883. From John R. H. Moorman, editor and translator, *A New Fioretti: A Collection of Early Stories about Saint Francis of Assisi* (London, 1809).
64. Armstrong, *Saint Francis*, 1252. From *The Mirror of Perfection*, translated by Leo Sherley-Price, chap. 113.
65. Armstrong, *Saint Francis*, 1252.
66. Christopher Dingle, *The Life of Messiaen* (Cambridge: Cambridge University Press, 2007), 6–10.
67. Dingle, *The Life of Messiaen*, 68–74.
68. Olivier Messiaen, quoted in David Rothenberg, *Why Birds Sing: A Journey through the Mystery of Bird Song* (New York: Basic Books, 2005)
69. Robert Fallon, "A Catalogue of Messiaen's Birds," in *Messiaen Perspectives 2: Techniques, Influence and Reception*, ed. Christopher Dingle and Robert Fallon (Surrey, UK: Ashgate, 2013), 113–146.
70. BirdNote, "Vivaldi's Goldfinch," October 5, 2015, http://www.audubon.org/news/vivaldis-goldfinch (accessed January 21, 2018).
71. Hollis Taylor, "Composers' Appropriation of Pied Butcherbird Song," *Journal of Music Research Online*, 2011, https://www.hollistaylor.com/ewExternalFiles/Composers%20appropriation.pdf (accessed January 21, 2018).
72. Rothenberg, *Why Birds Sing*, 209–227.

6
Extinctions and Apocalyptic Birds

Scientists estimate that during the last five centuries, more than 150 species of birds have become extinct because of human actions.[1] This chapter surveys expressions of the belief (and the real possibility) that birds and humans are caught in an apocalyptic spiral. From the Bible to *Silent Spring* and from Hitchcock's *The Birds* to contemporary forecasts of climate change, religions and cultures have depicted birds and humans plunging together toward death (Figure 6.1). Often these images have reflected unfortunate realities.

Death by Human Misappropriation of Birds

Deadly misappropriations of birds sometimes accompany the role of birds as spirit guides for humans. Julie Zickefoose, author of *The Bluebird Effect: Uncommon Bonds with Common Birds* (2012), is a bird rehabilitator who has been praised for her "legendary" ear for birdsong.[2] Zickefoose's book consists of stories of helping birds to heal and learning from them. After raising a motherless hummingbird, releasing the bird, and having the bird return to hover in front of her nose and land on her finger, she reflects:

> I cannot describe how it feels to have a free-living, essentially wild hummingbird seek me out for companionship. I search for an answer to this delightful conundrum. I decide that, lacking a mother, she simply needs to make contact with someone she knows. And somehow, having a person speak lovingly to her fills that need. Perhaps she made the connection between food and me during her confinement in the tent, and she still associates me with that form of comfort and fulfillment. Whatever is going on, I know that I will never be through learning about how birds' minds work, even the tiniest ones.[3]

Zickefoose respects and admires all the birds she rehabilitates. Mourning doves, she writes, are "not nearly as dumb as they look."[4] Watching a female bluebird

Figure 6.1 Vultures over Pennsylvania suggest apocalypse in the era of saturation bombing. Andrew Wyeth, *Turkey Buzzards Soaring*, about 1942-50, Tempera on Masonite. Shelburne Museum.

Photograph: Photo by Author, © 2023 Wyeth Foundation for American Art / Artists Rights Society (ARS), New York

find a new partner on the same afternoon when her mate, a bird Zickefoose rehabilitated seven years before, was carried off by a hawk, Zickefoose mourns for the missing male but takes a lesson: "I should be more like her, I think, willing to fast-forward to the next act."[5] Tree swallows, starlings, chickadees, barn swallows, Carolina wrens, ospreys, titmice, rose-breasted grosbeaks, scarlet tanagers, phoebes, piping plovers, least terns, grouse, white-throated sparrows, Savannah sparrows, orchard orioles, red-tailed hawks, cranes, northern cardinals, and turkey vultures (vultures are her totem birds, who seek her out)—all these birds teach Zickefoose as she heals them.

But her closest bond with a bird was ultimately negative. In 1989, "The first time my biological clock rang," Zickefoose bought a parrot because she wanted "something young and helpless to care for."[6] Twenty-three years later, she wrote, "Parrots can be delightful. But they are raunchy, awful pets."[7] Her parrot for a long while bit the man who became her husband, and tried to drive her older child out of the home after she had a second baby (the parrot seemed to regard Zickefoose as his mate, and the first child as their first brood). She wondered whether the parrot would outlive her, and whether she would be forced to pass the bird down to one of the children. "I stay away from pet stores, because I can't bear to see the bright, dark eyes of the latest crop of hand-fed nestlings, knowing the life of misunderstanding, alienation, and loneliness most of them will face once they grow up to be parrots." She could not release her own bird—"old, flightless, and half-naked [from nervously plucking his own feathers, a common behavior in captive animals] as he is—to the Peruvian Amazon," she reflected. Nor did she "have the forbearance to purchase another macaw to keep him company—logarithmically increasing the mess and noise of one."[8]

Amazingly, given the detailed and intimate relations between Zickefoose and the parrot she called "Charlie," the bird gave the woman a final surprise. As the book went to press, the macaw went into two months of nesting frenzy, tearing up newspapers and building mounds in corners. Then she turned out to be a female and spent hours passing a huge egg. "I held my little hen macaw in my arms past midnight, then, before dawn, rushed her to an avian veterinarian three hours distant."[9] However, an infection had already set in, and the bird died. Zickefoose deeply regretted her loss, but also regretted the bird's life:

> A pet, I've come to believe, is an animal whose emotional needs can be met by a human being. However much I loved her and tried to keep her engaged and happy, this little blue and green bundle of unmet needs was more inmate than pet, as are, I submit, all captive psittacines. Without mate and flock, without the joy of flight from flower to fruit to roost to nest, captive parrots are just marking time, time that felt at once too long and much too short to me.[10]

Mozart had a funeral for a pet starling he kept for three years, and who gave him the opening theme of his Piano Concerto in G, but that bird's story was likely also tragic. Among all the birds that live with humans, the hunting hawks, the pigeons, and the chickens have probably adapted best and formed the most genuine spiritual relations with people. Their lives have been at least partly free and expressive of their own strengths. Now, because of factory farming—a phenomenon less than a century old—relations between humans and chickens are also entangled with death and extinction, through the loss of chicken varieties and the incubation of bacteria and viruses. As Andrew Lawler has pointed out:

> The royal pet, the sacred symbol of the sun and herald of resurrection, the bird that cleansed us from sin and provided us with our models for courage

and self-sacrifice is quickly turning into a vital foodstuff. The chicken in China, for example, has long represented the five virtues of politeness, martial arts, bravery, benevolence, and faith, but its primary role today is feeding the country's 150 cities with populations in excess of 1 million—a number likely to double by 2030.[11]

Although human population growth increases demand for chickens, it also threatens the elimination of many varieties of chicken. The factory farming that took hold after World War II produces billions of nearly identical, hybrid birds that cannot fly, or, in many cases, even stand or walk, and has displaced hundreds of hardy subspecies that once flourished on small farms and in backyards. In her 2017 book, *Big Chicken*, journalist Maryn McKenna visited a farm in Marquette, Kansas, called Good Shepherd Poultry Ranch, where an elderly farmer named Frank Reese was keeping dozens of varieties of chickens and turkeys alive. As Reese watched some Rose-Comb White Leghorn chickens at his feet, he told McKenna, "There might be just 50 of those left in the world."[12]

Big Chicken also argues that threats to human health arise from our treatment of these birds. Because factory farming depends on heavy usage of antibiotics—in the United States, about four times the tonnage of antibiotics went into animals in 2015 as into humans[13]—factory farms incubate drug resistant strains of bacteria, especially *E. coli* and salmonella.[14] The bacterium known as MRSA, or methicillin-resistant *Staphylococcus aureus*, appeared almost simultaneously in hospitals and on farms.[15] Much less automated chicken farms, such as those of China, were probably the breeding ground for the virus of the worldwide, deadly flu of 1918, an epidemic that killed one hundred million people, about 5 percent of the world's population. Several instances of avian flu infecting humans have occurred in recent years.[16] If the survival of human civilization is ever threatened by disease, it is quite possible that birds will incubate and spread that threat. The Covid pandemic of 2020 gave only a hint of how much death and disruption could ensue.

Extinctions and Religious Attitudes

Extinctions—eliminations of an entire species of living things—have been occurring for billions of years on earth, but humans have recognized extinctions only since Darwin's discovery of natural selection and since the rise of paleontology, assembling its fossils, in the middle of the 1800s. Because extinction is a kind of Last Judgment, an ultimate confrontation with the reality of death, the concept of extinction has religious overtones. The human actions that determine which species go extinct and which do not are also entangled with our religions.

Scientists now count five *mass* extinctions—the disappearance of half or more than half of all species of living things, within one million years or less (sometimes much less)—in earth's history of about five billion years.[17] The fifth and most famous mass extinction, the one that ended the era of the dinosaurs, happened sixty-five million years ago, but many argue that we humans are now causing a sixth. This mass extinction (if it is real) began about fifteen thousand years ago, with the end of the last ice age.[18] It first manifested itself in the continents that came to be named the Americas, as large numbers of humans arrived on those continents and hunted most species of larger animals, such as saber-toothed cats, woolly mammoths, stilt-legged horses, and teratorn birds (some weighing 150 pounds, with wingspans of almost twenty-five feet)[19] to extinction.

Since Europeans arrived in the Americas in large numbers, beginning about five hundred years ago, some smaller species—notably among birds, the passenger pigeon, the ivory-billed woodpecker, and the Carolina parakeet—have gone extinct. There have also been tremendous reductions of numbers among species that are not extinct. It is estimated that by the early 1900s, 95 percent of the pre-Columbian bird population of the United States had disappeared.[20]

Many smaller bird species may soon vanish because of loss of habitat caused by climate change. According to the National Audubon Society of the United States, 314 out of the 588 bird species still present in North America are either endangered or threatened with extinction. The 126 "endangered" species are expected to lose at least 50 percent of their range by the year 2050, while the 188 "threatened" species may lose 50 percent of their range by 2080.[21]

These Audubon Society concerns might seem trivial to the more pessimistic climate scientists, who expect birds and lizards to be temporary survivors in a world that will soon see mass mammalian extinctions, on an earth that is baking in a carbon-rich atmosphere, suffering simultaneously from a drought of fresh water and floods from rising saltwater seas.[22] On the other hand, there are scientists who deny that a sixth, or Anthropocene, mass extinction has begun.[23] Some who have warned for decades about global warming nevertheless expect humans to engineer solutions, perhaps by blocking some sunlight or by recapturing carbon from carbon dioxide in the air.[24]

One undeniable, dramatic extinction of a bird happened in a very public way, in the midst of nations born of Western civilization, and quite recently by historic standards. In 1860, a single migrating flight of passenger pigeons passing over Ontario, Canada, was estimated to have included 3.7 *billion* birds.[25] The forests of North America then supported about four to five billion passenger pigeons. This was the most numerous vertebrate animal on earth. Its largest nesting site, which took place in 1871 in Wisconsin, extended to 850 square miles of trees, some of which were broken by the weight of birds, and of ground covered by pigeon dung.[26] Almost sixty years earlier, the bird painter and naturalist John James Audubon observed a flight of pigeons in Kentucky, thick enough to obscure the sun, which took three days to pass.[27] Yet, by 1914, the last passenger pigeon, a hen named Martha, died in captivity in a Cincinnati zoo, and the species was extinct.[28] Within a single century, the pigeon had fallen from awe-inspiring population densities to extinction.

Audubon saw massive hunting of the passenger pigeon, but believed that the species was so numerous that it could never be eliminated. However, those gigantic numbers of the 1800s and the subsequent crash may have both been caused by humans, and both may have stemmed in part from religious factors. Early European settlers in North America took note of the passenger pigeon, but with nothing like the wonder and terror of Audubon and nineteenth-century observers. For example, John Winthrop, the first English governor of Massachusetts, saw large flights of pigeons as instruments of God to reward or to punish. If they arrived after a harvest, to be eaten along with a crop, as Winthrop saw in 1648, the pigeons were a blessing; but if they arrived before a harvest and ate the crops of the colonists, as Winthrop saw in 1643, they were a punishment. But neither Winthrop nor other Americans of the colonial era described pigeons blotting out the sun, forests damaged by the weight of birds, noises like tornadoes from flocks arriving, or land covered for miles in pigeon dung. Winthrop estimated the flock that ate the corn in 1643 as "above 10,000"—a large roost of birds, but nothing approaching the numbers of the 1800s.[29]

The relative calm of colonial accounts of the passenger pigeon may have resulted from the religions and cultures of the humans indigenous to America. Native Americans, particularly the Seneca of northern New York and Pennsylvania, but also the Cherokee of the Southeast, the Ho Chunks (or Winnebago) of Wisconsin, and the Mi'Kmac of Nova Scotia, integrated passenger pigeons into their religious stories and rituals. For example every spring, between the tapping of trees for maple syrup and the first planting of crops, the Seneca held a pigeon festival. Seneca moved to the nesting sites of the birds and took many young pigeons (the squab, much tenderer than adult pigeons) with nets or by hand, allowing the older birds to live.[30] With several other Native nations holding similar ritual hunts, the numbers of pigeons were regularly reduced. Besides, native humans competed with pigeons for the nuts and fruits of the forest, further restricting the possible growth of the bird population.[31]

But by 1813, when John James Audubon witnessed pigeons darkening the sky for three days in Kentucky, European diseases, wars, and displacements had long since decimated the human population of Native Americans east of the Mississippi. It seems that, from the accounts of Audubon and others in the 1800s, the reduction in populations of Native humans may have led the pigeon population to explode. As Native human populations declined, so did the amount of land covered by forests in the eastern United States, so that flocks of migratory pigeons combined into larger groups with fewer places to roost.

Terror displaced wonder in an account of the arrival of pigeons from Columbus, Ohio, in 1855. As Frank Raper reported in the *Columbus Dispatch*, a "low-pitched hum" from the horizon grew steadily louder. What seemed to be clouds appeared, and the hum became "a mighty throbbing." Then the clouds came together and blotted out the sun. "Children screamed and ran for home. Women gathered their long skirts and hurried for the shelter of stores. Horses bolted. A few people mumbled frightened words about the approach of the millennium, and several dropped to their knees and prayed."[32] This was a relatively small flock for those days, probably on its way to join a larger nesting, but it blocked the sun for two hours before it left, leaving Columbus "ghostly in the now-bright sunlight that illumined a world plated with pigeon ejecta."[33]

Visitations from massive flocks of pigeons looked like biblical plagues, signaling something about the intentions of God. When European Americans thought they saw signs of the Apocalypse, they acted quickly. Mormons in Illinois headed west to build their Zion; Adventists in upstate New York gave away their goods and gathered on hills to be caught up in the Rapture. Julia Ward Howe saw the "coming of the Lord" as she watched the Union army from her hotel room near Washington, and she wrote "The Battle Hymn of the Republic" in a single night.

Terrified by masses of pigeons, European Americans began to kill every bird they could grasp or net or shoot, sometimes using fireworks to knock them out of the sky.[34] Greed also motivated mass killings. Unlike the Seneca, who took only young birds and limited themselves to the moment when the pigeons nested on their lands, European Americans had access to large markets for birds and technical means to exploit the bounty of pigeon meat. With railroads, barrels of salted pigeons could be shipped quickly to Chicago and New York. With telegraphs, crowds of hunters could follow the movements of the flocks.

Religious differences between Native and European Americans almost certainly contributed to the destruction of the passenger pigeon (Figure 6.2). Although Native Americans were not ecologists, working for conservation in a self-conscious fashion, they did have religions that presented the pigeons as a tribe of conscious beings with a leader, sometimes called the White Pigeon, and they had stories about the pigeons offering themselves as food during certain times of the year.[35] On the other hand, the religions of European

Figure 6.2 Hunters with guns and nets, guided by telegraph reports and sending their catch by railroad, reduced the passenger pigeon from a population of five billion to zero in about fifty years.
Science History Images / Alamy Stock Photo.

Americans, growing out of Jewish and Christian traditions, led people to think that God made the world, including animals, as a realm where humans would "have dominion" (Genesis 1:26, NRSV). The Bible also declared that "every moving thing that lives shall be food" for humans (Genesis 9:3, NRSV). No religious customs of observing seasonal cycles, taking only younger birds, or expressing respect for birds restrained the Europeans in the ways that the religions of Native Americans restrained them.

Passenger pigeons were very easy for humans to kill, especially when they nested. Their defense against predators was their sheer numbers, but pigeons could be harvested by cutting down the trees that held their nests or by netting or even by hand. Since each pair produced only one egg per year, the systematic harvests of the 1800s quickly reduced the species to extinction.

The same era that saw European Americans kill the passenger pigeon also witnessed the demise of the Carolina parakeet, the only parrot native to North America. Brilliantly colored in green, yellow, and orange, and so hardy they could fly through snowstorms, migrating over a range from Michigan and New York to Florida and Texas, these parrots traveled in large and noisy flocks that startled people from northern Europe. In the winter of 1780, Dutch settlers near Albany, New York, were so amazed by Carolina parakeets that they took them as a sign of "nothing less calamitous than the end of the world."[36]

By 1831, Audubon noted that the Carolina parakeet seemed to be in serious decline. The birds were prized for their feathers and kept as pets but hated for the effects that their visits could have on crops, especially fruit trees. They were easy for humans to kill in large numbers, because they traveled in large flocks and responded to an attack by gathering around fallen birds and calling out to each other, so that the rest of the flock could also be netted and killed.[37] As they became rarer, they became more valuable for capture as pets, but they did not survive well in captivity. The last tiny flocks, with a total of thirteen birds, were seen in Florida in 1904. Reports and rumors of sightings occurred as late as 1938, but no strong claims have been made since.[38]

Fortunately, the historical orientation of Judeo-Christian tradition also makes Christians and Jews amenable to change. The sudden loss of the passenger pigeon and the more gradual disappearance of the Carolina parakeet helped to launch the conservation movement. In 1918, the new Audubon Societies that had organized to study and to protect birds in many American states, worked together and spurred passage of the Migratory Bird Treaty Act, a law that now extends its protection to more than one thousand bird species and includes agreements of the United States with Canada, the United Kingdom, Mexico, Japan, and Russia.[39]

Since passage of the Migratory Bird Treaty Act, near extinctions of the snowy egret, the wood duck, and the sandhill crane from hunting have been prevented. In some important ways, an era of conservation was underway by 1920. The threat from a rage for feathered hats and clothing, which nearly extinguished the ostrich in the late nineteenth and early twentieth centuries, was avoided partly by the development of ostrich farming and partly by changes of fashion induced by shame. When British Petroleum accidentally killed almost a million birds in the 2010 oil spill at its Deepwater Horizon well in the Gulf of Mexico, BP was held liable under the Migratory Bird Treaty Act. In 2015, the corporation agreed to pay $100 million to support wetlands that help migratory birds flying over North America from the Gulf.[40] However, in 2018 Republicans in Congress and the Trump administration were seeking to amend the law to limit prosecution to those who deliberately and directly killed birds, while the National Audubon Society was lobbying against any such change. As of July 2018, the deaths of birds in oil pits were no longer being prosecuted by the government under the Migratory Bird Treaty Act.[41] This threatened to reverse considerable progress. By fining oil companies for every bird that landed on an open wastewater pit at an oil well and died, the Environmental Protection Agency of the Obama administration had induced enough companies to put screens over their pits to reduce the number of bird deaths from about two million to one million per year. In September 2021, the Biden administration reversed Trump's relaxation of the oil pit rule, again protecting birds.[42]

Underlying such sweeping changes of law and of behavior are changes of attitudes toward wild birds, at a level so deep that these attitudes could be called religious (defining religion as a system of nonrational commitments that holds life together). For example, Audubon loved birds, but he also killed every model for his bird paintings, so that he could study and pose and even trace them for his dramatically detailed pictures. Less than a century after the artist's death, his accounts of killing birds caused revulsion.[43] Audubon's religious values contrasted with those of the Taoist bird painters of China and Japan, whose rule was to observe their subjects for years in the wild and then to go into their studios and paint them quickly from memory, in order to express the chi or life force of the bird.[44] From the perspective of Taoist religion, Audubon's bird paintings are technically impressive but dead. Because of his methods, it has been charged that his paintings have no *chi*, the Chinese word for life force.

The creators and the wearers of fashions that included feather fans from eagles and egrets, whole birds on hats, and muffs and stoles made from four whole herring gulls sought to appropriate the spirits of the animals they killed and wore. But in a matter of two or three decades, from the 1890s to the 1920s, a fashion revolution took place. Clothing and accessories that would have been prized came to be looked upon as grotesque. Furs, including whole foxes as stoles, continued to be acceptable into the 1960s, but the bird and feather mania of the Gilded Age had passed into history by 1920.

Unfortunately, long before the rise of conservation movements, many species of birds had already been swept away, particularly as European explorers moved into new parts of the world. The bird most famous for its extinction, the dodo, disappeared within less than a century of the Dutch colonization of Mauritius, the Indian Ocean island where it lived. Since only about fifty humans lived on Mauritius before the dodo disappeared (in 1662 or 1693, depending on which last sighting is accepted), it seems likely that other invasive species introduced by the Dutch, such as rats, pigs, goats, and monkeys, were the direct cause of the bird's demise.

The story of the great auk (*Pinguinus impennis*) reflects more badly on humanity than that of the passenger pigeon, the Carolina parakeet, or the dodo. Once a numerous species ranging throughout the North Atlantic, up to the Arctic, as far south as Florida, and into the Mediterranean, this was the first bird to be called a "penguin." Like the Antarctic penguins known (and widely admired) today, the great auk walked upright and looked clumsy on land, but flew gracefully under water and lived on fish. Dense populations, as large as ten thousand breeding pairs, were reported on islands such as Funk Island, off Newfoundland, when Europeans first described the birds in the 1500s. The birds were easily killed when they bred on land, and they were prized for food and for their thick down. By 1753, the people of Newfoundland were asking the British to stop killing them, but no British ban was imposed until 1794, when the birds were nearly extinct. A last stronghold, the inaccessible island of Geirfuglasker near Iceland, was systematically plundered by the crew of a British privateer in 1808, then submerged by volcanic eruptions in 1830, so that only about fifty birds survived on nearby island of Eldey. In 1844, some fishermen were dispatched to Eldey to collect specimens for museums, and they apparently killed the last breeding pair.[45]

In 2015, the English writer Jessie Greengrass used historical accounts of the extinction of the great auk in her short story "An Account of the Decline of the Great Auk, According to One Who Saw It." Writing as a sailor who took part in killing the birds for the last twenty-five years of the species, she said that at first, "Looking at them, at the numbers of them, you would have thought them infinite," and that they served as a "larder" for sailors who were fishing and hunting whales. The sailors would reach the island of Geirfuglasker in a launch, then "find a flat place which we would clear of birds with a club swung about circular." Then they would use a board to drive birds from the shore into the ship's hold, where they were killed and salted for later consumption. After a while they came to the island not as part of another mission but specifically for feathers, plucking the birds and throwing the corpses into the sea. Though they noticed the numbers of birds declining, "We said it must be for some other reason than us and besides we had come two thousand miles and more so we could hardly just turn back." The sailor recalled finding the last two birds on Eldey Island, with a ship chartered by a naturalist because "The prices had become so enormous and it was cheaper probably to send us to where a few had been seen than it was to buy a stuffed one, even if there was one to buy." He recalled that this last pair "began to look around them, as if to find others of their kind to huddle with against us because they had always thought to find safety in numbers, but there were no others." The sailors caught and strangled the birds.

Greengrass imagined the sailor explaining the killing of the birds in terms of a madness that might be called religious zeal. Her description may well have also applied to the mass murders of the passenger pigeon and the Carolina parakeet.

> Here is the truth: we blamed the birds for what we did to them. There was something in their passivity that enraged us. We hated how they didn't run away. If they had run away from us we could have been more kind. We hated the birds. When we looked at them we wanted nothing more than to smash and beat and kill. We felt in them a mirror of our sin and the more we killed of them the cleaner we became. Sometimes it would be two days at the killing or three even and we wouldn't sleep. We would keep at our slaughter through darkness with the light from the fires only, and in the morning the bodies thrown from the cliffs would cover the sea for yards about the rock. The eggs we trampled, dancing across them in our boots. No matter what we did the birds stayed huddled to the rock, waiting for us

to reach them.... It was a kind of madness they caused in us and afterwards we would be exhausted and on the way home we wouldn't talk about what had happened but only about how much money we could make from the feathers. But alone with ourselves we blamed the birds.

The sailor felt some sorrow five years later, "because in any loss you can see a shadow of the way that you will be lost yourself." He marveled at the fact that there was no sign left of such a mass of life. "It used to be that on a warm day you could hear the rock before you saw it and smell it before you heard it but it's barely a hand of winters now since the last bird went and already the rock is clean." Although it was "three fingers deep" in bird dung, now "it is the colour of pewter and all the shit is washed clean by the rain."

Extinctions from hunting still threaten birds today. The ivory-billed woodpecker was last seen in the 1960s, and the whooping crane has been barely saved from the brink of disappearance. But in the last century, extinctions from systemic effects such as chemical pollution and climate change have become the primary threats to species of birds.

Chemical Threats and *Silent Spring*

World War II and its aftermath brought new threats of extinction. As Rachel Carson pointed out in her classic warning, *Silent Spring* (1962), before the war poisons were generally labeled with skulls and crossbones and kept in special sections of stores, to be used only in limited applications to address acute infestations.[46] After the war, chemicals developed to kill humans were found to have the capacity, in lower doses, to kill insects. Perhaps hardened by the war to the idea of dropping death from the skies, people began to spray poisons from airplanes over farms, forests, and suburban neighborhoods to control such "pests" as Japanese beetles, gypsy moths, fire ants, and mosquitoes.[47] By Carson's count, two hundred new chemical poisons had been developed and deployed in the two decades from 1942 to 1962.[48] She noted that these chemicals were not simply poisonous to the insects they targeted, but also to birds and mammals and humans: "They should not be called 'insecticides' but 'biocides.'"[49] She pointed out that insects often evolved to survive the poisons, requiring that new and more poisonous chemicals be developed, and that insects sometimes rebounded in greater numbers than before. She warned that humans were polluting the whole environment, even including our own bodies, possibly altering the genetics of our species "by something as trivial as the choice of an insect spray." Her language was as powerful as her thoughts:

> All this has been risked—for what? Future historians may well be amazed by our distorted sense of proportion. How could intelligent beings seek to control a few unwanted species by a method that contaminated the entire environment and brought the threat of disease and death even to their own kind? Yet this is precisely what we have done. We have done it, moreover, for reasons that collapse the moment we examine them. We are told that the enormous and expanding use of pesticides is necessary to maintain farm production. Yet is our real problem not one of *overproduction*? Our farms, despite measures to remove acreages from production and to pay farmers *not* to produce, have yielded such a staggering excess of crops that the American taxpayer in 1962 is paying out more than one billion dollars a year as the total carrying cost of the surplus-food storage program.[50]

Carson began her scientific work as a marine biologist, working for the US Fish and Wildlife Service, and her first writings were all about the sea. Her third book, *The Sea around Us*, won the National Book Award in nonfiction for 1951. Even in *Silent Spring*, water played a crucial role; she pointed out that poisons spread on land would reach underground aquifers and rivers and seas. "It is not possible to add pesticides to water anywhere without threatening the purity of water everywhere," she wrote.[51] *Silent Spring* has a chapter called "Surface Waters and Underground Seas," and another called "Rivers of Death."

But it was birds, and the idea of spring without birdsong that inspired the compelling title of *Silent Spring* and the three-page fable about a country town facing a "strange blight" that opened the book. Birds gave Carson her most compelling examples of poisoning from the air above. She described the elimination of grebes (a relative of the duck) from Clear Lake in California;[52] the destruction of the sage grouse on high western plains;[53] the spasms of a dying, poisoned meadowlark in Illinois;[54] and the effects of a campaign against fire ants in the South on blackbirds, dickcissels, woodcocks, bobwhite quail, and both wild and domestic turkeys.[55] She outlined the chemical mechanism whereby DDT makes the egg of a robin lifeless.[56] And Carson found a positive possibility among birds. When Carson explored alternatives to the use of chemicals to control insects, reintroducing birds that eat insects had its place among many other natural methods she suggested.[57]

The idea of a world without birdsong changed Rachel Carson from a scientist who wrote beautiful prose to a prophet with a Word of warning. Like the prophets of the Bible denouncing wicked kings, she denounced the rulers of her time:

> Who has decided—who has the *right* to decide—for the countless legions of people who were not consulted that the supreme value is a world without insects, even though it be also a sterile world ungraced by the curving wing of a bird in flight? The decision is that of the authoritarian temporarily entrusted with power; he has made it during a moment of inattention by millions to whom beauty and the ordered world of nature still have a meaning that is deep and imperative.[58]

Writing again as a prophet, she offered a clear choice. Natural alternatives for controlling insects abounded. But natural alternatives, from planting marigolds to introducing birds to developing bacteria, were not explored, "for the simple reason that they do not promise anyone the fortunes that are to be made in the chemical industry."[59]

Silent Spring raised the prospect that the extinction of birds through spraying of chemicals might portend the extinction of humanity. Quoting Dr. David Price, a scientist with the US Public Health Service, Carson warned, "We all live under the haunting fear that something may corrupt the environment to the point where man joins the dinosaurs as an obsolete form of life. And what makes these thoughts all the more disturbing is the knowledge that our fate could perhaps be sealed twenty or more years before the development of symptoms."[60]

Silent Spring belongs on a short list of books that have changed the world, arguably as much as *Uncle Tom's Cabin* and the *Communist Manifesto*. Because Carson's warnings about DDT were heeded, bald eagles and hawks that were nearly extinguished in the United States have returned to flourish, and robins were not exterminated. But more importantly for human civilization, the perspective of *Silent Spring* on "the ordered world of nature," a world of balance in which people realized that they should consider the systemic effects of their actions, became a scientific norm. The concept of an ecosystem became commonplace. As Carson wrote, the balance of nature was not "a state of affairs that prevailed in an earlier, simpler world," but rather "a complex, precise, and highly integrated system of relationships between living things which cannot safely be ignored any more than the law of gravity can be defied with impunity by a man perched on the edge of a cliff."[61]

This perspective was not mainstream in 1962. Only fourteen years before, in 1948, Dr. Paul Müller had been awarded the Nobel Prize in Physiology or Medicine for discovering the insecticidal properties of DDT. Dr. Robert White Stevens, a chemist at Rutgers University and American Cyanamid, a major producer of insecticides, dismissed Carson as "a fanatic defender of the cult of the balance of nature."[62] Stevens further observed: "The crux, the fulcrum over which the argument chiefly rests, is that Miss Carson maintains that the balance of nature is a major force in the survival of man, whereas the modern chemist, the modern biologist and scientist, believes that man is steadily controlling nature."[63] In the last paragraph of *Silent Spring*, Carson clearly stated her opinion of science like that of Stevens (or Müller):

> The "control of nature" is a phrase conceived in arrogance, born of the Neanderthal age of biology and philosophy, when it was supposed that nature exists for the convenience of man. The concepts and practices of applied entomology from the most part date from that Stone Age of science. It is our alarming misfortune that so primitive a science has armed itself with the most modern and terrible weapons, and that in turning them against the insects it has also turned them against the earth.[64]

More than half a century later, this argument continues. Critics of Rachel Carson, mostly on the right but some also on the left of the political spectrum, claim that her campaign against DDT in particular and insecticides in general has led to tens of millions or even hundreds of millions of preventable deaths from malaria and other insect-borne diseases. In 2014, when Google celebrated Carson's legacy on the fiftieth anniversary of her death, Breitbart News (then led by Steve Bannon, who was later chief strategist for President Donald J. Trump), compared her to Hitler, Stalin, and Pol Pot as a mass murderer.[65] Others characterized her as a "radical environmentalist" spreading a "fatal cult of antihumanism."[66]

As a woman who dared to challenge men, Carson was attacked in gendered terms. *Time* magazine characterized *Silent Spring* as "hysterically overemphatic" and filled with "emotion-fanning words." Ezra Taft Benson, who served both as President Eisenhower's secretary of agriculture and later as president of the Mormon Church, wrote to Eisenhower wondering "why a spinster with no children was so concerned about genetics."[67] The ordinary misogyny of our culture intensified when a woman raised apocalyptic alarms.

Birds of Prophetic and Apocalyptic Traditions

Birds were associated with desolation in the Bible before apocalyptic writing emerged. During the mid-700s BCE, the first prophet whose work was included in the book of Isaiah used birds to evoke God's "day of vengeance" on Edom, a southerly neighbor of Judah: "The hawk and the hedgehog shall possess it; the owl and the raven shall live in it.... There shall the owl nest and lay and hatch and brood in its shadow; there too the buzzards shall gather, each one with its mate" (Isaiah 34:11, 15).

In one of the earliest examples of apocalyptic writing—a genre of prophecy that describes war between cosmic forces of good and evil, with dark symbols displacing the clear language of classical prophecy—the prophet Ezekiel wrote that God commanded him,

> Speak to the birds of every kind and to all the wild animals: Assemble and come, gather from all around to the sacrificial feast that I am preparing for you, a great sacrificial feast on the mountains of Israel, and you shall eat flesh and drink blood. You shall eat the flesh of the mighty, and drink the blood of the princes of the earth—of rams, of lambs, and of goats, of bulls, all of them fatlings of Bashan. You shall eat fat until you are filled, and drink blood until you are drunk, at the sacrificial feast that I am preparing for you. And you shall be filled at my table with horses and charioteers, with warriors and all kinds of soldiers, says the Lord God. (Ezekiel 39:17–20, NRSV)

Dating from sometime around the destruction of the Jerusalem Temple and the exile of Jews to Babylon in 586 BCE, this vision of birds and animals at a "sacrificial feast" was the culmination of an invasion of Judah by the enemies called Gog and Magog, mysterious nations that appear again almost seven centuries later, in the Christian book of Revelation. In both Ezekiel and Revelation, the birds are summoned to clean up after a terrible, final battle of world history, after which (in Ezekiel) a new temple is built or (in Revelation) a New Jerusalem comes down from heaven for the sake of God's chosen people.

John of Patmos, the Christian visionary who wrote Revelation sometime around the 90s CE, had no doubt read Ezekiel, and Revelation gives the birds their charge in language similar to Ezekiel's. According to John, after the "kings of the whole world" are gathered "at the place that in Hebrew is called Harmageddon" (Revelation 16:14–16, NRSV), Jesus appears riding a white horse, with a sword coming out of his mouth, and leading "the armies of heaven" (Revelation 19:14–15).

> Then I saw an angel standing in the sun, and with a loud voice he called to all the birds that fly in midheaven, "Come, gather for the great supper of God, to eat the flesh of kings, the flesh of captains, the flesh of the mighty, the flesh of horses and their riders—flesh of all, both free and slave, both small and great." (Revelation 19:17-18, NRSV)

Next the "beast" and the "false prophet," who had misled the world in Revelation 13, are captured and thrown into a "lake of fire" (Revelation 19:20). The sword of Jesus kills "the rest" of those who gathered to oppose him at Armageddon, "and all the birds were gorged with their flesh" (Revelation 19:21).

Birds can also be independent agents, with their own agendas, playing independent roles in apocalyptic writing. In the Words of the Luminaries, a writing among the Dead Sea Scrolls, birds and wild land animals rebel against God and are vanquished by sheep, who obey God.[68] In the Apocalypse of Peter, one of the many early Christian books that were not included in the New Testament, vultures pursue the unchaste and tear their flesh.[69]

In an apocalypse of the Mayans, a heavy-beaked, heavy-lidded bird called Vucub Caquix, a name translated as "Seven Macaw," uses the destruction of the world by a flood as an opportunity to become "high god" and rule over everything. This usurpation takes place during the interval between the previous world and the present world, while a large group of supernatural beings labors at creation. Vucub Caquix flies above the floods that have drowned the previous world and settles himself at the top of the world tree, which is called the *ceiba*. He proclaims that he is the sun and the moon of this dimly lit world and asserts his authority over all. He is attacked by Hun Ahpu, one of the Mayan hero twins, and a bitter fight ensues. Vucub Caquix severs Hun Ahpu's arm but is eventually shot by a blowgun and falls from the tree. As the usurping bird falls, his body clears a path along the world tree to our present world and Itzam-Yeh, the bird spirit helper of the leading creator or sorcerer of the new world, Itzamna, flies up and assumes his rightful place at the crown of the tree. Both Vucub Caquix and Itzam-Yeh were identified by Mayan astronomers with the seven-star constellation known as the Big Dipper. This meant that these apocalyptic birds could be seen atop the world tree in summer, but would fall below the horizon in winter, just as the Big Dipper falls below the horizon in winter at latitudes below forty-one degrees north.[70]

Recent Apocalyptic and Sex: Hitchcock and *The Birds*

In the modern world, apocalyptic writing remains popular, for several enduring reasons. An account of an ending gives the world meaning; it makes history a plot, as opposed to a story that just goes on and on in which events mean nothing more than weather. Also, the sadness and fear arising from the knowledge that each of us must die as an individual are somehow abated by stories of everyone dying together, as if individual loss is absorbed by the collective. And some comfort is found in the details of apocalyptic destruction, just as horror stories and films frighten people, but leave audiences with a sense that they have survived a terrible event that killed others. Audiences like to be frightened because of the security they feel when the frightening scenes are over. The victims have all died before their eyes, and they are still alive.

People routinely name *The Birds* as the most frightening film ever made by Alfred Hitchcock (Figure 6.3). Hitchcock himself made the same claim. Among our families, friends, and colleagues, almost everyone has seen the movie once, but no one was willing to watch it again when we were researching this chapter.

Fear arises first in *The Birds* by the way the movie challenges viewers physically. Physical shocks abound. From the first attack, when a lone gull dives at the heroine on a beautiful day and leaves a bleeding gash in her head, through the discovery of a farmer eyeless and dead in his bedroom amid many dead birds, to the culminating scene of the heroine helpless in an attic, writhing under crows and seagulls that were thrown at her by stagehands until she broke down in reality as well as in the film, seven different, distinct assaults on people by birds are vividly enacted, with a skillful mixture of real and mechanical birds and cartoon effects.

156 WINGS OF THE GODS

Figure 6.3 A short story by Daphne du Maurier and an attack by poisoned birds on a coastal California town inspired Alfred Hitchcock to make a film that still creates fear sixty years after its release in 1962. Publicity poster for *The Birds*.
Universal Pictures / Photofest.

A second kind of fear, scientific fear, comes with the facts that the movie cites. Hitchcock made *The Birds* in part because he had heard of an attack of seagulls on a coastal town near Santa Cruz, California, on August 18, 1961. Apparently poisoned by shellfish who had in turn consumed algae containing a neurotoxin, the birds crashed into houses and cars and plunged onto lawns. When the birds of the movie begin attacking, characters in the movie discuss the real event that happened one year before.

And what could people do if bird attacks became widespread, systematic, and long lasting? When a man suggests getting guns and killing every bird on earth, an amateur ornithologist in the film replies, "We wouldn't have a chance." The film's expert argues that there are about 5.75 billion birds in the United States, and perhaps 100 billion worldwide. But scientists now estimate a world population of as many as 400 billion birds, or almost sixty birds for each human.[71] A general avian attack, coming without warning and persisting, could conceivably bring about the end of humanity, or at least of civilization.

Another kind of fear comes with guilt, the fear of judgment and of damnation, a deserved punishment. In his trailer for *The Birds*, Hitchcock dryly reviewed human mistreatment of birds, beginning with a (faked) cave painting of a bird transfixed by an arrow. He showed off hats that featured plumes and even whole birds. He picked up a hunting shotgun, sat down to eat a whole chicken, then got up and strolled to a cage where a bird bit his finger. Many who saw *The Birds* thought that the movie was a parable of Nature fighting back, and the director encouraged this view. As Hitchcock said in an interview, "The birds had been shot at, eaten, put in cages. They'd suffered *everything* from the humans, and it was time they turned *on* them. Don't mess about or tamper with nature."[72]

Fourthly, fear of sex courses through *The Birds*, as it does through much of Hitchcock's work, but here with a distinctively avian twist. The film intertwines birds and sex, from the opening scenes of the character Melanie Daniels, a notorious socialite buying a mynah (a bird she intends to teach shocking words to offend a prudish aunt). In the pet shop, Melanie meets lawyer Mitch Brenner, who is seeking a pair of "lovebirds" (*Agapornis*, a type of parrot that gained its name because males pass food from their beaks to females, in a gesture that resembles kissing) as a birthday present for his younger sister. Brenner mistakes Daniels for an employee of the store, and Daniels plays along, pretending to knowledge she doesn't have. When a bird gets loose in the shop and the lawyer catches it under his hat, then puts it back behind bars, he says, "Back into your gilded cage, Melanie Daniels." This reveals that he has recognized the woman, who had not told him her name, from seeing her answering charges in court and from reading gossip columns about her adventures in Europe.

In *The Birds*, sex involves men and women hunting each other, just as birds begin to hunt humans. And as cultural critic Camille Paglia suggested in her book on *The Birds*, the stiletto shoes and upswept hairdos of the women in the film are especially suggestive of birds. In British slang of the sixties, which was spreading across the Atlantic, attractive young women were commonly called "birds." The idea of sex with a bird can be powerful, as we have seen in the myth of Leda and the swan and in the various forms of *Swan Lake*, including *Black Swan*.

When Hitchcock was making *The Birds*, some colleagues working on the film warned him that putting together a romantic comedy and a horror film would not work. There was real plausibility in the warning, but ultimately the film does come together. In the plot worked out by Hitchcock and writer

Evan Hunter, romance blooms because of horror. Surviving the traumatic bird attacks creates a bond between the characters called Mitch Brenner and Melanie Daniels. Even more importantly, because Melanie proves helpful in the crisis but then becomes a victim of the birds, reduced to catatonia and being driven to the hospital, Mitch's mother Lydia Brenner comes to accept her as a daughter. According to Camille Paglia, Lydia is "the town's chief carnivorous bird" when she first meets Melanie,[73] but by the end Lydia is cradling Melanie's head in her lap as they look tenderly into each other's eyes.

Finally, *The Birds* generates a fifth kind of fear, the fear of apocalypse. Apocalyptic writing by definition involves catastrophe, and even cosmic destruction. Though the whole world is not destroyed in *The Birds*, the town of Bodega Bay is abandoned, and the bird attacks that have driven the humans away from that town seem to be continuing elsewhere. The central characters have come to love each other, and they escape the house where they have barricaded themselves, but their escape to safety is not assured. Civilization has not gained the upper hand against Nature.

At the end of the short story that started Hitchcock's thinking about avian apocalyptic—"The Birds" by Daphne du Maurier (published in 1952, as part of her collection *The Apple Tree*)—an isolated English family is waiting for another attack in their cottage on a farm where the people living in the main house have already been killed. The BBC is off the air, and there is no assurance that civilization will recover. Neither du Maurier's story nor Hitchcock's film ends with any definite resolution. Instead, each ends with a looming sense of apocalyptic threat. Both the film and the story were informed by traumatic experiences of hiding in bomb shelters during the German bombing of England in World War II and by the pervasive, Cold War worries that nuclear attacks would soon send people back into shelters.

In one crucial detail, the film was much more upbeat than the story. Daphne du Maurier's farm family gains nothing through the bird attacks, and they look doomed at the end. They are still in the cottage, barricaded behind boarded-up windows, and the man of the house tosses his last cigarette into the fire, with no plan but to hold out as long as possible. On the other hand, the family of the film has gained a member and the promise of love, both between Mitch and Melanie and between Melanie and Mitch's mother, and even between the lovebirds that sister Cathy brings into the car that carries them away from their cottage to possible freedom.

Accounts of apocalyptic destruction that attain broad popularity in a culture always seem to contain the seeds of rebirth. As Joseph Campbell and his inspiration Carl Jung have frequently observed, the mind refuses to contemplate death without resurrection. Perhaps because of this aspect of human nature, Hitchcock's combination of romantic comedy and apocalyptic horror in *The Birds* not only succeeded, but established a convention that has continued through contemporary zombie and vampire movies, superhero action epics, and science fiction films. In *Arguing the Apocalypse* (1994), Stephen O'Leary pointed out that the book of Revelation itself is not structured as a tragedy—with rising tension until a climactic event, after which comes a fall—but as a comedy, with a plot that spirals upward from conflict to triumph to conflict again until the end, a final revolt that results in Satan being thrown into a pit and the New Jerusalem descending from heaven.[74] This descent of the city of God is presented as a wedding between God and humanity, with the New Jerusalem "prepared as a bride adorned for her husband" (Revelation 21:2b, NRSV). Comedies often end with a wedding between antagonists (in this case God and humanity).

Both in Revelation and in *The Birds*, there are basic conflicts between male and female. Revelation makes heroes of 144,000 Israelite men. These males are worthy to sing the song of the Lord, a new song, because they "have not defiled themselves with women, for they are virgins; these follow the Lamb wherever he goes" (Revelation 14:3b, NRSV).

The dichotomy of women as virgins or whores is very prominent in Revelation. First comes the Christian leader referred to as "Jezebel" in Revelation 2:20, who is condemned by John of Patmos for teaching that Christians may eat food offered to idols, a sin to which he refers as "fornication." Next comes a good woman, the Woman Clothed with the Sun of Revelation 12, who gives birth to a future ruler of the earth and then is saved from Satan in the form of a dragon by God. In Revelation 17, a woman clothed in scarlet and gold appears, offering all nations a cup "full of abominations and the impurities of her fornication" (Revelation 17:4b, NRSV). She is named as "Babylon the great, mother of whores and of earth's abominations" (Revelation 17:5b). Finally another virgin, the New Jerusalem, completes the series. With two cosmically bad women, two cosmically good women, and 144,000 men who are good in part because they have avoided women, the misogyny of Revelation is hard to miss.

Hitchcock's movie also presents women as a source of tension that must be controlled. Recent revelations of how Hitchcock became obsessed with women, particularly Tippi Hedren of *The Birds*, and attempted to control and to dominate women as a kind of defense, raise the issue of whether the director saw his aggressive birds as the equivalents of women. In a print advertisement for the movie, Hitchcock alluded to a secret meaning: "There is a terrifying menace lurking right underneath the surface shock and suspense of The Birds," he wrote. "When you discover it, your pleasure will be more than doubled." Camille Paglia speculated that Hitchcock was referring to "the familiar Shakespearean paradox of shadow versus substance," and concluded that "for Hitchcock, I suspect, the menace is archetypal woman, who is also mistress of surfaces." Hitchcock's behavior during the shooting of bird attacks led some observers to suggest that the master of suspense was terrified both of women and of birds.[75]

In the age of modern warfare with its apocalyptic potential, birds could stand in for something deadlier than women. The three vultures of Andrew Wyeth's *Soaring* (1950), gliding birds seen from above as they soar over a landscape of rolling hills with a single farmhouse, gave a natural shape and an archetypal referent to the bombers of the Cold War with their nuclear threat. As Roberta Smith wrote in a review of the picture, it "can make the stomach lurch, first from the spatial plunge, then the sense of foreboding."[76]

Hopes for Overcoming Extinctions

Crows and gulls took the lead roles in six out of seven attacks in *The Birds*, with one exception, an invasion of the Brenner home by sparrows who came down the chimney. No bald eagles or condors or red-tailed hawks, no turkey vultures or peregrine falcons appeared. Because of environmental factors, and especially the widespread use of DDT after 1945, all of these large raptors and scavengers were very rare in California when the film was made in 1962.

According to the US Fish and Wildlife Service, about fifty thousand nesting pairs of bald eagles lived in the United States in 1782, the year when that eagle was chosen as the national bird. Only 487 nesting pairs of bald eagles remained in 1963, when *The Birds* was released.[77] Decline had begun in the nineteenth century, as some of the prey of eagles, especially waterfowl and shorebirds like gulls, were nearly extinguished by human hunting for feathers and other forms of decoration. Often, farmers shot eagles to protect their chickens, lambs, and other livestock and domestic animals. In 1940, Congress passed the Bald Eagle Protection Act, which stated that the bald eagle was "threatened with extinction" and forbade killing, selling, or possessing bald eagles. An amendment added the golden eagle in 1962, so that the law became the Bald and Golden Eagle Protection Act. But with the end of World War II came a new threat: DDT had been discovered to be very effective as an insecticide during the war, preventing many cases of malaria in Italy by killing the mosquitoes that carry the disease. Unfortunately, DDT also causes eagles (and many other birds) to produce eggs with shells too thin to survive the parent bird's weight in incubation.

Rachel Carson and *Silent Spring* (1962) helped to rescue the bald eagle, but not instantly. Arguments over DDT raged for ten years until 1972, when the Environmental Protection Agency finally banned its use in the United States. Thirty-five years later, in 2007, the Fish and Wildlife Service counted about ten thousand nesting pairs of bald eagles in the lower 48 US states, and on June 28, 2007, it removed the bird from its list of threatened and endangered species. Similar increases of hawks, vultures, falcons, and osprey took place, so that seeing a large raptor in the skies over North America has become much more common in the third decade of the twenty-first century than it was in the 1970s.

In Alaska, the bald eagle always maintained robust numbers, but Hawaiian native birds have not been so fortunate. Now called "the extinction capital of the world," the Hawaiian Islands once had about 142 bird species known nowhere else.[78] New islands have emerged from volcanic activity over the last five million years, and species specific to each island have evolved. But the arrival of Polynesian humans about one thousand years ago introduced the brown rat and malaria, both of which began to hurt the native birds. When Europeans arrived in the 1700s, they brought the black rat, a more efficient predator. Centuries of lost habitat from farming ensued, followed by spraying with DDT and other poisons meant to kill insects. As of August 2018, the American Bird Conservancy estimated that 95 of the 142 Hawaiian bird species known nowhere else had gone extinct since humans arrived. Out of 44 native birds still widespread in Hawaii, 33 were listed under the Endangered Species Act. Nevertheless, the Conservancy has also reported successes in sanctuaries provided for the Hawaiian petrel, Newell's shearwater, millerbirds, and palila, all native species of birds saved from extinction. A struggle for the Hawaiian crow (*Corvus hawaiiensis*, aka "alala")—partly a struggle against ornithologists who disrupted breeding by climbing trees to take pictures of crows in nests—saw the disappearance of the last Hawaiian crows in the wild in 2002 and their (apparently successful) reintroduction from a breeding program to the forest in November 2017.[79]

Another success in fighting extinction has brought the largest bird in North America, the California condor (*Gymnogyps californianus*) back from the very edge. In 1988, none of these condors was living in the wild. They had been killed indirectly, because of hunters using lead bullets and shot to kill animals. When condors ate the remains of these animals, they contracted lead poisoning. But fortunately, the US Fish and Wildlife Service and a number of other agencies and private charities banded together to breed the bird in captivity, and in 1992 they began to release condors to the wild. As of May 2018, the wild population had grown to 410 birds, and for the first time since 1988 there were more condors in the wild than in captivity.[80]

An Australian anthropologist and environmentalist named Thom van Dooren has written that the California condor's recovery owes something to marketing. In the nineteenth century, for example in Audubon's *Birds of America*, this bird was called the "California turkey vulture." Some referred to it simply as a "buzzard." But California condors do resemble the largest birds alive today, Andean condors (*Vultur gryphus*), and conservationists began to refer to the California birds as "condors" early in the twentieth century. According to Dooren, the new name "clearly captured a sense of majesty and grandeur that the older names had not" and it "helped to distance these birds from the other vulture species." The successful return of the condor to the skies above California gives "some hope for all the other struggling vultures around the world,"[81] he concluded.

No other vultures have struggled so desperately in recent times as the vultures of India.[82] Experts estimate that India and Pakistan had a vulture population of about thirty million birds in 1990, but within a decade it collapsed into the hundreds, with not even a single pair of vultures seen together. The cause of death was kidney failure, but the cause of kidney failure remained a mystery until 2003, when it was found that the vultures were dying from an accumulation of diclofenac, a painkiller given to cattle.

This near extinction involved religions both in its causes and its effects. For millennia, the vultures of India had cleaned up the carcasses of cows that died in the fields, because Hindus would not slaughter cows. The cow is a sacred animal for Hindus, an image of motherhood and harmlessness, and diclofenac appealed to Hindus as a means to spare cows from suffering. Meanwhile, the vultures that cleaned up the bodies of sacred cows also served in another religion, Zoroastrianism, practiced by Persians, or Parsis, who have lived in India since Persia (now Iran) became a Muslim country thirteen hundred years ago. For Zoroastrians (as we saw in Chapter 4), dead human bodies are a pollutant, and burial and cremation make the elements of earth and fire impure. To dispose of their dead, they build towers in which human bodies are placed above where dogs or rats can reach them, to be eaten by vultures. Until the near extinction of the 1990s, vultures would reduce the bodies to bones within hours. After the population crash of vultures, crows and other birds still came to the towers, but they lacked the powerful bills and claws of the vulture and could not do the job before decomposition made the sites unpleasant. Since 2006, India has tried to ban the use of diclofenac in cattle, and vultures are being bred in captivity, so there remains some hope for Indian vultures to come back from the brink.[83]

Beyond conservation, a nonprofit organization called Revive&Restore is working to reverse extinctions. By editing the genes of surviving species to accept genes culled from the dead remains of extinct species, this group hopes to revive the passenger pigeon, for example. Its website proclaims that the return of passenger pigeons would enliven the forests of North America, which have become stagnant without the repeated breaking of branches and opening of canopies that migrating passenger pigeons once provided.[84] Along with the passenger pigeon, Revive&Restore is undertaking similar projects reviving the heath hen (last seen on Martha's Vineyard in 1932), and the woolly mammoth (extinct ten thousand years, but well preserved in Siberia and closely related to modern Asian elephants). The group also seeks to prevent extinctions of the horseshoe crab and the black-footed ferret.

Revive&Restore features people prominent and qualified enough to inspire respect, from its cofounder Stewart Brand (creator of the *Whole Earth Catalog*, which he headed from 1968 through 1984) to scientists like Dr. Beth Shapiro, a professor at the University of California, Santa Cruz, who serves as adviser to the Passenger Pigeon Project.[85] In an age when elephants face extinction from poaching and loss of habitat, the idea of restarting woolly mammoths on a revived grassland area in Siberia can seem attractive, and research for that project has already yielded new ways to fight a virus that threatens Asian elephants. But there are skeptics. For example, Dr. Paul Ehrlich, who heads the Center for Conservation Policy at Stanford and who wrote *The Population Bomb* (1968), argues that there may not be enough genetic diversity in the (approximately fifteen hundred) passenger pigeon remains now held in museums, and that the starting population for reintroducing the species to the wild would have to be quite large.[86] Opponents of what Revive&Restore calls "de-extinction" generally contend that conservation of still viable species is much more cost-effective than attempting to bring back species that have disappeared. Stewart Brand replies that the funding of Revive&Restore comes from private sources unrelated to the conservation movement.

Hope to avoid extinctions, despite the drastic effects that humanity appears to be having on the planet, also arises from the birds themselves. Birds can be remarkably adaptable, as chimney swifts showed centuries ago when they took up residence in the chimneys built by humans who destroyed the dead and hollow trees that the birds had evolved to prefer as nest sites.[87] More recently, as climate change brought the time of maturity of grasses in the Arctic a month earlier than it had been, scientists have found that barnacle geese are flying much faster on their journeys north and skipping stops for rest and refueling they would normally have made.[88] And even more conclusively, a fifteen-year study that began in 2003, comparing modern nesting practices of 202 species to data from more than a century ago, showed that birds in North America today are nesting from five to twelve days earlier than they did. Since nestlings can be killed by too much heat, the birds have taken to nesting and laying when the weather is cooler. This strategy has enabled many species to remain at favorite nesting sites, rather than nesting farther north or higher up on mountains.[89]

But however adaptable birds prove to be, only a shift in religious and cultural attitudes can offer enduring hope to avoid a human-caused mass extinction. The era of John James Audubon (1785–1851) witnessed the integration of birds into a modern religion of nature, and this development is the subject of the next chapter.

Notes

1. BirdLife International (2017): "We have lost over 150 bird species since 1500." Accessed at: http://www.birdlife.org (accessed June 28, 2018).
2. Jane Alexander, *Wild Things, Wild Places: Adventurous Tales of Wildlife and Conservation on Planet Earth* (New York: Alfred A. Knopf, 2016), 94.
3. Julie Zickefoose, *The Bluebird Effect: Uncommon Bonds with Common Birds* (Boston: Houghton Mifflin, 2012), 88.
4. Zickefoose, *The Bluebird Effect*, 294.
5. Zickefoose, *The Bluebird Effect*, 14.
6. Zickefoose, *The Bluebird Effect*, 319.
7. Zickefoose, *The Bluebird Effect*, 321.
8. Zickefoose, *The Bluebird Effect*, 337–338.
9. Zickefoose, *The Bluebird Effect*, 339.

10. Zickefoose, *The Bluebird Effect*, 339–340.
11. Andrew Lawler, *Why Did the Chicken Cross the World? The Epic Saga of the Bird That Powers Civilization* (New York: Atria Books, 2014), 259.
12. Maryn McKenna, *Big Chicken: The Incredible Story of How Antibiotics Created Modern Agriculture and Changed the Way the World Eats* (Washington, D.C.: National Geographic, 2017), 158.
13. McKenna, *Big Chicken*, 254.
14. McKenna, *Big Chicken*, 27, 186.
15. McKenna, *Big Chicken*, 220, 232–239.
16. Rob Schmitz, "Why Chinese Scientists Are More Worried Than Ever about Bird Flu," *NPR Morning Edition*, April 11, 2017, https://www.npr.org/sections/goatsandsoda/2017/04/11/523271148/why-chinese-scientists-are-more-worried-than-ever-about-bird-flu (accessed March 16, 2018).
17. Peter Brannen, *The Ends of the World: Volcanic Apocalypses, Lethal Oceans, and Our Quest to Understand Earth's Past Mass Extinctions* (New York: HarperCollins, 2017), 3.
18. Illinois State Museum, "The Late Pleistocene Extinctions," http://exhibits.museum.state.il.us/exhibits/larson/lp_extinction.html (accessed June 28, 2018).
19. Natural History Museum of Los Angeles County, "Teratorns," https://nhm.org/site/research-collections/rancho-la-brea/about-teratorns (accessed June 28, 2018).
20. Kathleen Kaska, *The Man Who Saved the Whooping Crane: The Robert Porter Allen Story* (Gainesville: University Press of Florida, 2012), 10.
21. National Audubon Society, "Birds and Climate Change," September 9, 2014, http://climate.audubon.org/article/audubon-report-glance (accessed June 29, 2018).
22. Brannen, *Ends of the World*, 250.
23. Brannen, *Ends of the World*, 245.
24. David Wallace-Wells, "The Uninhabitable Earth," *New York*, July 10, 2017, http://nymag.com/daily/intelligencer/2017/07/climate-change-earth-too-hot-for-humans-annotated.html (accessed June 29, 2018).
25. Joel Greenberg, *A Feathered River across the Sky: The Passenger Pigeon's Flight to Extinction* (New York: Bloomsbury USA, 2014), 5–7.
26. Greenberg, *Feathered River*, 131–136.
27. Greenberg, *Feathered River*, 50.
28. Greenberg, *Feathered River*, 188.
29. Greenberg, *Feathered River*, 69–70.
30. Michael Edmonds, "Flights of Fancy: Birds and People in the Old Northwest," *Wisconsin Magazine of History* 83, no. 3 (Spring, 2000): 171.
31. Charles E. Kay, "Are Ecosystems Structured from the Top-Down or Bottom-Up? A New Look at an Old Debate," *Wildlife Society Bulletin* 26, no. 3 (Autumn 1998): 492.
32. Greenberg, *Feathered River*, 54.
33. Greenberg, *Feathered River*, 54.
34. Greenberg, *Feathered River*, 54.
35. Greenberg, *Feathered River*, 42–45.
36. Noel F. R. Snyder, *The Carolina Parakeet: Glimpses of a Vanished Bird* (Princeton, NJ: Princeton University Press, 2004), 1.

37. Julian P. Hume and Michael Walters, *Extinct Birds* (London: T. & AD Poyser, 2012), 187.
38. Hume and Walters, *Extinct Birds*, 187.
39. National Audubon Society, "The Migratory Bird Treaty Act, Explained," January 26, 2018, https://www.audubon.org/news/the-migratory-bird-treaty-act-explained (accessed June 29, 2018).
40. US Fish & Wildlife Service, "BP Deepwater Horizon Oil Spill Settlement Funds Migrate North," April 27, 2015, https://www.fws.gov/news/ShowNews.cfm?ID=FC61EB52-BF8A-45AA-C04D802711C4EF55 (accessed June 30, 2018).
41. Amy Walters, "Behind Trump's Energy Dominance," *Reveal* (The Center for Investigative Reporting and PRX, 2018), July 14, 2018, https://www.revealnews.org/episodes/behind-trumps-energy-dominance/ (accessed July 24, 2018).
42. Hawk Hammer and Jamie Rappaport Clark, "Biden Administration Reverses Trump Rule That Gutted Migratory Bird Protections," *Defenders of Wildlife*, September 29, 2021, https://defenders.org/newsroom/biden-administration-reverses-trump-rule-gutted-migratory-bird-protections (accessed March 7, 2022).
43. Anne Raver, "The Dark Side of Audubon's Era, and His Work," *New York Times*, March 30, 1997, https://www.nytimes.com/1997/03/30/style/the-dark-side-of-audubon-s-era-and-his-work.html (accessed July 25, 2018).
44. Alan Priest, *Aspects of Chinese Painting* (New York: Macmillan, 1954), 85, 103; George Rowley, *Principles of Chinese Painting*, rev. ed. (Princeton, NJ: Princeton University Press, 1974), 30.
45. Hume and Walters, *Extinct Birds*, 132.
46. Rachel Carson, *Silent Spring* (Boston: Houghton Mifflin, 1962), 155.
47. Carson, *Silent Spring*, 156.
48. Carson, *Silent Spring*, 7.
49. Carson, *Silent Spring*, 8.
50. Carson, *Silent Spring*, 8–9.
51. Carson, *Silent Spring*, 42.
52. Carson, *Silent Spring*, 47–48.
53. Carson, *Silent Spring*, 65.
54. Carson, *Silent Spring*, 99.
55. Carson, *Silent Spring*, 166–167.
56. Carson, *Silent Spring*, 205.
57. Carson, *Silent Spring*, 293.
58. Carson, *Silent Spring*, 127.
59. Carson, *Silent Spring*, 259.
60. Carson, *Silent Spring*, 188.
61. Carson, *Silent Spring*, 246.
62. Quoted in Terry Tempest Williams, "The Moral Courage of Rachel Carson," in *Courage for the Earth: Writers, Scientists, and Activists Celebrate the Life and Writing of Rachel Carson*, ed. Peter Matthiessen (Boston: Houghton Mifflin, 2007), 137.
63. Quoted in Al Gore, "Rachel Carson and Silent Spring," in *Courage for the Earth: Writers, Scientists, and Activists Celebrate the Life and Writing of Rachel Carson*, ed. Peter Matthiessen (Boston: Houghton Mifflin, 2007), 65–66.

64. Gore, "Rachel Carson," 297.
65. Clyde Haberman, "Rachel Carson, DDT, and the Fight Against Malaria," *New York Times*, January 22, 2017.
66. Robert Zubrin, "The Truth about DDT and Silent Spring," *New Atlantis*, September 27, 2012, https://www.thenewatlantis.com/publications/the-truth-about-ddt-and-silent-spring (accessed July 25, 2018).
67. Quoted in Terry Tempest Williams, "The Moral Courage of Rachel Carson," in *Courage for the Earth: Writers, Scientists, and Activists Celebrate the Life and Writing of Rachel Carson*, ed. Peter Matthiessen (Boston: Houghton Mifflin, 2007), 137–138.
68. Eyal Regev, "Sin, Atonement, and Israelite Identity in the Words of the Luminaries in Relation to 1 Enoch's Animal Apocalypse, *Hebrew Union College Annual* 84–85 (2013): 19.
69. Meaghan Henning, "Eternal Punishment as Paideia: The Ekphrasis of Hell in the Apocalypse of Peter and the Apocalypse of Paul," *Biblical Research* 58 (2013): 43.
70. Deborah Byrd, "Can You Find the Big Dipper?," *Tonight*, October 3, 2018, http://earthsky.org/?p=2806 (accessed July 19, 2018).
71. Kevin W. Gaston and Tim M. Blackburn, "How Many Birds Are There?," *Biodiversity and Conservation* 6 (1997): 615–625. Kevin Drum, "How Many Birds?," *Mother Jones*, March 23, 2011 http://www.motherjones.com/kevin-drum/2011/03/how-many-birds (accessed July 9, 2014).
72. Interview from the documentary *Inside Hitchcock* (1973), quoted in Camille Paglia, *The Birds* (London: British Film Institute, 1998), 88.
73. Paglia, *The Birds*, 40.
74. Stephen D. O'Leary, *Arguing the Apocalypse: A Theory of Millennial Rhetoric* (New York: Oxford University Press, 1994), 68–69, 83–84.
75. On Hitchcock's fear of birds: Peter Ackroyd, *Alfred Hitchcock: A Brief Life* (New York: Doubleday, 2015), 216. On his fear of women (especially Tippi Hedren), Ackroyd, 214–215 and Donald Spoto, *Spellbound by Beauty: Alfred Hitchcock and His Leading Ladies* (New York: Harmony Books, 2008), 243–277.
76. Roberta Smith, "New Light on Wyeth's Outer and Inner Landscapes," *New York Times*, May 29, 1998, https://www.nytimes.com/1998/05/29/arts/art-review-new-light-on-wyeth-s-outer-and-inner-landscapes.html (accessed July 25, 2018).
77. US Fish & Wildlife Service, "Bald Eagle Fact Sheet: Natural History, Ecology, and History of Recovery," June 2007, updated April 20, 2015, https://www.fws.gov/midwest/eagle/recovery/biologue.html (accessed July 26, 2018).
78. Sean Greene, "Extinction Looms for Native Bird Species on the Hawaiian Island of Kauai," *Los Angeles Times*, September 26, 2016, http://www.latimes.com/science/sciencenow/la-sci-sn-hawaii-native-birds-20160907-snap-story.html (accessed July 27, 2018).
79. Beverly Peterson Stearns and Stephen C. Stearns, *Watching, from the Edge of Extinction* (New Haven: Yale University Press, 1999), 41–55. On more recent developments, see Leslie Nemo, "A Year Later, It's Take Two for the Hawaiian Crow's Return to the Wild," *Audubon*, November 2017, https://www.audubon.org/news/a-year-later-its-take-two-hawaiian-crows-return-wild (accessed July 27, 2018). Also Russell McLendon, "Hawaiian Crows Return from Extinction in Wild," *Earth Matters*, January 28, 2018,

https://www.mnn.com/earth-matters/animals/blogs/hawaiian-crows-return-extinction-wild (accessed July 27, 2018).
80. US Fish & Wildlife Service, "California Condor Recovery Program," May 23, 2018, https://www.fws.gov/cno/es/CalCondor/Condor.cfm (accessed July 30, 2018).
81. Thom van Dooren, *Vulture* (London: Reaktion Books, 2011), 135, 137.
82. Chris Bowden, "Asian Vulture Crisis: It's Not Over Yet," *Conservation India* (April 2, 2018), http://www.conservationindia.org/articles/asian-vulture-crisis-its-not-over-yet (accessed July 31, 2018).
83. Vulture Conservation Foundation, "Indian Courts Ban Multi-dose Vials of Diclofenac," November 4, 2017, https://www.4vultures.org/2017/11/04/the-sanitary-workers-get-some-backup-in-india/ (accessed August 2, 2018). Also: Rachel Becker, "Cattle Drug Threatens Thousands of Vultures," *Nature*, April 29, 2016, https://www.nature.com/news/cattle-drug-threatens-thousands-of-vultures-1.19839 (accessed August 2, 2018).
84. Revive&Restore, "Passenger Pigeon Project," https://reviverestore.org/about-the-passenger-pigeon/ (accessed August 2, 2018).
85. Revive&Restore, "Staff / Board of Directors," https://reviverestore.org/about-us/ (accessed August 2, 2018).
86. Steph Yin, "We Might Soon Resurrect Extinct Species. Is It Worth the Cost?" *New York Times*, March 20, 2017, https://www.nytimes.com/2017/03/20/science/revive-restore-extinct-species-dna-mammoth-passenger-pigeon.html (accessed August 2, 2018).
87. National Audubon Society, *Guide to North American Birds: Chimney Swift*, https://www.audubon.org/field-guide/bird/chimney-swift (accessed August 2, 2018).
88. Kendra Pierre-Louis, "These Birds Are Racing to Their Mating Grounds. It's Exhausting," *New York Times*, August 1, 2018, D2.
89. Wallace Ravven, "Survival of the Shrewdest," *New York Times*, August 1, 2018, D3.

7
Birds in Romantic Arts, Sciences, and Religions

Death and Reverence

Birds are revered as angels, divine messengers, in a new religion of nature that has been developing since the Romantic era started, in the late 1700s. This gives hope, because religious commitments to helping birds could lead people to do things like cleaning up oceans that we are filling with plastic. But it is also terrible for birds to become angels, because birds used to be neighbors, companions, coworkers, and pests who were constantly present. Birds are angels now because people love them, but also because birds are often revered as exotic visitors, visions we seek on expeditions, or examples of a passive "nature" that must be preserved. To avoid completing our destruction of the world, humanity needs a religion of nature that includes birds as agents. We could allow birds to guide us, watching birds and listening to birds to show us how our actions can affirm life.

The Industrial Revolution contributed both to destruction and to reverence. As industry spread, wild habitats shrank, and wild birds retreated. On the other hand, industry grew alongside Romantic fascination with energies hidden in nature. As Jacob Bronowski noted in *The Ascent of Man*,[1] thrills of wonder accompanied the mining and burning of coal and channeling of electricity that displaced the descriptive sciences of the Renaissance and neoclassical eras.

In order for a religion of nature to take hold, in the world of mass media that began with the steam-powered printing press and extended to the internet, a new view of the universe was needed. Nature had to be explained clearly enough for humans to know how to serve it properly. This new cosmology was born with modern science, and especially in the evolutionary theory of Charles Darwin and his followers, which is to say all modern biologists. Meanwhile, Romantic currents of visual art and poetry also moved human cultures toward reverence for nature. Romantic art and evolutionary science shared a preoccupation with death, and the ultimate form of death is extinction. A series of bird extinctions (several described in detail as forms of apocalypse in the last chapter) resulted from the spread of Western empires, especially as those empires industrialized. First went the dodo, a stout flightless bird native to the Indian Ocean island of Mauritius. Dodos disappeared in the 1600s, probably destroyed less by humans than by other animals that European humans introduced to Mauritius. But direct human killing, by sailors seeking food and feathers and oil, and finally whole skins for trophies and museums, wiped out the only North Atlantic penguin, the great auk that lived in large colonies from Newfoundland and Iceland to Europe, by the early 1800s. Next, humans moved by their desires to decorate themselves with feathers and to protect their fruit trees and crops hunted the only parrot native to the United States, the Carolina parakeet, to near extinction by the mid-1800s and to complete oblivion in the early 1900s. Then with shocking suddenness, Americans armed with guns and nets and bombs, aided by the new technologies of telegraphs and railroads, killed and sold and ate into extinction the most numerous vertebrate in the world, the passenger pigeon. Only six decades separated its peak of population from its disappearance. The population of passenger pigeons rose to about five billion around 1850 (as compared to 1.2 billion humans at that time). They were still roosting in flocks of hundreds of millions in the 1870s, but their numbers fell to zero by 1914, when the last of the world's migratory pigeons died alone, twenty-nine years old, in a Baltimore zoo.

More than 150 species of birds have been exterminated in the last five centuries, and the decline of overall numbers of birds has been far greater. It is estimated that the number of individual birds in the land area of the United States fell by about 95 percent from 1492, when the first voyage of Columbus reached the Americas, to 1900.[2] The years since 1970 have seen a further decline of 30 percent—meaning that about three billion birds have died without being replaced—among the birds of North America.[3] In places where Native Americans once saw and heard hundreds or thousands of birds of a single species, our great-grandparents saw scores, our grandparents saw dozens, and birders now take note of individuals, couples, and families of birds in isolated nests. The "dawn chorus" has become a scattering of solo singers.

But fortunately, these waves of deaths provoked reactions. For example, species with spectacular plumes like the ostrich and the egret nearly disappeared around 1900, but both now flourish. The ostrich survives because of domestication in southern Africa, and the egret because of laws and international treaties forbidding hunting and organized campaigns to change fashion.[4] Raptors and scavengers such as the bald eagle, the California condor, the osprey, and many hawks and falcons were all nearly wiped out by the 1950s because of the insecticide DDT, building up through the food chain from crops to insects to rodents to large birds, but these predators have recovered in the last half-century as DDT has been banned. Even gulls, now often scorned by bird watchers because they are so common, were nearly killed off by the fashion of making hats and stoles out of whole birds. Campaigns to change fashion ensued, and flocks of gulls now roam ocean coasts and parking lots inland.

When Alfred Hitchcock filmed *The Birds* in 1962 (as detailed in Chapter 6), he used crows and gulls as his prime attackers of humans. It would have been unrealistic to include really ferocious birds like eagles and hawks, because so few of them were alive in the wild. A new version of *The Birds* could be much more vivid. It could show eagles stealing babies and peregrine falcons slashing adult human throats by striking at two hundred miles per hour.

Some birds have become agents of their own recovery by adapting to the conditions that humans have created. Before industrialization, the birds now called chimney swifts nested in hollow trees, cliffs, and caves, but they gained a new name by moving into chimneys.[5] Crows have learned to live in human cities so successfully that a book, *Crow Planet: Essential Wisdom from the Urban Wilderness* (2009), celebrates their triumph.[6] In Tokyo, crows have long been observed using automobile traffic to crack open nuts.[7] Massive night roosts of crows in cities, campuses, and forests have become problematic for humans,[8] and it seems possible that more crows are alive today than ever before. The success of nonmigratory pigeons, the settled cousins of the passenger pigeon, inspired a book called *Superdove: How the Pigeon Took Manhattan . . . and the World* (2008).[9] And although the Carolina parakeet was hunted to death in the United States, escaped pet parrots are now succeeding so well that *Forbes* magazine reported twenty-five non-native parrot species breeding wild, in states from Florida and California to the Canadian border, in 2019.[10]

The first human generations that destroyed whole species of birds also began to celebrate and even to venerate avian survivors. The same generations that conquered nature developed religions of nature. Birds have become embodiments of divine Nature, the only wild animals that most humans see and "one of the few aspects of nature that will come to you" (as novelist and birder Jonathan Franzen has observed).[11] Visual artists and poets began to express reverence for birds as part of their reverence for nature centuries ago, and their work has inspired activists who have formed organizations that are working to end and to reverse the long story of decline.

Audubon the Savior

At the center of the new religion of nature stands a savior armed with a rifle and a paintbrush. John James Audubon (1785–1851) lived and died at a crucial moment between the thoughtless destruction of species as Western empires expanded and the horrified realization that the most numerous bird species, and perhaps all wild birds, could be eradicated. Today, a loose network of national, state, and local societies in the United States bears the name "Audubon," and that name always stands for the appreciation and protection of birds. But Audubon himself killed almost every bird that he painted and thousands more. The heritage of John James Audubon—a killer who loved his victims and an artist who inspired conservationists—began the rhythm of death and resurrection that continues to run through the new religion of nature.

Audubon became a legend, an American wilderness hero like Daniel Boone and Davy Crockett, decades before his death (Figure 7.1). And Audubon left a legacy of art, paintings of birds that remain in demand today, selling for millions and displayed in museums and libraries. Also a scientist, he contributed no theories but wrote volumes of observations. His work, his art, and his legend led people to see birds not simply as animals who could be appropriated as symbols or in myths, but as agents in their own stories who could be seen with the seriousness of religion.

Audubon died surrounded by nature but close to the city, in a mansion within a wooded estate he owned on the West Side of Manhattan. Part of that estate is still known as Audubon Terrace, between 155th and 156th Streets, with Broadway on the east and Riverside Drive on the west (in Audubon's day, the forest extended from Broadway to the Hudson River, about thirty-five acres). His death provoked a rumor that he was the son of Louis XVI, king of France and husband of the infamous Queen Marie Antoinette, both of whom were guillotined in the French Revolution. That rumor gained force from the mysteries surrounding Audubon's origins.

BIRDS IN ROMANTIC ARTS, SCIENCES, RELIGIONS 173

Figure 7.1 John James Audubon in 1826, when he sailed to England to show his paintings and sell subscriptions for his massive folio *Birds of America*, which cost about $35,000. At age forty-one, Audubon dressed as the frontiersman he had become. Portrait by John Weir.
Photo by Alamy.

It was true that Audubon's parentage was at least partly French, but the details were obscured by the sexual effects of slavery and by forced migrations during a revolutionary era. The great American painter and explorer was born in Haiti while that nation was still a French colony. His father, Jean Audubon (1744–1818), worked as a French naval officer and merchant marine captain around the Caribbean and in New Orleans, which was also French at the time.[12] The elder Audubon acquired a sugar plantation in Haiti, where he had a slave mistress of mixed race named Bouffard, who bore his three daughters.[13] His only son, who would become our Audubon, was born to a French woman named Jeanne Rabin (1758–1785), who was brought to Haiti as a servant by Captain Audubon. She died a few months after giving birth.

Conditions both in Haiti and in France were becoming disordered in those years, and in 1788 Captain Audubon thought it best to take his three-year-old son—whose birth had been recorded without a name, and who was sometimes called Jean Rabin and sometimes Jean Fougère—to France, where Captain Audubon's childless legal wife lived in the center of Nantes, a port city on the Loire River near the Atlantic coast. Madame Audubon raised the boy until he reached young manhood. She saw that he was educated and confirmed as a Roman Catholic, finally acquiring his father's surname.[14]

Writing at fifty about his Catholic confirmation, Audubon showed a detached attitude toward religion:

> I was within a few months of being seventeen years old, when my stepmother, who was an earnest Catholic, took into her head that I should be confirmed; my father agreed. I was surprised and indifferent, but yet as I loved her as if she had been my own mother,—and well did she merit my deepest affection,—I took to the catechism, studied it and other matters pertaining to the ceremony, and all was performed to her liking.[15]

This passage exhausts the attention Audubon gave to formal religion in all of his voluminous writings. But later in that manuscript, as he described a life of poverty in America in 1820, when he had just buried an infant daughter and was surviving on bread and apples while traveling with two young sons, Audubon told of finding God among the birds:

> One of the most extraordinary things among all these adverse circumstances was that I never for a day gave up listening to the songs of our birds, or watching their peculiar habits, or delineating them in the best way that I could; nay, during my deepest troubles I frequently would wrench myself from the persons around me, and retire to some secluded part of our noble forests; and many a time, at the sound of the wood thrush's melodies have I fallen on my knees, and there prayed earnestly to our God.[16]

This became a pattern of spiritual life among the founders of the religion of nature that was beginning in Audubon's time. From the English Romantic poets to Walt Whitman and Emily Dickinson, T. S. Eliot and Robert Penn Warren and Mary Oliver, these writers were not drawn by Christian teachings to embrace a religion of nature. Dickinson wrote to her cousin Eugenia Hall that she hoped Eugenia loved birds, because "It is economical. It saves going to Heaven."[17] Like Audubon, Dickinson and other modern poets met divine power directly in birds.

For John James Audubon, the journey from Catholic confirmation in France to becoming a founding saint in the religion of nature proved long and difficult. In 1803, as France conquered Europe and the first successful slave revolt of the New World made Haiti independent, the eighteen-year-old Audubon escaped being drafted into the French armies of Napoleon by being sent by his father to the United States, where he claimed to have been born in Louisiana (by then an American territory, unlike Haiti) in order to avoid deportation. Passing through the port of New York, he made his way to an estate that his father had purchased in Mill Grove, Pennsylvania, near Philadelphia. The young man's French education had included instruction in "music, dancing, and drawing" (he was an accomplished flutist and violinist), and the Pennsylvania countryside gave him many opportunities to indulge interests in "shooting, fishing, and riding on horseback." He took special pleasure in hunting "fowls of every sort." He became an American outdoorsman with the style of an English or French dandy. As he recalled in 1835:

> I was ridiculously fond of dress. To have seen me going shooting in black satin smallclothes, or breeches, with silk stockings, and the finest ruffled shirt Philadelphia could afford, was, as I now realize, an absurd spectacle. . . . I purchased the best horses in the country, and rode well, and felt proud of it; my guns and fishing-tackle were equally good, always expensive and richly ornamented, often with silver.[18]

A physically imposing man of more than average height with a broad chest, thick hair falling below his shoulders, and an aquiline nose, Audubon was suited from youth to his legend as an explorer, scientist, and artist. His French taste in clothing quickly yielded to buckskins and furs, as he adopted the costume of an American frontiersman.

Among Audubon's new neighbors in Pennsylvania was Lucy Bakewell (1787–1874), herself born in England and the daughter of a landed family, whom he married in 1808. Bakewell and Audubon made a passionate couple, based on their surviving letters and the four children they had despite frequent separations. The first twenty years of their marriage were filled with harrowing adventures involving two failed businesses (a "mercantile house" and a steam logging mill) and transplantations of the family, with long-term residences in Louisville, Kentucky, and in New Orleans. Lucy ran grammar schools in her homes, and both Lucy and John James taught various skills to make money, while Audubon also hunted for food and sold portraits of people. Separations of up to fourteen months took place as Audubon went on expeditions "to purchase goods," but he was less intent on business than on enlarging a catalog of bird drawings that he always carried with him. The autobiography that he wrote for his sons in 1835, unpublished until 1893, confessed that "a hundred times and more," he was "driving several horses . . . laden with goods and dollars," when he "lost sight of the packsaddles, and the cash they bore, to watch the motions of a warbler."[19]

Early in these decades of travel, in 1810, Lucy Audubon's family connections led to a meeting of her husband with the Scottish-born naturalist Alexander Wilson (1766–1813), who was systematically seeking and drawing the birds of America. Wilson published five volumes of *American Ornithology* between 1805 and 1812, and he showed the first two volumes to Lucy Bakewell's uncle Benjamin, a glass manufacturer in Pittsburgh. Bakewell suggested that Wilson, who was always seeking collaborators who knew about birds, seek out his niece's husband in Louisville. There Wilson showed his work to Audubon, while Audubon showed Wilson some of his own drawings. Audubon nearly subscribed to purchase Wilson's series, but did not because he became convinced that his own drawings and observations of birds were superior. He was inspired by meeting Wilson with a dream that, one day, his own works would be reproduced in books surpassing Wilson's, with even the largest birds at full life size.

Audubon added emotion to Wilson's emphasis on accuracy, moving beyond scientific illustration into the realm of fine, imaginative art. He posed his birds in lively postures and action scenes, amid other birds and animals, plants and natural settings, and so foreshadowed (and probably inspired) the later dioramas of museums and the documentaries of film and television. While he was still living at the estate his father had bought at Mill Grove, Audubon invented the technique of mounting the bodies of birds on boards with wires so that he could pose them as though they were alive, then draw them in detail.[20]

With regard to the religious effects of Audubon's technique of posing and painting dead birds, Jonathan Rosen has commented,

> The impulse to kill and then resurrect is everywhere evident in Audubon's paintings. He was obsessed with bringing the creatures he shot back to life; it is the key to all his work. This connects him to modern-day birdwatchers. It also gives his work a quasi-religious component. . . . Audubon's birds are icons of an emerging American religion.[21]

The formal American religions of Audubon's time tended to value abstemious attitudes toward the material world, resisting all sensual pleasures with the nearly monastic discipline of capitalists that sociologist Max Weber described as "this-worldly asceticism." Weber's ideal capitalist—whom he found in that emblematic American, Benjamin Franklin—practiced self-denial for the sake of success and health, building the kingdom of God in this world, rather than to attain heaven.[22] Despite his French origins and youthful love of fine clothing, Audubon became not only an American (taking the oath of a citizen in 1812), but an exemplar of these new American, generically religious virtues like inventiveness, frugality, hard work, an intrepid spirit of exploration, and abstinence from alcohol and rich foods. On March 18, 1848, while the naturalist descended toward death in his New York mansion, *Scientific American* magazine published this note:

> It is said that when this distinguished naturalist arrived in the city of Cincinnati, his poverty was so extreme that he humbly requested permission of a drayman to pull a few hairs from his horse's tail. This novel request was granted, and these hairs Audubon manufactured into rings which he disposed of for a few cents, and thus laid the foundation of fortune and success in life.[23]

Sixteen years earlier, in 1832, when Audubon was just becoming famous for his enormous *Birds of America*, which was published in a series of "double elephant" folios from 1827 to 1838, the *Key West Gazette* published a reminiscence of Audubon from Dr. Benjamin Stroebel, an amateur naturalist who lived most of his life on Key West. Stroebel reported that during a visit of seventeen days to Key West in May 1832, Audubon revealed himself as "a most extraordinary man" whom "danger cannot daunt, and difficulties vanish before him." As the doctor recalled: "During his stay here his hour of rising was three o'clock in the morning; from that time until noon, and sometimes even until night he was engaged in hunting among the Mangrove Keys—despite of heat, sandflies and mosquitoes." Four years later, in 1836, Dr. Stroebel completed a book of Florida sketches that included a chapter on Audubon, and he added some details about diet, alcohol, and work during those days that started at 3:00 a.m.:

> During these expeditions he took no refreshments but biscuit and molasses and water, proving by his example that ardent spirits are never necessary to health even under the greatest exposure and fatigue. Before and after dinner, as soon as he returned from the morning jaunt, Mr. Audubon employed himself in drawing such birds as he might have procured during the morning, and in the evening he was on the hunt again.
>
> According to Stroebel, who knew Key West well and had his own interest in birds, Audubon explored "places, into which I question much, if any animal two legged or four legged, had ever before penetrated, unless it was the Pelican or Cormorant."[24]

Writing for his sons about his habits as a young man, Audubon claimed that he was "temperate to an *intemperate* degree." He specified that he "lived, until the day of my union with your mother, on milk, fruits, and vegetables, with the addition of game and fish at times, but never had I swallowed a single glass of wine or spirits until the day of my wedding." Audubon attributed "my uncommon, indeed iron, constitution" to this abstinence. His refusals to drink alcohol and to eat luxuriously sometimes "annoyed" others, especially in France, where he "never went to dinners . . . because often not a single dish was to my taste or fancy, and I could eat nothing from the sumptuous tables before me." But still approving of his premarital simplicity more than twenty-five years after his wedding, Audubon wondered why he had ever modified his diet to be more social, and asked, "Why should not mankind in general be more abstemious than mankind is?"[25]

In all of his writing, Audubon cultivated his legend. He told a story of meeting with Daniel Boone (1734–1820), including a vivid physical description of Boone that could not have been true, because when he invited Boone to join an expedition in 1814 the old explorer was already eighty, and Boone wrote back to say that his hunting days were past.[26] Other stories seem more likely, because they are less heroic, as when he spent a night in the cabin of a frontier woman and her two sons who tried to rob him, but Audubon was rescued by vigilantes who were pursuing his assailants and who hanged them. An episode from 1819 described how Audubon stabbed and nearly killed a man who had attacked him with a club in a dispute about the finances of a failed mill.[27]

One of the most powerful stories that Audubon told of himself appeared in his *Ornithological Biography* (5 volumes, 1831–1839), in the chapter on the golden eagle. Unlike most of the birds he painted, the eagle came into Audubon's hands in 1833, not through his rifle but by his purchase of a live bird that had been caught by one foot in a trap for foxes. Weighing the eagle, Audubon found that the bird was female, several pounds heavier than males. Nevertheless, he changed the bird's sex in his account, probably in deference to the gender expectations of his audience. Calling the eagle a "royal prisoner," and noting "[her] looks of proud disdain," Audubon felt tempted to set the bird free, so that he could "see [her] spread out [her] broad wings and sail away toward the rocks of [her] wild haunts," but was convinced by an inner voice that "seemed to whisper that I ought to take the portrait of this magnificent bird." To do this by the method he had developed, Audubon had to kill the eagle and mount her in a pose on wires.

After spending "a whole day in watching [her] movements," then another day in deciding how to mount the bird, on the third day the artist began an attempt to "take away [her] life with the least pain to [her]." A prominent medical doctor, George Parkman, advised "suffocating [her] by means of burning charcoal," but hours of confinement in a cage in a tiny room with a charcoal fire and blankets sealing the doors did not result even in unconsciousness: "There stood the Eagle on [her] perch, with [her] bright unflinching eye turned towards me, and as lively and vigorous as ever!" Audubon tried more charcoal, until midnight, found the bird "still uninjured," and then went on for ten more hours before going to sleep. The next day, he added sulfur to the fire, "But we were nearly driven from our home in a few hours by the stifling vapours, while the noble bird continued to stand erect, and to look defiance at us whenever we approached [her] post of martyrdom." At this point, Audubon resorted to "a method always used as the last expedient." He obtained "a long pointed piece of steel," a sharp needle, and thrust it through the eagle's heart.

Audubon then "sat up nearly the whole of another night to outline [her], and worked so constantly at the drawing, that it nearly cost me my life."

The project of killing, mounting, and drawing the eagle in its setting, on a mountain with a rabbit in its talons, took more than two weeks (observers commented on the stench that often accompanied Audubon's method of painting birds) (Figure 7.2). After completing the picture, he was "completely prostrated" for days, almost certainly because of a stroke or TIA (transient ischemic attack), since he was unable to speak or to hold anything in his hands. He thanked Dr. Parkman and two other friends for their "unremitting attention" in restoring his health,[28] but at age forty-eight Audubon began to decline, continuing to go on journeys to find birds, but never again working at full strength.

The resulting picture has been recognized as one of the greatest of the 435 color plates that appeared in *Birds of America*. The eagle is starting to fly, her beak facing the sky and open in a cry, as she holds the dead rabbit, one talon piercing its right eye. Along the whole bottom of the scene ranges a horizon of mountain peaks, and at the lower left corner a fallen tree bridges a gap from one peak to another.

A mystery surrounds that fallen tree. In the original watercolor painting, now in the collection of the New York Historical Society, a man with long hair, in buckskin clothing and cap (the wilderness outfit Audubon adopted, after his youthful dandy clothes) has mounted astride the log, apparently using it to get from one peak to another, with a rifle and an eagle strapped to his back. For some reason, that figure of a man was taken off the log when the London engraver made the plate used to print *Birds of America*. Given that the eagle came to Audubon by purchase as he visited the city of Boston, not by clambering on the eagle's native mountains of New Hampshire, it seems possible that the naturalist's concern for accuracy overcame the artist's first decision about composition. Biographer Richard Rhodes, citing art historian Theodore Stebbins, has noted that the pose of the bird in Audubon's *Golden Eagle* parallels that of the most famous painting of Napoleon, Jean-Louis David's *Napoleon Crossing the Alps*,[29] and that Audubon might have used the hunter crawling on the log as a parallel to soldiers dragging cannons in the background behind David's heroic Napoleon, pointing upward on his rearing horse. That reading is supported by Audubon's claim to have been taught painting by David during his adolescence in France. It has also been suggested that Audubon put himself into the eagle painting as a kind of confession to murder, but that the engraver found the figure of a frontiersman too much trouble, just a distraction from the eagle and its prey.

BIRDS IN ROMANTIC ARTS, SCIENCES, RELIGIONS 181

Figure 7.2 Killing this golden eagle without destroying it as a model took Audubon days, and painting it as it decomposed left Audubon disabled. The artist appeared in the painting but not in the engraved edition.
General Collection, Beinecke Rare Book and Manuscript Library, Yale University.

The only other human who appears in Audubon's bird paintings, and the only human who was transferred from his original drawings and watercolors into the plates for *Birds of America*, stands aiming a rifle at a snowy egret (also called a white or snowy heron). Here another level of editing took place. The hunter appeared in the original watercolor, and survived in the engraving by Nicholas Havell for the double elephant-sized, original English edition of *Birds of America* and also in the *Ornithological Biography*, the work that Audubon published in America as a commentary on *Birds*, but this hunter disappeared in the later, seven- and ten-volume editions of *Birds of America* that were printed in a large (Royal Octavo) but not enormous size in Philadelphia in the 1840s.

Audubon's mixed feelings about killing birds may have led him to edit the hunter out. In the *Ornithological Biography*, he gave an account of how a snowy egret acts when it has been shot. Audubon's writing has a specificity which suggests personal experience:

> When, on being wounded in the wing one falls into the water, it swims off toward the nearest shore, and runs to hide itself by the side of some log, or towards a tree which if possible it climbs, ascending to its very top. When seized, they peck at you with great spirit, and are capable of inflicting a severe wound.

Scientific Realism Affects the Uses of Birds in Poetry

The later 1800s saw science transform the literary treatment of birds. Poets of the English Renaissance, from Chaucer in his *Parliament of Fowls* through Shakespeare, had used birds to personify human feelings. Romantic poets of the 1800s on both sides of the Atlantic, such as the English Percy Shelley (in "To a Skylark") and John Keats ("To a Nightingale") and the American William Cullen Bryant ("To a Water Fowl"), saw birds as provocations of human envy, creatures who knew no sorrow and for whom God provided blissful lives in secure nests. But then something changed, as scholar and feminist Louise Pound (1872–1958) observed in 1930: "In the day of the ornithologist and of Audubon clubs the contrast of the older poets between the pure joy of the bird's destiny and the wretchedness of man's seems the pretty fiction that it is."[30] Birds were now seen as participants in the struggle for survival that Charles Darwin described. Birds of the scientific age had their own joys and sorrows.

Pound identified this change in a poem of Walt Whitman (1819–1892), written in 1859 (the year of publication for Darwin's *Origin of Species*), called "Out of the Cradle Endlessly Rocking." Whitman recalled how, as a boy, he had watched the nesting of two mockingbirds, the species that Audubon ranked as the greatest singers among all American birds. Whitman called these birds "guests from Alabama" who made their family home for the summer near Paumonok beach on Long Island. From May through August he had watched this couple lay and tend their "four light-green eggs spotted with brown," till one day suddenly the female bird was gone, the nest was empty, and he heard the male calling after his mate. Whitman gave eighteen stanzas to the bereft bird's song, ending with:

> O past! O happy life! O songs of joy!
> In the air, in the woods, over fields,
> Loved! loved! loved! loved! loved!
> But my mate no more, no more with me!
> We two together no more.

This was how Whitman the man of forty recalled himself as a boy learning of death. Six years later, in 1865, mourning President Lincoln, Whitman made verses translating the song of a hermit thrush into the framework of his 206-line elegy, "When Lilacs Last in the Dooryard Bloom'd."

No great poet has written of birds as equals more than Emily Dickinson (1830–1886). She mentioned birds in 220 poems, sometimes in passing, but often as the focus of her attention, as in "A Bird, came down the Walk" (1862):

> He did not know I saw –
> He bit an Angle Worm in halves
> And ate the fellow, raw.

For those who appreciate accurate observation of birds, the most perceptive lines in this poem are "And he unrolled his feathers, / And rowed him softer Home – / Than oars divide the Ocean." These lines show that Dickinson was interacting with a crow, because crows fly with a rowing motion, reaching ahead and drawing air back, unlike many birds who stroke straight down and up and then glide. Crows rarely glide, though they can soar. But accurate description of flight is not the main source of the poem's power. Rather, this poem evokes the crow personally and shows how well writers of Dickinson's time were coming to know birds. The juxtaposition of predatory murder, caution, fear, and beauty caused Dickinson scholar Helen Vendler to introduce the poem as a "bizarre little narrative."[31] Both bird and poet seem equally entangled in the "danger" and caution raised as Dickinson offers the crow a crumb.

Another relationship between a human and a bird features in one of Dickinson's most often quoted poems, "Hope is the thing with feathers."

> "Hope" is the thing with feathers –
> That perches in the soul –

The bird of this clear poem, joyful despite "gale" and "storm," is every bit as divine as the dove that embodied the Holy Spirit who landed on Jesus at his baptism in John 1:32, or "in bodily form, as a dove" in Luke 3:22. All four canonical Gospels have the dove as the incarnation of God in their accounts of this baptism, and Dickinson is writing about the same avian form of God here. In traditional theology, just as despair is the sin against the Holy Spirit, so hope is the sign of the Spirit's presence. But now a real bird stands in the place of God.

And a more cosmic, even pantheistic, version of God as a bird appears in the Dickinson poem numbered 653, also dated to 1862, the same year as "Hope is the thing with feathers." Usually titled "Of Being is a Bird" after its first line, this poem of twelve lines presents God as pervading the "General Heavens," showing itself in avian form and filling the air with music. As Dickinson scholar Stanley Plumly noted in 2014, "The concept of Being itself—as an ontological reality—is enacted as a bird, a bird gladly celebrated."[32]

The standard collection of Dickinson's poems dates "Of Being is a Bird" to the same year when she first sent samples of her work to Thomas Wentworth Higginson (1823–1911), a Civil War colonel and Unitarian minister who had left the pulpit and became an editor of the *Atlantic Monthly*. Higginson did more than anyone to make Dickinson's poems known to the world.

A year after he first read Dickinson, in 1863, Higginson published a book called *Out-Door Papers* that featured fourteen chapters on various subjects, from "Saints, and their Bodies" to "Gymnastics" and "The Health of our Girls." One of Higginson's last chapters, "The Life of Birds," anticipated recent books such as Jon Young's *What the Robin Knows* (2012) in its descriptions of the different languages of birdsong. Higginson observed that bird language was the only nonhuman communication that deserved to be called "language," because among animals only a bird or a human "employs its tongue, *lingua*, in producing sound."[33] He described and translated eight different groups of notes that a Robin sang to him in a few moments, when he took shelter from rain under an oak tree where the bird perched, and presented those messages as only a small sample of the Robin's "endless vocabulary."[34] Recalling conversations with Henry David Thoreau (1817–1862), who had only just died, Higginson praised Thoreau for his "unerring eyes" in identifying birds and their geographical distribution from Minnesota to New England.[35] Higginson quoted Darwin to remind his readers "how profoundly ignorant we are of the condition of existence of every animal." He added his own conclusion: "And from Humming-Bird to Eagle, the daily existence of every bird is a remote and bewitching mystery."[36]

Evolution and Birds as Agents

Higginson, Thoreau, and Emily Dickinson each took part in and responded to a scientific revolution that was transforming human thinking about birds: the revolution brought about by Charles Darwin's discovery of evolution through natural selection. Darwin's pathbreaking book, *The Origin of Species*, appeared in 1859. But before Darwin published, and within the evidence set forth by Darwin, birds had already been appearing to some visionaries as revelations of the most basic power of life. Variation among the beaks of finches on the Galapagos Islands helped Darwin to understand natural selection. Decades earlier, in 1836, geologist Edward Hitchcock wrote that the mysterious tracks in stone that had been found in 1802 along the Connecticut River belonged to ancient birds.[37] Uniformitarian principles of geology implied that the river and the bird tracks were both many millions of years old, not thousands as the Bible's genealogies implied. By 1844, Thoreau's friend and patron Ralph Waldo Emerson (1803–1882) was rejoicing in his most famous essay, *Nature*, that geology had exploded "our

Mosaic and Ptolemaic" understandings of time and set all forms of life into a new historical context:

> Now we learn what patient periods must round themselves before the rock is formed, then before the rock is broken, and the first lichen race has disintegrated the thinnest external plate into soil. . . . How far off yet is the trilobite! how far the quadruped! how inconceivably remote is man! . . . It is a long way from the granite to the oyster; farther yet to Plato, and the preaching of the immortality of the soul. . . . Nature is always consistent, though she feigns to contravene her own laws . . . Space exists to divide creatures, but by clothing the sides of a bird with a few feathers, she gives him a petty omnipresence. The direction is forever onward.[38]

In this new and vast expanse of time opened by geology, birds stood out as both ancient but also youthful animals, animals who mediated the life of the spirit to people. For example, Thoreau's journal for July 5, 1852, claimed that the song of the wood thrush makes everyone who hears it "young, and Nature is in her spring." Only the thrush among birds "declares the immortal wealth and vigor that is in the forest." For anyone who hears the wood thrush, "It is a new world and a free country, and the gates of heaven are not shut." The song of this thrush, wrote Thoreau, brings a power of redemption:

> He sings to make men take higher and truer views of things. He sings to amend their institutions; to relieve the slave on the plantation and the prisoner in his dungeon, the slave in the house of luxury and the prisoner of his own low thoughts.[39]

Without much doubt, most readers would conclude that Thoreau here deliberately overstated his knowledge of the intentions of the wood thrush. But Thoreau's suggestion that the thrush responded in some way to plantation slaves at work or to prisoners in cells, or to the moods of other humans, fit well with the perceptions of others who were being led by advances in science to listen to birds much more closely. Thoreau, Higginson, and Dickinson all heard messages in birdsong that were missed by Emerson, who had lamented, "We are as much strangers in nature, as we are aliens from God. We do not understand the notes of birds."[40] And even Emerson's complaint showed the direction of scientific and religious thought. Emerson *wanted* to understand birds, and he thought that understanding birds would bring humanity into a new relationship with nature and with God.

What Emerson desired, Thoreau claimed to have experienced in the relations with birds that he described in *Walden* (1854). Immediately after beginning to spend his nights in a cabin in the woods, just after July 4, 1845, Thoreau "found myself suddenly neighbor to the birds; not by having imprisoned one, but having caged myself near them."

> I was not only nearer to some of those which commonly frequent the garden and the orchard, but to those wilder and more thrilling songsters of the forest which never, or rarely, serenade a villager,—the wood thrush, the veery, the scarlet tanager, the field sparrow, the whip-poor-will, and many others.[41]

Months later, on a calm October afternoon, Thoreau had a long encounter with a loon on the surface of Walden Pond. He had often seen a loon early in the mornings, close to the shore, and "endeavored to overtake him in a boat, to see how he would maneuver," but the loon "would dive and be completely lost."[42] This time, Thoreau was already in his boat looking for a loon when one surfaced about six yards in front of him, then "set up his wild laugh and betrayed himself." As Thoreau paddled toward the loon the bird dove, "But when he came up I was nearer than before." Then the bird dove again, and Thoreau "miscalculated the direction he would take" and paddled in the wrong direction, finding himself almost three hundred yards away when the loon came up for air, "and again he laughed long and loud, and with more reason than before." Further efforts failed to get Thoreau any closer than about thirty yards.

> Each time, when he came to the surface, turning his head this way and that, he coolly surveyed the water and the land, and apparently chose his course so that he might come up where there was the widest expanse of water and at the greatest distance from the boat. It was surprising how quickly he made up his mind and put his resolve into execution. He led me at once to the widest part of the pond, and could not be driven from it. While he was thinking one thing in his brain, I was endeavoring to divine his thought in mine. It was a pretty game, played on the smooth surface of the pond, a man against a loon. Suddenly your adversary's checker disappears beneath the board, and the problem is to place yours nearest to where his will reappear

again. Sometimes he would come up unexpectedly on the opposite side of me, having apparently passed directly under the boat.[43]

When Thoreau decided to wait with his oars and stare out over the pond looking for the bird to surface, he "would suddenly be startled by his unearthly laugh behind me." For an hour the game went on, and when the loon was most successful at surfacing far away, "He uttered a long-drawn unearthly howl, probably more like that of a wolf than any bird." Thoreau concluded that the loon "laughed in derision of my efforts, confident of his own resources." A little later the sky became overcast, and the game ended with another of those howls, "perhaps the wildest sound that is ever heard here,"[44] a sound that Thoreau interpreted as the prayer of the loon:

> He uttered one of those prolonged howls, as if calling on the god of loons to aid him, and immediately there came a wind from the east and rippled the surface, and filled the whole air with misty rain, and I was impressed as if it were the prayer of the loon answered, and his god was angry with me; and so I left him disappearing far away on the tumultuous surface.[45]

When Thoreau read Darwin, he interpreted the account of how the many forms of life had evolved through natural selection as good news, a new gospel. Humans were not "strangers" in nature as Emerson thought, but participants in the same system of nature that produced other animals. Writing "The Succession of Forest Trees" in 1860, Thoreau concluded that evolution yielded a richer sense of life than his previous image of God as an omnipotent Artist. "The development theory implies a greater vital force in nature, because it is more flexible and accommodating, and equivalent to a sort of constant *new* creation."[46]

Listening to the loon on Walden Pond and reading Darwin, Thoreau took his place in the first generation that would ascribe both self-consciousness and intrinsic rights to birds. Modern science began with the Enlightenment rejection of ancient and medieval assumptions that the entire world, including animals, took part in a universal life force, and had consciousness with which to relate to gods or humans. Prescientific thinkers, from the writers of the Hebrew Scriptures and Aristophanes in *The Birds* to Attar in *The Conference of the Birds* and Francis of Assisi's sermons to the birds, saw birds as self-conscious agents, but without ascribing rights to them. The implicit panentheism of premodern worldviews enabled ancient and medieval thinkers to see all things as filled with divine life without developing scruples about how any animals, including humans, were treated. A sensibility that saw everything within God still allowed sinful humans to suffer forever in hell, and also for the crucifixion of human rebels, torture of heretics, public burning of witches, and drawing and quartering of traitors. In this view, the suffering of creatures raised no moral problems. If everything was divine, nothing was exempt from suffering, but divine power redeemed that suffering.

The focus of modern thinkers on self-consciousness as the crucial distinction of humanity from the rest of creation broke this continuity. René Descartes (1596–1650), whose *Cogito, ergo sum* ("I think, therefore I am") turned philosophy to focus on the process of reasoning, saw an absolute difference between humanity and the rest of nature. This enabled moderns to develop a sharp distinction between human beings with rights and all other beings in the world. Granting consciousness only to the realm of spirit and divorcing consciousness from the material world, Descartes concluded that animals had no consciousness of suffering. He performed vivisections to study physiological mechanisms. His followers at the seminary of Port-Royal, where the great philosopher and geometrician Blaise Pascal worked, nailed living animals to boards and cut them open, declaring that their cries were "the noise of a little spring that had been touched" and no evidence that they were self-conscious or even that their bodies actually had feelings.[47] Immanuel Kant (1724–1804), the most influential moralist of the modern era, taught in his lectures on ethics that "animals are not self-conscious, and are there merely as a means to an end. That end is man."[48]

As the Enlightenment progressed toward the Romantic era, some writers protested the denial of all rights to animals. David Hume, Voltaire, and Rousseau all argued that people should try to minimize animal suffering, but such arguments had only a few, partial results. Laws proposed to ban bull baiting and to regulate treatment of horses failed to pass the English Parliament in 1800 and 1821. But Jeremy Bentham (1748–1832), the founder of Utilitarianism, employed his principle that morality should seek "the greatest happiness of the greatest number" to shift the focus from whether animals had reason to whether animals could suffer, and here the evidence was harder (though not impossible, as among the followers of Descartes) to deny. A bill protecting horses and asses from mistreatment, but not including dogs and cats, passed Parliament in 1822, and the Royal Society for the Prevention of Cruelty to Animals was founded in 1824.

After Darwin's *Origin of Species* (1859) proposed that all life arose from common ancestors and developed by natural selection, and his *Descent of Man* (1871) explicitly included humanity in evolution, the great theorist published *The Expression of Emotions in Man and Animals* (1872), where he taught that animals were capable of "love, memory, curiosity, reason, and sympathy."[49] Darwin transformed theology almost as much as biology. Without intending to do so, he gave theologians who no longer took Genesis literally another way to defend the Christian doctrines of original sin and the human need for redemption. A week after Darwin's death in 1882, despite his expressed wish to be buried next to his older brother Erasmus and infant children in a family plot, Darwin was interred among the great English writers and thinkers in Westminster Abbey. As the London *Times* noted about his corpse, "The Abbey needed it more than it needed the Abbey."[50]

Meanwhile, the extension of the British Empire to India was increasing English and American exposure to Hindu doctrines of divine spirit inhabiting all life, karma, reincarnation, and vegetarianism. Although both Jeremy Bentham and Charles Darwin continued to eat meat, the nineteenth century saw the birth of some semivegetarian communities like Brook Farm (1841–1846) in Concord, Massachusetts, and of more extreme experiments like Fruitlands, where (for seven months) the famous Alcott family and others subsisted on nuts and fruits, avoiding even the killing of plants. Sylvester Graham's prescription of whole wheat flour and vegetarianism persisted to the present, as did the Seventh-Day Adventist movement, which from its birth in 1844 has taken the biblical prohibition against eating blood seriously enough to lead some to a vegetarian diet and to create a cereal industry through the Kellogg family. Religions and science both prepared the culture for movements to ban the killing of birds, even for food.

Women Win First Victories for the Bird Protection Movement

But before a new religion of nature could emerge, the male monopoly on religious authority needed to be at least weakened, if not eliminated. Why would the men who ruled have wanted any new religion? As scholars like Elaine Pagels, Elizabeth Clark, and Rodney Stark have found, Christianity rose out of the welter of religions in the ancient Roman world, in large part because women of the Roman upper classes and slaves both found in the faith a new vision of social life and a community that affirmed their own worth.[51] Christian mothers like Helena, the mother of Constantine, the first Christian emperor, and Monica, the mother of Augustine, the first major Latin theologian, helped bring their pagan sons to convert. Something similar happened in the 1800s, especially in the worldwide, cosmopolitan British Empire and in its breakaway province, the United States.

Scholars have written for half a century about the "feminization" of American culture in the nineteenth century,[52] and parallel developments took place everywhere that British culture touched. The age is called Victorian today, and at the center of Victorianism was Queen Victoria, a woman who reigned over the largest empire in history from 1837 to 1901 and who (with her beloved Prince Albert) brought a new global, middle-class culture, including the Christmas tree, the world's fair (ancestor of Disney World), and the modern chicken[53] into the world. In the realm of Christian thought, women began to write influential books, especially didactic novels like Mary Shelley's *Frankenstein* (1823), Harriet Beecher Stowe's *Uncle Tom's Cabin* (1852), and the many works of George Eliot (pen name of Mary Ann Evans), but also nonfiction statements like Margaret Fuller's *Women in the Nineteenth Century* (1845) and Elizabeth Cady Stanton's *The Woman's Bible* (1895). Roman Catholics of the 1800s launched hundreds of new orders of nuns. Nuns running Catholic schools seemed to be an aspect of nature by the 1920s, but the proliferation of nuns was really a new phenomenon. Parish schools run by nuns were largely invented in the United States, to enable Catholic families to avoid the anti-Catholicism of the American public schools.[54]

Within the world of birding, female leaders succeeded where males failed. Widowed by the death of John James Audubon in 1851, Lucy Audubon resumed her trade of teacher, this time in her mansion on the estate on the Upper West Side of Manhattan. Among her students was George Bird Grinnell (1849–1938), a neighbor of seven years old who brought her an abandoned, juvenile red crossbill.[55] Lucy told Grinnell about the bird, showed him an Audubon picture of the adult crossbill, and eventually took the boy out to find the other crossbills and set the bird free. She used that occasion to teach Grinnell to look at nature with reverence, and continued to teach him until he went to a boarding school at fourteen. "If I can hold the mind of a child to a subject for five minutes, he will never forget what I teach him," was Lucy Audubon's motto. This certainly proved true for George Bird Grinnell.

Grinnell went on to Yale, where he graduated from college in 1870, met paleontologist Othniel Marsh, went west with him to collect dinosaur bones, and received a doctorate by 1880. Meanwhile on the Great Plains, he had hunted with some of the last of the free Pawnee Indians and been deeply impressed by them. He accompanied General George Armstrong Custer into the Black Hills to survey for gold, but luckily turned down Custer's invitation to return and so escaped the annihilation of Custer's Seventh Cavalry in 1876.[56] By 1886 he was back in New York, trying to promulgate a vision of responsible use of the whole natural world, against the momentum of a culture that saw the rifle and the railroad as the primary tools and symbols of the progress of civilization. As founding editor of *Forest and Stream* magazine, Grinnell used that journal to promote conservation. He launched another periodical, the first magazine named Audubon, to recruit people into an Audubon organization that he also founded to preserve populations of wild birds, which were being destroyed both by commercial hunting for food and for the ornamentation of women's hats and clothes.

Grinnell recruited women from the beginning of his career, and women completed his work. Although he enrolled almost fifty thousand members within two years into the society he named for Audubon, he closed down that group and his bird conservation magazine in 1889. He had become discouraged by the effort to keep *Forest and Stream* going, with a focus on hunters, while simultaneously advocating care for wild birds to a predominantly female audience.

Historian Carolyn Merchant has discovered and documented a "gendered dialectic," with leadership moving back and forth between men and women, as nineteenth-century movements for bird conservation made gradual progress between the 1880s and the Migratory Bird Treaty Act of 1918.[57] At first men, beginning with Grinnell and continuing with others such as John Muir, who convinced Theodore Roosevelt to conserve redwood forests, and Frank Chapman, who began the dioramas of birds in the American Museum of Natural History in New York, recruited women to take actions toward conserving birds. Long before 1900, when Chapman began the annual Christmas bird count as a substitute for a traditional Christmas bird hunt, Chapman made a personal bird count (in February 1886) that involved two afternoon walks in "the uptown shopping districts" of Manhattan, during which he identified feathers or whole birds from more than forty species on the hats of 543 women, as opposed to only twenty-two women who wore hats without feathers.[58]

Some women were moved by being blamed for the killing of birds. As Celia Thaxter wrote, addressing dead birds in an essay, "Women's Heartlessness," which first appeared in Grinnell's *Forest and Stream* magazine in 1886 and was often reprinted elsewhere:

> Do I not see you every day ... writhing as if in agony around female heads, still and stark, sharp wings and tail pointing in stiff distress to heaven, your dried and ghastly head and beak dragged down to point to the face below, as if saying, "*She* did it."[59]

Many women went on wearing dead birds, in hats and as stoles or feathered dresses, for half a century after Thaxter's attack on the fashion. But some women picked up the cause of bird appreciation and preservation in women's clubs, beginning with a birdwatching group founded at Smith College by Florence Merriam in 1886. Merriam (later Florence Merriam Bailey) wrote the first field guide for birdwatching, *Birds through an Opera Glass* (1889), which remained in print into the 1900s, and has been revived for new editions in 2011, 2012, and 2016. Harriet Lawrence Hemenway and her (largely female) friends in Boston began the Massachusetts Audubon Society in 1896, and by 1899 Mass Audubon had been joined by fifteen other societies,[60] with their own magazine and memberships with a majority of women. Such clubs often recruited a prominent man to serve as president while women did the work of the organizations as secretaries.

Men failed to create lasting organizations to protect birds, in part because they had other jobs, and in part because they were mocked as "hermaphrodites" for being men who worked with women. Grinnell and Chapman also transgressed gender roles as men trying to protect birds for the sake of beauty and justice, against male hunting and business interests. John Muir was lampooned in a 1909 editorial cartoon from a San Francisco newspaper that depicted him in a flowery bonnet and a dress, attempting to sweep back a sea of water for a reservoir that was eventually created in Yosemite National Park. Another cartoon featured Chapman leading an army of women in featherless bonnets to protect birds from hunters.[61] Such mockery appeared even within the bird conservation community: the cartoon of Chapman was published in *The Condor*, an ornithological journal from California.

John Muir and his friend Theodore Roosevelt both kept their feelings about birds private, even as they worked to further the cause of bird conservation. On an expedition to Alaska in 1880, Muir feared that he and his party might perish in a canoe trapped by ice when a small brown songbird, a water ouzel (now called an American dipper) whom he praised as "the most complete of God's small darlings," flew around the canoe and sang, as if to say, "You need not fear this ice and frost, for you see I am here." Muir compared the bird to Jesus reassuring his disciples by walking on the water of the Sea of Galilee.[62] But in his public work to preserve forests, Muir rarely if ever brought up birds at all. Almost twenty years later, in a letter read aloud to the annual meeting of the New York Audubon Society in 1899, Theodore Roosevelt, then the governor of New York, said that he "would like to see all harmless wild things, but especially all birds, protected in every way." Even though the passenger pigeon and the Carolina parakeet were not yet extinct, those birds had disappeared from New York, and Roosevelt marked their absence: "The destruction of the wild pigeon and the Carolina parakeet has meant a loss as severe as if the Catskills or the Palisades [two prominent geological features of New York] were taken away."[63] But like John Muir, Theodore Roosevelt did not feature sympathy for birds in his general public statements. Praising mountains and forests and rivers, large mammals like mountain lions and grizzlies, and in our own day polar bears, made for more masculine images to promote conservation.

On the side of those who wanted to protect birds, however, the international trade in feathers and bodies of birds provided an appealing target. The Lacey Act of 1900 prohibited interstate transport of birds killed in violation of any state laws. Among the greatest triumphs of the period of internationalism that ended with World War I and the League of Nations was the 1918 Migratory Bird Treaty Act, both a law of the United States and an international treaty. It began in 1916 with the United States, the United Kingdom, and Canada, and eventually included Mexico, Russia, and Japan to effectively prohibit the killing of all migrating birds with specific, narrow exceptions for Native American rituals and scientists doing research.

The Migratory Bird Treaty Act of 1918 ended an era of extinctions of birds by direct human killing. After 1918, a century began in which culture, rather than law, has become the vehicle whereby birds have brought humanity closer to a religion of nature.

Audubon and Women in Twentieth-Century Literature

John James Audubon was observing egrets in South Carolina and Florida during 1832 and 1833, just before he bought and killed the golden eagle and endured a life-changing stroke, as described above. A century later, in 1938, Eudora Welty incorporated Audubon's account of shooting an egret into her short story "A Still Moment," a fiction in which Audubon interrupted a meeting of frontier preacher Lorenzo Dow (1777–1834) with famed criminal John Murrell (1806–1844). Welty's story exemplified how a female artist can make a real man into the one of the legends that a new religion needs.

Lorenzo Dow has been called the most widely traveled evangelist and the most famous American of his day.[64] He was among the first Protestant ministers to preach in Alabama, Mississippi, and other parts of the South, and he included slaves in his revival meetings. He was trying to redeem the whole nation.

When Eudora Welty first showed Dow to her readers, he was riding quickly on a "race horse" along the Natchez Trace, a route created by Native Americans hunting and following animals through the forest from the site that became Natchez, Mississippi, to the site of Nashville, Tennessee. Dow remembered encountering Indians who stopped him, and persuading them to let him go by bowing to them, humbling himself. God always protected him, he reflected. Animals of the forest seemed to ask him to save them, but he pressed on. Birds had a different, reassuring message for the evangelist:

> Birds especially sang of divine love which was the one ceaseless protection. "Peace, in peace," were their words so many times when they spoke from the briars, in a courteous sort of inflection, and he turned his countenance toward all perched creatures with a benevolence striving to match their own.[65]

In contrast to Dow, John Murrell was known as the worst criminal of his time, because he killed more than four hundred travelers, gaining the title of "land pirate."[66] One of Murrell's favorite games was to lure slaves to revolt and then to betray them to white authorities, in the process taking some of the money and goods that the slaves had seized. He plotted to forge slaves and criminals into a personal empire.

In Welty's story, Murrell met Dow and rode with him along the Natchez Trace. Murrell told Dow a long story of murder, something he notoriously did to his victims before revealing himself as the villain of the story and killing them. But Dow and Murrell stopped together and dismounted, then Audubon interrupted. He surprised them as he silently approached, looking for birds. Welty introduced Audubon as "a sure man, very sure and tender, as if the touch of all the earth rubbed upon him and the stains of the flowery swamp had made him so."[67]

Audubon's arrival caused Murrell to pause as he drew his gun to shoot Lorenzo Dow. Dow asked the newcomer who he was, but "Audubon said nothing because he had gone without speaking a word for days." To ask an Indian for venison, he would draw a deer, Welty wrote, quoting Audubon's own writings. Audubon's heirs published journals that he wrote at the end of every day, but he traveled alone and so rarely spoke. Audubon's silent concentration led Murrell and Dow to focus their own attention as "a solitary snowy heron flew down not far away and began to feed beside the marsh water."[68]

According to Eudora Welty, Dow and Murrell saw the bird as a sign that confirmed their own dreams. Dow thought that God's glory had "lighted in a marshland, feeding at sunset. Praise God, His love has come visible." Murrell "saw himself proudly . . . going down rank after rank of successively bowing slaves to unroll and flaunt an awesome great picture of the Devil colored on a banner." But "Audubon's eyes embraced" the bird, and "he could see it as carefully as if he held it in his hand." Welty wrote that for these three men, so different in their ways, the bird became a common center that brought them together in peace.

> What each of them had wanted was simply all. To save all souls, to destroy all men, to see and to record all life that filled this world. . . . It was as if three whirlwinds had drawn together at some center, to find there feeding in peace a snowy heron. Its own slow spiral of flight could take it away in its own time, but for a little it held them still, it laid quiet over them, and they stood for a moment unburdened.[69]

Audubon broke the spell. With "his mind going to his pointed brush," at the moment when he saw the "total beauty" of the heron, "he tightened his hand on the trigger of the gun and pulled it, and his eyes went closed." Now he held the whole bird in memory, "But it was not from memory that he could paint."[70] He needed a corpse to mount upon his wires.

When Audubon opened his eyes, he saw horror in the face of Lorenzo Dow, and realized that he had never seen "horror in its purity and clarity until now."[71] The painter went to the bird, put its warm body into his bag, and began to leave on foot, just as Dow remounted his horse and began to ride slowly away. Murrell felt proud and satisfied that the three men were parting, as though each had taken "the pride out of one another" and gone on their separate paths.[72] Murrell rode off gladly into the approaching night.

Recovering from the horror Dow had shown him, Audubon comforted himself by thinking about his art. "It was undeniable, on some Sunday mornings, when he turned over his drawings they seemed beautiful to him." He knew that "what he would draw, and what he had seen, became for a moment one to him then." But Welty decided that Dow's horror had shocked Audubon into a realization that "the best he could make would be, after it was apart from his hand, a dead thing and not a live thing, never the essence, only a sum of parts." The painter saw "his long labor most revealingly at the point where it met its limit." Still, Audubon continued walking into the darkening woods, "trained to see well in the dark . . . noting all sights, all sounds, and was gentler than they as he went."[73]

Eudora Welty ended her tale with a reflection on religion, seen through the faith of Lorenzo Dow. She imagined Dow unable to leave the place or to forget what he had seen. Instead, he rode back toward where the bird had died. A revelation of divine love and the unity of all things now became a lesson about death and separateness. Welty made her Dow reflect that for God, love and separateness must be the same, because "Time did not occur to God." Looking at the empty place where the heron had landed, Dow still saw the bird. "Its beauty had been greater than he could account for," he realized. A "sweat of rapture" broke out on his body, and the evangelist shouted, "Tempter!" into the dark marsh. Then he "whirled" in his saddle and rode "at high speed" toward the camp ground. There he would preach, by torchlight, to a crowd that awaited his message about the Last Judgment, "In that day when all hearts shall be disclosed" (1 Corinthians 4:5). In her last line, Welty noted that a new moon, "slender and white," white and female like the heron, "hung shyly in the west."[74] The dead bird lived again.

In 1969, more than thirty years after Welty's story was published, the scene of Audubon shooting the snowy heron, and Welty's use of that scene in her story, inspired poet Robert Penn Warren to write his final published work, which he called *Audubon: A Vision*. Seeing through Audubon's eyes, Warren gave an exquisite account of the birds Audubon painted. Because the birds appeared in natural actions, sometimes flying, Warren praised their "footless dance." He noted that Audubon's birds had eyes "bright as a jewel / And merciless," showing no compassion for their human viewers. Even the air of Audubon's paintings "glitters like fluent crystal" and seems "hard a perfectly transparent iron" which the birds cleave "With no effort."[75]

These words captured the iconic quality of Audubon's birds in action, yet frozen in time, suggesting the eternal. Here language, visual art, and a religious vision converged. And this passage came immediately before Warren's reflection on Audubon killing the snowy heron as it was described in Welty's short story.

According to Warren, the painter slew his models "at surprising distance, with his gun" then held them with his head bowed, "But not in grief." He slew the birds so that he could put them where they could live forever "where they are, and there we see them: / In our imagination." Audubon the killer and artist showed those who see his birds what love can be: "One name for it is knowledge."[76]

Birds mediated between humans and eternity for Robert Penn Warren, just as birds mediated the eternal for Stone Age cave painters, or for participants in ancient vulture funerals, or for Egyptians who hoped for immortality under the wings of Isis and Horus, with help from a sacred ibis mummy. Birds were taking their central place in a new religion of nature.

During the twentieth century, birds outgrew the roles of symbols and messengers of God to become divine themselves, incarnations of Life that people saw and so learned how to live. In 1986, Mary Oliver published "Wild Geese," a poetic statement of this new gospel: "You do not have to be good," wrote Oliver. Instead of walking on our knees through deserts, "You only have to let the soft animal of your body / love what it loves." The world assures us of this when we share the despair of others and offer our own despair, seeing that "the world goes on." Sun and rain move across landscapes, and "Meanwhile the wild geese, high in the clean blue air," call to us, "harsh and exciting." Their call announces that we have our place "in the family of things."[77]

Mary Oliver continued a lineage that links Audubon with Emily Dickinson and the Victorian women who revived bird preservation, to Eudora Welty and then to Robert Penn Warren, to Oliver herself and to us today. At the end of Warren's *Audubon: A Vision* (1969), the poem "Tell Me a Story" described a childhood revelation that foreshadowed Oliver's *Wild Geese*: "Long ago, in Kentucky," Warren wrote, he stood at dusk on a dirt road hearing "The great geese hoot northward." Those geese, unseen, made sounds that entered Warren's heart and made him a poet, leading him to see immortal life in Audubon's painted birds. In the very next and last verses of *Audubon: A Vision*, Warren used that moment to redeem the "mania" of history in the twentieth century: "In this century, and moment, of mania, / Tell me a story."

That story, given by the geese, should have "great distances" and "starlight" and "deep delight."[78]

In our twenty-first century, more moments of mania require another story of rebirth. Our arts and sciences are giving us new ways to integrate humans and gods, genders and sexes and nature, into a new religion. Birds still offer the elements needed for this integration, and we need to see them before our destruction of the world has gone too far.

Notes

1. Jacob Bronowski, *The Ascent of Man: A Personal View*, new ed. (London: BBC, 2011), 211–213.
2. Kathleen Kaska, *The Man Who Saved the Whooping Crane: The Robert Porter Allen Story* (Gainesville: University Press of Florida, 2012), 10.
3. Gustave Axelson, "Nearly 30% of Birds in U.S., Canada Have Vanished since 1970," *Cornell Chronicle*, September 19, 2019, http://news.cornell.edu/stories/2019/09/nearly-30-birds-us-canada-have-vanished-1970 (accessed October 13, 2019).
4. Sara Abreyvaya Stein, *Plumes: Ostrich Feathers, Jews, and a Lost World of Global Commerce* (New Haven: Yale University Press, 2010). On egrets and treaties, see Kurkpatrick Dorsey, *The Dawn of Conservation Diplomacy: U.S.-Canadian Wildlife Protection Treaties in the Progressive Era* (Seattle: University of Washington Press, 1998). Also Frank Graham Jr., *The Audubon Ark: A History of the National Audubon Society* (New York: Alfred A. Knopf, 1990) and Oliver H. Orr, *Saving American Birds: T. Gilbert Pearson and the Founding of the Audubon Movement* (Gainesville: University Press of Florida, 1992), 236–237.
5. Cornell Laboratory of Ornithology, "Chimney Swift," https://www.allaboutbirds.org/guide/Chimney_Swift/overview (accessed August 26, 2019).
6. Lyanda Lynn Haupt, *Crow Planet: Essential Wisdom from the Urban Wilderness* (New York: Little, Brown, 2009).
7. Gareth Huw Davies, "Bird Brains," https://www.pbs.org/lifeofbirds/brain/ (accessed August 26, 2019).
8. Annelise Eagleton, "A Murder of Crows: When Roosting Crows Come to Town," *Cool Green Science*, June 26, 2016, https://blog.nature.org/science/2016/06/28/murder-crows-roosting-wildlife-conflict/ (accessed August 26, 2019).
9. Courtney Humphries, *Superdove: How the Pigeon Took Manhattan . . . and the World* (New York: Smithsonian, 2008).
10. GrrlScientist, "Escaped Pet Parrots Are Now Established in 23 U.S. States," *Forbes*, May 21, 2019, https://www.forbes.com/sites/grrlscientist/2019/05/21/escaped-pet-parrots-are-now-naturalized-in-23-u-s-states/#70d6661154cb (accessed August 26, 2019). The article cites Jennifer J. Uehling, Jason Tallant, and Stephen Pruett-Jones,

"Status of Naturalized Parrots in the United States," *Journal of Ornithology*, 160 (2019): 907–921, https://doi.org/10.1007/s10336-019-01658-7.

11. Serena Renner, "Jonathan Franzen's Controversial Stance on Climate Action," *Sierra: The National Magazine of the Sierra Club*, January 7, 2019, https://www.sierraclub.org/sierra/jonathan-franzens-controversial-stance-climate-action (accessed January 23, 2020).

12. Roberta J. M. Olson and Matthew Spady, "In Quest of Audubon: Exploring Audubon's Monument in Trinity Cemetery and Mausoleum to Rediscover Its History," *New York History* 96, no. 1 (Winter 2015): 105.

13. Gregory Nobles, *John James Audubon: The Nature of the American Woodsman* (Philadelphia: University of Pennsylvania Press, 2017), 14.

14. Nobles, *John James Audubon*, 14–15, 19.

15. John James Audubon, *Selected Journals and Other Writings: John James Audubon*, ed. Ben Forkner (New York: Penguin Books, 1996), 9.

16. Audubon, *Selected Journals*, 27.

17. Emily Dickinson, "Dear Genie," early 1876, http://archive.emilydickinson.org/correspondence/hall/l455.html (accessed January 23, 2020).

18. Audubon, *Selected Journals*, 18.

19. John James Audubon, *Writings and Drawings*, ed. Christopher Irmscher (New York: Library of America, 1999), 786.

20. John James Audubon, "My Style of Drawing Birds," quoted in Hezekiah Butterworth, *In the Days of Audubon: A Tale of "The Protector of Birds," with an Appendix on the Formation of Audubon Societies* (New York: D. Appleton, 1901), 28–31.

21. Jonathan Rosen, *The Life of the Skies* (New York: Farrar, Straus, and Giroux, 2008), 39.

22. Max Weber, *The Protestant Ethic and the Spirit of Capitalism*, trans. Talcott Parsons (New York: Routledge, 1992), 105, 115, 180–181.

23. *Scientific American*, March 18, 1848, 205.

24. E. A. Hammond, "Dr. Stroebel's Account of John J. Audubon," *The Auk* 80, no. 4 (October 1963), 463–466.

25. John James Audubon, "Myself," in *Writings and Drawings*, 783–784.

26. William Souder, *Under a Wild Sky: John James Audubon and the Making of "The Birds of America"* (New York: North Point Press, 2004), 264–266.

27. Audubon, op. cit. note 24, 790–791.

28. John James Audubon, *Ornithological Biography*, chapter on the golden eagle, in *Writings and Drawings*, 356.

29. Richard Rhodes, *John James Audubon: The Making of an American* (New York: Alfred A. Knopf, 2004), 376.

30. Louise Pound, "Note on Walt Whitman and Bird Poetry," *English Journal* 19, no. 1 (January 1930): 33.

31. Helen Vendler, *Dickinson: Selected Poems and Commentaries* (Cambridge, MA: Harvard University Press, 2010), 157.

32. Stanley Plumly, "Wings," *Kenyon Review*, New Series, 36, no. 3 (Summer 2014): 168.

33. Thomas Wentworth Higginson, *Out-Door Papers* (Boston: Ticknor and Fields, 1863), 304.

34. Higginson, *Out-Door Papers*, 305.
35. Higginson, *Out-Door Papers*, 312.
36. Higginson, *Out-Door Papers*, 295–296.
37. Adam Vaccaro, "Millions of Years Ago, Western Massachusetts Was a Jurassic World," *Boston Magazine*, June 15, 2015, https://www.boston.com/news/local-news/2015/06/15/millions-of-years-ago-western-massachusetts-was-a-jurassic-world (accessed January 20, 2020). Also see Riley Black, "Hitchcock's Primeval Birds," *Smithsonian Magazine*, December 19, 2011, https://www.smithsonianmag.com/science-nature/hitchcocks-primeval-birds-9861470/ (accessed January 20, 2020).
38. Ralph Waldo Emerson, "Nature," in *The Collected Works of Ralph Waldo Emerson: Essays, Second Series* (Cambridge, MA: Harvard University Press), 105.
39. Henry David Thoreau, *The Writings of Henry David Thoreau*, vol. 4, *Journals, May 1, 1852–February 27, 1853*, ed. Bradford Torrey (Boston: Houghton Mifflin, 1906), 190–191.
40. Ralph Waldo Emerson, *Nature* (Boston: James Munroe, 1836), 81.
41. Henry David Thoreau, *The Writings of Henry David Thoreau*, vol. 2, *Walden* (Boston: Houghton Mifflin Company, 1906), 95.
42. Thoreau, *Walden*, 259.
43. Thoreau, *Walden*, 260.
44. Thoreau, *Walden*, 261.
45. Thoreau, *Walden*, 262.
46. Henry David Thoreau, "The Generation of Trees," quoted in Randall Fuller, *The Book That Changed America: How Darwin's Theory of Evolution Ignited a Nation* (New York: Viking, 2017). Excerpt at https://longreads.com/2017/07/13/late-in-life-thoreau-became-a-serious-darwinist/ (accessed January 19, 2020)
47. Peter Singer, *Animal Liberation* (New York: HarperCollins, 2002), 200–201.
48. Singer, *Animal Liberation*, 203.
49. Singer, *Animal Liberation*, 206, 211.
50. Quoted in Clifford B. Frith, *Charles Darwin's Life with Birds: His Complete Ornithology* (New York: Oxford University Press, 2016), 237.
51. Rodney Stark, "Reconstructing the Rise of Christianity: The Role of Women," *Sociology of Religion* 56, no. 3 (Autumn 1995): 229–244; Elizabeth Clark, "Women, Gender, and the Study of Christian History," *Church History* 70, no. 3 (September 2001): 395–426; Elaine Pagels, "What Became of God the Mother? Conflicting Images of God in Early Christianity," *Signs* 2, no. 2 (Winter 1976): 293–303.
52. Ann Douglas, *The Feminization of American Culture* (New York: Alfred A. Knopf, 1977).
53. Andrew Lawler, "The Bird That Flipped the World: Secret Histories of the Modern Chicken," *Salon*, December 7, 2014. Also see Andrew Lawler, *Why Did the Chicken Cross the World? The Epic Saga of the Bird that Powers Civilization* (New York: Atria Books, 2014), and Maryn McKenna, *Big Chicken: The Incredible Story of How Antibiotics Created Modern Agriculture and Changed the Way the World Eats* (Washington, DC: National Geographic, 2017).

54. Eileen Mary Brewer, *Nuns and the Education of American Catholic Women, 1860–1920* (Chicago: Loyola University Press, 1987), and also see Jenny Franchot, *Roads to Rome: The Antebellum Protestant Encounter with Catholicism* (Berkeley: University of California Press, 1994).
55. Carolyn Merchant, *Spare the Birds! George Bird Grinnell and the First Audubon Society* (New Haven: Yale University Press, 2016), 11.
56. Timothy Egan, "Gone West," review of John Taliaferro, *Grinnell*, New York Times Book Review, August 11, 2019, 8.
57. Merchant, *Spare the Birds!*, 22.
58. Pagels, "God the Mother," 28–29.
59. Celia Thaxter, "Women's Heartlessness" (Boston 1886; reprinted for the Audubon Society of the State of New York, 1899), http://www.seacoastnh.com/celia-thaxter-attacks-heartless-women-wearing-birds-as-fashion/ (accessed June 14, 2020).
60. Merchant, *Spare the Birds!*, 38.
61. Merchant, *Spare the Birds!*, 19–20. Also Adam Rome, "Political Hermaphrodites: Gender and Environmental Reform in Progressive America, *Environmental History* 11, no. 3 (July 2006): 440–463.
62. Mark I. Wallace, *When God Was a Bird: Christianity, Animism, and the Re-enchantment of the World* (New York: Fordham University Press, 2019), 120–121.
63. Quoted in Merchant, *Spare the Birds!*, 39–40.
64. Benjamin Brawley, "Lorenzo Dow," *Journal of Negro History* 1, no. 3 (June 1916): 265–273.
65. Eudora Welty, "A Still Moment," in *The Collected Stories of Eudora Welty* (New York: Harcourt Brace Jovanovich 1980), 190–191.
66. James Lal Penick, *The Great Western Land Pirate: John A. Murrell in Legend and History* (Columbia: University of Missouri Press, 1981).
67. Welty, "A Still Moment," 194.
68. Welty, "A Still Moment," 195.
69. Welty, "A Still Moment," 196.
70. Welty, "A Still Moment," 197.
71. Welty, "A Still Moment," 197.
72. Welty, "A Still Moment," 197.
73. Welty, "A Still Moment," 198.
74. Welty, "A Still Moment," 199.
75. Robert Penn Warren, *Audubon: A Vision* (Random House, 1969), 30.
76. Warren, *Audubon*, 30.
77. Mary Oliver, "Wild Geese," in *Devotions: The Selected Poems of Mary Oliver* (New York: Penguin Press, 2017), 347.
78. Warren, *Audubon*, 31–32.

8
Birds Leading Humans to Another New World

Birds have led people to new worlds before. Ravens led human hunter-gatherers to sources of food and water as they crossed Siberia and the Bering Sea land bridge into what some later called the "New World." Long before that, birds led humans in East Africa to beehives full of honey and became their partners in ritual. Birds gave people examples of how to sing, how to decorate our bodies, and how to build shelters of sticks. Birds showed humans that animals could fly, and after hundreds of millennia we joined birds in the sky.

Now human divisions impede action to end pollution and climate change and pandemics, but birds soar above boundaries. Human religious divisions are contradicted by the universal reverence for birds in human religions that appears in this book. We may be ready to work together to help birds, and so to heal our planet. If we can learn to help birds now, they may lead us to another new world, a renewed version of the world where birds first greeted us.

At this point in our ecological crisis, listening to birds has become a religious duty, a matter of life and death. Religions deal in life and death commitments, and as our world teeters between life and death we need new, less anthropocentric religious commitments. We need an external standard.

Millions hope for deliverance from alien visitors, or from escape to other planets. Some, including James Lovelock, author of the Gaia hypothesis that life is a self-regulating system, hope that artificial intelligence will emerge from our computers and force us to stop burning fossil fuels.[1] Almost four billion pray in hope that the God of Abraham will send Jesus, or the Mahdi, or Saoshyant, or the Messiah of Israel. About two billion hope and expect that Kalki the tenth avatar of Vishnu or Maitreya the cosmic Buddha will one day deliver all living things from suffering. These hopes and prayers help people to live, but do not show us how to act.

Wings of the Gods. Peter (Petra) Gardella and Laurence Krute, Oxford University Press. © Oxford University Press 2024.
DOI: 10.1093/oso/9780197691878.003.0008

Birds can guide our actions because they live here now, suffering with us and from things that we do, meanwhile talking to us with their songs, their beauty, and their examples. Because the lives of birds connect earth and wood with water and sky, their condition reflects the condition of all these primal elements and environments. Deep religious wisdom, apparent around the world from Rome to Kenya to Tibet to Japan to Turtle Island, says that a sky full of birds portends a good future. The Latin roots of the word "auspicious" are *aves*, birds, and *specere*, to look at. We should attend to birds as the voice of nature, and to a great extent we do. Our primate and human ancestors evolved to hear birdsong as a sign of safety, the absence of predators, and the presence of food and water. This chapter will discuss how we are listening to birds already and learning to listen better. It will also suggest how we might act differently in hope of sharing more lessons and more joy, more life with birds.

Chapter 1 defined religion as a "system of nonrational commitments that holds life together." In this last chapter, readers will see many nonrational commitments involving birds that have been made since the 1900s began. Although no formal religion of nature has declared itself, hymns and symbols of traditional religions increasingly feature birds. Birdwatching is practiced and praised as a form of meditation and a source of healing. Artists and thinkers often use birds to focus their commitments to nature.

But now, an explicit religion of nature seems necessary to keep people from destroying the world we share with birds. For a religion of nature to help life to flourish, a critical mass of people must recognize and fulfill our commitments to birds. One clear example of how birds are showing us the ways beyond current divides happened at the end of the 2020 campaign for president of the United States.

On Eagle's Wings: A Biblical Hymn for a God of Nature

On the Saturday after the 2020 election, when President-elect Biden looked for words to heal the United States after the news media had finally called him the winner, he concluded his speech with four lines from "On Eagle's Wings." This hymn was written by a Catholic priest, Michael Joncas, in the 1970s. Its popularity has reached across the spectrum of Christians in the United States, but its lyrics never mention Jesus. Instead, the song mixes bird images from the Bible with hopes of salvation within nature. "He will raise you up on eagle's wings." The words echo Exodus 19:4 ("I bore you on eagles' wings") and Deuteronomy 32:11 (where God "hovers" over Israel in the desert as an eagle, who then "takes them up, and bears them aloft").

This hymn would never have been written if eagles had gone extinct, or even vanished in the United States by the 1970s, as they would have were it not for humans listening to eagles. Rachel Carson and others paid attention to eagles, so Father Joncas could write a song inspired by eagles that did not evoke tragedy. In that sense, "On Eagle's Wings" is the voice of the eagle.

Moving from powerful eagles to fowl hunted for food and chicks being sheltered, the hymn goes on to evoke Psalm 91:3, "He will deliver you from the snare of the fowler" and "under his wings you will find refuge":

> The snare of the fowler will never capture you,
> And famine will bring you no fear:
> Under his wings your refuge,
> His faithfulness your shield.

Biden read the whole chorus, four lines that are repeated in the hymn four times:

> And he will raise you up on eagle's wings,
> Bear you on the breath of dawn,
> Make you to shine like the sun,
> And hold you in the palm of his hand.

Not only do these lyrics make humans and God into birds, they also make nature and humanity divine. God is an eagle, and also the light and wind that will "bear you on the breath of dawn." Though humans sometimes need "refuge" under God's wings (a shelter that Jesus offers the people of Jerusalem when he pictures himself as a hen in Mark 13:34 and Matthew 23:37), these people will be transformed "to shine like the sun." The sun will not melt their wings as it did the wings of the Greek legend Icarus, who crashed to earth and died. Instead, they will become immortal by mounting to heaven along rays of the sun. Reaching the sun has been a human hope since thousands of years before the Bible and the myth of Icarus were written, since the ages when Egyptians raised obelisks to mimic rays of the sun god Ra and built pyramids to connect their pharaohs to the sun.

The eagle of this hymn is both the biblical Jehovah and a transpersonal Power that delivers us from death. By asserting that forces working through and above this world will bring us beyond any harm, "On Eagle's Wings" has become a standard hymn for funerals. In the religions of nature that are now appearing in America, death is a moment in the Circle of Life (a sacred phrase since Disney's *Lion King*) and funerals stress triumph, not judgment or mourning. When Biden gave his first speech as president-elect, the American republic was close to death from a plague and a bitterly contested election, and the new president-elect used the hymn to assure the nation of rebirth.

On the morning after Biden's speech, the political talk show *Face the Nation* featured Peggy Noonan, former chief speechwriter for President Ronald Reagan, praising Biden for his choice of this hymn. Although herself a Catholic, Noonan stressed that "On Eagle's Wings" was also loved by evangelical Protestants. Scholars joined the chorus of praise. Writing for the broad audience of *Patheos*, a website with "channels" for everyone from pagans to evangelicals and columns, including "The Friendly Atheist," University of Michigan scholar Melissa Borja recalled that as a singer, she performed the hymn at weddings as well as funerals and regular services. Borja found that when this hymn was in a service, people always "stood up straighter and prepared to sing heartily."[2] On November 7, the day Biden spoke, Professor Robert Orsi of Northwestern University tweeted that he would brook no criticism of "On Eagle's Wings." Recalling how he had held the hand of a dying woman at a Good Friday service while singing the hymn, Orsi called it "cheesy, but very good cheese."

As Chapter 2 noted, the biblical God acts as a bird in the first account of creation, in Genesis 1:2. There God is said to "hover" (or "move" or "brood") over the primordial deep as a bird hovers over eggs in a nest, stirring the air with gentle wingbeats—Hebrew *merachefet*, a verb that recurs in the Bible only once, in Genesis 1:2. That verb appears in a feminine singular form of the verb *rachaf*, or hover, to go with the feminine noun *ruach*, which means "spirit" or "wind." But a masculine bird hovers, *yerachief*, in Deuteronomy 32:11, where God is said to have carried Israel out of Egypt in the way that a male eagle might use its wings to catch and carry fledglings who were falling. "On Eagles' Wings" and the Bible both present the eagle, which represents God, embodied in both genders.

Birds are particularly suited to unify genders, because birds exhibit a spectacular variety of gender expressions. Some species, like cardinals or robins, have dramatic sexual dimorphism, differentiations of color and other features like crests that suggest definite gender differences. But in other species, like pigeons and crows, the sexes can hardly be differentiated even by experts. As we have seen in Chapter 4, the hero pigeon who saved the Lost Regiment of World War I was misgendered as a male in her museum display for decades. Among predators like eagles and hawks, the male is usually about one-third smaller than the female and is often called a *tercel* or *tierce* because of this.[3] And as the discussion below of the documentary *March of the Penguins* (2005) will show, penguins cross many gender lines in the ways that they nurture their young.

Among the critical responses to Alfred Hitchcock's *The Birds* in Chapter 6, connections between women and birds appeared. Both women and birds inspired intense interest mixed with guilt and fear, leading to a need for control, in the director. Perhaps fear arose from Hitchcock's recognition of the gender ambiguity of birds, so that birds challenged the strict divisions of gender he needed to feel secure in his masculinity. Gulls and crows, birds with little sex dimorphism, were the main attackers of people in *The Birds*. Only a caged pair of "lovebirds," parrots named for the fact that they mate for life, remained unaffected by the manic hatred for humans that had seized all other birds as *The Birds* ended.

When the divine bird is an eagle, that eagle connects to a heritage of nationalism, and of nations turning into empires. But the bald eagle has not always been so important, and the recent near extinction and resurrection of bald eagles as a species connects the realms of civil religion and nature religion. The bald eagle was primarily saved by a woman, Rachel Carson.

The Bald Eagle as Icon of Empires, of the United States, and of Nature Religion

The Great Seal of the United States, printed on the back of every dollar bill, features a bald eagle with wings spread, grasping an olive branch in the right set of talons and thirteen arrows in the left. That eagle also appears on the presidential seal. By identifying with the eagle, the United States appropriated an ancient symbol of imperial power. Every Roman legion had an animal of metal on a pole as its standard, and the eagle was the most popular of such animals. Egypt and Poland now have eagles on their flags; Russia has a double-headed eagle on its coat of arms. In the United States, the bald eagle also stands for a new religion of nature.

In Europe, golden eagles are the dominant heraldic animal. The bald eagle lives only in North America, and so never appears on Old World flags or coats of arms. Even the eagle killing a snake on the flag of Mexico is a golden eagle. But the white head of the bald eagle gives it the power of instant recognition, and the bald eagle rules the sky in the United States.

American dollar bills and presidents of the United States both rose to greater prominence in the 1900s than they had before, and so did their symbol the bald eagle. Although the eagle had been part of the Great Seal since 1782, when Congress approved the design created by congressional secretary Charles Thompson,[4] eagles were no more important among the early symbols of American national life than the pyramid, the eye of God, the Latin slogans (*E pluribus unum*, *Annuit coeptis*, and *Novus ordo seclorum*), or the Roman numerals MCMLXXVI ("1776") that also appear in the seal. The eagle had barely won its place in the Great Seal over other possible images, such as Ben Franklin's (perhaps joking) suggestion of a turkey, Thomas Jefferson's idea of an image of Moses leading Israel, or the favorite of John Adams, a figure of Hercules choosing between pleasure and virtue.

The Civil War brought a few images of eagles into public discourse, but not often, and not always positively. A cartoon in the English newspaper *Punch* from 1861 showed the eagle as a torturer. In that drawing, King Cotton was chained by the Union blockade of Southern ports, just as Prometheus was chained in Greek myth, to be punished for giving humanity fire. King Cotton was having his intestines eaten by a bald eagle as Prometheus had his intestines eaten by the eagle of Zeus, only to have them grow back as he slept to be eaten again the next day.[5]

With the advent of air combat in the Great War of 1914 to 1918, the bald eagle was used more often to personify the United States (Figure 8.1). Airplanes dropping bombs became the most prominent weapons of World War II, from the Battle of Britain and the attack on Pearl Harbor to the atomic bombing of Japan. During the Vietnam War, which extended from 1963 to 1975, the United States alone dropped three times more bombs than had been dropped by all sides in World War II.[6] Days of bombing to create "shock and awe" preceded attacks by ground troops in both American wars with Iraq, in 1991 and 2003.

Wars fought from the air succeeded each other, contributing to the eagle's dominance as the symbol and messenger of the God of American civil religion. This God of the eagle was evoked by the motto "In God We Trust," which was adopted by Congress in 1956.[7] Unlike the doves of God in the Bible, the

BIRDS LEADING HUMANS TO ANOTHER NEW WORLD 209

Figure 8.1 The American eagle gained new prominence when the airplane became a weapon. Recruiting poster for the US Army Air Service in World War I. Charles Livingston Bull, 1874–1932, artist.

Photograph: Library of Congress.

ravens of Viking god Odin, or the peacock of Goddess Saraswati of India, the eagle is a top predator, one whose characteristic action is to dive from the sky bringing death in its talons, often stealing prey from other predators. The golden eagle belonged to the sky god living on Mount Olympus and hurling lightning bolts, and to Vishnu the sky god of India, and the bald eagle was the more striking American version. Americans of the twentieth century came to see themselves as allies of a sky god, looking down on the rest of the world from an Olympian height, intervening with violence to restore peace when oaths (or treaties) were broken. Zeus (and the Roman version, Jupiter or Jove) punished oath-breakers, disliked deception, and tended to favor the wealthy and powerful, as did the United States.

The spread of farming and the expansion of cities both threaten top predators. Panthers and mountain lions and wolves disappeared from states east of the Mississippi and retreated in the West as human populations grew and the frontier of North America closed. Farmers and hunters eradicated big cats and wolves. The bald eagle had a more secure niche and food supply near rivers and seacoasts because it preferred fish, but the spread of insecticides after World War II still drove it nearly to extinction.

Unfortunately, the status of the bald eagle as a symbol of the United States was insufficient to save eagles or the ecological systems where they lived. A Bald and Golden Eagle Protection Act was passed in 1940, forbidding the taking, selling, possessing, or transporting of eagles or their nests or eggs or feathers, but at about the same time the US Army began to use DDT to kill mosquitoes and so prevent the spread of yellow fever and malaria. Because DDT controlled deadly diseases and was generally efficient at killing insects, it became very popular. By the 1960s, eagle eggs had become so permeated by DDT that only about five hundred breeding pairs of bald eagles lived in the United States, as opposed to an estimated ten thousand pairs in 1782.[8]

The slide of the bald eagle toward extinction was halted largely because Rachel Carson's *Silent Spring* found its audience in a nation where many were already observing birds more carefully. Carson reported the details of a study by a banker from Canada named Charles Broley who retired to Florida, and who banded more than one thousand young eagles between 1939 and 1949, then kept following the birds as they migrated until his death in 1959. Before Broley, only 166 eagles had ever been banded so that their movements could be known. Broley documented a rapid decline in the numbers of young eagles hatching, and his reports to the Florida Audubon Society, combined with observations in New Jersey and at Hawk Mountain in Pennsylvania, supported what Carson called "the trend that may well make it necessary for us to find a new national emblem."[9]

Adult bald eagles were not bothered by DDT, and even laid eggs in the usual numbers, but the insecticide stored in the yolks killed eagle embryos before they hatched. Immature eagles made up 40 percent of the birds counted at Hawk Mountain between 1935 and 1939, but only 20 percent between 1955 and 1959, and in 1957 there was only one young eagle for every thirty-two adults observed. During the adolescence and young adulthood of one of the authors near the southwest Connecticut coast in the 1960s and 1970s, eagles were rarely seen or reported except behind bars in zoos or performing for human handlers and audiences in captive bird shows.

This near extinction was averted because sufficient numbers of Americans developed a new skepticism about the science they had been taught. As Carson asserted in the last lines of her world-changing book, the presuppositions of Cartesian philosophy and rationalistic science had both been discredited by measurable effects.

> The "control of nature" is a phrase conceived in arrogance, born of the Neanderthal age of biology and philosophy, when it was supposed that nature exists for the convenience of man.... It is our alarming misfortune that so primitive a science has armed itself with the most modern and terrible weapons, and that in turning them against the insects it has also turned them against the earth.[10]

When these words were published in 1962, professional scientists defended DDT in service of governments and corporations, and those organizations sought to maximize power for those who held office and profit for corporate leaders and shareholders. But with Rachel Carson's work to transform human attitudes toward ecology, the female-led aspect of Carolyn Merchant's "gendered dialectic" in bird preservation movements (discussed toward the end of the last chapter) reasserted itself. And as will appear below, most social reform efforts showed a similar dialectic of male pioneering and failure, female organization and success, and male consolidation and reaction.

The image in Figure 8.2 brings this dialectic to its culmination by the bald eagle. Unlike the fierce predator of the World War I recruiting poster, this eagle uses its beak and wing to protect all people in the United States. Viewing this logo at its unveiling in 1980, President Jimmy Carter described it as "the

Figure 8.2 Logo of the Department of Health and Human Services. As HHS says, "The symbol represents the *American People* sheltered in the wing of the *American Eagle*, suggesting the Department's concern and responsibility for the welfare of the people."

wings of the eagle sheltering the people."[11] The Department of Health and Human Services has adopted this description on its website.[12]

Formal religions at first lacked the tools of thought to participate. Theologians and religious thinkers depended on philosophy, and most modern philosophers had abandoned religious questions for logic and linguistic analysis, seeking to prove each other's statements wrong and paying no attention to the physical world. Few disciplines were as male-dominated as philosophy. But religion has more to do with art and language and music than with philosophy. In the twentieth and twenty-first centuries both female and male artists, especially poets and musicians and painters, began to see birds as messengers from nature to humanity.

The Deadly Century before 2020: Extinctions, Genocides, and Rebirths through Women

Rachel Carson knew that she was campaigning against powerful economic, scientific, and political interests. She knew herself as a female scientific writer with no job or doctorate. Even worse, wars dominated world history for most of Carson's life (1907–1964), and wars grew from and supported attitudes that encouraged people to treat nature as an enemy.

As Carson wrote in *Silent Spring* (1962):

> Our attitude toward poisons has undergone a subtle change. Once they were kept in containers and marked with skull and crossbones; the infrequent occasions of their use were marked with utmost care that they should come in contact with the target and with nothing else. With the development of the new organic insecticides and the abundance of surplus planes after the Second World War, all this was forgotten. Although today's poisons are more dangerous than any known before, they have amazingly become something to be showered down indiscriminately from the skies. Not only the target insect or plant, but anything—human or nonhuman— within range of the chemical fallout may know the sinister touch of the poison. Not only forests and cultivated fields are sprayed, but towns and cities as well.[13]

Carson then described the airborne spraying of thickly populated suburbs of New York City to control gypsy moths in 1957.[14] In her next chapter, entitled "Beyond the Dreams of the Borgias," she noted that poisons much stronger than many that would be restricted in a pharmacy had become common domestic items, sold alongside food in supermarkets and widely used in kitchens and gardens, impregnated into shelf paper and floor wax and mothproof blankets, and casually dispensed from portable sprayers inside homes.

Although Rachel Carson never mentioned the Holocaust, changing attitudes toward poisons connected directly to the killing of Jews during World War II. Fritz Haber, the German Jewish chemist who won a Nobel Prize for inventing a way to get ammonia from nitrogen in the air that made fertilizers abundant, also developed poison gases used in World War I. Haber later invented the poison gas used at Auschwitz and other Nazi death camps.

Modern philosophy supported this acceptance of poisons and of genocides. As noted in the last chapter, Enlightenment philosophers starting with René Descartes had established self-consciousness as the defining attribute of humans and denied its existence in animals, justifying any degree of animal suffering or mistreatment if the interests of humanity could be advanced. Humans also could be killed if they were seen as inferiors or subhumans whose existence impeded the ideals of society that philosophers developed. In her study of the Armenian genocide of 1915, historian of philosophy Siobhan Nash-Marshall has argued that the rationalism that began with Descartes and that continued through the French Revolution and the 1800s aimed to destroy and to remake the traditional world in a rational image, not simply to understand it. The revolutionary thinkers who justified killings of kings and aristocrats and priests in England and France were succeeded by German Idealists like Kant and Hegel, and German theories of reason driving history informed the work of Marx and other thinkers. These heirs of rationalism and Idealism included racists who appropriated Darwin's idea of natural selection to support their pretenses to share the new power of science in service of what Nash-Marshall called "demiurgical designs." Many revolutionaries of the Left and Right saw genocides not as crimes but as inevitable developments in natural selection, necessary but unpleasant cleansings carried out by representatives of superior civilizations on the way to a more perfect world.

Although genocidal actions against Native Americans, Africans, Pacific Islanders, and Asians accompanied the growth of Western empires from the 1500s into the 1900s, the word and the concept of "genocide" did not come into existence until the 1940s, to describe Nazi murders of Jews, and even then gained acceptance only gradually. Rather than proclaiming the intention to purify the world by killing the inferior, leaders and historians of genocide have hidden behind euphemisms such as "the Final Solution" (of the Jewish Question) or "Relocation and Resettlement" (of Armenians in Turkey) or "the Long March" (of Navajo to Oklahoma) or "the Middle Passage" in an "Atlantic trade" (of Africans to the Americas).[15] Unlike terrorists, who commit crimes in public to provoke response, perpetrators of genocide have sought their aims at least partly in secret, so that the denial of genocide becomes an essential aspect of the crime.

Denial continued for decades after World War II. In American mass culture, from the conformity and tensions of 1957 to the countercultures of 1966, the Sunday night news program that held the CBS time slot later occupied by *Sixty Minutes* was a series of 121 episodes, compilations from newsreels called *The Twentieth Century*. Narrated by Walter Cronkite, the anchor of CBS News, *The Twentieth Century* often dealt with topics related to World War II. But no episode of *The Twentieth Century* focused on the Holocaust, the first event ever called a "genocide."[16] As the twentieth century passed its midpoint, the victors and losers of World War II settled together into a stable order, anchored in the United Nations. Genocides of human populations and extinctions of animal populations proceeded, but were seen as mere shadows, insubstantial nightmares that made the shining images of progress featured at world's fairs and at Disneyland stand out more clearly. One of the most successful books about genocide, Samantha Power's *A Problem from Hell: America and the Age of Genocide* (2002), established that the United States did nothing directly in response to genocides against Armenians, Jews, Cambodians, Kurds, Rwandan Tutsi, or Bosnians.[17]

Now, as the middle decades of the twenty-first century approach, humanity has a new attitude toward birds, nature, and the divine. Many revere nature for its own sake as well as for any gods nature reveals. But this attitude came with great costs, and it remains fragile. Our new ethical norms are poorly defined, ineffective, and contested. Until humans routinely revere all species and all things on earth, we will not cease from temporarily profitable activities that cause animal (and sometimes human) deaths in massive numbers.

For an example of how moments of progress are succeeded by destruction and decline, consider the course of history since the Migratory Bird Treaty Act of 1918. Passed in response to the extinctions and near extinctions of many species, this unique example of international law brought together the United States, the United Kingdom, and Canada. It became part of a series of triumphs and disasters that succeeded each other throughout the century after its passage. Enacted in the same year when a global flu pandemic that claimed between fifty and one hundred million human lives began and a Great War that killed twenty million ended, the 1918 law has saved billions of individual birds and helped scores of species to survive. But the population of North American birds nevertheless fell by about three billion (or about 30 percent) between 1970 and 2020, and recent estimates say that 70 percent of all wildlife in the world has died in the last fifty years. Prohibiting the direct killing of wild birds ended extinctions caused directly by the fashion and food industries, but did not slow the extinctions resulting from the destruction of natural habitats because of suburban development or pollution from industrial agriculture and waste disposal. Birds have adapted far better than most species, but the insects many birds depend on for food are in especially steep decline. The Trump administration eliminated one protection of birds in the 1918 law, ending penalties for oil companies that fail to shield waste oil pits so that birds die after landing in them, mistaking them for ponds.[18] In 2021, the Biden administration restored those penalties to protect birds, but for how long remains to be seen.

When the twentieth century began, hopes were rising that bird life would flourish in a world of peace. In 1900, Frank Chapman of New York began the first Audubon Christmas bird count, which built on a British folk tradition of Christmas bird hunts, with twenty-seven birders listing species and counting at twenty-five locations that ranged across the United States and Canada from Ontario to California. Meanwhile, the most famously conservationist American president, Theodore Roosevelt, was expanding national parks and winning the Nobel Peace Prize of 1905 for his role as a mediator to end a war between Russia and Japan. Russia and Japan eventually joined the migratory bird treaty.

World peace would theoretically include equality and harmony between women and men. But the "gendered dialectic" that historian Carolyn Merchant noted in bird protection movements of the 1800s continued into the twentieth century, so that women after 1918 turned over the leadership in bird protection organizations that they held in the 1880s to men. Meanwhile, the first wave of feminism reached its goals and ended. Two of the many social reforms that feminists and female-led organizations like the Women's Christian Temperance Union had sought for decades finally arrived in 1919 and 1920, when the Eighteenth and Nineteenth amendments enshrined the prohibition of alcohol and women's right to vote in the US Constitution. In the United Kingdom, women over thirty gained the vote in 1918, and younger adult women in 1928. During four decades before 1920, female leadership of what has been called a "Purity Crusade" raised the minimum age of consent for sexual intercourse from ten, following the standard of the common law of England (one exception in the United States was Delaware, where the age of consent was seven), to current levels. Legal prostitution (now commonly called sex work), which had been accepted to the extent that guidebooks to New York City brothels were published and the US Army set up camps for sex workers near bases in the Spanish-American War, was banned in state after state through the efforts of the same women's groups. Laws against selling sex were passed despite support for legal sex work by the male-dominated American Medical Association.

But during the 1920s and 1930s, conflict between progressives and reactionaries began a century of wars, gendered repression, genocides, and new threats of bird extinction. In the United States, isolationists doomed President Woodrow Wilson's dream of a League of Nations to secure world peace, while a Red Scare crippled socialist domestic hopes. Prohibitions of alcohol and drugs fueled organized crime, and women's suffrage failed to transform politics.

Beyond the United States and the United Kingdom, fascists defeated democratic socialists in Italy, Germany, and Spain, and military nationalists led Japan to ally itself with them by 1940. In Russia, the revolutionary ideologue Lenin died in January 1924 and was replaced by the bureaucrat Stalin, who ruled until his death in 1953 and set the totalitarian pattern of Soviet Communism that shattered in 1991, only to be revived by Vladimir Putin after 2000. Civil wars and invasions of Russia, China, Ethiopia, and Spain in the 1920s and 1930s fed into World War II, which raged from 1939 to 1945, followed by limited, but interminable wars from the late 1940s to the present in locations including Korea, Indochina, Afghanistan, and Iraq. Chronic armed conflicts roiled in Israel and its neighborhood, in Latin America, and in Africa.

Fortunately, the wars since World War II have lacked the spirit of global crusades and claims of racial and ideological superiority that appeared on all sides during World Wars I and II. As European empires in Asia and Africa collapsed in the postwar decades, people from former colonies moved to the capitals of empire. The people, foods, and cultures of China, India, Japan, Thailand, Burma, and Korea spread across the globe, and so did the Muslim and Buddhist and Hindu religions. Attitudes toward animals that once seemed extreme to Westerners, such as the concept of an animal soul, spread as well.

Even in philosophy, despite its narrow, modern focus on reasoning expressed in verbal languages and abstract symbols, a new attitude was emerging. Martin Buber, the author of *Ich und du* (1937), which was translated into English as *I and Thou* in 1957 and which made Buber the first Jewish religious thinker most Christian theologians had ever read, directly affirmed the consciousness of animals. "The eyes of an animal have the capacity of a great language," wrote Buber.[19] He saw animals as inhabitants of a state "between the realms of plantlike security and spiritual risk." Interactions between animals and humans took part in the same "mutuality" that God had made "the gate of entry into our existence."[20]

Buber reflected on moments when he had returned the gaze of a cat, looking into the cat's eyes. He imagined the cat feeling his look and asking with its own eyes: "Can it be that you mean me? Do you actually want that I should not merely do tricks for you? Do I concern you? Am I there for you?

Am I there? What is that coming from you? What is that around me? What is it about me? What is that?"[21]

This new perspective on animals became important because Buber was a world-famous thinker, one of the "public intellectuals" of the midcentury West, alongside Reinhold Niebuhr and Jean-Paul Sartre. In the year when *I and Thou* first appeared in English, Buber did a tour of American campuses, lecturing at Princeton and Northwestern Universities and the University of Chicago and headlining the Fall Convocation at Drew University. His thought was so influential across disciplines that he addressed students and faculty at the Washington School of Psychiatry in the District of Columbia and engaged in a dialogue with psychologist Carl Rogers in front of four hundred scholars at the University of Michigan, during an April conference sponsored by the coordinator of religious activities. Buber made such a hit that he returned for another American tour in 1958.

Buber's emphasis on dialogue influenced other important thinkers, such as Nel Noddings, who published *Caring: A Feminine Approach to Ethics and Moral Education* in 1984. Noddings argued that a moral person must exercise care in concentric circles of relationship that began with the self and extended not only to other humans, both known and unknown, but also to the nonhuman world, including animals. While Peter Singer, a Princeton philosopher and author of *Animal Liberation* (1975) followed Jeremy Bentham and utilitarians in emphasizing obligations arising from the animal capacity for suffering, the school of thought that arose from Buber, Noddings, and French philosopher Emmanuel Lévinas stressed recognition and respect for animals as conscious agents. For Buber, in human interactions with "nature," communication "sticks to the threshold of language,"[22] but for those who have built on Buber's encounters with animals, that threshold has been crossed from both sides. People now hear messages from birds and talk to birds, and accounts of such messages proliferate in literature, film, and visual arts.

Birds and Gendered Spiritual Life in Popular Culture

People today groan at the mention of *Jonathan Livingston Seagull*, if they recall it at all. That tale in children's book format of a gull who cared more about flying than food belongs to the 1970s, along with bell-bottomed pants and disco. Birders note that the book isn't really about birds but about magical, New Age thinking projected onto birds. As birders say, there is no type of bird named "seagull," although there are many species called "gulls" in the family Laridae.[23]

But *Jonathan Livingston Seagull* used birds in ways that added to larger trends in the emerging religion of nature. It revealed elements of those trends, if intellectual scorn can be set aside. Behind the thirty million copies sold in twenty-two years, the *Time* magazine cover story of November 13, 1972, and the movie with a Grammy-winning score by Neil Diamond lay the ideas of Christian Science applied to animals. Because Christian Science grew from the work of Mary Baker Eddy, whose followers prayed to "Our Father, Mother God" in the late 1800s, *Jonathan Livingston Seagull* took part in the gendered dialectic that informed bird protection and other social reform movements. Its messages suited the masculine moment of the twentieth century, but also promoted the feminine school of spirituality that flowed through Eddy and her Mother Church and that would grow more prominent in the twenty-first century.

According to Richard Bach, the Christian Science lay leader, air force fighter pilot, and author of books on flight who wrote *Jonathan Livingston Seagull*, the book came to him in two visions, the first in 1959. In that vision, a gull named for the racing pilot John Livingston (a pilot Bach saw in childhood) dove faster than a falcon by holding in his wings. After Jonathan scattered his fellow gulls in a power dive, the flock banished him. Gulls should fly to find food, they said, but Jonathan lived for flight.

There the first vision ended for Bach, who left the air force because it gave him few chances to fly. He worked for Douglas Aircraft, then as an editor with two flying magazines. He barnstormed through the Midwest, taking passengers on flights in a biplane built in 1929. One day in 1967, a dream of gulls gave Bach the rest of the story. In that dream, Jonathan was living alone, practicing flying, when gulls who called themselves his "brothers" brought him to a gull called Elder Chiang. Chiang moved instantly to a spot fifty feet away, then returned "in the same millisecond" to Jonathan's shoulder. To travel that way, Chiang said, "You must begin by knowing that you have already arrived."[24] After Chiang taught Jonathan, he said to "keep working on love" and disappeared.[25] Jonathan saw that he must return to his first flock.

Back among normal gulls, Jonathan taught that "Each of us is in truth an idea of the Great Gull, an unlimited idea of freedom."[26] He healed a gull whose left wing was useless and raised another from the dead.[27] Then Jonathan vanished, leaving a disciple to teach that "a seagull is an unlimited idea of freedom, an image of the Great Gull, and your whole body, from wingtip to wingtip, is nothing more than your thought itself."[28]

These statements took the teachings of Christian Science, that Mind is God, God is Love, and Mind is the only reality, and refocused them on freedom. Christian Science began in 1875, with the publication of *Science and Health: With Key to the Scriptures* by Mary Baker Eddy. Eddy founded her church in the same period when women were rising to prominence everywhere in American Christianity. Along with Ellen Gould White of the Seventh-Day Adventists, Phoebe Palmer of the Holiness movement, Victoria Woodhull who ran for president on the platform of free love, and Frances Willard of the Women's Christian Temperance Union, Eddy belonged to the wave of women among religious reformers that Carolyn Merchant found in the bird conservation movement.[29]

Mind was the only reality, as Eddy and Christian Science taught, so illness could be cured by the power of Mind. Liberating many from unregulated, spurious medicines and procedures, Christian Science became a national phenomenon with churches everywhere. By 1945, Christian Scientists ranked highest in status, as measured by per capita income and professional and educational attainments, among all Christian groups in the United States.[30] The Christian Science complex near the center of downtown Boston still impresses visitors.

Bach focused the ideas of Christian Science on freedom. In the movie version, the theme song by Neil Diamond echoed the doctrines of Mary Baker Eddy, with film of a gull in flight. But the doctrines took on a more masculine tone, stressing Bach's individualism:

> Bach focused the ideas of Christian Science on freedom. In the movie version, the theme song by Neil Diamond began echoing Mary Baker Eddy, with film of a gull in flight and lyrics invoking "a theme that is timeless." But Diamond then gave the doctrines a more masculine tone, stressing Bach's individualism, assuring the bird that "the one God will make for your way."[31]

Religious themes implicit in the book became very explicit in the film, not only in songs but also in new dialogue, new plot points, and dramatic visuals. Much of the religious vocabulary came from Neil Diamond, whose songs repeated phrases like "Holy, holy" and its Latin equivalent, "Sanctus, Sanctus," as well as "Kyrie" and "Gloria." Diamond was born a Jew in Brooklyn, and his work brought both a Jewish sense of God and a Catholic awe before authority to the nature religion being taught by the script.

Moving farther in a masculine direction, the screenplay by Hall Bartlett, a Yale-educated, white, Anglo-Saxon, and Protestant independent filmmaker,[32] showed Jonathan resolving to "know all there is to know of this life" (39:30) after being banished. That began a hero's quest around the world, with the gull visiting whales and otters, pelicans and walruses and horses, deserts and mountains, an epic quest that never happened in the book. The quest gave opportunities to cinematographer Jack Couffer, a veteran creator of nature films.[33] Couffer's cameras made seagulls look like angels, sometimes by filming a flock from above (1:00, 1:12), and his work was nominated for the Academy Award for Best Cinematography. The movie's visuals worthily continued the iconic still images by pilot and photographer Russell Munson that occupied as much space as Bach's prose in the book. Though the book and movie of *Jonathan Livingston Seagull* drew deserved scorn, they brought talented men together to successfully glorify both nature and individual freedom.

The film had less commercial success than the book, perhaps because no critics reviewed the book until it became very popular, while critics were lying in wait when the movie came out. In 1973, famed critic Roger Ebert walked out of a screening less than halfway through, and his review called *Jonathan Livingston Seagull* "the biggest pseudocultural, would-be metaphysical ripoff of the year."[34] Yet at this writing in 2023, one can still rent or buy the film version of *Jonathan Livingston Seagull* on Amazon Prime, and a Blu-ray version went on sale in April of 2020 at Best Buy electronics outlets and Barnes & Noble bookstores. It was still available at Wal-Mart late in 2023.

Jonathan Livingston Seagull the film inherited some of the book's magic, but it would be surpassed among inspiring bird movies by a feature documentary, *March of the Penguins*. While *Seagull* generated only $1.6 million in revenues, barely covering the $1.5 million budget raised by Hall Bartlett, and failing to reach the $2.1 million that Paramount paid for rights to the film, *March* made $77 million on an $11 million budget. As of 2023, it remained the fifth-highest grossing documentary of all time, and it won the Best Documentary Oscar for 2006.[35]

Jonathan Livingston Seagull made birds speak as if they were humans, but *March of the Penguins* took another step in the popular religion of nature, speaking to humans about birds. At first, even the avian identity of the film's stars seemed in doubt. As narrator Morgan Freeman intoned with surprise, "The emperor penguin is *technically* a *bird*" (emphasis added). Film of penguins flying underwater helped to allay that doubt, as did the central theme of tending eggs.

The plot began with hundreds of penguins making a long walk from the sea to an inland mating ground. There the penguins mated and laid eggs, which the female penguins laboriously moved with their feet to the males, who sidled into position and slid the precious ovoids between their own feet and under their feathers. Then all the females walked back to the sea to feed, while the males with the eggs huddled together without food for 125 days, buffeted by an Antarctic winter. They crowded into a circular pack against the wind, taking turns as they shuffled with eggs between their feet from the inside to the outer ring of standing penguins, and then back inside again to preserve their own body heat. Many eggs were dropped and frozen during these shifts of position. But nature triumphed: when the winter ended and the eggs hatched, the male penguins even had a milky white substance in their digestive systems to feed the chicks. And when the females returned, epic struggles and triumphs continued. Before the newborn chicks could enter the water, they had to live for weeks on their own and walk to the sea along the paths their parents had trodden to the inland place where they had been conceived and hatched. Shots of cute toddling chicks alternated with grisly pictures of frozen chicks, chicks at play in the sun, and white down turning into gray feathers, which would eventually turn black if the bird lived.

Attempting to inspire humans, the scriptwriters stressed penguin love and endurance. As Morgan Freeman said, *March of the Penguins* was "a story about love"—the love of the penguins for each other, for their chicks, and so for life itself. Millions of years ago, as ice encased Antarctica, all the other animals left, he said. "The emperor penguin decided to stay to live—and love—in the harshest place on earth."

This message that love conquered all, especially when children were involved, was taken up by social conservatives in 2005 to vindicate political stances favoring traditional families and opposing both abortion rights for women and gay marriage. In 2004, the Massachusetts Supreme Judicial Court had ruled in favor of gay marriage, eleven years before the US Supreme Court, and that ruling caused panic in some states (especially Ohio, where a referendum to legalize gay marriage was on the 2004 presidential ballot) that probably cost John Kerry his chance to replace President George W. Bush (a switch of Ohio would have reversed the decision). Reviews of *March of the*

Penguins sometimes stressed its relevance to human families. For example, conservative Michael Medved recommended *March* as an antidote against liberalism, while gay activist Andrew Sullivan disagreed, pointing out that emperor penguins practiced monogamy only on an annual basis, with different couples pairing up each year.[36]

The year 2005 also saw penguins being used as ammunition for another salvo in the culture wars, in a children's book called *And Tango Makes Three*. Written by a gay male couple who eventually married, Columbia University psychiatrist Justin Richardson and playwright Peter Parnell, *Tango* is a children's book that tells the true story of two male penguins who raised an orphan chick in the Central Park Zoo in New York.[37] As in *March of the Penguins*, the focus is on penguins caring for an egg and then for a chick, but this time the parents were both males who were already a couple. The socially conservative lessons that *March of the Penguins* supposedly taught were directly contradicted by *And Tango Makes Three*.[38]

As University of Michigan scholar Lawrence La Fountain-Stokes documented, birds began to serve as vehicles for gay and trans authors. In 1999, gay actor and activist Harvey Fierstein wrote and acted in *The Sissy Duckling*, an HBO animated movie that was also released in 2002 as a children's book about a bird named Elmer who was called a sissy because of preferring domestic tasks like baking to sports, but who redeemed himself by caring for his injured father.[39] Stokes observed that between 2000 and 2004, a sexually explicit cartoon series called *Queer Duck* aired on the Showtime television channel, tackling many religious issues through encounters with cartoon versions of the Reverend Jerry Falwell and radio talk host Dr. Laura Schlessinger.[40] Stokes also found that Yiddish-speaking Jews and Spanish-speaking Puerto Ricans and others had developed a vocabulary of bird terms denoting roles in the gay community, such as *feygele* (little bird, Yiddish, origin of "fey") and *galinna* (chicken, from Spanish).[41] Although such discourse can be criticized as stereotyping, Stokes concluded that the bird cartoons and bird slang words moved the world "closer to a global project of liberation."

A craze for angels that began in the 1930s peaked in the 1990s, when trendy female college students (and occasional males) wore wings and halos to parties and to classes. Following a spate of straight male angels in movie comedies of the 1930s and 1940s, angels moved toward the female late in the 1900s, just as women returned to leadership in social movements, continuing

Carolyn Merchant's "gendered dialectic." Although biblical angels were male, at least by the gender of their names (Michael, Gabriel, Raphael), angels had become androgynous in Renaissance art and were usually female when painted or sculpted by Victorian and Pre-Raphaelite artists.[42]

Women always played the titular angel of Tony Kushner's *Angels in America: A Gay Fantasia on National Themes*, the two-night drama that brought AIDS to the Broadway stage in 1991 (HBO movie 2000, Broadway revival 2017). That female angel called herself a bird. Wrestling with a human (a gay male suffering from AIDS) who sought a blessing, she cried out:

> I I I I Am the
> CONTINENTAL PRINCIPALITY OF AMERICA,
> I I I I AM THE BIRD OF PREY I WILL NOT BE COMPELLED.[43]

But this angelic bird did allow the human who fought her to refuse to become a prophet. She then whispered, "The Body is the Garden of the Soul"[44] to the Mormon woman who had advised the human to fight, giving her an "enormous orgasm" (according to the stage directions). In an ineffectual reaction against this tide of culture, evangelicals continued to insist that angels were male and straight.[45]

Birds and spirits and transgressors of gender roles converged in a novel released to critical acclaim in November 2020, *The Thirty Names of Night* by Zeyn Joukhadar. Updating the Sufi classic poem *The Conference of the Birds* by Attar, which was discussed in Chapter 5, this novel is more a reflection on eternal patterns than a narrative, and it weaves birds and humans together from beginning to end. Both the author and the narrator are transmen, and the subject is Syrian-Americans searching for a lost world centered on Little Syria, a neighborhood now lost, which once stood near the site of the World Trade Center in lower Manhattan. At the heart of that culture lies the masterpiece of a painter named Laila from the middle of the twentieth century, a painting of a special ibis named *Geronticus simorgh*. The word *simorgh* can refer to an eagle or a peacock, but broken into two Persian words, *si* and *morg*, it means "thirty birds." Attar's *Conference of the Birds* told of the quest of thirty birds for a God named Simorgh. The painting of Simorgh has been lost and the narrator seeks it, and during the search many other things are found. For example, when a sanctuary for injured birds run by another Syrian immigrant is closed, the closure evokes a response from birds attempting to heal human culture:

As Aisha locks the door of the house, the birds fill the sky as though drawn to our sighing. They've been arriving every day from nowhere: orioles roosting on fire escapes, stray jays clinging to box air conditioners, dozens of ravens walking the shop awnings. People harbor different theories about what's bringing the birds to New York. They congregate like white blood cells to a wound, drawn to arson and eviction notices, to a pig's head hurled at a masjid door, to the murder of a Black trans woman deadnamed in a police report or the white man who set fire to a woman's blouse on Fifth Avenue for wearing hijab.[46]

Many incidents of birds swarming to answer human actions happen in the book. As developers "dig up the empty lot beside the last remaining tenement of Little Syria," a mass of goldfinches appears. They begin "as a flashing cloud of yellow gold that draws bystanders and cameramen for the evening news." A reporter enters the cloud, which has forced an Irish bar to close, and she "comes out screaming, her pink sheath dress shredded at the shoulders, her face tallied with scratches."[47] The goldfinches do not disappear until night falls. That incident spreads beyond lower Manhattan:

> One thing everyone's agreed on since the goldfinches arrived: never before has New York been so full of birds. . . . A week ago, some of the gentrifiers blamed a pair of brothers . . . who've got a pigeon coop on the roof of their building. But it isn't only pigeons that are filling the streets. Hordes of sparrows block traffic, circling the Brooklyn Public Library and soiling the gilded entrance. Snowy owls arrive out of season and roost in the rooftop gardens of brand-new apartment buildings, spoiling evening soirees with their swooping and screeching.[48]

The first sentence of *Thirty Names of Night* says that, on the fifth anniversary of the death of the narrator's mother, "forty-eight white-throated sparrows fall from the sky." As he stands on the roof, one of the sparrows "strikes my hand and gashes my palm." The birds become "companions in grief" for the narrator, "the omen that keeps me from leaning out into the air" to join his mother in death.[49]

Groups of birds, recalling the thirty birds of the Sufi poem, appear again and again. When the narrator first had a period, on "the day my body started conspiring against me"[50] as an adolescent, his struggles with his mother's advice to learn how to use a maxi pad and adjust to the changes in his body were

226 WINGS OF THE GODS

interrupted by sounds of wings at the bathroom window. "The air was filled with the *caaw-caaw-caaw* of grieving crows. There were hundreds" of crows in the air, and a special circle of mourners on the ground,

> a circular gathering of several dozen crows. In the center was the mangled body of the young dead crow. Both its wings had been ripped from its body, hanging by thin slats of red muscle.
> One at a time, each of the crows left the circle and hopped into the surrounding thicket, emerging with a small twig or a piece of dried grass. One by one, they placed their offerings on top of the body, hiding the twisted wings and the open beak. . . .
> Each bird laid their gift atop the dead crow and flew off. . . . I was left alone in the clearing with the body, buried under twigs and leaves and grass, my blood slick between my thighs.[51]

One night, just before the narrator cuts his hair in the transition from female to male, an owl taps on his window and wakes him up before dawn to walk from lower Manhattan through Brooklyn to Ozone Park in Queens, to see the place where his father died in an accident.

> When I look back, the single owl at my window has become dozens. We amass a cape of a hundred owls gliding behind us like a procession for the dead. I don't speak for fear of unraveling this enchantment. We continue down Atlantic in the middle of the empty street, and the white bellies of the owls are brighter than the streetlights.[52]

As the quest for Simorgh in this new version of *The Conference of the Birds* reaches its goal, the narrator finds the legendary painter Laila still alive in her nineties. His mother lost touch with Laila and herself tried to paint the rare ibis, *Geronticus simorghus*, but the newly named male Nadir is brought by Laila into a studio to see the goal of his mother's quest. Nadir's description of Laila's studio is addressed to his mother, who died more than five years before:

> The room is filled from floor to ceiling with canvases and papers, oil paintings and illustrations, piles of sketchbooks and spare frames, mountains of drawings. All these works have a single subject—*G. simurghus*, your birds. Laila has varied their features, sometimes giving them white wings

and sometimes making them dark, allowing the sun to bring out the iridescence of their feathers, positioning them with wings spread or heads cocked, walking a field after dusk or taking flight.... This is not a room, it is a menagerie, and standing in the midst of it, I am one of its birds.[53]

This scene echoes the climax of Attar's *Conference*, where birds who have traveled through valleys and over mountains and deserts finally come to the lake in the place where they hope to meet Simorgh. Gazing down, those birds see reflections of themselves and learn that God works through each of them. In a chapter of epilogue, Nadir the narrator and three friends paint a mural that represents *The Conference of the Birds* on an outside wall of Laila's building: "It's our own interpretation of the birds that follow the night, their contour feathers iridescent, their faces turned toward the east." East is the direction of flight for the thirty birds on pilgrimage in *Conference*, because one feather of Simorgh was found in China and the birds start in Persia, but west is the direction toward Mecca from Persia or toward New York from the Middle East. *The Thirty Names of Night* leaves its characters on the roof of Laila's building in Manhattan, dancing to the music of an oud under a sky filled with people who have flown west, as evoked in its final sentence: "On the edge of the city, planes are landing from Beirut and from Cairo, angling their enormous wings." Small mechanical birds appear in Joukhadar's story, and huge mechanical birds rule the sky, and birds and humans are all moving like the birds of Attar toward God. Perhaps in his next novel, if politics permit, Joukhadar will complete his quest with a journey back to the east through Syria to Mecca and Iran, the Persia of Attar's Sufi poem.

In *Thirty Names of Night*, another circle is closed, the circle between women and men. Nadir is a man, but a man who knows women very well, living in constant communion with his mother and with Laila, even before he finds her, and with other women in his family and the Syrian-American community. Within this novel, the alternation of leadership between women and men becomes one movement of humanity toward the divine, manifest among birds and humans of both sexes and all genders.

Visual Arts as Resistance on Behalf of Birds

Birds emerged as central subjects of visual art, rather than accompaniments of divine or human figures or embellishments of landscapes, only as the modern era of bird extinctions began. After the dodo and the great auk had already disappeared, but while the Carolina parakeet and the passenger pigeon were still regarded as pests, the Scot Alexander Wilson and the American John James Audubon started to seek out birds in the field, to paint birds for their own sake, and to publish books of engravings based on their work. Audubon thought that the passenger pigeon would never disappear, but he was concerned enough by the hunting he saw to wonder about its fate, and he knew and regretted that the Carolina parakeet was disappearing. Bird art began with resistance to extinction.

In the first decade of the twenty-first century, sculptor Todd McGrain took resistance to a new level with his "Lost Bird Project." McGrain, who held the position of artist in residence at the Cornell University Laboratory of Ornithology, worked for more than ten years to make and to distribute black bronze statues of five extinct bird species: the great auk, the Labrador duck, the passenger pigeon, the Carolina parakeet, and the heath hen. Each statue is much larger than life, somewhat taller than a human, and they were installed near places where the last living birds of each species were seen (which in the case of the great auk meant tiny Fogo Island, off Newfoundland). McGrain commemorated the making and the placements of the birds in a documentary video that premiered in 2011 and in a book published in 2014, both called *The Lost Bird Project*. The video and the book tell the story of how each of the birds lived and how they met extinction at the hands of humans, as well as how McGrain made the statues and negotiated with property owners and governments to find sites for them. The installations provoked rituals like that performed by schoolchildren on Martha's Vineyard, who were organized to blow over the necks of bottles to approximate the sound made by the last heath hen (called "Booming Ben" by the natives of the Vineyard).[54] That bird lived the final four years of his life alone, and was last seen perched in a tree and making his call in hope of attracting a mate in 1932. Now a statue stands in a field near the place where Ben called, and McGrain's video shows great prairie chickens, cousins of the heath hen, making a similar sound on the Great Plains, where humans of the Blackfeet and Cree nations still do a prairie chicken dance. Although the statues are beautiful and the stories compelling, the whole project evokes a sense of futility. Reading the book or watching the video, which features wistful music, leaves the reader or viewer sad but helpless. There is nothing more to be done, these bird species are lost. McGrain argues that forgetting the birds would be a new kind of extinction, and his bronzes should prevent that.

A more radical form of art as resistance began in China around 2008, when artist Xu Bing was commissioned to make a large piece for the atrium of the World Finance Center in Shanghai. Xu had already been exiled from China after the Tiananmen Square Massacre in 1989, but he had attained fame in the United States, then reconciled with the Chinese government and returned. When he went to the Shanghai construction site, he was appalled by the living and working conditions of the people building the World Finance Center. Workers who had migrated to Shanghai were living in tents and sleeping on wooden pallets, using hand shovels to dig huge foundations. The contrast between the ultramodern buildings of Shanghai's business district and the primitive dwellings and tools of the workers inspired Xu.[55] He designed two huge birds, representing the male and female aspects of the Chinese Fenghuang, an enormous and immortal bird who combined the female yin principle and the male yang and appeared as an auspicious sign of renewal, such as at the beginning of an imperial dynasty.[56] Xu Bing made his male bird (or *Feng*) ninety feet long and the female (called *Huang*) one hundred feet, and together they weighed twelve tons.[57] He used red hardhats to make combs and crests for their heads and grouped shovels as feathers, hung the toothed scoops of earth movers as claws under the bodies of the birds, and tied all the parts together with rubber hoses. Using materials left over from construction helped to express the energy and work associated with renewal. Connecting with stories of an immortal bird reborn in fire that had spread across the West since Herodotus brought them from ancient Egypt to Greece,[58] Xu Bing called his creation *Phoenix*.

Unfortunately, the visual effect seemed too rough and negative (especially after the 2008 financial crash) to those who ruled the gleaming new World Finance Center in Shanghai. Instead of flying through the sleek new atrium there, the birds found appropriate settings and receptive audiences in the West. They were displayed in a former electronics factory at the Massachusetts Museum of Contemporary Art (Mass MOCA), then for a year in the nave of the Cathedral of St. John the Divine in New York, and finally outdoors in Italy for the 2015 Venice Biennale.

Conceived as commentaries on a hypermodern center of capitalism, Feng and Huang flew in isolation within stark white walls at Mass MOCA. At Venice they were installed under a highway bridge, where they flew over water. But the Cathedral of St. John the Divine, the largest Gothic church in the world, with a nave so tall it could accommodate the Statue of Liberty (without the pedestal), provided the most evocative setting for the birds. Their flamboyance complemented the complex Gothic architecture and decor. They acquired strings of small lightbulbs to illuminate their bodies when the nave became dark. According to Deborah Fung, a daughter of immigrants from China to the United States who works as a psychotherapist (MA in art therapy) and holds degrees from two evangelical institutions (Wheaton College BA, Regent University MDiv), the placement of the phoenixes in St. John the Divine was a "quasi-liturgical act of offering and supplication, a prayer for blessing, an act that situates human beings in rightful relationship to the cosmos of which they are a part."[59] The birds were hung as if flying away from the high altar of the cathedral toward the door, going out into the world. These birds brought a Chinese sense that the world constantly renews its life into a sanctuary of the Christian hope for resurrection.

On Friday May 17, 2019, another example of art as resistance made news in New York. A wooden statue of a peregrine falcon, about eight feet tall, stood on the median island at Broadway and Seventy-Second Street, where it became the center of a ribbon-cutting ceremony for *Birds on Broadway*, an art installation of ten bird sculptures. The line of birds extended from a red-necked grebe with several chicks at Sixty-Fourth Street, directly in front of Lincoln Center, to a wood duck at 157th Street, the Broadway median closest to the place where John James Audubon lived the last ten years of his life and died in 1851.

At the ceremony, Kathryn Heintz, the president of New York City Audubon, gave a speech explaining that "the intersection of art and science is so perfect for Broadway malls." She pointed out that the huge sculptures, representing birds threatened by climate change, were all made from reclaimed wood, donated by companies that used wood in shipping and construction and furniture. "These birds have attitude," Heintz claimed, and the falcon that loomed over the audience bore silent witness. She then introduced sculptor Nicholas Holiber, who designed and built the ten birds in a donated studio. Holiber, a thin and fit man in his early thirties, then took the podium and thanked everyone, including New York City Audubon, the National Audubon Society, the Broadway Mall Association, the New York City Parks Department, and a man named Avi Gitler, whose studio has become a center both for art and for activism over the last few years. Gitler sees himself as a spiritual heir of John James Audubon.

Born in the Washington Heights neighborhood, north of Harlem in Manhattan, Gitler was raised an orthodox Jew and attended Yeshiva High School and University. He describes himself as a "nomad" like Audubon because he traveled for a decade around the world before settling into an upstate New York house. In 2014, he was running a small art gallery near 149th and Broadway when he had the idea of commissioning a mural of a bird on the vacant storefront next door to draw the attention of passersby.

That flamingo gave an idea to Mark Jannot, who was then director of communications for the National Audubon Society, headquartered on Varick Street in Manhattan. Audubon had just compiled a list of 314 bird species of North America (a majority of our total of 500) that are endangered by loss of habitat resulting from climate change. Jannot proposed to Gitler that he recruit artists to paint all 314 (the flamingo didn't count, since it is not a native North American bird) as public murals on walls and windows and security gratings in New York. This began the Audubon Murals Project, which included more than 120 murals by more than ninety different artists before the pandemic of 2020 delayed progress. A few murals are as small as window panes, and some are as large as the outside wall of a ten-story apartment building with no obstruction next door, but most are about as big as a small shop's front entrance. Usually they are colorful and realistic, but there are occasionally abstract or symbolic paintings. Realism meets surrealism in the mural of a common redpoll, a sparrow-like bird native to North America, hovering protectively beside a nest that contains four children whose clothing and skin colors are meant to indicate that they are immigrants to the United States. That group was painted much larger than life by a group of students supervised by arts therapist Jessie Novik on the wall of a public school, P.S. 192, facing the playground of Jacob Schiff School between 136th and 138th Streets on Amsterdam Avenue.[60]

Of course, the mural at New York's P.S. 192 didn't solve the dilemmas of the United States with regard to human immigrants or endangered native birds. The wooden statues made by Nicholas Holiber were dismantled in August 2020. As far as our research reveals, the phoenixes of Xu Bin that soared through the Cathedral of St. John the Divine have not been displayed since Venice in 2015, and they also have most likely been taken apart and lost. But the murals have made a lasting difference. Avi Gitler's gallery has closed, but the effects of its publicity campaign on the neighborhood remain. The grave of John James Audubon, in Trinity Cemetery near Broadway and 155th Street has been marked since 2015 by a painted Fish Crow (associated with death) four stories high on the east side of Broadway, facing the site on the west where Audubon lived and died and which is still called Audubon Terrace (Figure 8.3).[61] According to Gitler, the murals and the presence of

Figure 8.3 Painted by artist Hitnes in 2015 as part of the Audubon Mural Project, this fish crow is a traditional emblem of death that now faces Audubon Terrace, where John James Audubon died in 1851, at 155th Street and Broadway in New York.
Photograph by Andrew Maas.

Audubon have made the neighborhood of Washington Heights into a sacred space.

Physical Changes, Central Park, and Cultural Attitudes

In physical terms, New York and other American cities have made some progress in their treatment of birds. During the decades before 1900, when the last passenger pigeon was shot in the wild, barrels of pigeons packed in ice were sent in boxcars by rail from forests around the Great Lakes and the South to be eaten in the millions by the humans of Chicago, St. Louis, and New York. Then skyscrapers began to rise in cities, and migrating birds flew into them and died uselessly every year. Estimates reached 230,000 collisions in New York and six hundred million deaths each year across the continent. But in 2011, San Francisco passed the first law that suggested (not required) new buildings use windows treated with patterns to warn birds. By

December 2019, New York required that tiny ceramic lines or dots be applied to glass to break up reflections in all new construction and renovation; marks on as little as 7 percent of glass surfaces provides an effective signal.[62] In February 2018, almost two years before the legal requirement, the all-glass exterior of the Javits Convention Center had been retrofitted with six thousand bird-friendly glass panels. Estimates of the reduction of bird strikes at Javits range higher than 90 percent.[63] Ever since 1997, when a dead common yellowthroat in the Wall Street financial district surprised New York City Audubon member Rebekah Creshkoff, that activist chapter of the Audubon Society has run a program called Operation Safe Flight to encourage window treatments and more careful use of lighting at night to avoid misleading and killing birds as they pass over Manhattan.

The physical significance of New York's Central Park for birds has greatly increased during the last few decades, although the park was designed in 1858 and served as one of twenty-five locations in Frank Chapman's first Christmas bird count in 1900. A rectangle 2.5 miles long and 0.5 miles wide, Central Park contains 843 acres of landscaped woods, artificial hills, glacial erratic boulders, lawns, and water features, including a one-hundred-acre reservoir that has become a winter home for waterfowl.[64] Surrounded by the skyscrapers and apartment buildings of Manhattan, the park appears as a green oasis in a concrete desert when viewed from the air, the way that millions of migrating birds see it, traveling north or south along the Atlantic Flyway every May and October. Dense development between the District of Columbia and Boston on the coast and from New York to Montreal in the Hudson Valley has magnified the importance of this Central Park oasis for birds. Increasingly fierce winds and volatile weather patterns often focus on New York Harbor and western Long Island Sound, driving birds toward Central Park even if their normal flight paths would not have taken them there.

A new era of cultural prominence for Central Park as a place where humans see birds began in 1990, with the hatching of a male red-tailed hawk who came to be called Pale Male because of the light coloring of his head. He established a nest in December 1992, on the twelfth floor of a posh apartment building at 927 Fifth Avenue, near Seventy-Fourth Street on the eastern side of the park, and proceeded to raise about thirty chicks (with several different mates) over the next twenty-five or more years. Because Pale Male was "the first hawk to return to Central Park in longer than anyone can remember,"[65] his exploits drew extensive press coverage. Marie Winn wrote a book about

Pale Male and his courtships, *Red Tails in Love*, which was published in 1998 with an update on the hawk's activities ten years later. In 2004, when the board of the co-op association that owned 927 Fifth Avenue responded to complaints about bird droppings and parts of prey animals dirtying the canopy of the building's entrance by removing the eight-foot wide nest that Pale Male and his spouses had constructed, many humans including the television star Mary Tyler Moore (a resident of the building) protested, and the hawk was allowed to rebuild.[66] As late as 2019, many insisted that Pale Male still lived, although the identification was uncertain since he had never been banded.[67]

Crowds with binoculars came to watch Pale Male, and this began an explosion of Central Park birdwatchers. In 2012, the Home Box Office cable television network released a film called *Birders: The Central Park Effect*, featuring the bestselling author Jonathan Franzen, that documented how different New Yorkers searched the park for birds. These New York birders argued fiercely with each other. One guide called "Birding Bob," a PhD in botany named Robert DeCandido, has been leading groups in the park for twenty-five years, but his use of recorded calls to draw birds to show themselves infuriates others.[68] In the summer of 2020, Central Park birding made headlines because a white woman called police on a Black male birder for asking her to leash her dog, a request she interpreted as a threat on her life.[69] One side effect of the story was to publicize the popularity of birdwatching, especially among Black people, in the park. Meanwhile the white woman who called the police, named Amy Cooper but often called Karen because of a character in television comedies from 2004 and 2005,[70] lost her job and became a byword for white privilege and racism, while the birder she reported, a Harvard graduate named Christian Cooper, got a television series called *Extraordinary Birder* on the Hulu network in 2023.

In less than a decade, Central Park went from serving as the site of niche activities, urban oddities like the Pale Male craze, to a basic birding site of worldwide importance, exemplifying the new prominence of birding in general. The 2012 HBO video and story about Jonathan Franzen and others birding in the park mentioned 100 species of birds to be seen; by 2021 the count was 235 species.[71] No doubt, this difference reflected a growth of knowledge in the birding community, but the number of species may also have grown because loss of habitat through development causes increasing needs for a rest stop among migratory birds, while climate chaos brings more frequent visits by formerly distant species like pine siskins and snowy owls from the North and glossy ibises and Savannah sparrows from the South.[72] The increasing need of birds for Central Park and other urban rest stops was underlined in an interview with Scott Weidensaul, an ornithologist who published *A World on the Wing: The Global Odyssey of Migratory Birds* in 2021. According to Weidensaul, "We could potentially get much more bang for our conservation buck if we put more money and more effort into improving bird habitat in urban parks and urban greenspaces than protecting pristine areas in more rural or wilderness areas." Complimenting the Central Park Conservatory, the nonprofit group that oversees and promotes development in the park, Weidensaul added, "It's only going to become more important for migratory birds as the years go by."[73]

More than any physical changes, a cultural shift in birding over recent decades offers hope. Those who count species in Central Park and advocate for bird-friendly glass and lighting are doing great work, but changes in culture could result in more sweeping transformations of human behavior and public policy. If people continue to seek personal transformation through birds, perhaps birds may lead people to transform the world that birds and people share.

As recently as 2003, a book called *The Big Year*, followed by a Hollywood comedy based on the book in 2011, alerted the public to the phenomenon of competitive birding by people (almost all of them male) who were then pushing the record number of North American bird species seen in one year from the seven hundreds into the eight hundreds. There are about ten thousand surviving bird species in the world, and a handful of birders now claim life lists of nine thousand or more, with more than six thousand in a single year.[74] As dedicated as such birders are to seeing birds, their frenetic travel generates massive amounts of carbon dioxide, and publicity for their achievements appears to result in more competition rather than conservation, recovery of bird populations, or ecological health. The urgency of competitive birding may be increased by news of extinctions and diminutions of bird populations.

In 2013, an independent film called *The Birder's Guide to Everything* ranked humans who are interested in birds into three groups: feeders, listers, and watchers. Those who pursue record numbers of species are listers. The movie placed listers below watchers, who seek to see birds because they "want to achieve a transcendent connection between natures that erases any distinction between human and birds' souls." As the fifteen-year-old boy who was the hero of the movie explained to the girl he loved, "Most of us are just listers who strive to be watchers."[75]

Attitudes and actions conducive to becoming Watchers were prescribed by Claire Thompson, a staff member at the UK-based BirdLife International, in her book *The Art of Mindful Birdwatching: Reflections on Freedom & Being* (2017). She began by reminding readers that birds are sentient beings like ourselves, not objects. She urged everyone to practice an exercise of choosing one bird while looking out a window and focusing a wish for the bird: "May she be well, may she be happy, may she be free from suffering."[76] This echoed Buddhist formulations such as the Four Immeasurables and the *Metta* (or Lovingkindness) prayer for all beings, both of which are common in Buddhist meditation and worship.[77] And Thompson went on to recommend that people remember, while walking in a city, to look up occasionally rather than always looking down. She wrote that we should regard parks as better sites for meeting birds than our backyards, because "parks are a shared space" where "we interact with our feathered companions as equals."[78] Noting that evolution has given humans the innate knowledge that birdsong is "the music of safety," a signal that predators are not stalking us or the birds while we listen, she urged mindful listening to birdsong as a way to "relax our bodies but also enhance our concentration by stimulating our cognition."[79] Rather than responding to Rare Bird Alerts to grab binoculars and cameras and rush to a spot, Thompson advised her readers to find a sit spot, a comfortable place where they can "sit and remain still for at least twenty minutes" so that birds they disturb while walking can "begin to relax and return," convinced that they pose no threat.[80]

Even in the most threatening situation, a theater of war, birding can create some sense of peace. In *Birding Babylon: A Soldier's Journey from Iraq* (2006), Sergeant Jonathan Trouern-Trend of the Connecticut National Guard reflected, "Knowing that the great cycles of nature continue despite what people happen to be doing is reassuring."[81] Deployed with a medical unit for more than a year in 2004 and 2005, he reported the birds he saw in Baghdad, Mosul, Nasiriyah, and literally in the ruins of Babylon and in Ur, which the Bible calls Abraham's hometown. He found the presence of many familiar birds comforting, but also was excited to see new species like hoopoes, bulbuls, and laughing doves. Reflecting on his experience and hoping to return to Iraq someday in peace and to see more birds, Trouern wrote, "No matter how long it takes to get to that future, I know the birds will be waiting."[82]

Sergeant Trouern-Trend recorded his own Christmas bird count in Iraq, continuing the conservationist activity that Frank Chapman attached to that traditional religious holiday.[83] Birding can certainly bring out meditative feelings and connect to religions. Even academics, who are notoriously unlikely to take part in religious practices, seem compelled to adopt religious attitudes when they contemplate birds.

Ways of Looking at Birds: Scholars, Zoos, and Museums

Just as binoculars and telescopes isolate the object toward which they are directed from the rest of the world, birdwatching can isolate birds and so distort the reality of bird lives and the perspectives of those who use instruments to see birds. In *Binocular Vision* (2011), an English professor at the University of Illinois named Spencer Schaffner argued that field guides for birdwatching had identifiable agendas in how they treated birds and places where birds are found. For example, Schaffner noted that guides tended to regard birds as desirable or undesirable, good or bad, depending on whether or not the birds were found in geographic areas where their species could be seen as native. He also observed that pictures in field guides set birds against no backgrounds or idealized "natural" backgrounds, never showing how gulls, pigeons, crows, sparrows, chimney swifts, swallows, and many other birds still flourish in areas transformed by humans.[84]

An expansion of "binocular vision" into a program for action was recommended to those who seek to help birds more effectively by sociologist Elizabeth Cherry in her 2020 book, *For the Birds: Protecting Wildlife through the Naturalist Gaze*. Cherry's first book, *Culture and Activism* (2016), comparing movements for animal rights in the United States and France, gave credit to religion for giving energy to advocates of bird welfare in America. In *For the Birds*, she claimed that the birders she met through her research had long been altering their own diets and backyard landscapes and political positions in ways that would be fitting for adherents to a religion of nature.[85] Cherry's last sentences invoked inspiration, wonder, and attention, words that are often associated with prayer, worship, and meditation: "Finally, I hope that all readers will be inspired to get out and enjoy nature. The natural world holds many wonders, even in our own backyards. We just have to pay attention to it."[86] The words "nature" and "natural" here function as criteria for morality, playing the role of God in discourse.

Scholarly writing normally features verifiable facts, quantifiable data, and physical observations rather than emotions, but emotions appear when scholars write about religions of nature. In 2009, Bron Taylor published *Dark*

Green Religion, citing examples from the green movement to illustrate how holding nature sacred could lead to hatred and violence against humans.[87] Sarah Pike, another expert on religions and ecology, established in 2017 that members of the organization called Earth First! have resorted to suicide and violence to express grief as they mourn for nature or for specific trees and birds.[88] Both scholars acknowledge, even if they disapprove, the increasing importance of nature religions.

Central Park has shown that people can have profoundly positive relations with wild birds. One could say that the park is a place of magic called out of the earth by humanity, but this magic came without any recorded intention of landscape architect Frederik Law Olmsted or of the politicians and leaders of business and culture who ran New York City in 1858. By coincidence, 1858 also witnessed a great "Businessmen's Revival" of evangelical Protestants, led by a Methodist woman named Phoebe Palmer who ran prayer meetings in her home. That revival gave energy to the causes of abolishing slavery, prohibiting alcohol, and improving the legal status of women. It led thousands of businessmen to have moments of rebirth and join churches, but it seems to have done nothing for Central Park or for conservation in general. Historians have found schools of thought within liberal Protestant and Roman Catholic churches of the Romantic era that contributed to a growing reverence for Nature,[89] but little among the evangelicals who drove a steady rise of church membership in the United States from the early 1800s through the 1960s.[90] Two places that did become sacred for our generation of birders, Central Park in New York and Mt. Auburn Cemetery in Boston, were created by Victorian nature mystics, but without any direct intention of helping birds.

Two places where people could see birds, in hope that we might come to revere and to care for them, were deliberately created in the early twentieth century: the dioramas of the American Museum of Natural History in New York, and the Scripps Aviary in the San Diego Zoo. Despite the great work of their founders, Ellen Browning Scripps (1836–1932) and Frank Michler Chapman (1864–1945), the aviary and the dioramas have outlived their times. Both now need transformative changes to allow birds to act as messengers in an effective religion of nature.

Scripps led a life that extended through several phases of Carolyn Merchant's "gendered dialectic" of female and male leaders in social reform. Born a lower-middle-class Methodist in England, she came to America as a child, the youngest of six, and became the only person in her family who completed a program of higher education, at Knox College in Illinois. Then she worked with a brother on newspapers, first in Detroit and eventually across the United States, writing advice columns, syndicating her work, and (by her brother's account) building a great family fortune by several times saving newspapers from bankruptcy and helping to found what would become the Scripps chain of progressive publications. Always a spiritual seeker, Ellen Scripps left her last church membership in 1879, when Presbyterians refused to ordain women. She accepted many aspects of Christian Science, which had helped her sister Annie to deal with illnesses, and partially funded the building of the Christian Science church in La Jolla, California, near San Diego, where she also spoke at least once. Intrigued by Darwin and evolution but rejecting those who interpreted it in the "survival of the fittest" competitive mode promoted by Herbert Spencer, she became a believer in Life as a universal principle. "That there is no such distinction as the words spiritual and material imply seems to me unquestionable," she argued.[91] Settling in La Jolla for the last decades of her long life, she founded the Scripps Oceanographic Institute, Scripps College (a school for women at the center of five Claremont Colleges), and the San Diego Zoo, which some claim to be the greatest zoo in the world. In 1922, she gave the zoo "the Scripps Aviary, which, at eighty-two feet high, was the tallest flight cage in the world at the time."[92] That single tall cage grew over the next century into an enormous enclosure housing an artificial rainforest, a waterfall, and thirty-five species of birds, and connecting with the Parker Aviary and Owens Aviary, so that together the three hold ninety-five species and several hundred individual birds.[93] In May 2021, a hummingbird aviary was added to include three species of hummingbirds and fourteen species of other birds from South America.

A visit to the birds who lived in these environments in 2019 provided moments of wonder and an enduring sadness. Passing crowds of flamingoes, seeing Andean cocks greeting each other from inside and outside the cage, glimpsing the largest eagle in the world, a harpy eagle, on an artificial cliff, and meeting the stare of an ornate eagle hawk were all unforgettable experiences, made accessible by the gifts of Scripps and her successors. But to realize that having such moments means that these birds live out their lives in captivity, never stretching their wings for flights longer than a few yards, becomes depressing. Most human visitors do not seem awed or moved, but distracted and concerned for their own comfort.

Meanwhile, across the continent in Manhattan, the American Museum of Natural History features dioramas, small rooms separated by glass from an exhibit hall, where birds preserved by taxidermy and modeled into statuary stand amid models of other animals, rocks and plants and water features, in front of painted backdrops. Dioramas represented an advance on the practice of hanging the carcasses of birds in rows in wall closets behind glass doors, or even in drawers, modes of display that still continue in this and other museums. Frank Chapman, the self-taught ornithologist and conservation pioneer who was featured at the end of the last chapter, invented this way of displaying birds, probably inspired by John James Audubon's practice of painting and engraving his life-size birds in natural settings. Audubon's paintings and Chapman's dioramas both show birds in some version of their natural habitats, along with other species of animals and plants, and the practice was then applied to other animals in the New York museum and everywhere else. Twenty dioramas are included in the Hall of American Birds, and another twelve now appear in a hall called Birds of the World. According to signage in the museum, when Chapman's Hall of American Birds opened in 1902, "It was the only hall devoted to habitat groups in any museum of the world."[94] The signs also claim that "the power of the diorama has transformed museums across the world."

But the power of the diorama has severe limits. To enable dioramas to be seen clearly, without reflections on the glass, the larger rooms where they are set into the walls are kept dark, and the darkness keeps some visitors away. Only two years after Chapman's death in 1945, a biographical pamphlet published in 1947 by the museum said, "Most unfortunately, the main entrance to the gallery in which these exhibits are installed is located in a part of the Museum which is now reached by few visitors, and of these fewer still pass through the dark gallery."[95] When I visited in June 2019, some of the labels outside the bird dioramas had faded so badly that they were unreadable. The ceilings in the Hall of American Birds are very low, making the exhibit halls noisy when only a few people are in them, the air is musty, and the whole effect is funereal, discouraging to further interest in the birds and habitats depicted.

In an age of great nature documentaries, and of cameras that fly with live birds and record the life in their nests, the static scenes of dioramas have become too dull. A dead bison or bear or alligator can still exude enough power through sheer size to transfix many visitors to a museum, but all birds that can fly are small by comparison. Flying also means that birds on the ground are not in their complete natural habitat. For most birds, home includes the sky. Perhaps dioramas should be turned into settings for three dimensional, holographic projections that take the birds through their whole range of movements.

Commitments for Humans Who Practice a Religion of Nature

A better model than dioramas or zoos for integrating birds and people appeared over four days in the summer of 2017 in the neighborhood of Lenox, Massachusetts, where the Boston Symphony Orchestra has its summer home on an estate called Tanglewood. In a program called "Tanglewood Takes Flight," the BSO and Mass Audubon, the oldest Audubon society in the United States, combined four mornings and evenings of birdwatching walks led by experts, both on the Tanglewood grounds and at the nearby Pleasant Valley Wildlife Sanctuary, with many performances of works by Olivier Messiaen and other composers whose music integrates bird calls and birdsong.[96] An exhibit of bird paintings, drawings, photographs, and sculptures from the Mass Audubon museum of bird art was brought from its home near Boston to a large house on the Tanglewood grounds, and there were gallery talks about the art. That combination of music, visual art, and bird walks helped to inspire this book. If similar events could take place at prime migration times all over the world, a critical mass of influential people could come to realize that we share the world with birds.

Zoos should become bird hospitals and nurseries. At the Scripps Aviary in the San Diego Zoo, a placard identifying the prisoner harpy eagle says that "harpies hatched at the San Diego Zoo have been released in Central America."[97] The California condor came back from actual extinction (in the wild) in the 1980s through a three-decade program of captive breeding and release.[98] What if the physical infrastructure and staffing of these bird prisons were put in service of breeding many species of birds with the aim of increasing their numbers in the wild? Small numbers of people could still make reservations to visit the aviaries and see live birds in the places where the breeding took place, but these people could visit in good conscience, knowing that they are not seeing animals sentenced to life within large cages.

Dioramas and zoos have become much less necessary because of small cameras that do not impede birds as they fly and drones that can follow them, using telephoto lenses to collect records of their lives. Cameras focused on nests can take viewers into the natural homes and families of birds.

Instead of consigning such live feeds and footage to public broadcasting documentaries, we could integrate them into educational curricula and public service announcements on commercial television.

There is plenty of evidence that we are ready to stop torturing birds for companionship, amusement, and food. As Elizabeth Cherry noted in *For the Birds*, most birders are making changes in their diets, and the percentage of the general population declaring themselves vegetarians or vegans is rapidly growing.[99] In 1803, at the beginning of the Romantic era that began the religion of nature, the English poet and visionary artist William Blake wrote, "A Robin Red breast in a Cage / Puts all Heaven in a Rage / A Dove house filled with Doves & Pigeons / Shudders Hell through all its Regions."[100] No more should we allow people to buy and keep parrots as captives, living into their nineties without flocks or mates. No more should egg farms feature battery hens, with beaks chopped off and no chance to move, let alone fly into a tree. No more should people eat cheap, mass-produced chicken or turkey, but only meat from birds who led satisfying lives with love from each other and from us. Rather than the Purdue "oven-stuffer" roaster, which has more space when baking in an oven than it ever had in its life, we could discover that free-range chickens can be profitable to raise for food. France has already accomplished this by preserving traditional farms and chicken breeds.[101] Factory farming didn't take off until after World War II, and we could easily do without it now.

Planning human land development for wild birds would also mean planning better for ourselves. Our cities and our suburbs and our farms, our harbors and our airports and our industrial sites should all take birds into account. To avoid killing birds with invisible windows or jet engines or waste oil pools is a good beginning, but governments should also be setting aside flyways and rest areas for migratory birds. We should use public money, perhaps collected as a tax form checkoff or a rounding option in food markets, to ensure food and water and places to nest and roost for birds who are permanent residents. By creating landscapes for birds deliberately, as we have accidentally created one in Central Park, we will improve our own quality of life. A widely cited German study from December 2020 showed that people are happier when they are hearing and seeing more birds.[102] Instead of planning for more sterile environments, putting spikes on our buildings to discourage birds from nesting and paving all the land we can, we should plan in hope that neighborhoods and college campuses and cities will be shared with more and more numerous birds. If we plan to increase the bird population, we might avoid environmental catastrophes that will cause our own population to crash.

One way to plan for birds has been developed by an artist and landscape architect named Anina Gerchick. She has designed and created systems of bamboo racks holding thirty different plants, each rack ranging from one to twelve feet high along its thirty feet of length, with water supplies integrated into them, to encourage birds in urban areas. Ms. Gerchick calls these installations BirdLinks,[103] and she has placed them in several neighborhoods in New York City, with the cooperation of the New York Parks Department. In Gerchick's vision, BirdLinks would appear anywhere and everywhere, on flyways and in deserts, offering local plants that birds are accustomed to finding, whether on migration or close to their home nests.

As a minimum standard for success, we could aim to restore the numbers and balance of human and animal populations of the early twentieth century, after the Migratory Bird Treaty Act of 1918 and before the use of DDT. The century since the 1930s has brought great advances for human convenience, but also disasters of genocide, extinction, and pollution for all of life on earth (including human life). We should strive to repair some of that damage.

Audubon's Birds and Today's Issues of Religion, Gender, Race, and Nation

For as long as any movement committed to helping birds has existed in the United States, John James Audubon has been its patron saint. Today, a religion of nature centered on birds is coming into its own, but Audubon's place in the history of relations between birds and humans is being challenged. These challenges arise for good reasons, because Audubon and the movement founded in his name have not been perfect. But the work and heritage of Audubon, including the controversies over his life and character, can still help to show how birds point beyond divisions of religion, gender, race, and political nationalism.

Most basically, Audubon's life-size, vividly staged portraits of birds retain their power to spark what Hindus call *darshan*, the moment of seeing divine life shining through an image. "Audubon's real gift to us is awareness, and in that awareness is the beginning of all true conservation," according to Roger Tory Peterson, the father of modern bird guides.[104] Greek and Russian Orthodox Christians seek such contact with divinity in their icons, and

Audubon's paintings have been seen as icons by writers like Eudora Welty and Robert Penn Warren and by historians of religion and art, as appeared in Chapter 7.

Legitimate ethical, aesthetic, and religious objections arise from the fact that Audubon shot the birds that he painted, then used dead birds as models after posing their corpses in position with wires on a board. In contrast to Chinese and Japanese bird paintings, which according to tradition are done quickly and without models, in the studio after years of observing birds in the wild, Audubon's birds have been said to lack *chi*, or life force. But unlike East Asian bird painters, Audubon sought scientific accuracy in the details of feathers and bodily structures. Cameras that could record living birds with such detail have only recently become available. Because Audubon made glimpses of the eternal qualities embodied by living animals available to those who viewed his paintings, his guns and wires may be forgiven, along with the smell of decomposing subjects that often made the artist unwelcome in the homes and hotels where he worked. Those who do not see the life in Audubon's birds need to look less for the documentary photograph and more for the icon. What Audubon saw and recorded still has revelatory power for new generations.

Audubon transformed his own appearance, meeting his future wife in Philadelphia as a French dandy dressing in silk and lace and moving with her to Kentucky as an American woodsman in leather. His relations with women and his accounts of birds both led beyond narrowly limited gender roles. Beginning with Audubon's wife Lucy, women played enormous parts in launching the bird conservation movement that started with Audubon's work. First in Kentucky and then in Louisiana, Lucy ran grammar schools in her homes that paid for Audubon's expeditions to find birds. She came to England to supervise the collection of subscriptions from those who bought the double-folio edition of *Birds of America* that made him and her rich and famous. In the decade after Audubon's death in 1851, Lucy inspired her student George Bird Grinnell with a passion for birds that produced the first, failed Audubon society. And as historian Carolyn Merchant has demonstrated, the efforts of women who succeeded Grinnell, especially Muriel Lawrence Hemenway and Florence Merriam Bailey, made the name "Audubon" synonymous with societies that have succeeded in keeping many birds alive. Men then assumed leadership of the successful Audubon societies, but they met with few successes after the Migratory Bird Treaty Act of 1918, until Rachel Carson's *Silent Spring* was published in 1962.

Americans have urgently explored the distinctions between sex and gender, biology and behavior, in recent decades, but Audubon helped to demonstrate these differences two centuries ago, both by painting birds in such detail and also by observing and verbally describing their behavior. Plate 51 in *Birds of America* became famous for this violent image of a female red-tailed hawk holding a dead rabbit while she is attacked by another hawk. Not only did Audubon supply an image in this case, however. He also explained what the image said about gender roles among hawks and how those differed from the gender roles of eagles.

> The continued attachment that exists between Eagles once paired, is not exhibited by these birds, which, after rearing their young, become as shy towards each other as if they had never met. This is carried to such a singular length, that they are seen to chase and rob each other of their prey, on all occasions.[105]

When Audubon depicted passenger pigeons, his illustration highlighted sex differences between the male and female that do not exist among the nonmigratory pigeons that live among humans today. It also showed an unusual gendered behavior, with a smaller female feeding a larger male. Because many birds would follow an opposite pattern, in which males might feed females in order to secure their participation in sex and breeding, the accuracy of Audubon's staging of the birds here has been doubted. However, since Audubon actually watched passenger pigeons on several occasions, while the moderns questioning his accuracy have never seen the birds alive, Audubon probably deserves the benefit of the doubt. Besides, because hatchlings among birds frequently grow so fast that parents can be seen feeding children larger than themselves, the female bird in this picture may be the mother of the male.

As we deal with the fact that gender has become a major source of division in human society, birds offer transcendent perspectives for our discussion. Realizing that Audubon long ago showed that birds have many different gender roles and many ways to distinguish the sexes can help people to understand that new, more complicated classifications of human gender and forms of display are not "unnatural" deviations from a gender binary, but examples of the natural gender spectrum among all forms of life. Ornithologist Richard O. Prum has used the natural capacity for sex changes in ducks to argue that genetic sex is malleable in *Performance All the Way Down* (2023).

Audubon's personal history and his birds reveal similar possibilities with regard to race. Since 2014, when police shootings touched off a Black Lives Matter movement that continues at this writing, accelerating with the police murder of George Floyd in 2020, race has dominated all discussions of politics and culture in the United States. Every aspect of American life is being examined for evidence of systemic racism. In that effort, urgent questions have arisen about Audubon and the groups that bear his name.

Racially based slavery pervaded the United States (and the world) of Audubon's time, and Audubon's own racial identity is a matter of conjecture. It remains uncertain whether he was born in Haiti or Louisiana, but in either case he was born in a French territory where slavery was practiced, and where his French father had several children by at least one Black and enslaved woman. The most stable of the homes that Audubon's wife and children maintained while the explorer and artist traveled the country was in Louisiana. While Lucy Audubon made her living teaching a school in that Louisiana home, the family owned slaves who served as domestic help. On his explorations, Audubon himself sometimes had slaves carrying luggage and setting up camps. When traveling alone, he once spent a night with a family of escaped slaves who had fled a plantation because they had been sold to different owners. Audubon then convinced their original owner to buy them back so that they could resume life and stay together on the plantation, where they seemed "as happy as slaves generally are in that country."[106] Before setting sail for England in 1830, he sold several slaves along with the rest of his household goods. There is no evidence that Audubon ever decided to oppose slavery. In a letter from England to Lucy in 1834, he criticized the British government for acting "imprudently and too precipitously"[107] in abolishing slavery in its West Indian territories.

Critiques of Audubon for racism go beyond slavery. In 1837, only a year after the battles of the Alamo and San Jacinto took Texas from Mexico in 1836, Audubon passed through the region in search of birds. Already famous because *Birds of America* had begun to come out, he was shown a collection of human skulls belonging to Mexican soldiers whose remains were held by Texans who had no knowledge of their identities. He was offered some of the skulls and he accepted, eventually bringing them to the museum of Dr. Samuel Morton in Philadelphia. During the nineteenth century, many scientists in museums and universities of the United States and Europe were collecting skulls, especially from nonwhite people, in an effort to establish a science of "phrenology" that would predict character, intelligence, and aptitudes based on shapes in the skull. Phrenology was often used to seek arguments for racial superiority by comparing skulls from members of different ethnic groups. Dr. Morton in particular has been called the "founding father of scientific racism."[108]

At this writing, the racial attitudes Audubon revealed in his interactions with slaves and Mexicans are being cited as worthy of censure, or the modern exclusion from discourse called "cancellation."[109] Some argue that bird conservation groups could more effectively advocate for birds and recruit non-white members if the National Audubon Society and the state and local groups called "Audubon" dropped Audubon's name. Groups in Seattle and New York City have passed resolutions dropping Audubon from their titles, but the National Audubon Society has refused as of 2023, and New York City Audubon has chosen no new name.

Names that humans have given to birds have also come under attack, and again Audubon stands at the center of the storm. Credited with discovering twenty-five species, he named fourteen of them after people. One bird, the Audubon's oriole, was named for him by ornithologist Rene Primevere Lesson. In June 2020, a group called Bird Names for Birds was formed to advocate for replacing all human names attached to birds. Its website listed 150 such names, from Audubon's oriole, Bonaparte's gull, and Cooper's hawk to Zino's petrel.[110] The fact that all 150 birds listed were named for white men linked this tradition to racism and to sexism as well.

But ironically, an older controversy about Audubon and race has gone unnoticed, at least until now, in this discussion. There have been persistent claims that Audubon had African ancestry. He was listed in *The Negro Almanac* (fifth edition, 1989) among "Outstanding Black Artists."[111] He was cited by a stamp-collecting society among "African Americans on U.S. Stamps" with the note that "Audubon's mother was a Creole (mixed heritage) from Domenica." His portrait hangs on the wall of the African American Museum of Art and Culture in New Orleans.[112] On the other hand, one of the most thorough modern biographers of Audubon, Alice Ford, has argued that Audubon's mother, Jeanne Rabin, was a white, French maid brought by Captain Audubon to Haiti from Nantes, and most Audubon biographers of the last twenty years have followed her lead.[113] Audubon himself wrote that he had been told (presumably by his father) that his biological mother was a Spanish woman, not a French maid, and that he had been born in Louisiana, not in Haiti. That Spanish woman, according to Audubon, had accompanied his father to the Haitian plantation and died in the slave uprising that led to

Haitian independence and the transplantation of two of Captain Audubon's children to France. Another hint at Audubon's possibly mixed ethnicity appeared in the description on his (pre-photographic) passport for a trip to England in 1830, where his "oval face" was said to have had a "brown complexion."[114]

Whatever the truth of his heritage, there can be no doubt that once he settled on his family land near Philadelphia, the man now famed as John James Audubon stressed his deep connections to America. He boasted that his father Captain Audubon, as commander of French warships, had met George Washington during the Revolution, first before the winter at Valley Forge and later because he commanded a ship at the blockade of Yorktown that brought the surrender of the British in 1781. The elder Audubon claimed to possess a portrait of General Washington given to him by Washington himself.[115] His son described his arrival at New York harbor in 1803 as a journey "back to my own beloved country, the United States of America,"[116] even though evidence points to that trip being his first visit to the United States.

But a claim to American birth need not entail any claim to exclusively white ancestry. The United States was politically founded by English white supremacists, but it has never been a racially pure nation. The 1613 kidnapping of Powhatan princess Pocahontas and her 1614 marriage to Englishman John Rolfe started a line of descent that continued in President John Tyler and in Edith Wilson, the First Lady and functional president for the last years of Woodrow Wilson's second term, and Thomas Jefferson's six children by the half-white slave Sally Hemings also embodied that tradition of race mixing. Immigration and intermarriage have made the United States a model of racial combination, if not harmony.

Birds take no part in the human attempt to define "race," and birds transcend our attempt to divide them into types or species. Although birds can be classified by species, they often breed across species, especially within families, including corvids (ravens, crows, jays, and parrots), gulls, and ducks.[117] Birds nurture young from different species, as when strange eggs are left in their nests or when deaths of parents result in needy hatchlings. And birds cooperate by giving warning signals across species whenever individual birds can hear each other.

Birds fly across political boundaries between nations. Many traditional cultures celebrate birds for bringing crops from elsewhere, as appeared in Chapter 4. In the modern era, international diplomacy had one of its greatest triumphs with the Migratory Bird Treaty Act of 1918, an accomplishment bringing together the United States, Canada, the United Kingdom, Japan, and Russia that was celebrated in a classic study from 1998, *The Dawn of Conservation Diplomacy*. If humans are to learn how to moderate the current crises of global warming and ocean pollution and recurring pandemics, we will need to monitor the global movements and health of birds. Where the birds are, how much food they are finding, and what viruses they are carrying are all vital signs of planetary health. Evidence from recent publications, such as Scott Weidensaul's *A World on the Wing: The Global Odyssey of Migratory Birds* (2021), and the inclusion of satellite photography of millions of birds on major flyways in television weather reports, indicates that people are becoming more conscious of this aspect of life. Sonia Shah's *The Next Great Migration: The Beauty and Terror of Life on the Move* (2020) explicitly applies lessons from bird migration to human societies and politics. We need much more of such global thinking, and birds are leading us to do it.

In July 2019, the National Audubon Society held its biennial convention at Milwaukee, Wisconsin, and the keynote address was given by Winona LaDuke, a member of the Ojibwe nation of American Indians who is also a farmer, an author, a rural development economist with degrees from Harvard and Antioch, and an environmental activist. She was the first woman and the first Native American to give the keynote at an Audubon national meeting, and the content of her hourlong speech revealed how integrated the new religion of nature has become. Discussing birds alone only long enough for a joke about how native birds in Minnesota are treating invasive mute swans, LaDuke took for granted that the Audubon Society would respond to a universal message. "Whether we have wings, fins, roots, or paws—we are all in this together," LaDuke said. "One dish, one spoon, we all have the same dish. We are all related."[118] Birds have been showing us this from the beginning, and we may finally be learning it.

Notes

1. James Lovelock, interview with Stephen Sackur on *Hard Talk*, BBC July 16, 2021, https://www.bbc.co.uk/programmes/p09pm2lq (accessed August 9, 2021).
2. Melissa Borja, "'On Eagle's Wings': The Catholic Hymn for a Hurting America," *Patheos*, November 10, 2020, https://www.patheos.com/blogs/anxiousbench/2020/11/on-eagles-wings-the-catholic-hymn-for-a-hurting-america/ (accessed March 7, 2022).

3. See etymology of tercel: https://www.wordnik.com/words/tercel (July 26, 2021).
4. Peter Gardella, *American Civil Religion: What Americans Hold Sacred* (New York: Oxford University Press, 2014), 114.
5. *Punch* cartoon from 1861 can be found and purchased at https://www.amazon.com/American-political-cartoon-Cotton-Blockade/dp/B07HHMBVWR (accessed June 28, 2020).
6. Oliver Stone and Peter Kuznick, *The Untold History of the United States* (New York: Simon & Schuster, 2013), 387.
7. Andrew Glass, "'In God We Trust' Becomes Nation's Motto, July 30, 1956," *Politico*, July 30, 2018, https://www.politico.com/story/2018/07/30/in-god-we-trust-becomes-nations-motto-july-30-1956-741016#:~:text=On%20this%20day%20in%201956,become%20the%20nation's%20official%20motto (accessed June 28, 2020).
8. Rebecca Heisman, "Bald Eagle: The Ultimate Endangered Species Act Success Story," *Birdcalls: News and Perspectives on Bird Conservation*, May 24, 2018, https://abcbirds.org/bald-eagle-the-ultimate-endangered-species-act-success-story/ (accessed August 22, 2020).
9. Rachel Carson, *Silent Spring* (Boston: Houghton Mifflin, 1962), 119.
10. Carson, *Silent Spring*, 297.
11. President Jimmy Carter, quoted at the website of the company founded by the logo's designer, Malcolm Grear, https://www.mgrear.com/blog-2/identity-branding/united-states-department-of-health-and-human-services (accessed June 30, 2021).
12. "HHS Logo, Seal and Symbol Policies," US Department of Health and Human Services, https://www.hhs.gov/web/policies-and-standards/web-policies/logo-seal-and-symbol-policies/index.html (accessed July 1, 2021).
13. Carson, *Silent Spring*, 155–156.
14. Carson, *Silent Spring*, 158–161.
15. Siobhan Nash-Marshall, *The Sins of the Fathers: Turkish Denialism and the Armenian Genocide* (New York: Crossword Publishing, 2017), 52–55.
16. See the episode list for *The Twentieth Century* on the Internet Movie Database: https://www.imdb.com/title/tt0050072/episodes?season=1&ref_=tt_eps_sn_1 (accessed August 19, 2020).
17. Samantha Power, *A Problem from Hell: America and the Age of Genocide* (New York: Basic Books, 2002).
18. Celine Castronuovo and Rachel Frazin, "Trump Administration Proceeds with Rollback of Bird Protections Despite Objections of Scientists, Environmentalists," *The Hill*, November 27, 2020, https://thehill.com/policy/energy-environment/527735-trump-administration-proceeds-with-rollback-of-bird-protections (accessed June 14, 2021).
19. Martin Buber, *I and Thou*, trans. Walter Kaufmann (New York: Charles Scribner's Sons, 1970), 144.
20. Buber, *I and Thou*, 177.
21. Buber, *I and Thou*, 145.
22. Buber, *I and Thou*, 150.

23. Melissa Mayntz, "Fun Facts about Gulls," *The Spruce*, November 3, 2019, https://www.thespruce.com/fun-facts-about-gulls-385525 (accessed June 21, 2020).
24. Richard Bach, *Jonathan Livingston Seagull*, photographs by Russell Munson (New York: Macmillan, 1970), 55–56.
25. Bach, *Jonathan Livingston Seagull*, 67.
26. Bach, *Jonathan Livingston Seagull*, 76.
27. Bach, *Jonathan Livingston Seagull*, 83.
28. Bach, *Jonathan Livingston Seagull*, 93.
29. Carolyn Merchant, *Spare the Birds! George Bird Grinnell and the First Audubon Society* (New Haven: Yale University Press, 2016), 30ff.
30. Wade Clark Roof and William McKinney, *American Mainline Religion: Its Changing Shape and Future* (New Brunswick, NJ: Rutgers University Press, 1987), 110.
31. Neil Diamond, "Be," theme song from "Jonathan Livingston Seagull" (Paramount Pictures, 1973). http://www.absolutelyrics.com/lyrics/view/neil_diamond/jonathan_livingston_seagull (accessed July 23, 2020).
32. On Hall Bartlett, see https://www.tcm.com/tcmdb/person/10880%7C65200/Hall-Bartlett/#biography and https://www.amazon.com/Jonathan-Livingston.../dp/B08GKY1CH3 (accessed June 25, 2021).
33. On Jack Couffer, see https://www.imdb.com/name/nm0183307/bio?ref_=nm_ov_bio_sm (accessed January 12, 2021).
34. Roger Ebert, review of Jonathan Livingston Seagull, November 8, 1973, https://www.rogerebert.com/reviews/jonathan-livingston-seagull-1973 (accessed June 25, 2021).
35. On the success of *March of the Penguins*, see Adam Leipzig, "10 Lessons 'March of the Penguins' Taught Me about Success and the ROI of Risk" *Cultural Daily*, June 27, 2013, https://www.culturaldaily.com/10-lessons-march-of-the-penguins-taught-me-about-success-and-the-roi-of-risk/ (accessed June 25, 2021). Also Brian Welk, "15 Top Grossing Documentaries," *The Wrap*, October 7, 2020, https://www.thewrap.com/top-grossing-documentaries-box-office/ (accessed June 25, 2021).
36. Ed Caesar, "The Most Colourful Characters Are Black and White," *New Zealand Herald*, December 22, 2006, https://www.nzherald.co.nz/entertainment/the-most-colourful-characters-are-black-and-white/J6YS3DHFNKPZYUK6SXLVSR55DI/ (accessed June 29, 2021).
37. Dinitia Smith, "Love That Dare Not Squeak Its Name," *New York Times*, February 7, 2004, https://www.nytimes.com/2004/02/07/arts/love-that-dare-not-squeak-its-name.html (accessed June 29, 2021).
38. Ian Dooley, "Banned Books Week 2019: *And Tango Makes Three*," Costen Children's Library Princeton University, September 23, 2019, https://blogs.princeton.edu/cotsen/2019/09/banned-books-week-and-tango-makes-three/ (accessed June 29, 2021).
39. See *The Sissy Duckling*, https://www.amazon.com/Sissy-Duckling-Sharon-Stone/dp/B01MRILXWC, Amazon Prime Video (accessed June 29, 2021).
40. Susan Dunne, "Filling the Bill," *Hartford Courant*, July 17, 2006, https://www.courant.com/news/connecticut/hc-xpm-2006-07-17-0607170492-story.html (accessed June 29, 2021).

41. Lawrence La Fountain-Stokes, "Queer Ducks, Puerto Rican *patos*, and Jewish-American *feygelekh*: Birds and the Cultural Representation of Homosexuality," *Centro Journal* (March 2007), https://www.researchgate.net/publication/26486089_Queer_ducks_Puerto_Rican_patos_and_Jewish-American_feygelekh_Birds_and_the_cultural_representation_of_homosexuality (accessed January 24, 2021).
42. Peter Gardella, *American Angels: Useful Spirits in the Material World* (Lawrence: University of Kansas Press, 2007), 133.
43. Tony Kushner, *Angels in America* (New York: Theatre Communications Group, 1995), 251.
44. Kushner, *Angels in America*, 252.
45. Gardella, *American Angels*, 166. Also Peter Gardella, "Spiritual Warfare in the Fiction of Frank Peretti," in *Religions of the United States in Practice*, ed. Colleen McDannell (Princeton, NJ: Princeton University Press), 333.
46. Zeyn Joudhakar, *The Thirty Names of Night* (New York: Simon & Schuster Atria Books, 2020), 151.
47. Joudhakar, *Thirty Names of Night*, 99.
48. Joudhakar, *Thirty Names of Night*, 151–152.
49. Joudhakar, *Thirty Names of Night*, 1–2.
50. Joudhakar, *Thirty Names of Night*, 71.
51. Joudhakar, *Thirty Names of Night*, 73.
52. Joudhakar, *Thirty Names of Night*, 160.
53. Joudhakar, *Thirty Names of Night*, 284.
54. Todd McGrain, *The Lost Bird Project* (Lebanon, NH: University Press of New England, 2014), 77.
55. Deborah Fung, "The Phoenix in the Cathedral: Xu Bing and the Citizen Migrant Crisis in 'Boomtown' China," *Arts: The Arts in Religious and Theological Studies* 30, no. 2 (January 1, 2019), https://www.societyarts.org/in-the-study-the-phoenix-in-the-cathedral.html (accessed June 15, 2021).
56. The Editors of Encyclopaedia Britannica, "Fenghuang," *Encyclopedia Britannica*, April 7, 2010, https://www.britannica.com/topic/fenghuang (accessed July 14, 2021).
57. Christopher Jobson, "Xu Bing Arrives at Mass MoCA with His 12-ton Birds Made of Construction Equipment," *Colossal*, July 10, 2013, https://www.thisiscolossal.com/2013/07/xu-bing-arrives-at-mass-moca-with-his-12-ton-birds-made-of-construction-equipment/ (accessed July 14, 2021).
58. Helen Schumaker, "The Phoenix through the Ages," *Swarthmore College Bulletin*, October 2008, https://www.swarthmore.edu/bulletin/archive/wp/october-2008_the-phoenix-through-the-ages.html (accessed July 14, 2021).
59. Fung, "Phoenix in the Cathedral."
60. See images and account at https://gothamtogo.com/audubon-mural-project-flys-into-jacob-schiff-park-in-harlem/ (accessed August 22, 2019).
61. National Audubon Society, "Audubon Mural: Fish Crow by Hitnes," *Audubon*, March 20, 2017, https://www.audubon.org/news/fish-crow-hitnes (accessed July 5, 2021).

62. Linda Poon, "New York City Will Require Bird-Friendly Glass on Buildings," *Bloomberg CityLab*, December 13, 2019, https://www.bloomberg.com/news/articles/2019-12-13/nyc-is-making-its-buildings-bird-friendly (accessed July 3, 2021).
63. "The Jacob Javits Center Renovation—Setting an Environmental Example," *A Sharp Eye*, February 5, 2018, https://www.asharpeye.com/jacob-javits-center-renovation-setting-environmental-example/ (accessed July 3, 2021).
64. Phil Jeffrey, "Central Park Birding: About the Park," http://www.philjeffrey.net/cpb_about.html (accessed July 5, 2021).
65. Bodrum Mediterranean Restaurant, "Pale Male: NYC's Favorite Father," https://bodrumnyc.com/pale-male-central-park-hawk/ (accessed July 6, 2021).
66. Andy Newman, "When Mary Tyler Moore Stood Up for Pale Male the Red-Tailed Hawk," *New York Times*, January 26, 2017, https://www.nytimes.com/2017/01/26/nyregion/mary-tyler-moore-pale-male-hawk-animal-rights.html (accessed July 6, 2021).
67. Lauren Evans, "Pale Male Is a Legend—but Is He Still Alive?," Audubon, June 7, 2019, https://www.audubon.org/news/pale-male-legend-he-still-alive (accessed July 6, 2021).
68. Jake Sumner, "Ruffled Feathers among the Birders of Central Park," *New York Times*, May 25, 2021, https://www.nytimes.com/2021/05/25/opinion/bob-of-the-park-new-york-birders.html (accessed July 6, 2021).
69. Jan Ransom, "Amy Cooper Faces Charges after Calling Police on Black Bird-Watcher," *New York Times*, July 6, 2020, https://www.nytimes.com/2020/07/06/nyregion/amy-cooper-false-report-charge.html (accessed July 9, 2021).
70. Rachel E. Greenspan and Kieran Press-Reynolds, "How the Name 'Karen' Became a Stand-in for Problematic White Women and a Hugely Popular Meme," *Business Insider*, October 26, 2020, https://www.insider.com/karen-meme-origin-the-history-of-calling-women-karen-white-2020-5 (accessed November 17, 2023).
71. Pat Leonard, "Birders: The Central Park Affect," in *All about Birds*, Cornell Laboratory of Ornithology, July 11, 2012, https://www.allaboutbirds.org/news/birders-the-central-park-effect/ (accessed July 11, 2021). For the 235 number, see "Bird Watching" at https://www.centralpark.com/things-to-do/sports/bird-watching/ (accessed July 11, 2021).
72. Robert DeCandida, "Anticipation: Migrants Are Trickling In and a Central Park Birdwalk Is the Place to See Them," *Birding Bob*, April 18, 2018, updated March 1, 2020, https://www.birdingbob.com/post/2018/04/18/anticipation-migrants-are-trickling-in (accessed July 15, 2021).
73. Rebecca Pou, "In Conversation with Ornithologist and Author Scott Weidensaul on Bird Migration," *Central Park Conservatory Magazine*, April 22, 2021, https://www.centralparknyc.org/articles/in-conversation-with-scott-weidensaul (accessed July 12, 2021).
74. Jesse Greenspan, "Birding the World: What Drives Big Listers," *Birdwatching*, January 8, 2019, https://www.birdwatchingdaily.com/news/birdwatching/birding-the-world-what-drives-big-listers/ (accessed July 15, 2021).

75. Rob Meyer and Luke Matheny, "A Birder's Guide to Everything," 2013, minutes 34 and 44:48, https://www.amazon.com/Birders-Guide-Everything-Kodi-Smit-McPhee/dp/B00IXE6LNK (accessed July 15, 2021).
76. Claire Thompson, *The Art of Mindful Birdwatching: Reflections on Freedom & Being* (London: Leaping Hare Press, 2017, 38.
77. For the Buddhist Four Immeasurables, see https://www.padmasambhava.org/sermon/four-immesurables/ (accessed July 15, 2021). For the *Metta* prayer, see https://www.heartsongyoga.com/newsletters/may-all-beings-be-happy-healthy-and-free-from-suff/new-item/ (accessed July 15, 2021).
78. Thompson, *Art of Mindful Birdwatching*, 40–41.
79. Thompson, *Art of Mindful Birdwatching*, 51.
80. Thompson, *Art of Mindful Birdwatching*, 65.
81. Jonathan Trouern-Trend, *Birding Babylon: A Soldier's Journal from Iraq* (San Francisco: Sierra Club Books, 2006), 10.
82. Trouern-Trend, *Birding Babylon*, 12.
83. Trouern-Trend, *Birding Babylon*, 59.
84. Spencer Schaffner, *Binocular Vision: The Politics of Representation in Birdwatching Field Guides* (Amherst: University of Massachusetts Press, 2011), 17. 83.
85. Elizabeth Cherry, *For the Birds: Protecting Wildlife through the Naturalist Gaze* (New Brunswick, NJ: Rutgers University Press, 2019), 109, 192.
86. Cherry, *For the Birds*, 192.
87. See http://www.brontaylor.com/environmental_books/dgr/DarkGreenReligion.html (accessed July 20, 2021).
88. Sarah M. Pike, "Mourning Nature: The Work of Grief in Radical Environmentalism," *Journal for the Study of Religion, Nature and Culture* 10, no. 4 (January 2017): 419–441, https://doi.org/10.1558/jsrnc.v10i4.30627.
89. Mark R. Stoll, *Inherit the Holy Mountain: Religion and the Rise of American Environmentalism* (New York: Oxford University Press, 2015).
90. Roger Finke and Rodney Stark, *The Churching of America, 1776–2005: Winners and Losers in Our Religious Economy* (New Brunswick, NJ: Rutgers University Press, 2006).
91. Molly McClain, *Ellen Browning Scripps: New Money and American Philanthropy* (Lincoln: University of Nebraska Press, 2017), 72.
92. McClain, *Ellen Browning Scripps*, 189.
93. Stephanie M., "Into San Diego's Lost Forest," July 29, 2014, https://ladyofthezoos.com/2014/07/29/into-san-diego-zoos-lost-forest/ (accessed July 22, 2021).
94. See information at the museum website: https://www.amnh.org/exhibitions/permanent/north-american-birds (accessed July 22, 2021). Also: https://www.amnh.org/exhibitions/permanent/birds-of-the-world (accessed July 22, 2021).
95. William King Gregory, *Biographical Memoir of Frank Michler Chapman, 1864–1945* (National Academy of Sciences, 1947), 122.
96. See details at https://blogs.massaudubon.org/yourgreatoutdoors/tanglewood-takes-flight/ (accessed July 29, 2021).
97. See the harpy eagle sign at https://drive.google.com/file/d/1KM-VQSnszdNvof7EZcO4S03f192Lqh-2/view?usp=sharing (accessed July 30, 2021).

98. See the story of saving the California condor: https://wildlife.ca.gov/Conservation/Birds/California-Condor (accessed July 30, 2021).
99. Elizabeth Cherry, *For the Birds*, 170; Lacey Bourassa, "Vegan and Plant-Based Diet Statistics for 2021," *Plant Proteins.Co*, January 13, 2021, https://www.plantproteins.co/vegan-plant-based-diet-statistics/ (accessed August 3, 2021).
100. William Blake, "Auguries of Innocence," https://www.poetryfoundation.org/poems/43650/auguries-of-innocence (accessed August 3, 2021).
101. Maryn McKenna, *Big Chicken: The Incredible Story of How Antibiotics Created Modern Agriculture and Changed the Way the World Eats* (Washington, DC: National Geographic Partners, 2017), 211–215.
102. German Centre for Integrative Biodiversity Research (iDiv) Halle-Jena-Leipzig, "Biological Diversity Evokes Happiness: More Bird Species in Their Vicinity Increase Life Satisfaction of Europeans as Much as Higher Income," https://www.sciencedaily.com/releases/2020/12/201204110246.htm (accessed August 5, 2021).
103. See Anina Gerchick, "Bird Link," https://birdlink.world/ (accessed September 27, 2023).
104. Roger Tory Petersen quoted in Al Reinert, *Audubon*, documentary film (WETA, PBS, 2017), minute 0.50.
105. John James Audubon, "Red Tailed Hawk," from *Ornithological Biography* (1831). Excerpt here from John James Audubon, *Writings and Drawings*, ed. Christopher Irmscher (New York: Library of America, 1999), 258.
106. Gregory Nobles, "The Myth of John James Audubon," *Audubon*, July 31, 2020, https://www.audubon.org/news/the-myth-john-james-audubon (accessed August 11, 2021).
107. Nobles, "Myth of Audubon."
108. Komol Patel, "Penn Museum to Remove Morton Cranial Collection from Public View after Student Opposition," *Daily Pennsylvanian*, July 12, 2020, https://www.thedp.com/article/2020/07/penn-museum-morton-cranial-collection-black-lives-matter (accessed August 11, 2021).
109. Daryl Fears, "The Racist Legacy Many Birds Carry," *Washington Post*, June 3, 2021, https://www.washingtonpost.com/climate-environment/interactive/2021/bird-names-racism-audubon/ (accessed August 11, 2021).
110. List accessed at https://docs.google.com/spreadsheets/d/1Q_IJTLYWe0WWmMZueSftKUTJ4wTyuTYTeLk7ELiGiUY/edit#gid=2072416291 (accessed August 11, 2021).
111. Harry A. Ploski and James Williams, eds., *The Negro Almanac* (Detroit: Gale Group, 1989), 1035.
112. J. Drew Lanham, "What Do We Do about John James Audubon," *Audubon*, Spring 2021, https://www.audubon.org/magazine/spring-2021/what-do-we-do-about-john-james-audubon (accessed August 11, 2021).
113. Gregory Nobles, *John James Audubon: The Nature of the American Woodsman* (Philadelphia: University of Pennsylvania Press, 2017), 11.
114. Nobles, *John James Audubon*, 16–18.
115. Nobles, *John James Audubon*, 21.

116. Nobles, *John James Audubon*, 24. Quoted from the autobiographical sketch by Audubon, "Myself," which was never published in his life but which can be found in *Writings and Drawings*, 772.
117. Kaeli Swift, "Can Crows and Ravens Hybridize?," *Corvid Research*, September 6, 2018, https://corvidresearch.blog/2018/09/06/can-crows-and-ravens-hybridize/ (accessed August 10, 2021).
118. Winona LaDuke, quoted in Dominic Arenas, "More Than 600 People Flocked to Milwaukee for the 2019 Audubon Convention," *Audubon*, August 9, 2019, https://www.audubon.org/news/more-600-people-flocked-milwaukee-2019-audubon-convention (accessed August 10, 2021). Video of the entire address is available at https://www.youtube.com/watch?v=HGVjvLCAcrk&t=335s or through the Audubon website.

Epilogue: How the Cover of This Book, the Artist Who Painted It, and the Albatross He Painted Embody a Religion of Nature

The painting of an albatross skimming the ocean on the cover of this book could be an icon in the religion of nature. The life of artist Arthur Singer, the poem by Samuel Taylor Coleridge that made albatrosses famous, and the wonders of albatrosses themselves have all contributed to that religion.

In several Christian traditions, icons work as paintings with sacred power. While contemplating icons, an act that often takes place before services of worship, Christians of Greek, Armenian, and Russian traditions glimpse divine grace shining through the faces of saints or of Jesus. Hindus seek similar moments of seeing the divine, a blessing that they call *darshan*, as they pray before statues or paintings (which they call idols) of their gods. In a Christian icon or a Hindu idol, the power and message of an entire faith can appear at once.

The painting of a wandering albatross reproduced on the cover was created by Arthur Singer (1917–1990) an American artist inspired by the work of John James Audubon (1785–1851). Although Singer, born in a Jewish family in Manhattan, wrote nothing religious about the birds he painted, his work expresses a reverence that historians and imaginative writers have seen in Audubon, with whom he has many connections. Singer was born on Audubon Avenue in Manhattan, fifteen blocks above the building on Audubon Terrace where Audubon died, and where Audubon's widow for decades taught children who carried on the work of bird conservation that her husband had begun. As a twenty-year-old art student at Cooper Union in New York, Singer was "overwhelmed" at his first sight of the edition of Audubon's *Birds of America* in the life-sized, double-elephant folio edition that the college owned. "It had an enormous impact on me and shifted my attempts from mammals to birds."[1] Decades after graduation, as he worked on bird paintings more than a century after Audubon's death, Singer borrowed skins of birds from the American Museum of Natural History to mount as models in his home studio, and his son Alan Singer noted that these skins came in boxes labeled with the signature of John James Audubon.[2] This kind of direct lineage prevails in the traditions of icon painting and in the leadership of many religions, as among some Christian bishops, the passing of *samadhi* from the Buddha through all Zen *roshis*, and the rabbinical leadership of Hasidic groups. Lineages also figure in the story of bird conservation movements that is told in Chapters 7 and 8. But lineage wouldn't matter if the final product, the icon itself, did not have inherent power to evoke religious feeling. Singer's painting of the albatross has such power.

As Singer's albatross flies low over the ocean, picking up speed it will use to rise on updrafts of warm air and then to soar, the wings and body of the bird form axes that divide the scene into four parts, reminiscent of the ancient Indo-European solar symbol or swastika that resembles both the Christian cross and the central symbol of the Nazi flag. In Singer's painting, the axes of the symbol are not straight but slightly tilted to suggest motion, their ends curved as in India. The pattern both separates and unites the light of the sky with the dark of the sea.

A bird flying over the sea features in creation stories of many peoples, from the Hindus, whose Rig Veda 10 describes a waterbird laying a golden egg that contained the world, to the Haudenosaunee (or Iroquois) of the American Northeast, where waterbirds catch a falling woman for whom they try to make land, to the Finns, who see the world beginning with a teal duck laying eggs on the ocean. Even Genesis 1 says that the spirit of God "brooded" or "hovered" over the primordial sea as a bird broods over a nest. Sunlight breaks through clouds above, suggesting a high God in the heavens. The combination of dazzling brightness and clouds echoes the description of God's throne and glory in chapter 6 of the prophet Isaiah. Eyes are always important in icons, and here one eye of the albatross turns toward the viewer of the painting, inviting a response.

Because albatrosses soar and glide primarily over the oceans near Antarctica, the albatross was not named by Europeans until 1769,[3] and came to widespread attention only as global shipping became common in the late 1700s. This was also the moment of the Romantic revolution in art, music, literature, and science that gave birth to the religion of nature that this book connects with birds. A single poem, *The Rime of the Ancient Mariner*, published by Samuel Taylor Coleridge in 1798, introduced albatrosses to most readers in the English-speaking world. For Coleridge and his readers, the albatross functioned both as an agent of salvation and as an instrument of penance.

Early in the *Ancient Mariner*, the bird appears over a sailing ship driven too far south by weather and lost near Antarctica. Trapped in ice and fog, the sailors fear for their lives, but the albatross gives hope. As Coleridge wrote, in the voice of the one who survived the trip:

> At length did cross an Albatross,
> Through the fog it came;
> As if it had been a Christian soul,
> We hailed it in God's name.[4]

Cheered by their new companion, the sailors feed the albatross. The bird takes food from them, "And round and round it flew." Then "The ice did split with a thunder-fit; / The helmsman steered us through!"[5] Good fortune continued as "a good south wind sprung up behind." The albatross remains, "And every day, for food or play, / Came to the mariner's hollo." Nine days go by, with the bird each night resting on the ship's masts or sail shrouds, until one day, as the old sailor says without explanation, "With my cross-bow, / I shot the ALBATROSS."[6]

At first the crew was angry that the albatross was dead, but later its mood changed. While "the good south wind still blew behind," the seamen missed their "sweet bird." But then the ship reached the shortest day of the year, and the sun hung low in mist and disappeared. When it rose again the shooter was praised, for "all averred, I had killed the bird / That brought the fog and mist."[7]

Perhaps the sailors doomed themselves by praising the killer, but in any event the ship became becalmed and had no fresh water. With "Water, water every where, / Nor any drop to drink,"[8] the sailors cursed the shooter with their looks. Unable to speak from thirst, they marked him with the bird's corpse: "Instead of the cross, the Albatross / About my neck was hung."[9] Soon all two hundred of the crew except for the shooter fell down dead. Alone with dead sailors still staring at him, their bodies not rotting but remaining where they fell, the mariner tried to pray but found that he could not. A week went by in this horror, but then he saw in the ship's shadow a mass of water snakes and found them beautiful. "A spring of love gushed from my heart, / And

I blessed them unaware."[10] This blessing of the snakes, which the mariner attributed to the intercession of his saint, delivered him from the curse:

> The self-same moment I could pray;
> And from my neck so free,
> The Albatross fell off, and sank
> Like lead into the sea.[11]

About four hundred lines of supernatural adventures remain before the poem's end, but eventually the mariner returns to the port from which he left. Sentenced to do penance by traveling the world finding people who need to hear his story, he teaches a religion of nature. As the mariner concludes:

> He prayeth well, who loveth well
> Both man and bird and beast.
> He prayeth best, who loveth best,
> All things both great and small;
> For the dear God who loveth us,
> He made and loveth all.[12]

In 1848, fifty years after *The Rime of the Ancient Mariner* first appeared, a woman named Cecil Frances Alexander used a slight variant on these lines ("All creatures great and small") in her *Hymns for Little Children*. Alexander's hymn, "All Things Bright and Beautiful" became a standard in Anglican and other Christian services of worship.[13] It later provided a title for veterinarian James Wight, who took the pen name James Herriot in his reminiscences of a practice with large animals in 1930s Yorkshire, *All Creatures Great and Small*.[14] Samuel Taylor Coleridge wanted religion to move beyond the churches into the culture, led by intellectuals he called a "clerisy" (as opposed to "clergy" of the church), and his poem helped that to happen.

This chain of inspirations to reverence for nature began with the albatross itself, a bird that can seem superior to the earth. As an article in *Smithsonian* magazine claimed in 2007, "They spend the first six or more years of their long lives (which last upwards of 50 years) without ever touching land."[15] This statement seems false, because a young albatross may not even leave the nest on land where it was born for eleven months, growing as large as its parents without beginning to fly.[16] But there is also much truth in the statement that young albatrosses avoid land, because once an albatross does fly, it flies amazing distances, as much as four hundred miles a day,[17] learning where food (particularly squid) is plentiful in the ocean. Albatrosses only use land to gather with others, find a mate, build a nest on the ground, and breed, and many do not breed for five to seven years, so the young bird spends those years after fledging entirely in the air or floating on the water. Unlike the sailors who had "nor any drop to drink" in the Coleridge poem, albatrosses can live on saltwater because they have a gland that extracts salt.[18] Even their sleep takes place in the air. An albatross can soar to nearly forty thousand feet, then lock its wings in position and sleep as it glides for hours, moving twenty-two units of distance forward for every unit of altitude it loses.[19] Sensitive channels in the tubes of its beak, capable of detecting a food source from twelve miles away,[20] also keep the albatross informed of its speed and altitude.[21]

The bird in *The Rime of the Ancient Mariner*, which soared above the ship and answered the sailors when they called, was behaving in the manner of a wandering albatross, the largest variety of albatross, with wingspans up to thirteen feet. While most albatross varieties circle the globe near Antarctica and breed on particular Pacific islands or places in New Zealand, and some have found their way to live and feed over the Aleutian Islands near Alaska but still breed in the South Pacific, wandering albatrosses may live anywhere, because they follow ships and eat squid and fish that are churned up and garbage or trash thrown out by human crews. One such bird found a home with a flock of gannets in the extreme North Atlantic, touching down on the Faroe Islands, a Danish territory well above the Shetlands near the Arctic Circle, in 1860. Shot by a hunter in 1894, its body is now displayed in a Copenhagen museum.[22]

Estimates of albatross lifespans are uncertain. In December 2021, a banded Laysan albatross (a variety named for an island a thousand miles west of Hawaii) laid an egg in her habitual place on Midway Atoll (near the site of the Battle of Midway) at age seventy. This bird, called Wisdom by the ornithological community, was banded on one leg by Chandler Robbins (1918–2017) in 1956, when she had just laid her first egg. Since albatrosses never undergo menopause, she may continue laying an egg every two years for an unknown period in the future. "She's definitely learned to avoid predators out in the ocean, and she's learned to forage very efficiently and also maybe avoid plastic these days and potentially fishing vessels," according to Midway biologist John Klavitter,[23] who gave Wisdom her name in 2006.[24] Though endangered by ships, airplanes, and plastic cigarette lighters that humans have dumped into the Pacific, albatrosses still manage to survive and reproduce. In December 2022, Wisdom appeared on Midway without meeting her husband of ten years (called in Hawaiian Akeamakai, or "lover of Wisdom") and laid no egg, but hope remained that she would find another mate and return to nest late in 2023.

The stories of recovery from near extinction that conservation movements brought to other bird species, and especially to shorebirds, have parallels among albatrosses. A variety of short-tailed albatrosses that once numbered five million on the Japanese island of Torishima (literally "bird island") were clubbed into near extinction for feathers and oil in the nineteenth century, but began again to breed there in 1951 and continue to recover.[25] The albatrosses of Midway Atoll were endangered by aircraft traffic during World War II and after, but landscaping to separate their nests from runways has mitigated that situation.[26]

Sailors in the days of Coleridge sometimes said that albatrosses were deceased crewmates who followed ships because they liked to look at how things were going. Chandler Robbins compared himself more wistfully to Wisdom. He had banded her first in 1956, then again in 1966, 1985, 1993, 2002, and 2006. At age ninety-four in 2012, five years before Robbins died, he said, "While I have grown old and gray and get around only with the use of a cane, Wisdom still looks and acts just the same as on the day I banded her."[27]

Albatrosses and other birds are signs of eternity, forms of awareness that dominate time and space. They are indeed wings of the gods, and we humans are learning to see them. If we watch and work with them, perhaps get back to millions on Torishima, together we may save our world.

Notes

1. Paul Singer and Alan Singer, *Arthur Singer: The Wildlife Art of an American Master* (Rochester, NY: RIT Press, 2017), 18.
2. Alan Singer, The Cornell Lab Bird Academy, *Arthur Singer: 50 Years of Wildlife Art*, videorecording November 6, 2017, minute 55, https://academy.allaboutbirds.org/live-event/arthur-singer-50-years-of-wildlife-art/ (accessed February 14, 2023).
3. Mark Cocker and David Tipling, *Birds and People* (London: Jonathan Cape, 2013), 99.
4. Samuel Taylor Coleridge, "The Rime of the Ancient Mariner with line numbers," lines 63–66. http://shsdavisapes.pbworks.com/w/file/fetch/115519318/Rime%20of%20the%20Ancient%20Mariner%20Text%20with%20line%20numbers.pdf (accessed February 14, 2023).

5. Coleridge, "Rime," lines 68–70.
6. Coleridge, "Rime," line 82.
7. Coleridge, "Rime," lines 91–102.
8. Coleridge, "Rime," lines 121–122.
9. Coleridge, "Rime," lines 141–142.
10. Coleridge, "Rime," lines 282–285.
11. Coleridge, "Rime," lines 288–291.
12. Coleridge, "Rime," lines 614–617.
13. John Julian, *Dictionary of Hymnology*, 1907, https://hymnary.org/person/Alexander_CF (accessed February 14, 2023).
14. British Telly Dish, "Who Is James Herriot and How 'True' Is All Creatures Great and Small?," *Thirteen*, January 9, 2023, https://www.thirteen.org/blog-post/all-creatures-great-and-small-james-herriot-true/#:~:text=Alf%20Wight's%20first%20two%20books,All%20Things%20Bright%20and%20Beautiful (accessed February 14, 2023).
15. Kennedy Warne, "The Amazing Albatrosses," *Smithsonian*, September 2007, https://www.smithsonianmag.com/science-nature/the-amazing-albatrosses-162515529/ (accessed February 13, 2023)
16. Steven Rodabaugh, Don Turowski, Michael S. Martin, William Child, and Marvin Eicher, *Birds of the World*, vol. 1 (Crockett, KY: Rod and Staff Publishers, 2009), 17.
17. Cocker and Tipling, *Birds and People*, 99.
18. Rodabaugh et al., *Birds of the World*, 13.
19. Simon Barnes, *The Meaning of Birds* (New York: Pegasus Books, 2018), 19.
20. Barnes, *The Meaning of Birds*, 35.
21. Barnes, *The Meaning of Birds*, 20.
22. Oliver L. Austin Jr., *Birds of the World* (New York: Golden Press, 1961), 32.
23. Bill Chappell, "Wisdom the Albatross, Now 70, Hatches Yet Another Chick," *NPR*, March 5, 2021, https://www.npr.org/2021/03/05/973992408/wisdom-the-albatross-now-70-hatches-yet-another-chick (accessed February 13, 2023).
24. Elena Passarello, "Seventy Never Looked So Good: The Long, Wondrous Life of Wisdom the Albatross," *Audubon*, Spring 2021, https://www.audubon.org/magazine/spring-2021/seventy-never-looked-so-good-long-wondrous-life (accessed February 21, 2023).
25. Cocker and Tipling, *Birds and People*, 104.
26. Austin, *Birds of the World*, 34.
27. Martha Johnson and Jay McDaniel, "Hope from the World's Oldest Known Bird," *Open Horizons*, https://www.openhorizons.org/hope-from-the-worlds-oldest-known-bird-wisdom-the-albatross.html (accessed February 14, 2023).

Bibliography

Ackroyd, Peter. *Alfred Hitchcock: A Brief Life*. New York: Doubleday, 2015.

Aguilar, Mario I. "The Eagle as Messenger, Pilgrim and Voice: Divinatory Processes among the Waso Boorana of Kenya." *Journal of Religion in Africa* 26, no. 1 (1996).

Alexander, Jane. *Wild Things, Wild Places: Adventurous Tales of Wildlife and Conservation on Planet Earth*. New York: Alfred A. Knopf, 2016.

Anderson, Natali. "Brown Skuas Can Recognize Individual Humans, New Study Shows." *Science News*, March 28, 2016.

Aristophanes. *Birds*. Translated by Ian Johnston. Arlington, VA: Richer Resources Publications, 2008.

Armstrong, Edward A. *The Life and Lore of the Bird: In Nature, Art, Myth, and Literature*. New York: Crown Publishers, 1975.

Armstrong, Edward A. *Saint Francis: Nature Mystic*. Berkeley: University of California Press, 1973.

Arrowsmith, William. "Aristophanes' Birds: The Fantasy Politics of Eros." *Arion: A Journal of Humanities and the Classics*, New Series, 1, no. 1 (Spring, 1973).

Attar. *The Conference of the Birds*. Translated by Sholeh Wolpé. New York: Norton, 2017.

Audubon, John James. *Selected Journals and Other Writings*. Edited by Ben Forkner. New York: Penguin Books, 1996.

Audubon, John James. "Myself." In *Writings and Drawings*, edited by Christopher Irmscher. Library of America, 1999.

Irmscher, Christopher, ed. *John James Audubon: Writings and Drawings*. Library of America, 1999.

Audubon Society, National. "Chimney Swift." In *Guide to North American Birds*. Accessed at https://www.audubon.org/field-guide/bird/chimney-swift (August 2, 2018).

Audubon Society, National. "The Migratory Bird Treaty Act, Explained." *Audubon*, January 26, 2018. Accessed at https://www.audubon.org/news/the-migratory-bird-treaty-act-explained (June 29, 2018).

Awolalu, J. Omosade. "Yoruba Sacrificial Practice." *Journal of Religion in Africa* 5, no. 2 (1973).

Axelson, Gustave. "Nearly 30% of Birds in U.S., Canada Have Vanished since 1970." *Cornell Chronicle*, September 19, 2019. Accessed at http://news.cornell.edu/stories/2019/09/nearly-30-birds-us-canada-have-vanished-1970 (October 13, 2019).

Axtell, James, ed. *Indian Peoples of Eastern America: A Documentary History*. New York: Oxford University Press, 1981.

Bach, Richard. *Jonathan Livingston Seagull*. Photographs by Russell Munson. London: Macmillan, 1970.

Bahti, Tom, and Bahti, Mark. *Southwestern Indian Ceremonials*. 10th ed. KC Publications, 1997.

Barber, Joseph. *Chickens: A Natural History*. Ivy Press, 2012.

Barnes, Simon. *The Meaning of Birds*. Pegasus Books, 2018.

Bassett, Molly H. *The Fate of Earthly Things: Aztec Gods and God-Bodies*. Austin: University of Texas Press, 2015.
Beal, Richard. "Hittite Oracles." In *Magic and Divination in the Ancient World*, edited by Leda Ciraolo and Jonathan Seidel. Brill, 2002.
Beard, Mary, North, John, and Price, Simon. *Religions of Rome*. Vol. 1, *A History*. Cambridge: Cambridge University Press, 1998.
Becker, Rachel Becker. "Cattle Drug Threatens Thousands of Vultures." *Nature*, April 29, 2016. Accessed at https://www.nature.com/news/cattle-drug-threatens-thousands-of-vultures-1.19839 (August 2, 2018).
Bellah, Robert N. *Religion in Human Evolution: From the Paleolithic to the Axial Age*. Cambridge, MA: Harvard University Press, 2011.
Bender, Kelli. "Dancing Flamingo 'Pinky' Killed by Busch Gardens Visitor." *People*, August 5, 2016.
Benson, Elizabeth P. "The Vulture: The Sky and the Earth." *Palenque Round Table* 10, no. 310 (1996).
Bernas, Frederick, and Trevino, Amado. "Voladores Ritual Is Flight for Survival for Mexico's Totonacas." *BBC News Magazine*, October 11, 2013.
Bernish, Claire. "Drilling for Oil in the Israeli-Occupied Region of Syria's Golan Heights, a Violation of International Law." *Global Research*, June 25, 2016.
Bever, Lindsey. "How Killer Birds Forced Pope Francis to Change a Vatican Tradition: Releasing Doves of Peace." *Washington Post*, January 26, 2015.
Bieniek, Adam. "Cher Ami: The Pigeon That Saved the Lost Battalion." United States World War One Centennial Commission, 2016.
Bittel, Jason. "Think Crow Funerals Are Strange? Wait Until You See the Wake." *Audubon*, July 23, 2018.
Black, Riley. "Hitchcock's Primeval Birds." *Smithsonian Magazine*, December 19, 2011.
Borja, Melissa. "'On Eagle's Wings': The Catholic Hymn for a Hurting America." *Patheos*, November 10, 2020.
Bowden, Chris. "Asian Vulture Crisis: It's Not Over Yet." *Conservation India*, April 2, 2018. Accessed at http://www.conservationindia.org/articles/asian-vulture-crisis-its-not-over-yet (July 31, 2018).
Boyer, Pascal. *The Naturalness of Religious Ideas: A Cognitive Theory of Religion*. Berkeley: University of California Press, 1994.
Bradway, Kay, and McCoard, Barbara. *Sandplay: Silent Workshop of the Psyche*. London: Routledge, 1997.
Brannen, Peter. *The Ends of the World: Volcanic Apocalypses, Lethal Oceans, and Our Quest to Understand Earth's Past Mass Extinctions*. New York: HarperCollins, 2017.
Brawley, Benjamin. "Lorenzo Dow." *Journal of Negro History* 1, no. 3 (June 1916).
Breason, Robert C. "Mechanisms of Magnetic Orientation in Birds." *Integrative and Comparative Biology* 5, issue 3 (2005).
Breunig, Elizabeth. "Then the Birds Began to Die." *The Atlantic*, July 22, 2021.
Brewer, Eileen Mary. *Nuns and the Education of American Catholic Women, 1860–1920*. Loyola University Press, 1987.
Bronowski, Jacob. *The Ascent of Man: A Personal View*. London: BBC, 2011.
Buber, Martin. *I and Thou*. Translated by Walter Kaufmann. New York: Charles Scribner's Sons, 1970.
Butterworth, Hezekiah. *In the Days of Audubon: A Tale of "The Protector of Birds," with an Appendix on the Formation of Audubon Societies*. New York: D. Appleton, 1901.

Carson, Rachel. *Silent Spring*. Houghton Mifflin, 1962.
Carter, Mike. "In Tanzania with Africa's Last Hunter-Gatherers." *Financial Times*, August 21, 2015.
Castronuovo, Celine, and Frazin, Rachel. "Trump Administration Proceeds with Rollback of Bird Protections Despite Objections of Scientists, Environmentalists." *The Hill*, November 27, 2020.
Cherry, Elizabeth. *Culture and Activism: Animal Rights in France and the United States*. New York: Routledge, 2016.
Cherry, Elizabeth. *For the Birds: Protecting Wildlife through the Naturalist Gaze*. New Brunswick, NJ: Rutgers University Press, 2019.
Chung, Tsai Chih. *The Tao of Zhuangzi: The Harmony of Nature*. Translated by Brian Bruya. New York: Doubleday, 1997.
Clark, Elizabeth. "Women, Gender, and the Study of Christian History." *Church History* 70, no. 3 (September 2001).
Cocker, Mark, and Tipling, David. *Birds and People*. London: Jonathan Cape, 2013.
Coleridge, Samuel Taylor. "The Rime of the Ancient Mariner." In *The Poetical Works of S.T. Coleridge*, edited by Henry Nelson Coleridge. W. Pickering, 1834. Accessed at https://rpo.library.utoronto.ca/content/rime-ancient-mariner-text-1834 (September 26, 2023).
Conze, Edward, trans. *The Buddha's Law among the Birds*. Bruno Cassirer, 1955.
Copping, Jasper. "Honoured: The WW1 Pigeons Who Earned Their Wings." *The Telegraph*, January 12, 2014.
Cornell Laboratory of Ornithology. "Chimney Swift." Accessed at https://www.allaboutbirds.org/guide/Chimney_Swift/overview (August 26, 2019).
Crair, Ben. "What Birds Taught Me about Covid." *New York Times*, August 15, 2021.
Cutter, Robert Joe. *The Brush and the Spur: Chinese Culture and the Cockfight*. Chinese University Press, 1989.
Darg, Christine. "Two Miracle Dove Stories: From Gaza 2014 and Yom Kippur War 1973." *Jerusalem Channel*, February 12, 2017.
Davies, Gareth Huw. "Bird Brains." Accessed at https://www.pbs.org/lifeofbirds/brain/ (August 26, 2019).
Dickinson, Emily. "Dear Genie." Early 1876. Accessed at http://archive.emilydickinson.org/correspondence/hall/l455.html (January 23, 2020).
Dingle, Christopher. *The Life of Messiaen*. Cambridge: Cambridge University Press, 2007.
Dooren, Thom van. *Vulture*. Reaktion Books, 2011.
Dorsey, Kurkpatrick. *The Dawn of Conservation Diplomacy: U.S.-Canadian Wildlife Protection Treaties in the Progressive Era*. Seattle: University of Washington Press, 1998.
Douglas, Ann. *The Feminization of American Culture*. New York: Alfred A. Knopf, 1977.
Dove, Michael R. "Uncertainty, Humility, and Adaptation in the Tropical Forest: The Agricultural Augury of the Kantu.'" *Ethnology* 32, no. 2 (Spring 1993).
Driesch, Angela von den, Kessler, Dieter, Steinmann, Frank, Berteaux, Véronique, and Peters, Joris. "Mummified, Deified and Buried at Hermopolis Magna—the Sacred Birds from Tuna el-Gebel, Middle Egypt." *Ägypten und Levante / Egypt and the Levant* 15 (2005).
Drum, Kevin. "How Many Birds?" *Mother Jones*, March 23, 2011. Accessed at http://www.motherjones.com/kevin-drum/2011/03/how-many-birds (July 9, 2014).
Eagleton, Annelise. "A Murder of Crows: When Roosting Crows Come to Town." *Cool Green Science*, June 26, 2016. Accessed at https://blog.nature.org/science/2016/06/28/murder-crows-roosting-wildlife-conflict/ (August 26, 2019).

Eason, Cassandra. *Fabulous Creatures, Mythical Monsters, and Animal Power Symbols: A Handbook*. Greenwood Press, 2008.
Edmonds, Michael. "Flights of Fancy: Birds and People in the Old Northwest." *Wisconsin Magazine of History* 83, no. 3 (Spring 2000).
Egan, Timothy. "Gone West." Review of John Taliaferro, *Grinnell*. *New York Times Book Review*, August 11, 2019.
Ellington, Scott A. "The Sustainer of Life: The Role of the Spirit of God in Creation." *Australasian Pentecostal Studies*, 2009, 9–24. Accessed at https://aps-journal.com/index.php/APS/article/download/5/2?inline=1 (July 7, 2021).
Embry, Jessie L., and Wilson, William A. "Folk Ideas of Mormon Pioneers." *Dialogue: A Journal of Mormon Thought* 31, no. 3 (Fall 1998).
Emerson, Ralph Waldo. *Nature*. James Munroe and Company, 1836.
Emerson, Ralph Waldo. "Nature." In *The Collected Works of Ralph Waldo Emerson*, vol. 3, *Essays, Second Series*. Cambridge, MA: Harvard University Press, 1984.
Evenden, Matthew D. "The Laborers of Nature: Economic Ornithology and the Role of Birds as Agents of Biological Pest Control in North American Agriculture, ca. 1880–1930." *Forest & Conservation History* 39, no. 4 (October 1995).
Fallon, Robert. "A Catalogue of Messiaen's Birds." In *Messiaen Perspectives 2: Techniques, Influence and Reception*, edited by Christopher Dingle and Robert Fallon. Ashgate, 2013.
Fears, Daryl. "The Racist Legacy Many Birds Carry." *Washington Post*, June 3, 2021.
Feduccia, Alan. *The Origin and Evolution of Birds*. New Haven: Yale University Press, 1996.
Feher-Elston, Catherine. *Ravensong: A Natural and Fabulous History of Ravens and Crows*. Northland Publishing, 1991.
Feld, Steven. *Sound and Sentiment: Birds, Weeping, Poetics, and Song in Kaluli Expression*. Thirtieth Anniversary Edition. Durham, NC: Duke University Press, 2012.
Finke, Roger and Stark, Rodney. *The Churching of America, 1776–2005: Winners and Losers in Our Religious Economy*. New Brunswick, NJ: Rutgers University Press, 2006.
Fisher, Albert K. *The Hawks and Owls of the United States in Their Relation to Agriculture*. Division of Economic Ornithology and Mammalogy, Bulletin no. 3. United States Department of Agriculture, 1893.
Forest, Dylan. "Cannibalism, Sacrifice, and Hunting in National Parks." *Animal People*, April 2001.
Franchot, Jenny. *Roads to Rome: The Antebellum Protestant Encounter with Catholicism*. Berkeley: University of California Press, 1994.
Frith, Clifford B. *Charles Darwin's Life with Birds: His Complete Ornithology*. New York: Oxford University Press, 2016.
Fruchter, Rabbi Yaakov, and Steinberg, Rabbi Sholom Dov. *An Illustrated Guide to Kobonos and Menochos*. Torah Umesorah Publications, 1993.
Fung, Deborah. "The Phoenix in the Cathedral: Xu Bing and the Citizen Migrant Crisis in 'Boomtown' China." *Arts: The Arts in Religious and Theological Studies* 30, no. 2 (January 1, 2019).
Gabel, Pearl. "The Chickens Under the Bridge." *New York Daily News*, August 21, 2015.
Gambino, Megan. "What Was on the Menu at the First Thanksgiving?" *Smithsonian*, November 21, 2011.
Gardella, Peter. *American Civil Religion: What Americans Hold Sacred*. New York: Oxford University Press, 2014.
Gardella, Peter. *Domestic Religion: Work, Food, Sex, and Other Commitments*. Pilgrim Press, 1998.

Gardella, Peter. "Spiritual Warfare in the Fiction of Frank Peretti." In *Religions of the United States in Practice*, edited by Colleen McDannell. Princeton, NJ: Princeton University Press, 2001.

Gardella, Peter. "Two Parliaments, One Century." *Cross Currents* 44, no. 1 (Spring 1994).

Gaston, Kevin W., and Blackburn, Tim M. "How Many Birds Are There?" *Biodiversity and Conservation* 6 (1997): 615–625.

Geertz, Clifford. "Deep Play: Notes on the Balinese Cockfight." *Daedalus* 134, no. 4 (Fall 2005, reprint of 1972).

Gimbutas, Marija. *The Civilization of the Goddess*. HarperSanFrancisco, 1991.

Gipson, Rosemary. "Los Voladores, the Flyers of Mexico." *Western Folklore* 30, no. 4 (October 1971).

Glass, Andrew. "'In God We Trust' becomes nation's motto, July 30, 1956." *Politico*, July 30, 2018.

Goggin, John M. "Notes on Some 1938-1939 Pueblo Dances." *New Mexico Anthropologist* 3, no. 2 (November–December 1938).

Gore, Al. "Rachel Carson and Silent Spring." in Peter Matthiessen, ed., *Courage for the Earth: Writers, Scientists, and Activists Celebrate the Life and Writing of Rachel Carson*. Houghton Mifflin, 2007.

Graham, Frank Jr. *The Audubon Ark: A History of the National Audubon Society*. New York: Alfred A. Knopf, 1990.

Grant, R.G. *Battle at Sea: 3,000 Years of Naval Warfare*. New York: Penguin, 2011.

Gregory, William King. *Biographical Memoir of Frank Michler Chapman, 1864–1945*. National Academy of Sciences, 1947.

Green, Steven J. "Malevolent Gods and Promethean Birds: Contesting Augury in Augustus's Rome." *Transactions of the American Philological Association* 139, no. 1, Spring, 2009.

Greene, Sean. "Extinction looms for native bird species on the Hawaiian island of Kauai." *Los Angeles Times*, September 26, 2016.

Greenberg, Joel. *A Feathered River Across the Sky: The Passenger Pigeon's Flight to Extinction*. New York: Bloomsbury USA, 2014.

Greenhouse, Linda. "Court, Citing Religious Freedom, Voids a Ban on Animal Sacrifices." *The New York Times*, June 12, 1993.

Grimes, Ronald L. *The Craft of Ritual Studies*. New York: Oxford University Press, 2014.

GrrlScientist. "Escaped Pet Parrots Are Now Established in 23 U.S. States." *Forbes*, May 21, 2019. Accessed at https://www.forbes.com/sites/grrlscientist/2019/05/21/escaped-pet-parrots-are-now-naturalized-in-23-u-s-states/#70d6661154cb (August 26, 2019).

Guernsey, Julia. *Ritual and Power in Stone: The Performance of Rulership in Mesoamerican Izapan Style Art*. Austin: University of Texas Press, 2006.

Haberman, Clyde. "Rachel Carson, DDT, and the Fight against Malaria." *New York Times*, January 22, 2017.

Habig, Marion A., ed. *St. Francis of Assisi: Writings and Early Biographies: English Omnibus of the Sources for the Life of St. Francis* Franciscan Herald Press, 1983.

Hammer, Hawk, and Clark, Jamie Rappaport. "Biden Administration Reverses Trump Rule That Gutted Migratory Bird Protections." *Defenders of Wildlife*, September 29, 2021. Accessed at https://defenders.org/newsroom/biden-administration-reverses-trump-rule-gutted-migratory-bird-protections (March 7, 2022).

Hammond, E. A. "Dr. Stroebel's Account of John J. Audubon." *The Auk* 80, no. 4 (October 1963).

Haupt, Lyanda Lynn. *Crow Planet: Essential Wisdom from the Urban Wilderness*. Boston: Little, Brown, 2009.
Heinrich, Bernd Heinrich. *Ravens in Winter*. Summit Books, 1989.
Heisman, Rebecca. "Bald Eagle: the Ultimate Endangered Species Act Success Story." *Birdcalls: News and Perspectives on Bird Conservation*, May 24, 2018.
Henning, Meaghan. "Eternal Punishment as Paideia: the Ekphrasis of Hell in the Apocalypse of Peter and the Apocalypse of Paul." *Biblical Research* 58, 2013.
Hitakonanu'laxk (Tree Beard). *The Grandfathers Speak: Native American Folk Tales of the Lenape People*. Interlink Books, 1994.
Hannon, Elliott. "Vanishing Vultures a Grave Matter for India's Parsis." *All Things Considered*, September 5, 2012.
Higginson, Thomas Wentworth. *Out-Door Papers*. Ticknor and Fields, 1863.
Hodder, Ian. "Mysteries of Catalhoyuk." Science Museum of Minnesota, 2003.
Hornum, Michael. "Asis Rimoni." *asisrimoni.blogspot.com*, February 3, 2012).
Howe, C. D. "Service of the Birds." In *Seventh Annual Report of the Commissioner of Agriculture for the State of Vermont, 1915*. St. Albans, VT, no date.
Horsfall, Nicholas. "From History to Legend: M. Manlius and the Geese." *Classical Journal* 76, no. 4, April-May 1981.
Hume, Julian P., and Walters, Michael. *Extinct Birds*. T. & AD Poyser, 2012.
Humphries, Courtney. *Superdove: How the Pigeon Took Manhattan . . . and the World*. New York: HarperCollins, 2008.
Irigaray, Luce. "Animal Compassion." In Matthew Calarco and Peter Atterton, editors, *Animal Philosophy: Essential Readings in Continental Thought*. Continuum, 2004.
Jobson, Christopher. "Xu Bing Arrives at Mass MoCA With His 12-ton Birds Made of Construction Equipment." *Colossal*, July 10, 2013.
Johnston, Ian. "Humans and wild birds 'talk' to each other as they hunt for bees' honey." *The Independent*, July 21, 2016.
Joukhadar, Zeyn. *The Thirty Names of Night*. New York: Simon & Schuster, 2020.
Jung, Carl. *Memories, Dreams, Reflections*. New York: Vintage Books, 1961.
Karnik, Madhura. "India has a grand plan to bring back its vultures." *Quartz India*, June 8, 2016.
Kaska, Kathleen. *The Man Who Saved the Whooping Crane: The Robert Porter Allen Story*. Gainesville: University Press of Florida, 2012.
Kawagoe, Aileen. "On the trail of the torii's origins." *Heritage of Japan*. WordPress, 2013.
Kay, Charles E. "Are Ecosystems Structured from the Top-Down or Bottom-Up? A New Look at an Old Debate." *Wildlife Society Bulletin* 26, no. 3, Autumn, 1998.
Kearsley, Rosalinde. "Octavian and Augury: The Years 30-27 B.C." *The Classical Quarterly, New Series* 59, no. 1 (May 2009).
Killgrove, Kristina. "These Ancient Headless Corpses Were Defleshed By Griffon Vultures." *Forbes*, June 9, 2017.
King, Gilbert. "The History of Pardoning Turkeys Began With Tad Lincoln." *Smithsonian*, November 21, 2012.
Kushner, Tony. *Angels in America: A Gay Fantasia on National Themes. Part Two: Perestroika*. Theatre Communication Group, 2005.
LaDuke, Winona. Plenary address quoted in Dominic Arenas, "More Than 600 People Flocked to Milwaukee for the 2019 Audubon Convention." *Audubon*, August 9, 2019.
La Fountain-Stokes, Lawrence. "Queer ducks, Puerto Rican *patos*, and Jewish-American *feygelekh*: Birds and the cultural representation of homosexuality." *Centro Journal*, March 2007.

Laufer, Berthold. *Bird Divination among the Tibetans*. E.J. Brill, 1914.
Lawler, Andrew. "The bird that flipped the world: Secret histories of the modern chicken." *Salon*, December 7, 2014.
Lawler, Andrew. *Why Did the Chicken Cross the World? The Epic Saga of the Bird that Powers Civilization*. Atria Books, 2014.
LeBaron, Geoffrey S. "The 118th Christmas Bird Count Summary." *Audubon*, November 29, 2018.
Leeming, David Adams, and Leeming, Margaret Adams. *A Dictionary of Creation Myths*. New York: Oxford University Press, 2009.
Leipzig, Adam. "10 Lessons 'March of the Penguins' Taught Me about Success and the ROI of Risk." *Cultural Daily*, June 27, 2013.
Lewis, Charlton T., and Short, Charles. *A Latin Dictionary*. Oxford: Clarendon Press, 1969.
Lin, Derek. "Tao Living: The Giant Peng Bird." http://www.truetao.org/living/2000/200 011.him (January 17, 2018).
Linderski, Jerzy. *Roman Questions: Selected Papers*. Franz Steiner Verlag, 2007.
Mabuchi, Toichi. "Tales concerning the Origin of Grains in the Insular Areas of Southeastern Asia." *Asian Folklore Studies* 23, no. 1 (1964).
Macdonald, Helen. *Falcon*. Reaktion Books, 2016.
Macdonald, Helen. *H is for Hawk*. Grove Press, 2014.
Madsen, David B. and Madsen, Brigham D. "One Man's Meat Is Another Man's Poison: A Revisionist View of the Seagull 'Miracle.'" In *A World We Thought We Knew: Readings in Utah History*, edited by John S. McCormick and John R. Sillito. Salt Lake City: University of Utah Press, 1995.
Marlowe, Frank W. *The Hadza: Hunter-Gatherers of Tanzania*. Berkeley: University of California Press, 2010.
Marzluff, John, et al. "Lasting Recognition of Threatening People by Wild American Crows." *Animal Behavior* 79 (December 2009).
Marzluff, John M. *Welcome to Subirdia: Sharing Our Neighborhoods with Wrens, Robins, Woodpeckers, and Other Wildlife*. New Haven: Yale University Press, 2014.
Mascaro, Juan, trans. *The Dhammapada: The Path of Perfection*. New York: Penguin Books, 1973.
Masterman, E. W. Gurney, and Driver, G. R. "Quail." In *The Hastings Dictionary of the Bible*, rev. ed., edited by Frederick Grant and H. H. Rowley. New York: Charles Scribner's Sons, 1963.
Matthiessen, Peter, ed. *Courage for the Earth: Writers, Scientists, and Activists Celebrate the Life and Writing of Rachel Carson*. Houghton Mifflin, 2007.
Mayntz, Melissa. "Sounds That Attract Birds." *About Home*, November 7, 2016.
Mayntz, Melissa. "Fun Facts about Gulls." *The Spruce*, November 3, 2019. Accessed at https://www.thespruce.com/fun-facts-about-gulls-385525 (June 21, 2020).
Mazariegos, Oswaldo Chinchilla. "Of Birds and Insects: The Hummingbird Myth in Ancient Mesoamerica." *Ancient Mesoamerica* 21 (2010).
McCaine, David. "Israel's History Is Inundated with Examples of Supernatural Protection from God." *San Jose Christian Perspectives Examiner*, September 13, 2013.
McClain, Molly. *Ellen Browning Scripps: New Money and American Philanthropy*. Lincoln: University of Nebraska Press, 2017.
McGrain, Todd. *The Lost Bird Project*. Hanover, NH: University Press of New England, 2014.
McKenna, Maryn. *Big Chicken: The Incredible Story of How Antibiotics Created Modern Agriculture and Changed the Way the World Eats*. National Geographic, 2017.

McLaughlin, William. "How Holy Geese Saved the Republic during the First Sack of Rome (390 BCE)." *War History Online*, March 24, 2016.

McLendon, Russell. "Hawaiian Crows Return from Extinction in Wild." *Earth Matters* January 28, 2018. Accessed at https://www.mnn.com/earth-matters/animals/blogs/hawaiian-crows-return-extinction-wild (July 27, 2018).

Merchant, Carolyn. *Spare the Birds! George Bird Grinnell and the First Audubon Society.* New Haven: Yale University Press, 2016.

Miles, Christopher, with Norwich, John Julius. *Love in the Ancient World.* New York: St. Martin's Press, 1997.

Mings, Lonnie. "Dove Saves Soldiers from Death." *Israel News Digest*, August 2014.

Minunno, Giuseppe. *Ritual Employs of Birds in Ancient Syria-Palestine.* Ugarit-Verlag, 2013.

Mir, Mustansir. "Elephants, Birds of Prey, and Heaps of Pebbles: Farahi's Interpretation of Surat al-Fil." *Journal of Qur'anic Studies* 7, no. 1 (2005).

Mitchell, Chris. "Former Israeli Commander: God Protected Us in Battle." *CBN News*, September 16, 2013.

Moberly, R. W. L. "Why Did Noah Send Out a Raven?" *Vetus Testamentum* 50, no. 3 (2000).

Moleon, Marcos, with Jose A. Sanchez-Zapata, Anthoni Margalida, Martina Carrete, Norman Owen-Smith, and Jose Donazar. "Humans and Scavengers: The Evolution of Interactions and Ecosystem Services." *BioScience* May 2014.

Monkman, Betty C. "Pardoning the Thanksgiving Turkey." The White House Historical Association. Accessed at https://www.whitehousehistory.org/pardoning-the-thanksgiving-turkey (January 22, 2017).

Montanaro, Domenico. "The Strange Truth behind Presidential Turkey Pardons." *NPR: WSHU*, November 25, 2015.

Montanaro, Domenico. "Why Presidents Pardon Turkeys—a History." *PBS: CPTV*, November 26, 2014.

Moorman, John R. H., ed. and trans. *A New Fioretti: A Collection of Early Stories about Saint Francis of Assisi.* London, 1809.

Mortensen, Eric. "Raven Augury from Tibet to Alaska: Dialects, Divine Agency, and the Bird's-Eye View." In *A Communion of Subjects: Animals in Religion, Science, and Ethics*, edited by Paul Waldau and Kimberly Patton. New York: Columbia University Press, 2006.

Montgomery, Sy. *Birdology: Adventures with a Pack of Hens, a Peck of Pigeons, Cantankerous Crows, Fierce Falcons, Hip Hop Parrots, Baby Hummingbirds, and One Murderously Big Living Dinosaur.* New York: Free Press, 2010.

Munita, Thomas. "Pitting Heaven and Earth in a Fierce Andean Rite." *New York Times*, August 10, 2013.

Nash-Marshall, Siobhan. *The Sins of the Fathers: Turkish Denialism and the Armenian Genocide.* Crossword Publishing, 2017.

Nassen-Bayer, and Stuart, Kevin. "Mongol Creation Stories: Man, Mongol Tribes, the Natural World, and Mongol Deities." *Asian Folklore Studies* 51 (1992).

Neihardt, John G. *Black Elk Speaks: Being the Life Story of a Holy Man of the Oglala Sioux.* Lincoln: University of Nebraska Press, 1979.

Nemo, Leslie. "A Year Later, It's Take Two for the Hawaiian Crow's Return to the Wild." *Audubon*, November 2017. Accessed at https://www.audubon.org/news/a-year-later-its-take-two-hawaiian-crows-return-wild (July 27, 2018).

Nobles, Gregory. *John James Audubon: The Nature of the American Woodsman.* Philadelphia: University of Pennsylvania Press, 2017.

Nobles, Gregory. "The Myth of John James Audubon." *Audubon*, July 31, 2020.

Norenzayan, Ara. *Big Gods: How Religion Transformed Cooperation and Conflict.* Princeton, NJ: Princeton University Press, 2013.

O'Brien, Jane. "Unwrapping the Ancient Egyptian Animal Mummy Industry." *BBC News Magazine*, November 17, 2011.

O'Leary, Stephen D. *Arguing the Apocalypse: A Theory of Millennial Rhetoric.* New York: Oxford University Press, 1994.

Olson, Roberta J. M., and Spady, Matthew. "In Quest of Audubon: Exploring Audubon's Monument in Trinity Cemetery and Mausoleum to Rediscover Its History." *New York History* 96, no. 1 (Winter 2015).

Orr, Oliver H. *Saving American Birds: T. Gilbert Pearson and the Founding of the Audubon Movement.* Gainesville: University Press of Florida, 1992.

Owen, John. "Egyptian Animals Were Mummified Same Way as Humans." *National Geographic News*, September 15, 2004.

Pagels, Elaine. "What Became of God the Mother? Conflicting Images of God in Early Christianity." *Signs* 2, no. 2 (Winter 1976).

Paglia, Camille Paglia. *The Birds.* British Film Institute, 1998.

Palmer, Douglas. *A History of Earth in 100 Groundbreaking Discoveries.* Firefly Books, 2011.

Parrinder, Geoffrey. *Sex in the World's Religions.* New York: Oxford University Press, 1980.

Passarello, Elena. "Seventy Never Looked So Good: The Long, Wondrous Life of Wisdom the Albatross." *Audubon*, Spring 2021.

Penick, James Lal. *The Great Western Land Pirate: John A. Murrell in Legend and History.* Columbus: University of Missouri Press, 1981.

Perkinson, James W. "Protecting Water in the Anthropocene: River Spirits and Political Struggles in Detroit, Standing Rock, and the Bible." *Cross Currents* 66, no. 4 (December 2016).

Pierre-Louis, Kendra. "These Birds Are Racing to Their Mating Grounds. It's Exhausting." *New York Times*, August 1, 2018.

Pike, Sarah M. "Mourning Nature: The Work of Grief in Radical Environmentalism." *Journal for the Study of Religion, Nature and Culture* 10, no. 4 (January 2017).

Plato. *Phaedo.* Translated by Benjamin Jowett. P.F. Collier and Son, 1909.

Ploski, Harry A., and Williams, James, eds. *The Negro Almanac.* Gale Group, 1989.

Pound, Louise. "Note on Walt Whitman and Bird Poetry." *English Journal* 19, no. 1 (January 1930).

Power, Samantha. *A Problem from Hell: America and the Age of Genocide.* New York: Basic Books, 2002.

Plumly, Stanley. "Wings." *Kenyon Review*, New Series 36, no. 3 (Summer 2014).

Priest, Alan. *Aspects of Chinese Painting.* London: Macmillan, 1954.

Prum, Richard O. *Performance All the Way Down: Genes, Development, and Sexual Difference.* Chicago: University of Chicago Press, 2023.

Rasmussen, Susanne William. *Public Portents in Republican Rome.* L'Erma di Bretschneider, 2003.

Raver, Anne. "The Dark Side of Audubon's Era, and His Work." *New York Times*, March 30, 1997.

Ravven, Wallace. "Survival of the Shrewdest." *New York Times*, August 1, 2018, D3.

Rawski, Evelyn S. *The Last Emperors: A Social History of Qing Imperial Institutions*. Berkeley: University of California Press, 1998.
Regev, Eyal. "Sin, Atonement, and Israelite Identity in the Words of the Luminaries in Relation to 1 Enoch's Animal Apocalypse." *Hebrew Union College Annual* 84–85 (2013).
Renner, Serena. "Jonathan Franzen's Controversial Stance on Climate Action." *Sierra*, January 7, 2019. Accessed at https://www.sierraclub.org/sierra/jonathan-franzens-controversial-stance-climate-action (January 23, 2020).
Revive&Restore. "Passenger Pigeon Project." Accessed at https://reviverestore.org/about-the-passenger-pigeon/ (August 2, 2018).
Revive&Restore. "Staff / Board of Directors." Accessed at https://reviverestore.org/about-us/ (August 2, 2018).
Rhodes, Richard. *John James Audubon: The Making of an American*. New York: Alfred A. Knopf, 2004.
Robertson, Pat. *Miracles Can Be Yours Today*. Integrity Publishers, 2006.
Rome, Adam. "Political Hermaphrodites: Gender and Environmental Reform in Progressive America." *Environmental History* 11, no. 3 (July 2006).
Roof, Wade Clark, and McKinney, William. *American Mainline Religion: Its Changing Shape and Future*. New Brunswick, NJ: Rutgers University Press, 1987.
Rosen, Jonathan. *The Life of the Skies*. New York: Farrar, Straus, and Giroux, 2008.
Rothenberg, David. *Why Birds Sing: A Journey through the Mystery of Bird Song*. New York: Basic Books, 2005.
Rowley, George. *Principles of Chinese Painting*. Rev. ed. Princeton, NJ: Princeton University Press, 1974.
Rudgard, Olivia. "Exclusive: Could the Legend Come True? Tower of London Raven Allowed to Fly Free." *The Telegraph*, May 15, 2017.
Sadler, Richard W. "Seagulls, Miracle of." In *The Encyclopedia of Mormonism*, edited by Daniel Ludlow. London: Macmillan, 1992.
Santangelo, Federico. *Divination, Prediction and the End of the Roman Republic*. Cambridge: Cambridge University Press, 2003.
Saunders, William E. "The Value of Predatory Birds." In *Sixty-Ninth Annual Report of the Ontario Entomological Society*. T. E. Bowman Printer, 1938.
Sax, Boria. *City of Ravens: The Extraordinary History of London, the Tower, and Its Famous Ravens*. Duckworth Overlook, 2011.
Scalf, Foy. "The Role of Birds within the Religious Landscape of Ancient Egypt." In *Between Heaven and Earth: Birds in Ancient Egypt*, edited by Rozenn Bailleul-LeSuer. Chicago: University of Chicago Press, 2012.
Schaffner, Spencer. *Binocular Vision: The Politics of Representation in Birdwatching Field Guides*. Amherst: University of Massachusetts Press, 2011.
Schumaker, Helen. "The Phoenix through the Ages." *Swarthmore College Bulletin*, October 2008.
Scientific American. "Audubon." March 18, 1848.
Sharma, Pandit Vishnu. *Panchatantra*. Translated by G. L. Chandiramani. Rupa Publications, 1991.
Shavit, Ari. "Dear God, This Is Effi." *Haaretz*, March 20, 2002.
Shawn, Ted. *The American Ballet*. New York: Henry Holt, 1926.
Shelton, Jo-Ann. "Beastly Spectacles in the Ancient Mediterranean World." In *A Cultural History of Animals in Antiquity*, edited by Linda Kopf. Berg, 2007.

Sherman, Jane. "The American Indian Imagery of Ted Shawn." *Dance Chronicle* 12, no. 3 (1989).
Simek, Jan et al., "Sacred Landscapes of the South-eastern USA: Prehistoric Rock and Cave Art in Tennessee." *Antiquity* 86, no. 336 (June 2013).
Simpson, Wayne. "And the Spirit of God Moved upon the Face of the Waters." *jasher.com*, September 19, 2010.
Singer, Peter. *Animal Liberation*. New York: HarperCollins, 2002.
Smith, Jonathan Z. "The Domestication of Sacrifice." In *Violent Origins: Walter Burkert, René Girard, and Jonathan Z. Smith on Ritual Killing and Cultural Formation*, ed. Robert G. Hampton-Kelly. Stanford University Press, 1987.
Smith, Roberta. "New Light on Wyeth's Outer and Inner Landscapes." *New York Times*, May 29, 1998.
Snelling, John. *The Buddhist Handbook*. Inner Traditions, 1991.
Snyder, Noel F. R. *The Carolina Parakeet: Glimpses of a Vanished Bird*. Princeton, NJ: Princeton University Press, 2004.
Souder, William. *Under a Wild Sky: John James Audubon and the Making of "The Birds of America"*. North Point Press, 2004.
Spoto, Donald. *Spellbound by Beauty: Alfred Hitchcock and His Leading Ladies*. Harmony Books, 2008.
Sproul, Barbara C. *Primal Myths: Creation Myths Around the World*. HarperOne, 1979.
Stark, Rodney. "Reconstructing the Rise of Christianity: The Role of Women." *Sociology of Religion* 56, no. 3 (Autumn 1995).
Stearns, Beverly Peterson, and Stearns, Stephen C. *Watching, from the Edge of Extinction*. New Haven: Yale University Press, 1999.
Stein, Sara Abreyvaya. *Plumes: Ostrich Feathers, Jews, and a Lost World of Global Commerce*. New Haven: Yale University Press, 2010.
Stephan, Claudia, Wilkinson, Anna, and Huber, Ludwig. "Have We Met Before? Pigeons Recognise Familiar Human Faces." *Avian Biology Research* 5, no. 2 (2012).
Stoll, Mark R. *Inherit the Holy Mountain: Religion and the Rise of American Environmentalism*. New York: Oxford University Press, 2015.
Stone, Oliver, and Kuznick, Peter. *The Untold History of the United States*. New York: Simon & Schuster, 2013.
Sundstrom, Bob. "Birdsong Therapy." *BirdNote*, August 13, 2021. Accessed at https://www.birdnote.org/listen/shows/birdsong-therapy (August 20, 2021).
Tacon, Paul S. C., Langley, M., May, S., Lamilami, R., Brennan, W., and Guse, D. "Ancient Bird Stencils Discovered in Arnhem Land, Northern Territory, Australia." *Antiquity* 84, no. 324 (2010): 416–427.
Tate, Peter. *Flights of Fancy: Birds in Legend, Myth, and Superstition*. Delacorte Press, 2007.
Taylor, Hollis. "Composers' Appropriation of Pied Butcherbird Song." *Journal of Music Research Online*, 2011. Accessed at https://www.hollistaylor.com/ewExternalFiles/Composers%20appropriation.pdf (January 21, 2018).
Teilhard de Chardin, Pierre, S.J. *The Phenomenon of Man*. New York: HarperCollins, 1959.
Thaxter, Celia. "Women's Heartlessness" (Boston 1886). Reprinted for the Audubon Society of the State of New York, 1899. Accessed at http://www.seacoastnh.com/celia-thaxter-attacks-heartless-women-wearing-birds-as-fashion/ (June 14, 2020).
Thompson, Claire. *The Art of Mindful Birdwatching: Reflections on Freedom & Being*. Leaping Hare Press, 2017.

Thoreau, Henry David. *The Writings of Henry David Thoreau*. Vol. 2, *Walden*. Houghton Mifflin, 1906.

Thoreau, Henry David. *The Writings of Henry David Thoreau*. Vol. 4, *Journals, May 1, 1852–February 27, 1853*. Edited by Bradford Torrey. Houghton Mifflin, 1906.

Thoreau, Henry David. "The Generation of Trees." In Randall Fuller, *The Book That Changed America: How Darwin's Theory of Evolution Ignited a Nation*. New York: Viking, 2017.

Trouern-Trend, Jonathan. *Birding Babylon: A Soldier's Journal from Iraq*. Sierra Club Books, 2006.

Tsai, Michelle. "Wherefore Turkey?" *Slate*, November 25, 2009.

Tudge, Colin. *Consider the Birds: Who They Are and What They Do*. New York: Penguin Books, 2008.

Tzp, Melissa. "Ha-azinu: A Hovering Bird." *Midrash Torah*, September 18, 2017.

Uehling, Jennifer J., Tallant, Jason, and Pruett-Jones, Stephen. "Status of Naturalized Parrots in the United States." *Journal of Ornithology* 160 (2019): 907–921. https://doi.org/10.1007/s10336-019-01658-7.

United States Fish & Wildlife Service. "Bald Eagle Fact Sheet: Natural History, Ecology, and History of Recovery." Updated April 20, 2015. Accessed at: https://www.fws.gov/midwest/eagle/recovery/biologue.html (July 26, 2018).

United States Fish & Wildlife Service. "BP Deepwater Horizon Oil Spill Settlement Funds Migrate North." April 27, 2015. Accessed at https://www.fws.gov/news/ShowNews.cfm?ID=FC61EB52-BF8A-45AA-C04D802711C4EF55 (June 30, 2018).

United States Fish & Wildlife Service. "California Condor Recovery Program." May 23, 2018. Accessed at https://www.fws.gov/cno/es/CalCondor/Condor.cfm (July 30, 2018).

Vaccaro, Adam. "Millions of Years Ago, Western Massachusetts Was a Jurassic World." *Boston*, June 15, 2015.

Vendler, Helen. *Dickinson: Selected Poems and Commentaries*. Cambridge, MA: Harvard University Press, 2010.

Vitello, Paul. "Peter Marler, Graphic Decoder of Birdsong, Dies at 86." *New York Times*, July 28, 2014.

Voth, H. R. "Notes on the Eagle Cult of the Hopi." *Publications of the Field Museum of Natural History, Anthropological Series* 11, no. 2 (February 1912).

Vulture Conservation Foundation. "Indian Courts Ban Multi-dose Vials of Diclofenac." November 4, 2017. Accessed at https://www.4vultures.org/2017/11/04/the-sanitary-workers-get-some-backup-in-india/ (August 2, 2018).

Walker, Alice. *The Chicken Chronicles: Sitting with the Angels Who Have Returned with My Memories. Glorious, Rufus, Gertrude Stein, Splendor, Hortensia, Agnes of God, the Gladyses, & Babe. A Memoir*. New York: New Press, 2011.

Wallace, Mark I. "The Pileated Woodpecker: Avian Divinity in a Time of Chaos." *Kosmos: Journal for Global Transformation*, Summer 2021.

Wallace, Mark I. "The Wild Bird Who Heals: Recovering the Spirit in Nature." *Theology Today* 50, no. 1 (April 1993).

Wallace, Mark I. *When God Was a Bird: Christianity, Animism, and the Re-enchantment of the World*. Fordham University Press, 2019.

Wallace-Wells, David. "The Uninhabitable Earth." *New York*, July 10, 2017.

Walters, Amy. "Behind Trump's Energy Dominance." *Reveal*, July 14, 2018. Accessed at https://www.revealnews.org/episodes/behind-trumps-energy-dominance/ (July 24, 2018).

Warne, Kennedy. "The Amazing Albatrosses." *Smithsonian*, September 2007.

Watts, Jonathan. "Fight of the Condor: Peru Bull Fiestas Threaten Future of Rare Andean Bird." *The Guardian*, January 29, 2013.

Weber, Max. *The Protestant Ethic and the Spirit of Capitalism*. Translated by Talcott Parsons. London: Routledge, 1992.

Welz, Adam, "Jonathan Franzen: Egypt Is the Worst Place to Be a Migratory Bird." *The Guardian*, July 13, 2019.

Wijk-Bos, Johanna W. H. van. *Reimagining God: The Case for Spiritual Diversity*. Louisville, KY: Westminster John Knox Press, 1995.

Williams, Terry Tempest. "The Moral Courage of Rachel Carson." In *Courage for the Earth: Writers, Scientists, and Activists Celebrate the Life and Writing of Rachel Carson*, edited by Peter Matthiessen. Houghton Mifflin, 2007.

Williams, Terry Tempest. *Refuge: An Unnatural History of Family and Place*. New York: Vintage Books, 1992.

Wood, Michael, *Legacy: A Search for the Origins of Civilization*. Network Books, 1992.

Yin, Steph. "We Might Soon Resurrect Extinct Species. Is It Worth the Cost?" *New York Times*, March 20, 2017.

Yong, Ed. "Not a Human, but a Dancer." *The Atlantic*, July 8, 2019.

Yoskowitz, Jeffrey. "Goose: A Hanukkah Tradition." *New York Times*, December 24, 2016.

Young, Jon. *What the Robin Knows*. Houghton Mifflin, 2012.

Zickefoose, Julie. *The Bluebird Effect: Uncommon Bonds with Common Birds*. Houghton Mifflin, 2012.

Ziolkowski, Adam. "Between Geese and the Auguraculum: The Origin of the Cult of Juno on the Arx." *Classical Philology* 88, no. 3 (July 1993).

Zubrin, Robert. "The Truth about DDT and Silent Spring." *New Atlantis*, September 27, 2012.

Index

For the benefit of digital users, indexed terms that span two pages (e.g., 52–53) may, on occasion, appear on only one of those pages.

Figures are indicated by *f* following the page number

Ahura Mazda or Fravashi, 4, 5*f*
Ainu religion, 16
Albatross (*Diomedeidae sp*), 257–62
   Discovery by Europeans in Romantic age, 258–59
   Wisdom, albatross mother at, 70, 261–62
American Museum of Natural History, 239–41
Andean Condor (*Vultur gryphus*), 67–68, 68*f*
apocalypse. *See* Christianity; Hitchcock, Alfred; Mayan religion
Aristophanes (*The Birds*), 95–99
Armstrong, Edward, 126–27
Army Air Service, U.S., eagles in recruiting poster, 208–10, 209*f*
art as resistance to extinctions
   Audubon murals project, and Gitler, Avi, 230–31
   Bing, Yu, and *Fenghuang*, 229–30
   Birds on Broadway project, 230
   Lost Bird Project and McGrain, Todd, 228
Audubon, John James, 145, 146–47
   ancestry of, 173–74, 247–48
   contemporary ethical challenges, 243–45
   death of, 172
   life and art, 175–77, 180–82, 198
   painting of Golden Eagle, 181*f*, 182
   portrait at 41 years old, 173–74, 173*f*
   racial issues relevant to, 239–40
   religious and philosophical attitude, 174, 177
   See also Bakewell, Lucy

Audubon Society, 203, 247
   See also Grinnell, George Bird
Augur Buzzard (*Buteo rufofuscus*), 53–54
Augury, 42
   See also Christianity; Greek and Roman religion; Hinduism; Hittite religion; Kantu; Waso Boorana
Australian aboriginal religion, 36
   birds in rock art of, 35–36
Aztec religion, 23
   hummingbirds in, 23
   Quetzals in, 48–49
   Voladores, 49–51

Bakewell, Lucy, 244 and *passim*
Bald Eagle (*Haliaeetus leucocephalus*), 151–52, 190–91, 208–10, 209*f*
   "On Eagle's Wings" (hymn), 204–6
   role in American civil religion, 207, 208–12
Bali. *See* Cockfighting; Geertz, Clifford
Bateleur Eagle (*Terathopius ecaudatus*), 53–54
birds
   adaptability of, 164, 171
   as bringers of fire, 100
   as bringers of rice, 80
   and early humans, 27–28
   evolution of, 25–26
   foretelling weather, 28–29
   gender expression and cross-species behavior, 223, 248
   as guards, 4
   intelligence of, 69
   land use planning for, 242–43
   in Paleolithic art, 32–34

280 INDEX

birds (*cont.*)
  as people, 2
  in poetry, 182–84 (*see also* Dickinson, Emily)
  in rock art, 34
  role in contemporary music, 133 (*see also* Messiaen, Olivier)
  saving human crops, 79
  sex with, 105 (*see also* Greek and Roman religion; Leda and the Swan)
  as spirit guides, 115, 116
  symbolic heritage of, 69
  vehicle for gay and trans culture, 206–7
  See also extinctions
  birding (Bird Watching), 68–69
  cultural impact of birding guides, 237
  role in conservation and conservation movements, 235–36
Black Elk. *See* birds as spirit guides
Bower birds (*Ptilorhynchidae sp.*), 59
Buber, Martin, 217–18
Buddhism
  birds as models of Enlightenment in, 121
  Tibetan, 121–23
  vultures and funerary practices, 45–46

California Condor (*Gymnogryphus Californianus*), 162
California Gull (*Larus Californicus*), 78
Carolina Parakeet, (*Conuropsis carolinensis*), 145
Carson, Rachel (*Silent Spring*), 149–55, 161, 212–13
  forward, 210–11
  impact of work, 152
Catal Huyuk, 44–45
Central Park, significance for birds, 233–35, 238
Cher Ami (Hero pigeon of World War I), 88–90, 90*f*
Cherry, Elizabeth, (*Culture and Activism and For the Birds*), 10, 237, 242
Cheyenne and Lakota, birds in the Great Race, 21–22
Chicken (*Gallus gallus domesticus*), Alice Walker, 118
  contemporary relations with, 139–40
  roles in religion, 13

Christian Science, 220, 238–39
Christianity, 60, 205
  Armageddon, 154
  augury in, 56–57
  creation and Genesis, 12–13
  Holy Spirit as dove, 111
  Matthew and Luke, gospels of, 13
  See also doves
cockfighting, 118–19
Coleridge, Samuel Taylor (*The Rime of the Ancient Mariner*), 257–62
Common Drongo (*Dicrurus adsimilis*), 46–47
Condor, *see* Andean Condor, California Condor, Yawar festival.
Conference of the Birds. See Sufism; *See also* Joukhadar, Zeyn
creation, birds in. *See* AInu religion; Christianity; Iroquois religion; Japanese religion; Lenape religion; Mongol religion; Ojibwe religion; Samoyed religion; Yakuts religion; Yoruba religion
Crow (*Corvidae*). *See* Ravens and crows
  See also Cheyenne and Lakota; Hinduism; Judaism; Kwakiutl religion; Lenape religion; Mesopotamian religion; Tlingit religion

Darwin, Charles, 8, 140–41, 169–70, 182–83, 184–86, 188–89, 190, 238–39
DDT (Dichlorodiphenyltrichloroethane), insecticide poisoning birds, 116, 150–52, 160–61, 210–11, 243
Department of Health and Human Services, U.S., logo, 211–12, 212*f*
Descartes, René, 189, 213–14
Dickinson, Emily. *See* birds: in poetry
Dove (*Columbidae*) , 94–95, 111
  Carl Jung and, 111–13
  in modern wars of Israel, 86, 88
  in New Testament, 91, 110, 156
  in Old Testament, 91, 94–95, 153
  release by Pope, 66–67
  See also Christianity: Holy Spirit as Dove

Egyptian religion, 3, 14–15
  mummification of Birds, 64

INDEX 281

Emperor Penguin (*Aptenodytes forsteri*), 221–23
Ethiopian Snipe (*Sarcoramphus papi*), 34–35
Eurasian Teal (*Anas crecca*), 16–17
extinction, modern, 141–42, 169–71
  See also Carolina Parakeet; Great Auk; Hawaii; Hinduism; passenger pigeon; Wampanoag religion

Feld, Steven. *See* Kaluli
Finnish religion, 16–17
  See also *Kalevala*
Fish Crow (Corvus ossifragus), symbol of death and mural, 231–32, 232*f*
Flamenco dance, 47–48
Flamingo (Phoenicopterus sp), 47–48

Geertz, Clifford, 119
  See also cockfighting
gendered dialectic. *See* Merchant, Carolyn; women in conservation movements
Giotto, painting of St. Francis of Assissi with birds, 125, 125*f*
Global Hawk (drone), 3, 4*f*
Gobekli Tepe, 36–37
Golden Eagle (Aquila chrysaetos), 51–52, 160–61, 181*f*, 182, 208
  Goose (*Anatidae*), 198–99
  See also Greek and Roman Religion: Rome saved by
Goshawk (Accipiter gentilis), 112–14, 113*f*
Great auk (*Pinguinus impennis*), 148–49
Greek and Roman religion, 3
  Augury in, 54–56
  Leda and the swan, 80–105
  Prometheus, 100
  Rome saved by geese, 84–86
  Socrates, bird offering at death, 99–100
  See also Aristophanes (The Birds)
Grinnell, George Bird, 191–92
  See also Audubon Society

Hadza, 43*f*–44
  cooperation with Honeyguides, 43
  sacrifice among, 58–59
Hawaii, extinction of indigenous birds, 161

Hebrew(s). *See* Judaism
Higginson, Thomas Wentworth, 184–85
Hinduism, 3, 119–20
  augury and role of ravens in, 57–58
  creation, 15
  cult of Kali, 63
  gods protected by birds, 100–1
  Vulture decline and conservation, 162–63
Hitchcock, Alfred (The Birds), 155–60, 156*f*
Hittite religion, 57
Holocaust, as sin offering of birds in ancient Israel, 61–62
  as event that increased use of poisons, 213–15
homing pigeons, in World War I, 88–90
Honeyeater (*Meliphagidae sp.*), 35
Honeyguide (*Indicator indicator*), 43, 44*f*
Hoopoe (*Upupa epapa*), 4, 7*f*, 93, 123–24
Hopi religion, 24–27
  Eagles in, 51, 52–53
Hummingbirds (*Trochilidae sp.*), 23
  See also Aztec Religion; Mayan Religion

Icons, and cover painting, 257–58
Ireland, folk traditions, 126
Irigaray, Luce, 117–18
Iroquois religion, 15–16
Islam, Swallows and defense of Mecca, 82–84
  See also Sufism

Japanese religion, 16
Jatayu, hero vulture of the Hindu epic *Ramayana*, 100–1, 102*f*
Jonathan Livingston Seagull, 218–22
Joukhadar, Zeyn (*The Thirty Names of Night*), 224–27
  See also Sufism
Judaism, 3, 91–94, 204–5, 206
  Birds and kashrut, 58
  Ecclesiastes, 3
  Egypt, 14
  Elijah and ravens, 19–20, 92–93
  Genesis, 12–13, 94
  kaporos (Kaporot), 62–63
  Quail, 91–93
  sacrifice, 60–62
  Turtledove, 62–63
  See also doves

Kalevala. See Finnish Religion
Kaluli, 27–28, 31, 35, 36
Kantu religion, 54
King Vulture (*Sarcoramphus papa*), 34
Kushner, Tony, *Angels in America*, 105
Kwakiutl religion, 18

Lascaux cave, 32–34, 33f, *See* birds: in Paleolithic art
Lenape religion, 18–19
Lincoln, Abraham, 64–65

Macaw (*Psitttacidae sp.*), 22–23
Macdonald, Helen (H is for Hawk), 112–14
Magpie (*Corvidae sp.*), 21–22
March of the Penguins, 221–23
Mayan religion, 49
   Birds in apocalypse, 154–55
   Hummingbirds, 24
   King Vulture, 34
   Macaw, 22–23
Merchant, Carolyn, 8–9, 192, 207, 211, 216, 220, 223–24, 238–39
Mesopotamian religion, 20–21
Messiaen, Olivier, 130–33
Migratory Bird Treaty Act, 145–46, 215, 248–49
Mongol religion, 13
Montgomery, Sy (*Birdology*), 114–15, 116–17
Mormonism, role of gulls, 77
Muir, John, 192, 193–94

Nash-Marshall, Siobhan, 213–14
nature, religion of, emerging. *See* religion of nature, emerging
New Testament. *See* Christianity

Obama, Barack, pardoning Thanksgiving turkey, 64–65, 65f
Ojibwe religion, 15–16
Old Testament. *See* Judaism
Oliver, Mary (*Wild Geese*), 198–99

Parsee. *See* Zoroastrianism
Passenger Pigeon (*Ectopistes migratorius*), 142–45, 144f

Penguin (*Spheniscidae*), 221–23
Pigeon (*Columbidae sp.*), 59–60, 61–62

Quail (*Cothurnus cothurnus*), 91–93

Ramayana, Hindu epic, 100–1f
Ravens and crows (*Corvidae*), 17–18, 19–20
   British history and tradition, 80–82
   as tricksters, 18
   See also Cheyenne and Lakota; Hinduism; Judaism; Kwakiutl religion; Lenape religion; Mesopotamian religion; Tlingit religion
religion, definition of, 2–3, 140, 204, 212
religion of nature, emerging, 169–70, 172, 175, 190–91, 204
   role of birders, 237, 242
   role of zoos, 241
   See also Buber, Martin; Cherry, Elizabeth; *Jonathan Livingston Seagull*; *March of the Penguin*s
Resplendent Quetzal (*Pharomachrus mocinno*), 48–49
ritual, definition of, 42, 47
Roman religion. *See* Greek and Roman religion
Roosevelt, Franklin, 69
Roosevelt, Theodore, 192, 193–94, 216

Sacred Ibis (*Threskiornis aethiopicus*), 15, 64, 171–72
sacrifice and birds. *See* Hadza; Hinduism; Judaism; Vodun; Yoruba religion
Saint Francis of Assisi, 125–30, 131–32
   Sermon to the Birds, 128
Samoyed religion, 15–16
San religion, 34–35
Scandanavians, traditional religion of, 3
   See also Finnish religion
Scripps, Ellen Browning, and Scripps Aviary, 238–39
Singer, Arthur, bird artist of cover painting, 257–58
Snowy egret (*Egretta thula*), 146, 182, 194–96
Snowy heron (see Snowy egret)

Southeast Asian religions. *See* birds: as bringers of rice
Sufism and Conference of the Birds, 123–25
Swallow (*Hirundinidae sp., prob. Riparia sp.*), 82–84, See Islam, Swallows and defense of Mecca
Swan (*Cygninae sp.*), as protectors, and in Opera and Dance, poem *Leda and the Swan*, 101–4, 105

Taoism, birds as models in, 121
Thanksgiving and turkeys, 64–66, 65*f*
Thompson, Claire (*The Art of Mindful Birding*), 236
Thoreau, Henry David, 184–85, 186–89
Tibetan religious practice, 57–58
Tlingit religion, 18
Trouern-Trend, Jonathon (*Birding Babylon*), 236–37
Turkeys. *See* Thanksgiving
Turtledove (*Streptopelidae sp.*), 62–63

Voodoo, 63–64
Vulture (New World *Cathartidae sp*; Old World *Accipitridae sp.*), 45–46
   See also Buddhism; Catal Huyuk; Wyeth, Andrew (*Soaring*); Zoroastrianism

Wagtail (*Motacillidae sp.*), 16
Wampanoag religion, 69
   And Heath Hen, 70–71
Warren, Robert Penn (*Audubon: A Vision*), 197–99
Waso Boorana religion, 53–54
Welty, Eudora (*A Still Moment*), 194–97
White-billed Diver, also known as Yellow-billed Loon (*Gavia adamsii*), 15–16
Whitman, Walt, 183
Williams, Terry Tempest (*Refuge*), 117
women in conservation movements, 192–93
   See also Merchant, Carolyn
Wyeth, Andrew (*Turkey Buzzards Soaring*), 138*f*, 160

Yakuts religion, 15–16
   Funerary practice, 33–34
Yawar festival, and condors, 67–68, 68*f*
Yeats, William Butler, *Leda and the Swan*, 105
Yoruba religion, 15–16, 59

ZIckefoose, Julia (*The Bluebird Effect*), 137–39
Zoroastrianism, 4, 6–7, 7*f*, 37